MW00885641

SAMADHI

THE DEEP MEDITATION HANDBOOK

Volume 1 – YOGIC SCIENCE

Peter Marchand

Independently published by Peter Marchand in 2024
Cover image of a Sadhu in Samadhi by Pieter Weltevrede.

This book has been crowdfunded by numerous backers on Kickstarter. AI has not been used in its content creation.

Aum Gajananam, bhootaganadi sevitam

Kapittha jambo phalacharu bhakshanam

Uma sutam shoka vinasha karakam

Namami vighanesh shwara padpankajam

Aum

DEDICATION

To Harish Johari, who shaped my life like no other.

ACKNOWLEDGMENTS

As most of the teachings in this book were transmitted by my original teacher Harish Johari, humbling gratitude to him for his patience in teaching us.

Special gratitude is due to Tania Gordon Golad, who can be seen as the person that initiated the creation of this work. Out of the blue, she sent me a fully typed out transcript with over 15 hours of my teachings on meditation. How could I then not write this book?

Special thanks to Andra Irimia, Joyce Berg, Natacha Martins and Régine Deruyver, who not only gave me valuable content feedback, but also spent so many hours optimizing the language. As English is not my mother tongue, this help was invaluable.

Further thanks for providing more content feedback to Alina Konstantinova, Brando De Courten, Eric Bennewitz, Evgeny Dziatco, Michael Warshaw, Rodrigo Elizon, Sherzade Syed and Stephanie Rees Squibb. Such fun we had discussing all this.

To my guru brother Pieter Weltevrede→A9, I feel so honored that you allowed the free use of your paintings for the cover image and so many illustrations in this book. Harish Johari's teachings so much included that visual aspect, which you have mastered so well. Gratitude also to his daughter, the late Sapna Johari, for painting some of the Hindu symbols used in this book.

Gratitude to the many backers from around the world that supported the 'Deep Meditation Handbook' project through the crowdfunding platform Kickstarter.

Gratitude to the truth of yogic science, to Sanatan Dharma→A1, to the original, eternal, ever-changing and never-changing path and reality.

CONTENTS

Volume 1 - YOGIC SCIENCE

Volume 2 - SAMADHI PRACTICE

INTRODUCTION

I would like to start where this book concludes: the transformation brought about by the deepest state of meditation - known as Samadhi - is everyone's birthright. And clearly, we are entirely free to find our own way inside. Yogic science has an answer and a practice at the ready for every question that we might encounter on this path. I have tried achieving the same in this book. It is based in over 40 years of meditation practice, as well as in the experiences with my students.

In wellness meditation we are quite free in what to do and it might give us a really nice experience. From the point of view of yogic lore, achieving a state of mental relaxation is however just the beginning. To reach the really deep state of altered consciousness called Samadhi requires a rather clear if personalized methodology. If the transformative power of actual yogic meditation is our objective, there truly is a lot to learn in easing the process of withdrawing towards our very center.

Even though it is best not to talk about our achievements, I have no problem confirming that I have experienced multiple Samadhis over the past 2 decades. That is anyhow not such a miraculous thing. It happens to many, especially in India, as on average just a few years of regular practice may lead us to master the meditation phases that allow Samadhi to happen. Samadhi is not some elusive state that is only reserved for renunciates that are willing to give up on everything else. This book empowers anyone that takes up the challenge to start practicing actual meditation at home.

When I started writing this book, I thought I needed about 200 pages. They became more than 600. In part this is because I am trying to be clear and complete, as I plan only one book on meditation. The other reason is found in the very necessary personalization of the meditation process, meaning that I need to offer different solutions to a wide variety of readers. As the practice on our meditation mat must be complemented with a variety of practices and attitudes in life, there really is a lot to consider. And then especially when applying the ancient yogic principles to the lifestyle of the modern-day householder yogi.

I am aware that a book like this is not often written, because of the idea that people are not up to dealing with that much information, insight and what could be called spiritual ambition. Yet I have found that many seekers are remarkably devoted to understanding how everything fits together. I expect nothing from the reader, except for all to live up to our tremendous potential within the limitations of each moment. This book offers no quick fix, but a clear if far from straight path forward. How much time we have to practice is irrelevant once we accept ourselves as a work in progress.

This book is based on the teachings that I have received from my teachers, with additional understanding gained from scripture. Any word written cannot however escape my subjectivity. Hence only the errors are mine. Anyhow this book concerns the unspeakable. May it bring the reader to the practice and from there to their own insights.

Nothing in this book should thus be accepted by the reader because it is written here. Only by working with it, the understanding becomes ours. It is mainly based in the teachings of Harish Johari[1]*, complemented by the other teachers that followed in his wake*[2]*. The main paths, phases and practices of meditation taught here correlate with the principal teachings found in the ancient Yoga Sutras of Patanjali*[3]*. I also often refer to Ramana Maharishi*[4] *and Nisargadatta Maharaj*[5]*, whose teachings inspired much clarity.*

This is not a scholar's study on the subject of Samadhi, rather the viewpoint of a practitioner. As yogic scriptures number in the thousands and often disagree on many subjects, I have refrained from referring my sayings to particular texts. Finding some idea in scripture simply does not prove any statement. If for some of the more controversial subjects I do refer to specific teachers or scriptures, it is to absolve myself of too much responsibility, not to prove a point. I stay as close as possible to the original teachings. When as a Westerner I discuss this most essential body of knowledge from the Indian heritage, I am aware of the danger of cultural appropriation, as explained in Appendix 1.

I hope the reader may enjoy the reading, as I have enjoyed translating the ancient science to the here and now. Certainly the reader should develop personal preferences regarding the practices and attitudes proposed here, but to discover our path we must know our options. May it all inspire to try out some of the described practices. It will not only bring real insight, yet also the direct experience of our truly blissful divine nature. Any more lofty objectives aside, may it help all to be more happy, healthy and wise.

Peter Marchand

---

[1] Harish Johari is my original teacher, whom I met at the age of 20. More details in Story1 and in many other stories of this book.

[2] Baba Dwarka Das (Story 4), Narayan Rishi (Story 17), Narvada Puri Mataji (Stories 27, 29 & 38) and Kathia Baba (Story 3).

[3] The Yoga Sutras of Patanjali is a world-famous ancient text on yoga and especially deep meditation. The author is the sage Patanjali of India, often seen as the 'father of yoga' and who especially created the foundation for Ashtanga Yoga.

[4] Ramana Maharishi (1879-1950) is perhaps the most famous Indian saint of the past century. His teachings have very much defined modern understanding of nonduality, typically known as Advaita Vedanta.

[5] Nisargadatta Maharaj (1897-1981) is a contemporary of Ramana, a householder yogi with direct teachings on nonduality.

AUTHOR'S NOTES

This handbook aims at guiding the reader over a longer period of practice, regularly returning to some chapter or other. A handbook is a book to keep at hand. Hence it contains over 1000 internal references that make it easy to retrace some information:

→5.4.8 ←5.4.8	*Reference to a chapter in the following or previous pages.*
→P23 ←P23	*Reference to a practice in the following or previous pages.*
→A3	*Reference to an appendix at the end of the book.*
(8)	*Reference to a footnote on the same page.*

To facilitate the reading for people that are unfamiliar with Sanskrit, most of the terminology of this book is in English. I have given the original Sanskrit term of any main concept as a (SANSKRIT SUBTEXT) for further reference, so that the reader may easily research alternative approaches and opinions. More details on the use of the Sanskrit language are found in Appendix 2 and Appendix 8 offers an index of all Sanskrit words used.

For some Sanskrit words there is however simply no clear translation in English available, because the concept itself does not exist, neither in the language nor in the culture. Aside of already quite familiar words such as yoga itself, only the following 20 Sanskrit words - that seem hard to translate into one clear English word - are commonly used in this book without always being explained, except in their actual chapters:

- *Apana: the outgoing air*→4.2.2
- *Asana: a posture or seat*→7.2
- *Dharma: our natural role*→2.4.3
- *Dosha: an imbalance in the body*→4.3.3
- *Guna: a quality of energy*→4.2.1
- *Karma: action and reaction*→2.4.1
- *Kundalini: our most subtle energy*→4.2.5
- *Mantra: a Sanskrit sound object*→10.3
- *Ojas: our storehouse of energy*→4.2.3
- *Prana: the life force*→4.2
- *Rajas: the active energy*→4.2.1
- *Rasa: emotional essence*→4.1.5
- *Sadhana: sustained practice*→5.4
- *Samadhi: deep meditation trance*→2.1.5
- *Sattva: the light energy*→4.2.1
- *Tamas: the passive energy*→4.2.1
- *Tantra: transformation of energy*→2.7.1
- *Tejas: the energy of seeing*→4.2.3
- *Yantra: a geometric visual object*→10.4.5
- *Yogi : a master in yoga*→1.6

1

WHY MEDITATE?

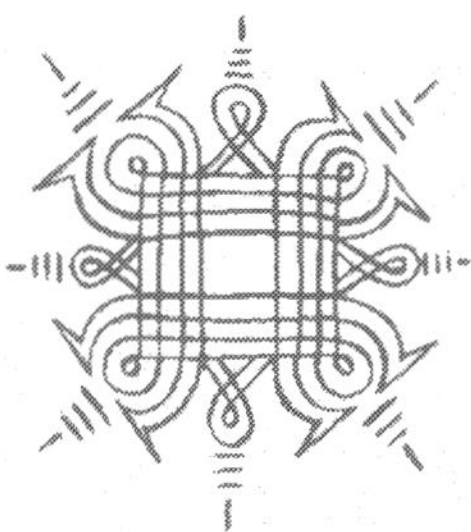

In meditation, we seek a happiness that is independent of what happens. Giving peace a real chance allows us to see beyond thought and meet our ever happy inner cosmic being. Discarding layers upon layers of individuality, we aim at reaching the deepest states of meditation, miraculously boosting our spiritual evolution. We thus grow into a life with enough peace and happiness to be really worth living, while also becoming extraordinarily magical.

1.1. Happiness

The central question that leads us upon the path of yoga and meditation is if we can be happy independent of what happens. It is a life changing yet logical quest, as we cannot fully control what happens. As long as our happiness depends on what is outside of us, we cannot durably escape unhappiness.

To meditate means to seek happiness inside rather than outside. It rests upon the most important spiritual experience that happiness is ours if we can actually stop our mind from seeking it outside of us. As we thus discover our endless smile in the spiritual heart(HRIDAYA), we can learn to keep that inner connection. Only then we may actually truly enjoy whatever is happening. We can still care about what happens around us, better than ever, while our happiness no longer depends on it. Through the path of meditation, happiness becomes self-existent, while a minimal level of peace is needed to maintain it.

1.2. Giving Peace a Chance

Happiness or unhappiness are experienced as pleasant or unpleasant emotions, which partially relates to their level of peace. Unpleasant emotions are usually rather devoid of peace. While pleasant emotions are not always very peaceful, they still require some peaceful basis to endure. Even our anger will be more palatable if it has some element of peace. In peace, happiness comes easily.

Peace is our key to live a happy life. We all need it and to some degree we all want it and occasionally cry for it, yet few truly have it. Meanwhile, nothing is needed to get some peace. If we let everything go, then peace is what remains.

Our mind is like an AI computer that is talking non-stop. It can give us plenty of good advice, but it just does not want to stop. We cannot turn it off nor run away from it because it is plugged directly into our brain. And it is so far advanced that it produces not only thoughts, but also a variety of pleasant and painful feelings, to maximally engage us in its storytelling. What thus sounds like a science-fiction story is a daily yet natural reality in most people's heads.

Primarily what we need is peace of mind. Mind is our great servant, programmed to always seek the fulfilment of our desires. By its nature, it does not seek nothingness. It always looks for some thing to make us more happy. Yet that something is always outside of us, beyond our control. To just enjoy what is makes a lot of sense most of the time. Mind is the main obstacle when we want to be happy with what we have.

Fortunately, our mind can definitely be made more peaceful. That alone will already increase the level of happiness in our feelings. And if we can regularly have some real peace from mind, then also on a deeper level more bliss can be generated.

To unplug our dear brain computer, meditation is the key. We can blame others or even society in general for our lack of peace, while peace we can all have, if we give peace a chance. By itself, it is not demanding. Everything else will naturally attract our attention when needed, so we do not even need to remain that much aware of it. But peace requires some time, some energy, some purposeful action towards inaction.

Getting more peace in our lives is thus the first objective of meditation, the short-term goal. From the moment that we start some meditation practice, peace will increase, even if that practice is still far from truly peaceful. Meditation will thus improve our lives on every level. We will quite rapidly see its benefits in our work, relationships and health. Our happy feelings will become more peaceful and durable, and they will not lead to unhappy feelings so easily.

While these are all very good reasons to meditate, there is also that world famous long-term objective generally known as enlightenment. That is a much more mysterious story of spiritual development, which is also a whole lot more ambitious. Through meditation, we may seek to become truly happy independent of anything else, like literally. Most people are not up to entertaining that notion. This objective however rests upon the ancient discovery that a powerful peaceful happiness already exists inside of us, literally.

1.3. The Thinker

The words 'man' and 'human' originate with *Manu*, the name of the first man of the new human race that emerged after the great flood, according to ancient *vedic* scripture. This name is referring to *manas*, the Sanskrit word for our mind. The *vedic* tradition thus defines us humans as thinkers, ruled by the mind. It is also quite the modern view.

Even though animals also have thought processes of some kind, humans have developed thought as no other species on earth, as far as we know. According to evolution theory, the advanced thinking capacity of our frontal brain lobes has made us into the most dominant animal on the planet. Thinking has allowed us to subjugate nature to quite some degree, while it has not brought much progress in mastering ourselves.

Thinking obviously has a place in our lives. However, it is not the only feature that makes us human. First of all, we are also very much feeling creatures. Thoughts and feelings always interact, for better or worse. Thinking thus comes very naturally to us, like breathing, eating or sleeping. But to think continuously, from the time we wake till we go to sleep, may not be the best way to use our brain.

Our mind is programmed that way, but also gives us the freedom to question and reprogram ourselves. Contrary to the other animals that are largely driven by instinct, our thinking capacity gives us the freedom to make our own choices. So how do we want to evolve as human beings? What could be the benefits of not thinking, at least now and then? Modern culture may be rightfully proud of the many achievements brought about by thinking and science, yet is the time then not right to also move beyond? Would it further our goals?

1.3.1. THE TWO-EDGED SWORD

We have this incredible tendency to believe that we can solve every problem through our thinking. When dealing with practical matters that usually holds true, though it might sometimes take a while or even many generations. The value of thinking in managing other issues is however much more limited. When we wonder how to get from here to there, we might use our mind and google it or something, sure. Yet when we ask the question where to go, our thinking may not bring a clear answer as there are just too many options and parameters. Then we have to feel where to go.

We try to outthink all of our problems, even though very often this is shown not to work very well. Sometimes we might think the same thought 100 times and still believe it is worthwhile to keep repeating it. Every so often we just cannot stop unpleasant thinking about past or future, even though we are quite aware it is not going to bring us anything. Thoughts thus appear as extremely addictive→4.1.7.

The ability not to think about the things that we feel are useless to think about, may be the first advantage of learning how to stop thinking. It would save quite some time and energy for starters. However greatly our brains have evolved, they are still just tools like our hands. If we cannot master our thoughts, our thinking capacity may often be more of a problem than part of a solution.

We can see this very clearly for example in how humankind now seems poised to fully destroy its own environment. The freedom of choice that our thinking brings us obviously carries great responsibility. It allows us to pursue even the most imaginary desires, while animals living natural lives are not often involved with what they cannot have. They usually display more common sense than we do.

Through our thinking, our desires appear as unlimited, though obviously fulfilling them is not. That conflict produces much unhappiness in itself, creating a state of rather permanent dissatisfaction in many people, even if they have so much to be happy about.

Thinking about all of this is obviously part of the game and has led to many auspicious movements and revolutionary scriptures. Nevertheless we can wonder, if thinking can lead to wisdom, why does it so often bring people in the opposite direction? Honestly, all ancient wisdom presented in this book has not stopped me from being quite stupid sometimes.

The very nature of the thinking process is in fact impartial and can lead anywhere. Through association and reasoning, our brain is basically just computing thoughts, very much like a computer would. Thinking is a two-edged sword, which can cut either way. We can prove anything through our thinking, hiding the fact that at the basis of every thought pattern lies an essential thought or axiom, which is not based in rationality at all.

1.3.2. BEYOND THOUGHT

At the origin of our thought patterns and opinions lie deeper subconscious feelings and insights. For example, for too many people, a forest is just a bunch of trees, a source of firewood maybe, not a living community. We can give grand lectures about taking care of the environment, but all these words will do little to convince those who do not feel a more profound connection to nature.

Thinking brings our feelings from the subconscious to the conscious. That may be useful, allowing us to translate a deeper feeling into some concept that we can work with. It is often where a solution starts, but truly not where it ends. Our spiritual insights may have a hard time to overrule our deeper fears, frustrations and desires.

Thinking differently very often is not enough to feel differently. Nothing in the universe seems more complex than our feelings. They are affected in so many ways, subject to so many parameters→4.1.1, that rational thought can only scratch the surface of their true meaning. Their most essential source lies within our subconscious programming, the so-called *karmic* impressions(VASANAS) of the past→3.6.1.

As we try to find our happiness inside, independent of what happens outside, our past programming clearly stands in the way. Our feelings often generate endless cycles of thought, expanding now this way, then that way, hardly bringing any significant result. As we may nevertheless keep trying to make some sense of it, should we not first learn to better listen inside? What happens if we can stop thinking about how we feel, allow those feelings to talk for themselves?

What comes out is definitely open for interpretation, so can we remain open-minded about it? Or will we try to control everything by labeling it within our thought constructs? Life and the feelings it brings is not very suitable for scientific analysis. There are just too many data for science to work with. So what if we listen just a while longer, before we again start talking to ourselves about what we have heard? What if we can really remain silent, let go of the tendency to analyze, the illusion of control? What if we can refrain from adding to any unpleasantness by commenting on it? What might come out of our silence?

In science it is well known that the most revolutionary discoveries are not made through rational thinking. Rather, they come as more accidental and strange intuitions from somewhere beyond our conscious mind. What if we could more consciously tap into that subconscious potential? Imagine what scientific progress we could generate by making meditation a standard part of the training of scientists?

Since AI is anyhow going to do much of the data-based analytical thinking for us in the nearby future, should we not look into developing something more juicy ourselves? When asked, AI confirms it will never have intuition. Whatever options it may so nicely display before us, we will still need to choose between them from deeper inside, from what can be called our 'II' or Intuitive Intelligence.

In dealing with our feelings, if thinking can be alternated with not thinking, it might just work better. Thinking will be very useful to make more concrete our understanding that emerges more clearly from the subconscious by not thinking. And why not simply add not thinking to thinking and thinking to not thinking, make them one?

1.3.3. TO SEE

The power of not thinking comes as an ability to see, which is the literal translation of *Dhyana*, the Sanskrit word for meditation. This seeing is not based on book loads of thoughts, weighing this and that. It is a doubtless knowing, a connection to that intuitive intelligence, which traditionally is called the cosmic intellect(BUDDHI). It can be used to see inside as well as outside.

We will explore the subject of developing intuition further on→2.6.1. To truly understand our complex feelings though, intuition is a must. It will allow us to reduce some issue to its essence and hence resolve it. That way we can really move forward in becoming more happy independent of what happens.

As thinkers, we can thus understand the value of moving beyond our thinking, towards our even greater intellectual capacities. That ability to access our higher intellect and bring its insights to the light - into our thinking process - may be the ultimate human potential.

And as we thus may learn how to stop thinking, we will also discover the unexpected treasure of our true divine nature, the cherry on the cake. Yet we have to very fundamentally stop thinking of ourselves as thinkers only. We are so much more than that.

1.4. Our True Being

I have written so often about this unspeakable truth[6], that I am at a loss now where to begin, without overly repeating myself. Since the central subject here is meditation, let us look at what I usually call the Self(PARABRAHMAN) from that point of view.

1.4.1. TEARS OF BLISS

When we meditate, we want to find out what is hidden behind our thoughts and feelings. Many secrets can be discovered there, yet the jewel of our dreams is our true beingness. It is the witness of everything that happens, the inner eye of pure consciousness. And it is simultaneously the most essential energy through which everything happens, from which everything manifests. As such, it is who we are in essence, our purest conscious energy or energized consciousness. I most often call it the Self, while it comes with many names such as awareness, presence, beingness, the heart, the holy spirit, cosmic consciousness or even god.

When in meditation we finally stop all that thinking, we still feel to exist and know that we do. It may be a strange experience, as we suddenly acquire a new sense of reality and all else seems to fade away as unreal. This new peaceful empty fullness brings joyful tears to our eyes. We have closed them at the start of our practice, while now we truly move our attention away from them and rejoin our heart of hearts. We then hold on to it for as long as we can, which is a long and complex love story.

When the thoughts have come back, something nevertheless has changed. Some sense of that Self remains, especially directly after meditation. It is the most precious thing that we take away from our practice. It may still be fragile, almost like a phantom, elusive when chased, impossible to catch, yet so nearby. It is even easily simply forgotten, within the maze of our thoughts and the business of our lives.

As we evolve in our practice, it becomes easier. At some point we realize that we have always known the Self, that it is actually nothing very special, this consciousness that remains in the gaps between our thoughts. Every individual knows of his own conscious existence, this sense of 'I am'. It is so self-evident that it seems totally unimportant. Why would we then seek it? Most people see something worthless there, negligible as a

---

6 Mainly in 'The Yoga of Truth – The Ancient Path of Silent Knowledge' by Peter Marchand, Destiny Books 2007, and 'Tantric Advaita, energizing nonduality', by Peter Marchand, self-published at Amazon 2021.

grain of sand. It is however a diamond far greater than any diamond.

So then we laugh and know to have found that which will ever bring our smile back. Some unhappiness may be unavoidable till the illustrious end→4.1.4, but we already feel free from it. We know to be free to be happy whenever we want, whatever happens. It is a wealth greater than any king's, truly destined for a god. Whatever we can say or think about it matters nothing but that one understanding, that we have found liberation. To hold onto it is in part a learning process, yet at least the pathway to heaven→3.8.4 is ours.

People who have never really meditated often believe that this stopping of our thoughts means that the plus of happiness and the minus of unhappiness are brought together into one big zero. They feel that while meditation might bring peace, it can bring no happiness, reducing our existence to that of a rock[7]. There is some logic there, but reality is different. Because if we can bring ourselves to this zero, this pure beingness without thoughts, then an unbeatable happiness emerges that can only be experienced. It appears for no reason at all but its own existence. In zero, that emptiness is full of unlimited beingness. It makes us want to laugh, to scream, to make fun of everything including ourselves.

Part of our evolution also includes answering a new question that starts dominating our mind. Why does the Self have this power, which is undeniable, to so lighten our heart? It is hard to believe in what we do not understand. The answer will teach us about its nature and how to embrace it, put it in our pocket, make it ours. All practice leads to it as it emerges from it, as it teaches us.

Empty of thoughts, the Self is empty of judgement and thus indeed beyond like and dislike, happiness and unhappiness. The blissful feeling of the Self is never influenced by whatever happens. We cannot even be sure if it vibrates at all or not, but it is the essence of life.

Silence is the sound of that pure awareness, which gives meaning to all other sounds, including words and thoughts. Unmoving, it is ever peaceful. Desire is absent, not even triggered by change. Time itself seems to disappear into that bottomless well.

There are no words for the Self, except to say what it is not, in fact then naming everything else. Only poetry can somewhat communicate the truth of it, leaving it mostly to our imagination, as we sense for it. We cannot see, hear, taste, smell or touch it. It cannot be drawn nor photographed and yet it can be meditated

[7] Sorry rock.

upon→10.6. Even the most advanced scanner that humankind might ever develop will never be able to detect the Self, as the perceiver lies beyond perception.

1.4.2. WE ARE ONE

The Self is in everyone's awareness, while it is nothing, no thing. It is formless, like an invisible cloud. It is more subtle than the most subtle of particles and yet bigger than any multiverse. We might say it is unmanifested beingness within manifested beingness, even while the very definition of these words remains unclear.

And since we most essentially are that, we cannot do anything without it, while it does nothing. We cannot even take a step forward without our awareness of that movement being present. In meditation doing nothing means being exclusively with the Self. Nevertheless, in all else the Self is also needed: in thinking, in feeling and in doing. That goes for everyone, which brings about a major realization.

That Self which we find inside of ourselves, must be present in everyone, since without it nothing can be done. And since it is without form, there cannot be any difference between that Self in each of us. There is no way to compare my Self to the Self of anyone else. One might just as well compare two invisible clouds. That Self which we found through our meditation within ourselves, seems to extend well beyond, into the entire universe. That Self which so much feels like our own, is our own, while it also belongs to the universe, which we are. We are all one in the Self. It is from this feeling of union with everything that we smile.

To truly see that Self behind another's eyes is beyond description. Because we recognize ourselves there, beyond similarities, as if we were looking in a mirror. It cannot even be compared to meeting one's identical twin, because there is only one, not two. Blessed is the one who comes out of the inside only to meet himself outside. And then it happens again and again, till we wink at ourselves behind the eye of a chicken, identify ourselves in a flower or a mountain, in whatever is.

1.4.3. TREASURE ISLAND

Now we know that we are all one, in essence, this one pure happy beingness. For the first time, we feel 100% connected. We have never been alone, that was just an illusion. Love arises from beyond conditioning, beyond wanting or needing. Love is the energy or *shakti* of the Self, the source of our smile, the answer to our question about that happy power of the

Self. Everything is perfect and we love all of it.

And then again we lose that connection. Having discovered our quintessence does not mean that we have excluded whatever else we are. Everything else has just lost some power, some relevance. The other aspects of our being however have not disappeared. They still hold great power and their relevance to us cannot be ignored so easily.

The light of the Self is thus still covered by the layers of our individual beingness. That is why, among other things, deepening our meditation practice is needed to lift these veils. The diamond is ours, if we want to work for it. The pirates have found Treasure Island, but where to dig and how deep?

1.5. Layers & Patterns

'Layers within layers' is another essential aspect of manifested reality that I have touched upon in all my books till now. These are the different layers of our individual being, the so-called sheaths of consciousness(KOSHAS). They stand in the way, so to speak, of the full encounter with the Self in the deepest state of meditation that is known as *Samadhi.*

This understanding is the basic *vedic* psychology. It is very different from Western psychology, which is mostly developed by people studying other people with severe mental issues. *Vedic* psychology originates with healthy people studying themselves through *Samadhi* meditation, which is the ultimate practice of inner observation.

The descriptions of our personalities, struggles and behaviors in Western psychology are usually produced by looking at ourselves from specific angles. Typical examples are the famous psychologist Freud, who looked at us from the point of view of sexuality, or Adler, who explained all of our behaviors from the angle of a power struggle. Each of the famous Western psychologists thus promotes their unique model of the human psyche, while none of these models seems able to singularly explain all of our complex psychological issues. Western psychology commonly does not even believe in a universal psychological model, while finding universal formulas is central to all science.

Vedic psychology on the contrary is essentially based upon self-observation in the deep meditation trance. It originates with the ancient *vedic* seers(RISHIS), yet anyone can have the same observations. The most important source of this knowledge comes when we look from the inside to the outside. In the trance state, our awareness is fully centered in itself, providing a uniquely objective view upon our own psychology.

Especially when moving out of the deeper meditation state, as different layers of our being again manifest, we can see them emerge with absolute clarity. Some of that objective experiencing of our being may also continue when observing ourselves and others in the normal waking state. Last but not least, when returning towards the center of our being in meditation, we also get a telling perspective, as these layers are being peeled of and discarded one by one.

It is always amazing how the *vedic* psychological model is so easily, instinctively recognized by anyone learning about it. This knowledge appears not as a particular and thus relative point of view on who we are. When observing ourselves, everyone can easily perceive these layers, which can be seen as truly universal. According to *vedic* philosophy, they do not only exist within our human psychology, but are the essential layers or dimensions found in anything manifested in the universe.

As sheets of cloth covering a lamp, or sheaths enveloping a knife or sword, these layers are what we are made of, as individuals. They obscure the light of the non-individual Self shining from within. These layers are particular forms of energy and the more close they are to the Self, the less dense and more subtle they are.

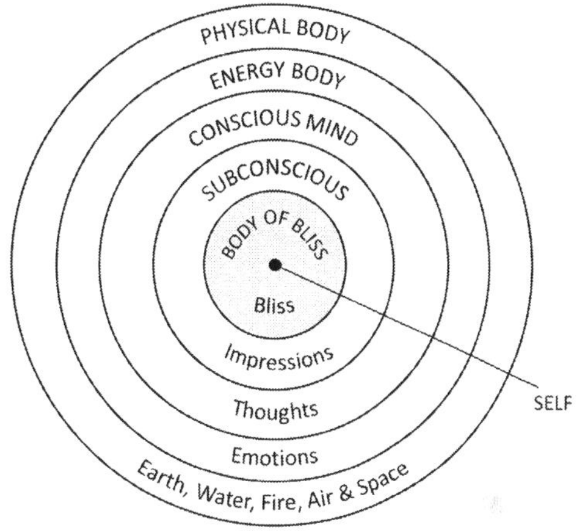

Image 1 - The sheaths of consciousness.

Our outermost layer is the physical body, made of the five elements. Next is our raw energy body, where we experience a variety of emotions. The conscious mind tries to make sense of life, thinking of solutions. The subconscious has wordless, energetic opinions about all of it, based in past experiences. It covers the gentle vibration of the body of bliss, directly generated by the Self.

As energies, the vibration of these sheaths typically ever changes. As our awareness identifies with these changes, they cloud our understanding and bring forth a variety of feelings. These are all too often far removed from the peaceful bliss of our innermost being. The different mental, emotional, behavioral, energetic and biochemical habitual patterns that we can find in ourselves, all relate to interactions between these layers. To change these patterns, we need to understand their components.

The central objective of yoga and meditation is to be happy whatever happens$_{\leftarrow 1.1}$. That is impossible without full access to the bliss of the Self, which may dissolve any unhappy feelings generated within the layers of our individuality. Some understanding of these layers is thus a requirement, so that they literally become more transparent. Each has different properties and separate ways in which they can be troublesome. Especially to reach deeper meditation, we cannot easily let go of these layers without clearly recognizing them.

As we thus divide ourselves into different densities of energy, we should always remember the unity inherent within these layers. What appears here as five separate aspects of our individual psychology is actually one thing, which we could call the bodymind. Each layer is in continuous interaction with the other layers and no behavior within one layer can be explained without referring to all other layers. These interactions happen so fast that they can only be perceived as a continuous interplay of energies. They manifest from the one energy of the bodymind, our vehicle into this world.

To separate our experiences of the different layers of our being is nevertheless useful in so many ways. Especially for the meditation process, each of these layers brings particular phases, obstacles and techniques. For example, the physical body poses the issue of sitting painlessly$_{\rightarrow 7.4}$, while releasing the *pranic* body requires breath retention$_{\rightarrow 8.6}$. Each sheath of consciousness plays a particular role within the process of meditation.

In trying to bring happy harmony to these layers, the more subtle inner sheaths outrank the more gross outer layers. If the physical body feels miserable, we can still breathe a good feeling into the emotional energy of our *pranic* body. When our emotional energy feels unhappy, some constructive thoughts in the mental body may overrule it. If our thoughts become hectic and desperate, we may still generate peace from the depths of our subconscious soul. And if our very soul is disturbed, the Self remains peaceful as ever.

The more deep inside we work on the very subtle levels of our manifested existence, the more this happy harmony that we seek may be durably established from the inside. Still, every layer requires some attention.

1.5.1. THE PHYSICAL BODY

What we generally regard as our body (ANNAMAYIKOSHA) is made out of the food(ANNA) we eat. It contains the five elements earth, water, fire, air and space, which correspond to the solids, liquids, fire, gasses and space of Western science. It is the earth element that gives it a particular form. Its many tissues, organs, systems, biochemistry and electro-magnetism are extremely complex and their limitless interactions are hard to fully understand. Also in our body, too many data.

The central hurdle in meditation created by the physical body is to develop a comfortable sitting posture. It should remain stable even if we are no longer in control of the body during the trance of deep meditation→13.2.4. The somewhat daunting ultimate objective is to be able to sit without moving for 3 hours, which is usually seen as the minimal duration of a truly successful deep meditation session→7.4.

Sitting on our spine is essential to reach the trance state. If we lie down or support the body too much, we usually fall asleep as our mind shuts down. Further on we will dig at length into the methods available to gradually develop a rock-solid sitting posture. If needed we can start with an already comfortable Cross-legged Posture with props and we usually end into the full Lotus Posture→7.4.4.

For this to work however, the body needs to be relatively healthy. In the chapter on physical balance→4.3 we will go into the related solutions, even if sometimes temporary. We also recognize how our emotions may cause physical imbalances→3.3.1. We can learn how to detach from some pain or discomfort that we may be unable to avoid→7.6.5.

Balancing the elements in the physical body will also help us to better balance our desires and direct them towards the upper energy centers→4.4. It may also be a requirement to achieve the basic emotional balance→4.1. that is needed to attain the deep meditation phase. Imbalances in the physical body may create or support unpleasant feelings and reduce the duration of our stay in more uplifting emotional states. Science points here to the many information molecules known as neurotransmitters, such as serotonin, endorphins and adrenalin. They communicate emotional information within the nervous system and towards other types of body cells as well.

Another major task is to sufficiently remove stress from the physical body prior to our meditation practice→7.2.1. Otherwise, when the body relaxes in meditation, the release of stress energy will disturb our concentration and might also trigger strong emotional responses from the subconscious mind.

1.5.2. THE ENERGY BODY

As we move further inwards towards the Self, our first subtle body(PRANAMAYIKOSHA) is entirely made out of the vital energy called *prana*. The life force of the energy body is primarily absorbed by our continuous breathing. It permeates the physical body and creates like a force field around us. This *pranic* body extends about an armlength from the physical body and is often named the *aura* in more Western spirituality.

It is here that we experience our emotions in nine essential emotional flavors→4.1.5, which we can directly affect through breathing exercises. The origin of these emotions however is also found in the other layers. Still, our vital energy vibration(GUNA) can be experienced as low, high or balanced→4.2.1, which will have a major impact on the quality of our feelings. Connecting to the feeling of the Self is hard when our energy vibration is either low or high. Real meditation is only possible when our energy vibration is balanced, while meditation is a great tool to bring it into balance.

The life force vibrates because of its basic polarity, which is traditionally expressed as a fluctuation between solar and lunar energies→4.2.4. It is quite normal however that our energy is either more solar or more lunar, more expanding or more contracting. Sometimes we are more rational, verbal, extroverted and creative, reflecting the more electrical and heating solar energy. Or we can be more emotional, visual, introverted and sensitive, because of the more magnetic and cooling lunar energy. That again depends on the other layers, together creating our more solar or more lunar personality in each moment, as it is needed→4.4.3.

The idea of individual separation, which is usually named the Ego→1.5.4, is very much based in our particular energy vibration. If that energetic aspect of the Ego cannot be sufficiently flexible to deal with changing circumstances, the basic polarity of our energy becomes imbalanced and the neutral feeling of the Self is lost.

Fortunately, breathing exercises and other practices can at least temporarily restore neutrality in the *pranic* body and our feeling. That is also essential to keep the physical body in a healthy state. In the meditation process the solar and lunar energies may become so well balanced that the life force becomes neutral or non-polar. Only then the energy can rise to a higher and more subtle level. That process usually starts in the *pranic* body, for example with alternate nostril breathing→8.5.2. Many more aspects of working with the *pranic* body will be discussed further on→8. They will all help us to relax, reducing the stress where we are most directly experiencing it.

In deeper meditation, after losing awareness of the physical body, our attention is also withdrawn from the *pranic* body towards the center. While we can then still experience subtle feelings, they are no longer so emotional in nature. In that phase, breath will ultimately stop and the *pranic* body will be temporarily shut down, set on standby. It is thus reduced to its most subtle essential form, which is like a pilot light or a seed.

1.5.3. THE CONSCIOUS MIND

We usually believe that thinking takes place in the brain, while according to *vedic* science this is both correct and incorrect. Conscious thought requires the electrical currents in the neural patterns of our brain cells, as well as their more emotional interplay with all kinds of information molecules in the cerebrospinal fluid. Yet in the *vedic* model, our thoughts are experienced in a more subtle energy body: the mental body (MANOMAYIKOSHA) of the conscious mind(MANAS).

Whatever happens in the brain is thus seen as the connection between this thought field made of subtle *prana* and the *pranic* and physical bodies. The mental body itself is the subtle energy of those thoughts as they appear to us. It is further connected inside through the body of the subconscious mind→1.5.4.

Hence our thoughts are affected from everywhere within the bodymind. That soup we just ate, the energy of a place or some old trivial memory may all in part be responsible for whatever thought comes to our mind. While it appears as if there is only one person thinking, there are actually many partners in this inner dialogue, which also happens between distinct parts of the brain.

The usually endless stream of thoughts should thus never be taken too seriously. A thought in itself has no validity and it is up to us to discard it or accept it. Thoughts are not only happening through association and reasoning. They originate in some particular part of the bodymind and are thus always partial, even if sounding rational and impartial.

The most important quality of our thoughts is definitely energetic and emotional in nature. Rationality is only trying to make some sense of it. Both the most stupid as the most elevated thoughts may originate with the deeper layers. The one who tries to understand is the Ego, feeling responsible to make informed decisions.

Understanding is the great illusion created by the conscious mind→3.4. If we can remember that, then it does pay off to improve our understanding. Relatively wise concepts may reduce the restlessness of mental confusion→3.4.1. We feel less of a need to think all the time and to understand equally means we know what to do, how to practice→3.5.

Stopping thought is the most direct method to increase Self-awareness, while when we are thinking both coexist. To stop the high-speed train of thoughts may thus begin with slowing it down. To pull the emergency brake is possible, but it might give us a headache and depends so much on willpower that the inner silence usually cannot last more than a few seconds in the less advanced practitioner→10.1.1.

Mind is by its nature excited, restless and whimsical. To gradually slow it down means to focus it somewhere, not allowing it to roam around as usual. Prior to that it is generally advisable to first calm down the energy vibration of the *pranic* body, as it is from there that the mental body is primarily powered.

Yet at some point it becomes merely a decision to stop thinking. On the one hand, this emerges as a phase during the meditation process. On the other hand, it is also an ability that one may acquire through practice, which no longer requires any prior practice and can be applied on the fly in daily life. So yes, some people move through life with the power to hold on to inner silence.

If the silence in our inner dialogue can last long enough, the meditation trance truly starts and we really dive into ourselves, beyond the conscious mind. In the deeper stages of deep meditation, the mental body will be shut down in the same way as explained earlier for the *pranic* body, being reduced to its seed.

1.5.4. THE SUBCONSCIOUS

What to say about the subconscious, which lies beyond thinking, talking or writing? For sure what follows cannot be taken too literally. The conscious mind is the part of our bodymind about which we are conscious. We only get some idea of what can be found in the subconscious on the basis of what seems to emerge from it into the conscious mind. The mystery remains however when we ask ourselves how all these things are organized within the catacombs of the subconscious (VIJNANAMAYIKOSHA).

As two layers of the bodymind, there is quite a grey zone in between the conscious and the subconscious mind. They are hard to separate, as without the subconscious content, the conscious mind simply cannot function. Equally in absence of a conscious mind, the subconscious has no way to express itself. In a more nerdy way, we might compare the conscious mind to the software of a computer, using the data stored on the hard drives of the subconscious.

Beyond memory

The subconscious first of all holds our memories. These impressions consist of words and concepts, stories of the past, including signals from all senses, as well as recollections of related emotions. All personal content of the subconscious originates with our processing of past impressions, while it goes way beyond a storehouse of memories.

All our past experiences, as well as everything we have thought, felt and learned about them, have also created another kind of subconscious content that is no longer directly related to our memories. Much of it even seems not to be primarily present as words, nor as remembered images or smells for example, but rather as content of a more energetic nature. We might also call it personality.

We can imagine our subconscious as a galaxy of star systems, not just very wide but also terrifyingly deep. Some areas are radiating peace or blooming love, while other parts may create violent eruptions or show like dark stagnant black holes, surrounded by foul gases. Some subconscious issues are clearly more active, while many others are rather dormant. And all together they also influence each other and the whole of the subconscious, which may then appear as more or less peaceful.

Atomized words

Moving deeper inside we clearly move beyond words. Nevertheless, part of the subconscious definitely still holds words. These words exist there as the building blocks of the endlessly computed sentences that we find in the conscious mind. Yet, in the subconscious there is no linear train of thoughts. Rather, the words there exist as definitions, ideas, concepts and memories. Very much like an encyclopedia, however without alphabetical ordering. So rather like a search engine, the subconscious seems based on a kind of keyword recognition, which is usually called association.

Also the associations between these words exist as concepts somehow, so the subconscious contains simple phrases made out of a few words, such as 'Italians eat pasta' or 'I don't like jazz'. Our inner ideas also contain opposing views such as 'I cannot trust anybody' or 'I have to give everyone the opportunity to be nice'.

There are even entire songs, poems and stories recorded into the subconscious, which we can recall from memory. Repetition of thoughts in the conscious mind seems like a main process through which our content is firmly engraved within the subconscious.

All these words, basic concepts and stories are continuously available to be used by the conscious mind. Without them we simply could not think. All apparently random associations made by the conscious mind are also based in these subconscious relationships, making free association an important tool in therapy to understand our subconscious drives.

As the subconscious holds our memories, it thus also contains the conclusions we more or less consciously distilled from them. Like we might remember in full detail something that happened yesterday, but within a month that memory will have partially faded, depending on the value it has to us. At some point the actual memory may thus move beyond our reach, but the seed of it will remain available, as the ultimate conclusion that we have drawn from it.

Vedic scripture calls part of the subconscious content atomized, reduced to the smallest form or seed(BIJA). As atomized 'words', our past experiences may help us in more instinctively judging new experiences, without needing to remember those past adventures. Given how many things happen in just a single day, it is actually the only workable way in which the sum total of all our memories can be truly helpful to us.

Quite some information stored in the subconscious originates with learning processes that are mostly subconscious themselves. For example, our conscious understanding of the meaning of facial expressions and other body language is usually low. Meanwhile subconsciously, we all have that knowledge to some degree and it will affect our interactions with others without us being very aware of it.

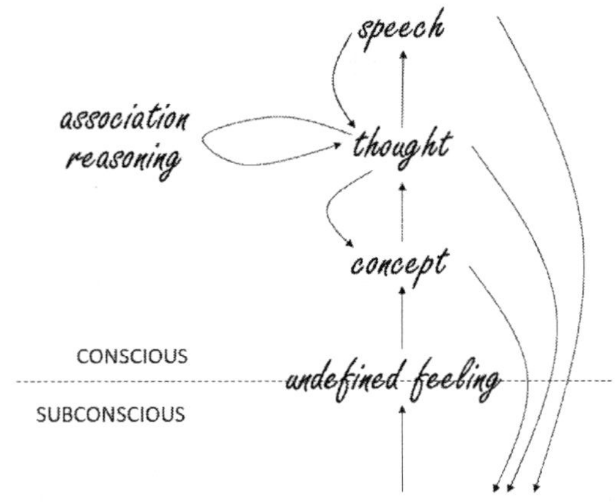

Image 2 - Interaction between conscious and subconscious.

As per *vedic* science, as shown in Image 2, thoughts are created when such atomized words emerge from the subconscious as not very clearly defined intuitive feelings(PARA). They are translated by the conscious mind into the actual concepts or words out of which our thoughts are made→10.3.1. Sentences emerge through association and reasoning, eventually also while speaking.

Emotional values

Words also have values attached to them, based in those past experiences. These are first of all sensory such as sounds, visuals, smells, tastes and textures, while they also have an emotional component. Like and dislike primarily are present here in a highly refined fashion, including an infinite variety of levels of harmfulness or attractiveness for example. This must go well beyond a system of words with clear definitions. Who can name all variations to the color blue?

This way, the understanding that is stored subconsciously is very emotional in nature, energetic in fact. We might say that a particularly flavored feeling is attached to every word. It is what gives the words in our personal encyclopedia meaning. Some words will have a lot of meaning or value, whether positive or negative. Other words are far less important, mere facts of the past or the knowledge gained from them, without much consequence.

Words of music

Words are made out of sound syllables. Hence also the words in the subconscious are sounds. And because of the emotional values attached to them, they are not just sounds, but songs, music. The entirety of the subconscious thus might sound like fire or a waterfall, with the overall sound as an interplay of so many little sounds. The music is continuous, yet only the loudest sounds are heard by the conscious mind and they are often triggered from there as well, as well as by the sense organs.

The power of sound is one of the greatest powers of yoga, especially when used in *mantra* or seed sound meditation→10.3.1. It can very directly affect the music of the subconscious, which is also its atomized understanding. Just like the sound of a *mantra* is more powerful than its meaning, the energy of our inner music is more powerful than whatever conceptual understanding is attached to it.

Thus, the words in our subconscious not only become more abstract as we move deeper inside. They are also increasingly reduced to their essential energies, expressed as sound frequencies→9.1.2. In deeper meditation, this may be directly experienced→10.3.1.

Narrow-mindedness

When we move about in life, we tend to look for that which we deeply know as pleasurable, while trying to avoid that which we remember as painful or uncomfortable. The subconscious however naturally mistrusts anything which is so new that it cannot be understood through past experiences. Whatever is thus not recognized, is often feared, hated, or simply labeled as 'irrelevant' or even 'nonexistent'.

Some historians believe that language development in prehistory did not start with common, practical things, which could more easily be pointed at than named. The first words thus would not have been apple, tree or stone, but rather sun, moon, stars, river, water, light, death. Naming these rather incomprehensible things not just gave a feeling of understanding them. It also brought a sense of power, a way of controlling that fear of the unknown. Oh that, that is the sun, case closed, nothing important. While the mystery has not disappeared, it feels as if known once we name it.

The subconscious may thus block us from accepting the unknown, the intangible, the truth beyond words. Accepting the unknowable is contrary to the very function of the subconscious, which is to classify and value everything, safely put it in a labeled box. We have to be always aware of this tendency of the subconscious to reject that which does not yet fit within its prior programming, also while reading any book.

The origin of the Ego

At the center of it all, we find the most essential word 'me' or 'I', to which all other words are related. That relationship is there in the fundamental separation between 'me' or 'not me'. It is here that we find our dear Ego[(AHAMKARA)] , the 'I-maker', in its most essential form.

We identify as 'me' with the physical body, with the feelings in our energy body, with the thoughts in our conscious mind, with the impulses produced by the subconscious and maybe also with the next layer, the blissful energy emerging from the Self. The Ego thus has no body of its own, being just like a bunch of ideas in the subconscious taking their totality very seriously.

The Ego is a reflection of the Self in the subconscious, when the awareness of 'I' seeks an answer to the question 'Who am I?' in our various bodies. It is like the reflection of the moon in a puddle of water, which a child might take for real as it tries to grab it. We cannot find the Self in the bodymind, only in the 'I am' of our awareness.

Still, we mostly identify with what we see as personal, which for most people starts in the physical body. From the identification with the physical body, we also tend to identify with things outside of us, start seeing physical things as part of us. This identification manifests in 'mine' and 'not mine', 'I want' and 'I don't want', 'I like' and 'I dislike'. This process is not limited to physical things. It includes opinions for example, which depend on identification with some content of the conscious and subconscious minds. And it obviously also includes other beings.

While a majority of the concepts thus

stored in the subconscious may be labeled as 'irrelevant', the number of 'important' identifications that make up the entirety of our Ego is still vast. And all tend to produce and reproduce in us certain more or less powerful tendencies(VASANAS) to think, feel and act in particular ways, whether uplifting or not. Some of them we may easily change, just by changing our mind about them. Others are more resistant to the power of the conscious mind and we keep repeating them from the subconscious, such as bad habits.

Desires and aversions may emerge from all layers of our being. The elements of the physical body are a primary source, triggered by the life force as it interacts with the elements in the energy centers of the *pranic* body→4.4.1. Desires and aversions may be further amplified by the capacity for fantasy of the conscious mind. Yet it is in the subconscious that these truly gain power, as we attach to them, which is primarily a subconscious identification process.

Fortunately, we do not only repeat our mistakes. Every day we also try to repeat our successes. Our Ego gets to decide which is which. To change our tendencies, desires and aversions at their source is the true spiritual growth→3.8. Whatever we come to understand in our conscious mind, it can only gain true meaning if the subconscious accepts to be reprogrammed accordingly.

It is truly mysterious how the subconscious is said to contain our *karmic* impressions→3.6.1. They produce not just our *karmic* tendencies to act in certain ways, but also *karma* as destiny itself. Whatever happens to us is thus said to be attracted by our own inner vibrations. The songs of the subconscious are ever heard by the universe and somehow it responds. Life provides us with the experiences needed to bring the music into the conscious and allows us to finetune our inner tunes.

Impersonal programming

Not all of that Ego content is personal however. Some of it clearly relates to the body we are born in. The subconscious holds genetic memories of our bloodline. It has information that is available to large ethnic groups, such as a talent for Salsa. Some is typical for humanity at large, such as the ability to appreciate music, which is of course at the same time influenced by personal experiences.

As humans and chimps share a surprising 98.8 percent of their DNA, especially our animal nature is found here, like in possessiveness or territorial behavior. These animal instincts are usually associated with the reptile brain, while the desire to cuddle comes more from our mammal programming.

It is said that gods only give, demons

only take and human beings do the business of give and take. We can thus see our animal nature also as that which makes us into takers→4.10.3. Humans usually feel that stealing is really bad, while among animals it is shamelessly common, both in between species, as within the same species, and even in a clan or family. Just watch the birds in the garden fight over the food offered to them. We can see this as natural and harmless since animals do not have the human brain that allows taking that selfishness to the next level. Selfishness is nevertheless in origin a survival trait programmed within our bodymind.

Sometimes we may feel surprised to see our behavior explained through that of animals and vice versa. How is it possible? Because we share some part of our subconscious programming, which still very much rules our conscious actions. As those animal instincts keep us alive, we should be grateful for them, yet also see how they may lead us astray from a happy human life.

Many of our actions, such as breathing, digesting or walking, are usually regulated subconsciously. Even more complex actions such as driving can be done without thinking about them. Many of our reactions to what others do or say just happen from beyond thought. We are not robots that cannot move beyond their original programming, nevertheless even our conscious decisions are largely preprogrammed. Very much like in an AI computer, our programming and the related understanding just evolves.

Some of this programming must also be recognized as a conscious conditioning by others, found in raising kids, school education or media manipulation. With good or bad intent, we are taught to fear or hate this and that, as well as to want or need certain things to feel good about ourselves, or to feel accepted by others. Conditioning is a terrible word, while also fairly natural, part of a learning process. Continuously we program, deprogram, reprogram.

The Russian scientist Pavlov showed us long ago how dogs could be conditioned to salivate at the sound of a bell, if that sound was repeatedly presented at the same time that they were given food. We must thus realize that our conditioning does not only manifest in us through conscious thought. A lot of understanding is subconscious, existing beyond thought and created beyond thought. This is especially true during childhood, but it is still happening.

Our soul

Where are our subconscious data thus stored as words, sound frequencies or energies? Science will mostly point to the midbrain, hindbrain and brain stem. Some information that is more common, inherited from various life forms that precede us, is directly found in our DNA and all related information molecules in the physical body. Yet according to *vedic* science, the subconscious mind is not limited to the parts of the body it uses. The song of the subconscious is heard within our very soul, which is the subtle body of the subconscious.

The soul(JIVA) is defined in *yogic* science as the energy body that travels from one physical body to the next, in the mysterious process of reincarnation→2.7.2. The subconscious layer of our soul is thus personal, while the Self is impersonal. The soul is our most central individual beingness, as shown in Image 3. It also 'contains' the impersonal Self and the layer of bliss.

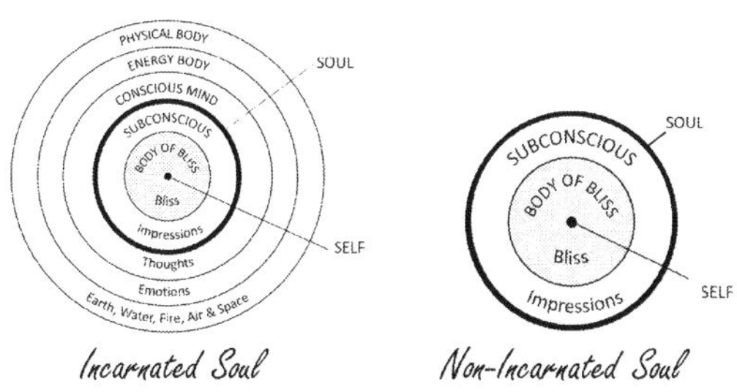

Image 3 – The individual soul.

Some of the tendencies we are born with originate in past lives. They are not just the result of the random recombination of the genes of our parents. Any parent knows that a baby shows a highly unique character within weeks of being born. The journey of the soul through many lives and spiritual dimensions is described further on→2.7.2. The subconscious can thus be seen as our soul's very database, based in its personal history throughout many lives.

Cosmic Intelligence

The layer of the subconscious mind sort-of has an outside and an inside. The outside of the layer is the interface with the conscious mind. Its words are more concrete and the content is more personal and memory related. On the inside however, words become more abstract and universal. They are called the cosmic intellect(BUDDHI), from which the name Buddha originates.

This knowing is impersonal and is seen as a manifestation of cosmic intelligence, the most pure 'wording' that the awareness of the Self may trigger in our subconscious mind. The cosmic intellect is like a universal potentiality rather than some kind of divine encyclopedia, as it does not hold words. The seeing of the Self manifests cosmic intelligence in our subconscious, producing some more essential understanding there. When those new insights are accepted by the subconscious, they become in a way again personal, even if their language might remain more abstract and universal.

The more close we move within the layer of the subconscious in the direction of the Self, the more the understanding that we find is thus truly universal, no longer time-bound even. Our cosmic intelligence makes us see beyond what all happened in the past, towards what always is, has been and will be, in every now. Pure seeing, the essence of intuition, is found here→2.6.1. For most people however, the outer layer of the subconscious produces too much noise to hear the subtle whispers of the innermost layer.

Within the layer of the subconscious, *vedic* science will thus often separate the more personal content of the Ego from the universal content inspired by the cosmic intellect. In the theatre of our inner dialogues, they play very different roles. A rather revealing old metaphor sees the physical body as a country, managed by the conscious mind as its administration. Our deep Ego is then the king who has to take all decisions, advised upon by the wise advisor that is the intellect, and inspired by the Self, which is god almighty.

Transforming Karmic Tendencies

The rather logical task at hand is to bring the subconscious into the conscious and reprogram it. The challenge may feel truly overwhelming, given the vastness of our inner content. Thinking and feeling are not the same thing, precisely because of the immense power of this content. While part of it is personal and our own doing, some of it as explained is even impersonal, a burden shared by all, in DNA, etc. It seems like an impossible endeavor to unravel all that, until we realize that there is another way, which does not depend on handling each little inner sound one by one.

As explained before, every word stored in the subconscious relates to the single word 'I'. It is the Ego, the identification and attachment that gives power to these words. If we can exclude the central player in this game, it ends. The words and memories may still exist, but without the Ego they will have no more power. They will all basically be labeled as 'irrelevant' in the subconscious.

In the words of Ramana Maharishi - who was introduced in the Introduction - 'All *karmic* tendencies are attached to the Ego and it is thus that they can also be dissolved through disidentifying from the Ego.' Thus we may escape from the impact of our earlier programming, from our childhood, from our past lives, from the reptile brain, even from our very DNA. Only then can we truly move from 'I am number one' to 'we are one'.

This is the path of yoga and meditation, and especially of deep meditation. Again quoting Ramana: 'Through a deeper state of deep meditation(NIRVIKALPA SAMADHI) all the knots of the *karmic* tendencies are loosened and all past *karmas* destroyed, so that the light of the Self is experienced without effort, inwardly and outwardly, and at all places and times.' This deep transformation of ourselves, which also increasingly brings access to our cosmic intelligence, is the true objective of this book.

1.5.5. THE BODY OF BLISS

This is the deepest layer of our individual beingness, centered around the Self. Yet the Self is not limited to that layer or place, as it is omnipresent, in every layer and place. The body of bliss (ANANDAMAYIKOSHA) holds the energy that is the most direct manifestation of the Self, while it is not the Self. The Self also has an energy, but that energy is unmanifested, a potentiality, which is a rather abstract story[8].

The body of bliss holds the essential manifested energy from which all other energies are manifested. So all layers of our being originate in our most subtle body, which is ever peacefully happy. It holds no words and is unaffected by any pleasure or pain experienced in the other layers. Its energy is directly 'fed' by the Self on a continuous basis. Contrary to the *pranic* energy out of which all other bodies are made, the energy of this blissbody is beyond polarity→4.2.4. Hence it exists beyond action and inaction→4.2.1, as all action is created by the polarity of *prana*.

We can indirectly experience the bliss of this layer when through increasing Self-awareness its gentle vibration starts influencing the other layers. To fully and directly experience this subtle body, we have to really withdraw all of our attention from all other layers. That is only possible in the deepest phase of deep meditation→13.2.4.

Even then, the body of bliss is part of the illusion, with the risk of attachment to this peaceful happiness. So we even have to let go of the desire for that feeling to reach the end point. If after meditating we attach to the resulting bliss, we destroy it.

What more to say? We're in this yoga game for the bliss, for that happiness which is Self-sustained. I can only wish for everyone to succeed in that objective. Knowing however that even the auspicious desire for bliss must ultimately meet our equanimity, it is all part of a letting go of everything, rather than a seeking. What we seek is right here, right now. We are that.

---

[8] See Chapter 2 of 'Tantric Advaita, Energizing Nonduality', by Peter Marchand, self-published at Amazon 2021.

1.6. Deep Transformation

Life itself teaches us, transforms us, shapes us all the time. Yet that can go either way, towards more blockage or more flow, attachment or detachment, illusion or Self. All *yogic* and other disciplines, all therapies and healings, all wisdom and ideals, thus serve the same goal. They gradually transform our subconscious programming towards more universal intelligence, peace and happiness, whether more or less directly.

Nevertheless, without the ultimate transformation power of deep meditation, letting go of the multitude of profound attachments of our subconscious personality is an impossible task. The Yoga Sutras of Patanjali, the most central yoga scripture[9], clearly state that the observer can only fully know itself, if the attention can be entirely withdrawn from its objects, meaning everything else.

The English term 'deep meditation' is actually quite misleading, as it just gives the impression of a really good meditation. The original word *Samadhi* is very clearly described as a highly specific and entirely abnormal state of inner absorption→13.2.1. Simultaneously it is regarded as our most natural original state, our seed state→13.5.1. *Samadhi* is the culmination of all practice, bringing us beyond practice. *Samadhi* is the principal *yogic* practice that makes a *yogi* into a master of yoga or union.

1.6.1. ALL IS AS ONE

Samadhi literally means that all is perceived as one→13.2.1. It is called the fourth state of being, next to the waking state, the dream state and deep sleep. It is like a peculiar kind of sleep, a trance, where we lose awareness of the physical body without losing awareness altogether at all. In this state of deep meditation, the Ego seems temporarily lost, leaving only the awareness of the Self, experienced in the body of bliss and even beyond→13.2.4.

There are no words that come close to this experience. It is just a passing phase of course, a mere taste of enlightenment. Body consciousness, our emotions, the conscious mind, the subconscious and the Ego are naturally revived at the end of it→13.2.5. Yet, *Samadhi* only needs to happen once to change everything.

That 'I', which is the central creator of all valued content in the subconscious, will have gained a lot of power and confidence. But it will also be so much more relaxed and detached from this content as a result of it. Automatically, in

[9] Yoga Sutras of Patanjali, verse 1.4.

one clean effortless sweep one might say, all those innumerable little songs of the subconscious will have changed tone. As the one central parameter in our programming is altered by the deep meditation experience, the entire program adjusts→13.4.4.

Following that experience, people's personalities tend to show quite fundamental changes. A rather doubting, timid nature may fully disappear, astonishing everyone. Some kind of self-sabotage, such as frequent resistance against taking proper care of our body, suddenly is no more. New talents in art and music may be discovered. Spiritual books that before were hard to get, now seem entirely transparent. And above all, a smile comes so much more easily.

In the first hours or days after a true *Samadhi* experience, that smile seems glued to our faces. While we are back in the waking state, we still feel very connected to that other place we just visited. The entire universe looks ridiculous as a result and yet so very lovable. Hence the smile. We will talk more about coming out of a deep meditation experience, so that we do not block its naturally manifesting effects→13.3.3.

The state of *Samadhi* is in some ways similar to the hibernation of animals. It likewise involves the shutting down of the physical body, which is not the case in deep sleep. After a while even the heart will stop, breath will stop, everything but the tiniest vibrations will stop. In the chapter on deep meditation we will explore at length what all this means→13.2.4. The more the body shuts down, the more we lose our awareness of it, which is the key to enter *Samadhi*.

Samadhi starts when the conscious mind falls asleep and we lose our awareness of the body, along with our connection to the sense organs. It is like sleeping without sleeping, but it is different from dreaming because the conscious mind is no longer active. Any other deep experience, while we are still aware of sitting there, is not that.

1.6.2. EVOLUTIONS IN SAMADHI

Our first *yogic Samadhi* will be a life changing experience, while it is only a new beginning. To attain the ultimate objective of enlightenment, the cumulative effect of multiple *Samadhis* will be needed. *Samadhi* is also not the end point because it has many levels, a gradual letting go of all layers of our existence→13.2.4. While the first experience may only take a few minutes, we gradually move towards ever longer trances that may last many hours, if not more.

At often astonishing speed, this process will change our personality, until it finally becomes so relaxed and flexible that it ceases to have relevant existence. Hence it is said that we attain natural *Samadhi*, where the trance state extends even to the waking state→13.5.

1.6.3. PRAY FOR PATIENCE

We will further on explore how to detect the occurrence of *Samadhi* in our meditation practice→13.2.2. Yet *Samadhi* is not something that can be done→12.2. We can only create the circumstances for it to happen. So while we should never lose sight of that precious jewel, we cannot be too eager for it. Ultimately, willpower has nothing to do with it. Tiptoe inside, don't make a sound, don't scare away that which cannot be found[10].

After getting our first tastes of deep meditation, which might happen quite rapidly, it becomes more difficult again. Honestly, it will take most people years of sustained practice to master *Samadhi*, even if some beginner's luck is involved→13.2.3. To have the power to consciously bring ourselves to the point where the grace of *Samadhi* can happen, it takes time and effort.

For my original teacher Harish Johari→Story1, it only took about 10 minutes to enter *Samadhi*, after which we could no

Story 1 Meeting My Teacher of Truth

Once upon a time, I met master Sri Harish Johari, who became my principal teacher (SATGURU). He was a successful author, a gifted painter and sculptor, a splendid cook, an ayurvedic massage miracle, a wonderful chanter of mantras and a unique composer of Indian music. To me he was mostly such an inspiring teacher, but he did not think that to be very important. He was a magical person, stirring things inside of me with a warmth that was really addictive. He effortlessly combined universal beingness with individual character, always so clear about the subjectivity and objectivity of his teachings. His knowledge was so vast that it felt like he could answer any question in full detail. My limited understanding is entirely shaped by him and this book would not exist if I had not been fortunate to meet him when I was only 20 years old. If that would not have happened as it did, for sure the course of my life would have been entirely different.

---

[10] Paraphrasing myself here from the last chapter of 'The Yoga of Truth – The Ancient Path of Silent Knowledge' by Peter Marchand, Destiny Books 2007.

longer detect any heartbeat or breath. It takes quite a bit longer for most practitioners that are already able to attain such a state. It still takes me half an hour to one hour or longer for *Samadhi* to make its appearance, and there is no guarantee. Anyhow the first *Samadhi* is just a start. Who knows how long the full enlightening of our programming will take? We embark here on quite a long journey, which may last more than a lifetime.

So, we hold our horses. We realize that this is the greatest of ambitions, the practical expression of the ultimate desire for liberation. Most people are not at all ready to accept this challenge. Most people that are interested in meditation are not able to deal with that kind of expectation and the frustrations that it may bring. Many people picking up this book now, may only be ready for it many years later. Let it remain on their bookshelf until the time is right. Expectation is the trap.

1.7. The Divine Ego

Any impatience thus represents wrong understanding, wrong method, the wrong approach altogether. We have to hold our spiritual Ego→2.8.3 in check and that is not easy, because this path does require quite some effort. We will have to sacrifice at least some other attachments to walk the full length of it. We may tend to compensate for that by inflating our self-image, hiding our Ego in spiritual wrapping paper.

The objective of *Samadhi* must be simultaneously forgotten and always remembered. Very essentially, we accept ourselves the way we are, while improving, moving further, as indeed we can. We enjoy our own song, yet that just motivates us to compose the next one.

We all have this incredibly funny and tragic tendency to keep searching for the ultimate instant solution. We want to jump right now straight to the end point, from wherever we are. That is also why many teachers are still selling such so-called ultimate solution.

Yet no *mantra*, idea, exercise or power will be sufficient on its own. Such ultimate, powerful practice - and there are many - can only fulfill its promise after we have followed the path to the point where we are ready. When all obstacles have been removed, only the last non-step needs to be taken. There are no true shortcuts and very often it is only our impatience that causes us to disagree with anything other than an instant path→10.6.1.

Whoever keeps looking for some ultimate solution forgets that there is no ultimate problem. That which we truly are, is enlightened already. However dark our days may sometimes appear, that light is indestructible, always at hand in our presence. The Ego and its programming are just a natural thing, an assumed identity that suits our manifested existence. Along with the entire universe, it is itself a manifestation of the unmanifest Self. There is nothing wrong with the theatre of life as long as we do not take our roles in it too seriously. Our desired transformation is actually a matter of natural evolution.

1.7.1. SPIRITUAL EVOLUTION

This gradual relaxation of the Ego can be seen most clearly in the natural maturing of its desires. As our life force continuously interacts with the five elements of the body in the energy centers called *chakras*→4.4, a variety of desires are experienced in the bodymind. The Ego's attachment to these desires naturally evolves, as they are satisfied to some degree and more refined and rewarding tastes are developed.

Actions and efforts to fulfill our desires are part of this process of spiritual growth. As a desire is fulfilled, the experience causes us to look for something better. The understanding of the desires of the *chakras* shown in Image 4 brings so much insight into life and ourselves.

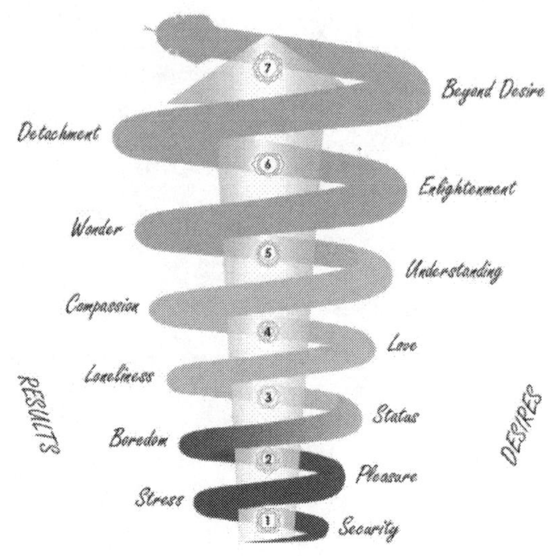

Image 4 – The desires of the elements in the chakras & the results of fulfilling them.

The density of the earth element creates the fixed physical form of the body, producing the 1st *chakra* desire for security of this form. As we secure our needs and survival through the fruits of our work, that desire becomes less. It then matures into wanting some enjoyment to compensate for the never-ending stress of working to secure ourselves, as our security will never be 100%.

The juice of the water element generates a variety of feelings, producing the 2nd *chakra* desire for enjoyment. As we thus satisfy mind and the senses in high variety, that desire becomes less. It then matures into wanting to achieve something to compensate for the satiation or boredom produced by endless sensory and mental entertainment.

The light of the fire element makes us

aware of what people see in us, producing the 3rd *chakra* desire for social status. As we achieve our social goals and a feeling of popularity, that desire becomes less. It then matures into wanting real love to compensate for the loneliness that we experience in the emptiness of people's congratulations, labels and opinions.

The life force in the air element brings a feeling of kinship with other living beings, producing the 4th *chakra* desire for real, unconditional love. As we gather some loving family or community around us, that desire becomes less. It then matures into seeking better understanding to compensate for the suffering caused by lack of harmony in both ourselves as in our community. The more we open our heart, the more it seems to bleed and we want answers.

The distance produced by the space element manifests as the 5th *chakra* desire for observation and understanding. As we contemplate, listen and read, that desire becomes less. It then matures into the desire to fundamentally transform ourselves through meditative processes, seeking to compensate for the limited power of words to harmonize our ever-changing feelings.

The harmony in the super element that holds all elements(MAHA TATTVA) generates opportunities for real bliss, producing the 6th *chakra* desire for enlightenment. As we practice meditation and gain a level of emotional stability, that desire becomes less. It then matures into giving up all desire to compensate for the tendency of any desire to break our inner silence, even the desire for silence.

In between the 6th and 7th *chakras*, the reprogramming of the Ego is happening in the most fundamental way, until in 7th *chakra* there are no words nor desires left. *Samadhi* is the main tool that produces this fundamental transformation.

There is more to say about our desires of course→4.4 and as the true spiritual desire for enlightenment evolves, it also brings with it quite particular phases, called the seven steps to heaven→3.8.4. This ancient wisdom offers the main framework for evaluating our spiritual progress and adapting our practice accordingly. This evolution is a process that chiefly occurs in the subconscious.

1.7.2. THE HERO OF THE PATH

Yet who is climbing this stairway to heaven? And what is the role of deep meditation on the way? *Samadhi* cannot be done and to learn nondoing by doing seems illogical. The Self is who we already are, so what to do? The Self will not be doing anything about it, though its mere presence is sufficient to fulfill its endlessly inspiring role.

In some stages leading towards full

Self-awareness in *Samadhi*, the Ego's willpower is definitely needed. The doing that is required is however an undoing, at least a temporarily letting go of all our attachments and related stories and desires. The illusion of being someone separate must be deprogrammed before the truth of union can be fully accepted. The Ego is destroyed by the fire of Self-knowledge, only to rise like a phoenix from the ashes→13.4.4. Then we just play our individual role in manifesting that universal Self.

One might say that the Ego is a hopeless case. Whatever solution it sees for its problems holds the seed of future problems. It is like a person fearing to drown in a river and seeking to hold on to a variety of weeds growing on the shore. Yet time and again their impermanent nature causes them to break, while the Ego desperately tries to catch some others, instead of just going with the flow.

There are phases in spiritual growth where self-study reveals that useless nature of our Ego games, which may create a feeling of nihilism. Nothing makes sense anymore, no doing seems worthwhile. Our desires, though still clearly present, seem not worth any more effort. Yet we have only lost an illusion to gain the reality of the Self. This feeling of disdain for our pointless Ego games will be turned to love. It will bring full awareness of the beauty of life and the naturalness of the spiritual growth of the Ego.

This undoing of itself is a glorious task that only the Ego can fulfill. Only the Ego can decide to meditate and let go. The Ego must sacrifice itself upon this path, freely offer up all its attachments. The Ego is thus the true hero of all spiritual progress[11]. The doer may be an illusion, while the illusion must find its own solution. Time is an illusion, but the illusion still requires it to merge into timeless reality.

Hence, in this process of reaching deep meditation, we take our time, but try not to waste it. Sometimes we will be more involved with it. Sometimes we will need or desire more involvement elsewhere. When we have some free time or even a lengthy holiday, we are free to invest some of it in this long-term project during a retreat→5.6. While we are actually just fine as we are, there is always room for growth.

Samadhi cannot be a goal in itself, as it is a new beginning, no end point. We will benefit as much from the path towards it, as from what comes after. *Samadhi* is thus the medium-term objective of our meditation practice, while from the start this activity will bring more peace and

[11] See also 'Love Your Ego' by Peter Marchand, self-published at Amazon 2019.

happiness in our lives.

In every second, our Ego is showing its lovable, divine, original nature through the effort of relentlessly pushing upward, like a tree trying to grow more branches into the sky. It only requires us not to cling to any results, lest it becomes just a new Ego game. We know who we truly are and let our light manifest ever more brightly. It is not even exclusively ours, so why attach to any achievement? Our Ego carries the burden of choosing every move or non-move. To move forward, we must love the mover, our dear divine Ego. We are the heroes that walk the *yogic* path.

1.7.3. THE MEANING OF LIFE

While we have come this far, why not also answer the rather ultimate question? Since our life is bound to fundamentally change by the path described here, should we not first know what is the actual purpose of the game, the meaning of life?

It will always feel like a mystery of course, but somehow the *vedic* seers have given an explanation that is both logical and workable. It is a four-part answer that rests upon the absolute reality of Self-awareness:

1. The universe manifests from the Self.
2. This happens naturally, without reason.
3. The meaning of life lies with the players.
4. Enlightenment is the last level of the game.

So first, the universe is a manifestation of the unmanifested Self. If the universe would not manifest from the Self, it would be a reality by itself. Yet there can be no two absolute realities existing separately from each other. The Self is the absolute reality and the universe is the relative illusion that it creates.

Second, the manifestation of the universe happens naturally, without particular meaning, purpose or expectation. This is only logical since the Self has no desire and thus never does anything with a purpose 'in mind'. The seers usually point to the blissful energy(ANANDA) of the unmanifested Self as the source of universal creation. While it is beyond change in the Self, this unmanifested energy or *shakti* has the tendency or potential to change and thus naturally manifests the universe. Just like feeling really good makes us dance and do things without particular reason, the universe manifests from the bliss of the Self simply because it can. The question on the meaning of life is thus more a matter of 'Why not?', rather than one of 'Why?'.

Third, as there exists no inherent or ultimate meaning to the game of life, only we can give meaning to it and are entirely free to do so. That purpose can be found within the entertainment that the universe has to offer. Consisting of the five elements, it brings the natural desires related to the *chakras* already discussed←1.7.1. All these desires ultimately serve our desire for happiness, which thus ever matures as our energy rises. Most will agree that the highest happiness that can be found within the illusion of the universe is in togetherness, love. It is the experience of unity in actual diversity, a game of hiding, seeking and finding.

Fourth, to find happiness independent of what happens in the universe is the last level of the game of life. This is the search for the undying happiness of the Self, known as enlightenment. It can thus be seen as the ultimate purpose of life, yet the manifestation of the universe is obviously not needed for it, since the Self is enlightened by itself. Hence the summum bonum can be found in a state of being manifested in life while being simultaneously anchored in full Self-awareness. This state is also known as natural(SAHAJA) *Samadhi*→13.5, the result of multiple deep meditation experiences, the goal of this book.

Thus the game of life(LEELA) can be seen as a divine entertainment for us to enjoy. It was not created for us to escape from. The illusionary nature of the game(MAYA) is confusing, which is part of the fun. This

Story 2 The Game of Hide and Seek

Once upon a time, Shiva and Shakti were floating through nothingness in their eternal embrace. Somehow, Shakti said to Shiva: 'Oh dearest beloved, it is so nice to be together in endless peace, love and bliss. But sometimes it gets a little boring. Can we not play a game? My nature is energy, which is ever changing, so I would love to create a universe where my energy can play in endless variety.'. Then Shiva wondered 'Oh my dear, I am the consciousness that is never changing. So how can I enjoy that ever changing universe of yours?'. Shakti however had her answer at the ready: 'No worry honey, I will place you inside of everything, so that you are at the center of every thing and everything. The center never needs to change, only my energies swirling around it will change. Thus you can remain never changing and I can be ever changing. We will then lose and find each other again and again and we will have so much fun.'. Thus Shiva agreed, Shakti created the universe and the divine love game of hide and seek called Leela began.

love game of hide and seek between consciousness and energy is beautifully illustrated in one of the many *vedic* creation stories←Story2.

While playing, we can nevertheless escape from the unhappiness caused by the ever-changing nature of the game. The clue is to remain detached from anything happening in the game and identified with the absolute reality inside. The path that leads towards this heaven on earth is the path of *Samadhi*. And we are all free to walk it.

2

THE MEDITATION PROCESS

Our meditation practice always needs to be adapted to the practitioner, and not vice versa. Nobody can tell us how to meditate. We all have to develop our own ideal meditation series, which will gradually evolve. As our objective is the same, we will also move through the same phases along the way, travel similar roads. It is a great journey of finding our own path among many, following that light inside.

2.1. Meditation Phases

While the way to do it is totally individual, what has to happen during the meditation process is the same for all. Some dislike that idea, preferring an entirely individual kind of magic in meditation. Yet we are all human beings and only in accepting that starting point we can move forward. The methods that we use to move through the meditation phases are our own, while the phases themselves are universal.

We all have the same Self as our goal and we all have to deal with the same layers of our individual existence, which are blocking the full and free access to the Self. If *Samadhi* is our objective, we have to move through the same meditation phases, letting go of these layers one by one. The duration of each phase depends on how fast we can reach its objective.

As shown in Image 5, we start with the firm intent to meditate. Then we relax body, breath and the senses, so that they minimally distract the conscious mind. That allows us to fully focus our awareness on the object of our meditation. Once concentration is stable, we enter the effortless state of real meditation. Finally, deep meditation can manifest and we automatically move beyond the conscious mind, pass through the subconscious and merge with the Self. In a nutshell, that is what needs to happen, even if for advanced practitioners many of these phases pass by so quickly that they are hardly noticed.

Image 5 - The process of meditation.

Whatever changes the practice brings to our subconscious programming, it will bring changes to our lives. The way we live obviously will also very much determine what can happen on the meditation mat. The one who thinks otherwise can never move beyond the relaxation of mind, merely compensating for a stressful life.

Too many meditation teachings actually do not move beyond some mental wellness. Obviously, teachers need to somewhat cater to their students. If we cannot make them fly, maybe they can learn to jump. At some point however, the practitioners must accept the need to put some effort into it, or they will never move forward. The true, deepest relaxation can only be reached if we get a firm hold on that chattering mind.

PHASE	FOCUS
Intention	forceful
Relaxation	relaxed
Concentration	forceful
Meditation	relaxed
Samadhi	effortless

Table 1 - Evolution of our focus through the meditation phases.

This process represents an alternation between tension and relaxation, as shown in Table 1. We find a similar approach in posture practice→7.2.2 and in many breathing exercises→8. While some focus is always needed throughout the practice, a phase where we are more forcefully concentrated is always followed by another with a more relaxed focus. In the last phase of deep meditation, the focus is strong, unwavering, yet there is no more effort, as the doer has left the scene.

2.1.1. INTENTION

Even if it only takes a few seconds, we all have to decide to meditate, make our intention(SANKALPA) perfectly clear. It is advisable to contemplate a little longer on this decision, gather our willpower. We have to be properly motivated to let go of our lives and not step into the practice half-heartedly. From being always fully mesmerized by what happens in our lives, we have to temporarily lose all interest.

Before we start our practice, we also have to know exactly what we want to do. We can change our mind about it along the way. But if all the time we will wonder what to do next, we cannot meditate. Repeating a series of practices for longer periods of time is generally advisable, so the plan will often be to repeat the same series as yesterday→5.4. At a more advanced stage, we will more or less follow the same path as always, rapidly moving through the meditation phases towards the point where we usually can go no further. For that last part then, we might plan something new.

Usually the intention phase takes the form of some fixed phrases, mentally repeated at the beginning of every session→6.3. As any expectation will destroy the results of our efforts, it is auspicious to surrender our practice to the divine in some way or other. Adding some optional ritual, the formulation of our intention speaks in a language that is more convincing to our subconscious and might even bring valuable spiritual support→6.4.

2.1.2. RELAXATION

Only the more advanced practitioners can enter the next phase of concentration without some prior relaxation. As relaxation exercises require focusing the mind here and there, we can easily use them to measure our concentration level of the moment. It is the phase that must be the most adapted to our stress level, as it changes day by day. Whenever some part of ourselves brings lots of mental activity that disturbs our focus, it first needs more attention.

It is logical to start with the physical body, our outermost layer. We work on it until we sit comfortably and solidly, which might take less than a minute for some, while others may spend over one hour on the deep relaxation of the body in posture (ASANA) practice→7. Next we relax the *pranic* body through breathing exercises (PRANAYAMA), until our breath is slow and deep, generating a profound feeling of calmness and slowing down our thoughts→8. We then start relaxing the next layer of the conscious mind by removing its connection to the outside world (PRATYAHARA), purifying the senses, followed by withdrawing our attention from them→9.

This phase ends with a feeling of relative detachment from everything. We witness our environment, breath and body in equanimity, hardly mentally commenting on our experiences. We are then primarily aware of the witnessing and the witness, of the Self. We also observe our thoughts and feelings, without too much adding to them. This state is commonly called mindfulness, when the mind is still full of impressions from the environment, but we are no longer full of them→9.3.

Many make the beginner's mistake of ending the practice here, as it feels rather good already. They believe to have reached the destination, while they have merely arrived at the departure gate. It is only in the next phase that we will move beyond wellness meditation and actually start emptying our mind.

Nevertheless, for people that are still struggling with emotional stability, it is very advisable to first repeatedly learn to create & enjoy a state of happy mindful relaxation. As that becomes easier, including getting that glimpse of the Self, they may be able to muster the willpower needed in the next phase and really start conquering their minds.

2.1.3. CONCENTRATION

Control over mind is the main real challenge in the process of meditation. One cannot let go of something without first holding it. We cannot stop the theatrics of the mind if we let it run anywhere it wants. This concentration phase(DHARANA) is like a mental workout and many are not up to it. They first need to become more relaxed. Yet if we want to be mentally strong, ready to face life square on, the arrow of our mind needs to be sharpened, concentrated. We need to become one-pointed.

While we all have the power to stop our train of thoughts by sheer willpower, we usually cannot hold onto that silence for very long→10.1.1. The moment we relax into it a little, some thoughts easily arise. Thus in meditation practice it is common to focus on the same idea, image or sound repeatedly or continuously, holding on to one meditation object for a longer period of time. That means we are still thinking, but the usual train of thoughts, moving forward through association and reasoning, has stopped. Our Ego's storytelling truly ends here.

The very function of our mind is to always look for something new, so it will naturally resist this boring focus on just one object. The creative capacity of the mind in bringing up new stories will be quite astonishing. From the most trivial to the most significant aspects of our lives, we may experience that it is really hard not to get caught by our inner dialogues.

We must persevere. The only answer to every question is the object of our meditation. Whenever we experience thoughts coming, we just again focus on our meditation object. Its energetic quality may help to gradually calm down the mind and make it easier.

If too many thoughts keep coming, we might give our mind more to do at first, using particular mindlocks→11.2. Combining more than one meditation object into one synchronized concentration practice may be required. If we have to stand on our head to be able to mentally repeat a *mantra* without thinking, so be it. Gradually we will become more concentrated. This phase ends in being fully focused on a single meditation object, experienced solely by the inner senses→12.1.1.

Frustration, desperation and other ways of not accepting the very nature of our mind, are the real blocking factors→11.1.2. In the end, mind will bend to our will. Disidentifying from our mind is the key both to stop thinking, as to not make a personal issue out of any temporary lack of concentration. We should also understand ourselves as children of a culture that rather promotes a hyperactive mind. We can be patient when also in this way reprogramming ourselves.

Even if sometimes we do not get to a really concentrated state, we will still have gained more mastery over mind. Even if we do not feel pleased with the results of our practice, we can be satisfied to have made the effort. We let the means become the end.

During this phase, the quality of our meditation object is extremely important→10. It should be maximally attractive, which is largely a personal matter. Its repeated use will imprint an energetic quality on the bodymind. Some sound objects for example are clearly able to silence the thought burping of the subconscious mind→11.3.2.

To stop our mind from flying around, it must be grounded. An object is needed and the more concrete it is, the easier it will be for the mind to hold onto it. Using the vehicle that is our object, we move from the form to the formless, from that with quality or *guna* to that which is beyond all qualities→13.2.4. It is like teaching a child the abstract character 'a' through the concrete image of an apple, as in 'a for apple'. Thus the object ultimately brings us to the Self.

As the Self is formless, many prefer to concentrate on a formless object, yet that is an illusion. Objects naturally have form, even if we can also meditate on more abstract forms→10.5. We will always concentrate on something, even if that something is the nothingness, the silence, the breath, a lotus, space or whatever. Even if we take the subject or Self as our object, it will be an object of mind→10.6. The need to concentrate our mind will not be lessened by it. Anyhow, we are free to choose our meditation object and we will go through the many options at length→10.

2.1.4. MEDITATION

In the phase of actual meditation(DHYANA) we remain fully focused on our meditation object, while gradually releasing willpower. Through the prolonged absence of the usual storytelling by mind, the sounds of our subconscious programming become more peaceful. No longer agitated by mind, the Ego can now fully relax. As it exists only as the story of stories, the quiet wordless silence of this phase makes the Ego forget itself.

We ease into the practice without losing our attention. Like at the end of the relaxation phase, when we witnessed a still rather distracted mind, we finally observe a fully focused and quiet mind. Mind is now in fact doing the practice, singing itself more and more to sleep, mesmerized by the meditation object. Thus, a trance develops in which the Ego can let go of doership and the one who is meditating may disappear.

2.1.5. DEEP MEDITATION

Samadhi then suddenly takes us by surprise, as if we are absorbed inside from the inside. We are no longer aware of sitting there, because we are no longer connected to the outside. We see no more difference between what is witnessed, the witnessing and the witness. Our meditation object becomes more abstract, energetic, until our experience of both existence as meditation becomes very subtle.

The subconscious is now so quiet that we can easily pass through it into the body of bliss→13.2.4. Then in a state of formless beingness, existing as the Self only, time disappears, until it reappears. We do not remember much of it, yet as a result of this temporary enlightening experience, full Self-realization remains. The new identity has a strong but relaxed nature.

Through that powerful relaxation of the Ego or Self-identity in deep meditation, the deprogramming and reprogramming of the subconscious happens all by itself. It occurs when gradually coming out of our *Samadhi* trance→13.2.5. It will continue even as we again enter the conscious mind, which also has a role to play in the resulting transformation process. The impact might even take months to fully manifest. And as the cocooning in one *yogic* trance session follows another, the great metamorphosis of the caterpillar into a butterfly becomes ever more pronounced.

2.1.6. LIFE

As our meditation practices evolve, our new programming has to find its way into our thinking, relationships, habits, attitudes, and feelings. The old attachments, thought patterns and bioelectrochemical fluctuations may nevertheless tend to repeat themselves, requiring some clear yet compassionate confrontation.

Hence the peace that we seek evolves into one practice, both happening in life, as when we step out of it in meditation. Progress through the meditation phases is not primarily a technical matter. It follows our energetic transformation, as it is digested and manifested in life.

Emotional→4.1, energetic→4.2 and physical balance→4.3 are keys to allow that maturing of peace. There are things to do→4.8 and stop doing→4.9. Food→4.5 and habits→5.3 must be optimized to a reasonable degree and we can use home remedies→4.6, fasting→4.7, retreats→5.6 and many more tools to accelerate our progress. Regular tasks such as cleaning are now also performed differently, no reason needed to sing or dance along. Our desires→4.4. and relationships→4.10. become more harmonious and the story of our life gets more real. We definitely should not forget to live life to the fullest, transcend our desires by fulfilling them.

As we thus overcome the numerous impediments to our meditation produced by the mind→3.3., we can uncover many treasures→3.2. that support our meditation power. One-pointed confidence is the result of sustained practice→3.1., alignment with natural cosmic rhythms→5.2., increasingly refined and applied understanding→3.4., as well as the power of *karma*→3.6..

Then finally any distinction between life and our meditation practice ends and we always reside in the same state of pure natural beingness. The bodymind is still operated in playing the game of life, but there is no one left to be fooled by any of it. Not so many people may attain this state of natural *Samadhi*→13.5., while it is everyone's birthright. Not a single reader should ever doubt it.

2.2. Personalization

Teaching everyone the same meditation series is rather useless, which basically explains the volume of this book. Group practices can only give people some experience, leading to some insights in the process. Thus also the practices in this book must be seen as example practices. We are all unique and if our differences are not taken into account, many will get stuck in some meditation phase or other. The example practices thus lead us to developing our own optimal series of practices.

There is the old Christian saying that 'all roads lead to Rome' and it also rings true here, as we are all having the same destination. Yet we all arrive from different airports and to reach Rome from Belgium I could even just walk. So the differences in the paths we need are as great as the differences that exist between us in terms of where we are as individuals.

Obviously, this is first of all a matter of ability. Our ability to let go of tension will affect the time needed for relaxation. Our ability to concentrate will determine when we can start relaxing into real meditation. Our ability to let go of control will decide when the deeper meditation trance manifests. Our meditation exercise series must thus naturally evolve and the time spend on each phase will vary accordingly→6.2. As general Self-awareness grows through the practice, the overall practice will mature.

2.2.1. DIFFERENCES

These abilities depend in part on our meditation experiences. Meanwhile also our general level of peace will very much determine what is possible. Some people are born with more peace than on average. Many are caught in very stressful lives, while life may be far less demanding of others.

Some practitioners have chosen to be renunciates→2.4.2, having hardly any responsibilities in the world. Others are householder *yogis*→2.4.2 and many depend on them. The time that we can actually spend on our meditation practice totally determines the ideal series of practices. What worked when on holiday in an *ashram* may often not work back at home.

Some people are more stress resistant than others, simply because of their particular biochemistry. This is partially expressed by the body chemistry they are born with or have developed on the way→4.3. Body chemistry may equally create a particular need for love and devotion in the practice, the ability to focus our willpower or a tendency to overthink. In some people we generally find too much activity, while in others passivity is the principal trap→4.2.1.

The personal dominance of lunar or solar energies will make us more easily engaged by visual or sound objects respectively→4.2.4. It will also affect willpower and the ability to let it go. The objective is to bring the solar and lunar energies more in balance, so that our energy can become neutral. That neutrality is however not generated in the same way for everyone.

Our general emotional state will equally define the process. Are we rather happy or not, when we start to meditate? When unhappy, do we tend to be angry or depressed, or are fear or sadness predominant? A particular relaxation or meditation object may be most suited in each case. Especially if these emotions seem to trigger many thoughts during meditation→4.1.6, such differences matter.

People that are still in the process of releasing serious trauma may be quite limited in meditation→4.1.9. While they may be very motivated to practice, any relaxation may automatically bring forth their turbulent suppressed emotions and memories→12.3.2. Some might end up crying, feeling anxious or severely frustrated and may then often seem truly worse off than before. Yet in the long run, this release of emotion may prove to be helpful, especially if the practice is adapted to the situation.

Our more general personalities are also at play. Do we identify ourselves with the archetypes[12] of leaders, mothers, scientists, rebels, players, hedonists, philosophers, servants, warriors? It means we will easily identify with some practices and not at all with others. Real lovers are hedonists, who will dread the boredom they associate with meditation and will always be most engaged in the practices that bring them some kind of entertainment. Born leaders, scientists and warriors will easily stick to the meditation plan, while players and hedonists may rapidly lose track and rebels will do so on purpose. Philosophers and scientists tend to try to understand everything which happens, destroying the actual practice with their endless questions and comments. Mothers, players and servants may more easily lose confidence if their concentration level is too low, while in others that will primarily generate more motivation.

These general images that we have of ourselves, the principal roles that our Ego has identified with, are not so easy to bypass. Our characters are very much at the center of our subconscious programming, self-illusions defined in very refined ways. Obviously, we usually

[12] These examples are inspired by the Vedic planetary archetypes.

identify with more than one of such roles. As the situation demands, we take on the personalities of parents, children, teachers, students, carpenters, gardeners or influencers.

In all these ways, the different energetic qualities found in the many layers of the bodymind, as well as the particular attachments of the Ego, will determine which practice series works best. The Self that we seek is the same for all, but meditation is not a seeking. It is a releasing of everything else. All that stands in the way of the pure experience of the Self has to be dissolved during meditation. We all have very different things to let go of and thus need tailor-made techniques to achieve each of these goals.

2.2.2. OPINIONS

Last but unfortunately not least, beliefs and opinions probably affect people's choice of practices the most. Nonduality believers want to focus only on the Self, in some way or other→10.6. Others believe in the magic of *mantras*→10.3.3 or *yantras*→10.4.5. Some feel that loving surrender to a preferred form of the divine is the only true meditation→10.1.2. Others experience truth in a perfect posture→7.2.1 or the energy of breath→8.1. If there is no love for what we are doing, if it feels contrary to our beliefs, how to do it?

Yet we must be open minded and not exclude anything on a purely theoretical and principally egoic basis. These opinions are but expressions of our programming. That which we are trying to get rid of, will thus also stand in our way, hidden behind these stories.

It is not because we passionately believe in one thing, that something else cannot work for us. The variety of practices found in all traditions has been developed precisely to answer different needs. Personalization of the meditation process is largely a matter of trial and error. If we do not wholeheartedly try something out, how can we judge it? If some practice works for us, then it does the job. Our choices of the many complementary paths and practices should be largely based on experience.

2.2.3. PATHS & TRADITIONS

As we thus try out different meditation techniques, we may feel quite overwhelmed by the high variety of practices offered by so many spiritual traditions. It helps to see that all in all they are not so different. Each tradition has to deal with the same layers of our individual beingness, developing techniques for passing through the same related meditation phases.

Likewise, each tradition has to provide

some answer on how to deal with thinking, feeling, doing, nondoing and the combination of all of these, which is like magic. These five aspects of our existence cover the totality of our human activity. For each, a particular *yogic* path^(MARGA)^ or approach can be discovered within any tradition, as shown in Table 2.

Thinking	Jnana Yoga
Feeling	Bhakti Yoga
Doing	Karma Yoga
Nondoing	Ashtanga Yoga
Magic	Tantra Yoga

Table 2 - The 5 yogic paths.

Traditionally, Bhakti, Jnana & Karma Yoga are seen as the 3 main paths, yet many schools will also add Ashtanga Yoga and Tantra Yoga - or one of its branches - to the list.

While these paths also exist as particular *yogic* traditions along various lineages of teachings, we should not confound them with mere traditions, to be followed or not. They are truly universal, because they offer the essential answers that any practitioner needs. There is no escape from any of these 5 paths, even if it is natural to prefer only one of them.

Our spiritual attitudes towards thinking, feeling, doing, nondoing and their magical combination will directly affect the meditation phases, techniques and objectives. Incorrect attitudes towards the principals of these paths will give both Ego and mind a multitude of meditation obstacles→2.8.3 to choose from. They offer a variety of useless excuses.

Personalization most essentially happens in how we walk these paths, which all together lead to the destination. That also involves many purely energetic, balancing practices for the bodymind→2.8.2, which make all paths easier to follow. Thus with a unique combination of all paths and practices, we will end up with our very own yoga→2.8.4, creating the most holistic approach to our own unraveling.

2.3. Nondoing in Ashtanga Yoga

Nondoing most directly relates to the meditation process. The *yogic* path that is generally associated with nondoing is the eightfold path of *Ashtanga Yoga*, leading up to the final stage of *Samadhi*. The eight[(ASHTA)] limbs[(ANGA)] are very similar to the meditation phases upon which the structure of this book is based, as shown in Table 3.

In *Ashtanga Yoga*, all layers←1.5 of our manifested being[(KOSHAS)] are methodically brought to inaction. *Asana* relates to the physical body, *Pranayama* to the *pranic* body, *Pratyahara* and *Dharana* to the sheath of the conscious mind, *Dhyana* to the subconscious and *Samadhi* to the sheath of bliss.

ASHTANGA YOGA	PHASES	C
Yama (restraints) Niyama (activities)	Life	4
Asana (posture) Pranayama (breath) Pratyahara (senses)	Relaxation	7 8 9
Dharana (concentration)	Concentration	11
Dhyana (meditation)	Meditation	12
Samadhi (absorption)	Deep meditation	13

Table 3 - Comparison of the 8 limbs of Ashtanga Yoga to the meditation phases put forward in the chapters (C) of this book.

Ashtanga is thus largely an expression of meditation technology, a logical process of increased nondoing. The Ego is countered here more indirectly, through the full relaxation and elimination of all layers of the bodymind, which are the principal source of the illusion of separation.

Compared to the *ashtanga* system brought forward by Patanjali[13], the only real difference is in my choice to emphasize some initial intention[(SANKALPA)], which is anyhow common in all traditions→6.3.

Ashtanga Yoga exists as a particular yoga tradition and teaching lineage, also known as the royal *Raja Yoga* or *Patanjali Yoga*. Nevertheless, the eight limbs put forward by Patanjali, the 'father of Yoga', are essential to understand and finetune any meditation practice. It thus has a place within all spiritual traditions.

Too many *ashtanga* schools have unfortunately reduced this tradition to the sole practice of postures and breathing exercises. That may be a good place to start for many, but why deny people the fruits of moving further? How can one leave out any of these eight steps and still call it *ashtanga*? It is a contradiction in terms, a restaurant menu promising 8 dishes yet ending with the starters.

As nondoing is the central subject of this book, we can leave it at that here. Without however also understanding the other essential *yogic* paths, we cannot understand meditation. Without knowing what to do with doing, feeling and thinking we cannot meditate, as doing, feeling and thinking will remain present to some degree in our meditation practices. Some doing is needed while we work towards that state in which real and durable nondoing manifests→12. And while the main practice in *ashtanga* is to turn away from all that doing, the other paths show us how to make it easier.

[13] Yoga Sutras of Patanjali, verse 2.29.

2.4. Doing in Karma Yoga

Whenever we do something, *Karma Yoga* or selfless service may free us from Ego-centered activities, at least now and then. While there is nothing wrong with naturally meeting our needs and pursuing our desires←1.7.1, the usual focus on what we need or want always puts our Ego in a rather stressful condition. The yoga of doing, which is named *Karma Yoga*, may provide some relief.

It is natural to expect some result out of the effort of doing something. However, that result is not always in our hands and even those might be shaky, mistakes may happen. Expectation is the mother of all disappointments and tends to postpone our happiness to some uncertain future. For sure, now and then, our Ego can use a break and be happy in the now, simply by doing, reveling in the action, but without expectation of a result.

2.4.1. KARMA

Karma first and foremost means action or doing. As we do our work, we fulfil our *karma*. The jobs that naturally come to us are our *karma*. Thus while the word *karma* is usually translated as 'destiny', it reveals itself first of all as our required contribution to life and the universe, the roles that we have to play to basically stay alive, function within the whole. Meanwhile our *karma* as action does produce our *karma* as destiny, through the *karmic* impressions in our subconscious soul. How that happens is a true mystery→3.6.

Since keeping the body alive depends on our environment and our ability to productively interact with it, our *karma* produces certain duties towards the whole. Our vulnerable body needs food and water, as well as protection from physical harm. While some loners may try to take care of themselves all by themselves, most people choose cooperation with others as the most secure way to meet our needs. Exchanging services, we thus perform our *karma* towards society, in part purely out of the natural first *chakra* desire to survive.

Yet also our other desires for enjoyment, status, love, understanding and bliss, as they relate to the *chakras* above the first←1.7.1, are part of the *karma* of life. They directly originate with the interaction between the life force and the elements our body is made off. Not fulfilling such desires does not threaten our lives, which is the difference with our actual needs. Nevertheless, fulfilling these desires to some degree is truly needed by the life force in order to retain its vitality, as our body cells need some enjoyment, as our digestive fire needs achievement, as our nerves need love, as our inner eye needs that seeing. In the long run, we need to feel alive in order to stay alive.

Desire is the natural power that makes everything in the universe move. While we usually see a desire as something which is chosen consciously, that is not its real nature. We usually do not choose to breathe, while when we decide to stop breathing the desire still manifests. Hence everything in the universe follows its nature to move and change[14]. The natural evolution of our desires follows a generally upward movement of energy that gives life meaning every step of the way←1.7.1. Without objective, without desire, no power.

Our *karmic* jobs thus also serve in fulfilling our various desires, with again much that can be better achieved together. Hence destiny includes our contribution towards society in ever further developing common enjoyment, achievement, love, understanding and bliss. Our *karma* ultimately means to serve the universe, including ourselves and our own spiritual evolution, which serves the serving. That is why we also subconsciously identify with our roles and jobs in society, producing some deep-seated personal character, with quite particular characteristics.

It seems needless to say that too many people in modern society are far too much mesmerized by their *karma* or work. We should neither run away from our work, nor run into it, becoming too stressed about it. Whatever we desire requires work. Even what we already have, may need maintenance. At some point we must realize how crazy it is to keep running through life, chasing stuff. Simple living, high thinking. Consuming less, working less. Renounce at least that which is pretty useless.

2.4.2. RENUNCIATE & HOUSEHOLDER

The *karmas* involved with living a meaningful life are thus infinitely more complex than those that keep us alive. As we wish to move the energy upward, that also brings the *karma* or action of yoga, meditation and related practices. As our desire for spiritual growth increases, our *karma* as destiny will change, triggering the actions or *karmas* that we need to perform to achieve our goal.

Renunciates, known as monks, *sannyasis* or *sadhus,* will thus try to stay away from all desires except in the desire for the bliss of enlightenment. They perform actions only in service to that goal

[14] See Chapter 14 of 'Tantric Advaita, Energizing Nonduality', by Peter Marchand, self-published at Amazon 2021.

or when needed for survival. Thus they largely live outside of society. They hardly need it and feel also not particularly responsible towards it. They believe that spiritual growth is their only true responsibility, which ultimately serves everyone.

It is no use however to permanently withdraw to the desert as long as we are still longing for an oasis. The idea is to free ourselves, not to confine ourselves to a mental cage of our own making and pretend to be happy about it. There is a huge difference between detachment and non-attachment. Detachment indicates attachment and is always forceful. Some willpower is clearly needed if we want to accelerate our spiritual growth. Yet to declare death to all desires except the ultimate one can work only if we are ready.

If all we want is the light of the Self indeed, renunciation moves beyond the action of detachment into simply being non-attached→3.8.4. It usually takes time to get there, but when we do, then why not spend the rest of our life in renunciation indeed? It is anyhow only one of many lives and we might again choose differently in the next→3.6.1.

Most people however recognize many desires simultaneously and thus they lead the more normal lives of householders. They work to support their needs and desires and this *karma* is very natural and found in all creatures. They associate with family and other groups of people, which brings more *karmic* responsibilities. It is then maybe more towards the end of life that they naturally retreat from it→3.8.5.

The householder *yogi* is only different from other householders as the desire for the bliss of enlightenment has a place within a variety of desires, traditionally summarized as pleasure(KAMA), wealth (ARTHA), harmony(DHARMA) and enlightenment (MOKSHA). Desires are thus balanced rather than renounced and any actions to fulfill them must be brought into harmony as well. Householder *yogis* can be said to follow the middle path, in between renunciates and regular householders.

Temporary renunciation, for an hour, a day, a week, a year, etc., has always been part of the spiritual game. Yet the idea to professionally renounce everything for life is fairly recent. This kind of monkhood originates with *Buddhism* over 2000 years ago, while the *yogic* culture is usually estimated to be at least tens of thousands of years old, even if opinions differ and yoga is truly timeless.

The most famous saints that produced the essential *vedic* body of knowledge were all married. The image that many people now have of the ideal *yogi*, as someone who lives entirely outside of life, is thus historically incorrect. The householder *yogi* is actually the original principle, letting renunciation naturally grow→3.8.4. Also here, we are free to make our own choice, as no one can stop us from attaching, neither from detaching.

2.4.3. DHARMA

Many different traditions have different names for the balancing of our *karmas* or actions in relationship with each other and everything else. In the *vedic* tradition, the rather unique concept of *dharma* is thus put forward as the ideal way in which to deal with our individual natures, desires and actions or *karma*.

Dharma is often translated as righteousness, but that is only limited to the *dharma* in moral issues. Nonviolence, speaking truth, respecting other people's freedom, etc. are universal ideals→4.9. These aspects of universal *dharma* are said to always lead to discussion and to be mostly an inspiration to ourselves and others. In the *vedic* tradition, morality is seen mostly as a matter of personal *dharma*, which is the right or *su-dharma*.

As it is the *dharma* of fire to burn and that of water to flow, it is our *dharma* to eat when hungry, clean the dishes afterwards and otherwise behave naturally. It means living in harmony in relation to our place within the whole. It is the *dharma* of the cow to be a vegetarian and that of the tiger to eat meat. We follow our nature as every creature does, so there is no universal law of *dharma* that applies to all, except the one of love. Through this law, we are as much supposed to love ourselves as to love others.

This ultimate *dharma* emerges from the spiritual truth of oneness, togetherness, love, found behind every eye we meet←1.4.2. *Dharma* is love in practice. Whatever goes against love is then considered *adharma*, the opposite of *dharma*, actions that destroy love, harmony and peace. They quite literally cut our connection to the Self, to the love in our heart of hearts.

To meet our *karma* in near-perfect *dharma* is a main spiritual requirement. We may not be in control of what *karmas* or jobs come to us, while we can re-act in harmony with ourselves and others. No desire can be more important than peace and love, because without these two how to appreciate even the greatest thing in the universe? To meet our *karma* in perfect *dharma* simply means that all troubles of life are no excuse for behaving like an a-hole. I wish everyone in the world would understand their *karma* thus and stay out of unnecessary trouble.

Our *karmas* or actions always serve some needs and desires and we can thus try to fulfill these in *dharma* or harmony. It is anyhow the best way to live a reasonably happy life, as *adharma* ultimately only leads us to unhappiness.

2.4.4. KARMA YOGA

Typically as householder *yogis*, we are advised to produce some 'good' *karma* through selfless service or *Karma Yoga*. At least now and then this practice may remove the stress felt by the Ego in working for all its needs and desires. Even many renunciates enjoy that blessing, selflessly serving their teaching lineage, spiritual community or any beings in need of help.

Hobbies are similarly relaxing us on the first *chakra* level of financial security, yet all other desires and attachments can still disturb our peace there. *Karma Yoga* is thus even more relaxing than a hobby and known as a great healer of our Ego.

First of all, *Karma Yoga* means doing something other than for ourselves. That is vital for this yoga to work. The Ego should not get any personal benefit out of the action, otherwise it is too hard to relax about it. *Karma Yoga* equally requires that while the action serves others, life, the universe, we should remain unconcerned about whether that service is successful or not. Only in giving up the fruits of our action, our Ego gets a break from all responsibility and our *Karma Yoga* becomes true.

That then of course also means that the Ego takes the break, and does not seek some gratification through that action, such as in our public image, the appreciation of others. We do the best possible job, but we take no credit for it. We do not involve ourselves as separate individuals in the practice and leave it all up to the divine *karma*. It is ideal if we can perform our *Karma Yoga* without telling anyone. And if we are wondering how we could be of service, our talents usually show the way.

Even if our *Karma Yoga* is truly helpful in solving other people's problems, we always have to remember that there is only one little problem named the Ego. A main trap in this yoga is to consider our selfless service in itself a reality. Suffering is only a matter of naturally forced detachment, even if it is from the life force itself→3.6.2.

Pushing us forward on the path, our pain is a blessing in disguise. Only the feeling of suffering is relatively real, so it is good to be kind, but we cannot expect it to change *karma*. What comes has to go, so all attachment must lead to detachment. Compassion is our prime motivation, as a full acceptance of all suffering, in ourselves as in others. We can dry each other's tears without needing to stop them.

Our *Karma Yoga* primarily serves in relaxing our own Ego. Whatever we can then do to help others who cannot help themselves, is just some added value. It may *karmically* compensate for some of the suffering that we may have caused through past actions. Meanwhile, we cannot do *Karma Yoga* just to improve our *karma*, merely investing in the beauty and bounty of our own future. That miracle can only happen if love itself is our motivation for the action, and we entertain no expectations.

The most effective service lies in spiritual teaching→3.7.8, sharing our understanding on how to escape from our common Ego-suffering altogether. These days, true free teaching is rare, as the economy has largely usurped also this most precious of human activities. It may be hard to imagine, yet there used to be a time when spiritual teaching was just a hobby, a natural sharing. Money so much rules people's attention through modern media these days, that free teaching hardly even gets noticed, except maybe by the most sincere seekers. Anyhow, if our teaching cannot thus be a true *Karma Yoga*, it can try to be not too damned commercial→3.7.8.

The real *Karma Yogi* is another matter altogether. Aside of meeting their minimalized needs, all other desires are renounced. All free time thus goes to serving some projects that are useful to society, animals, the environment or whatever suits our talents and abilities.

Full *Karma Yogis* are extremely rare. If they have not fallen into the Ego trap of this game, if they have truly sacrificed their individuality on the altar of universal love in service, their mere presence is known to bring peace and joy to all. Their actions become truly magical, with miracles happening apparently beyond their knowledge or doing. They smile the smile of a totally relaxed and desireless Ego, the divine light shining right through.

2.4.5. MEDITATION IN KARMA YOGA

If we thus can live in relative union with others and our Ego is not feeling too much stressed by the expectation of continuous successful performance, our meditation stands a chance of being successful itself. While meditation essentially is a nondoing, in most people it will require some doing to reach a state of being in which durable nondoing becomes possible. Moving through the phases of meditation until we can reach *Samadhi* is thus also an action or *karma*.

If it becomes *Karma Yoga,* then we are no longer meditating for ourselves, not desperate for some expected peace and bliss. Our practice then serves the entire universe, both energetically and in maximally reducing our own contribution to the suffering that is our common *karma*. Meditation thus also becomes *dharma*, a naturally good thing to do.

We then also meditate without any expectations regarding the result of this action towards inaction. For most people, that is actually highly advisable. As a result, yes, of letting go of our lofty expectations, we may experience reaching our meditation goals much more easily. Meditation is then something for which we regularly make some effort→5.4, while we do not let our mind dwell on any results. We just concentrate on doing the practice.

Some phrase may integrate that understanding into our meditation intention→6.3, affirmed before starting the daily practice. It is however mostly a matter of general attitude, avoiding a main trap for the spiritual Ego←1.7.2. Also our meditation practice is part of the game of life, which means it doesn't really matter who wins what.

2.5. Feeling in Bhakti Yoga

As all our actions aim at some happiness or other, feelings are very central to our lives. Even our yoga and meditation basically serve the feelings of love, peace and bliss. So why not change our emotions more directly?

To achieve some relative emotional balance is essential for reaching deep meditation, which will provide even more balance in turn. To durably cultivate happy emotions takes practice. To dissolve rather than suppress→4.1.6 unpleasant feelings equally requires experience. Yet if we already feel quite happy when starting to meditate, it will be so much easier to move inside. We will discuss this main subject in far more detail further on→4.1.

The feeling of love and connection is the most powerful of all happy feelings. Some devotional schools say that love is the source of all emotions and that it is enough to generate love in order to produce all flavors of happiness→4.1.5. We can experience joy, wonder, courage, peace or even love all on our own, fortunately. Nevertheless, feeling alone may put a lot of weight on our Ego's shoulders.

As we identify more with others, the natural responsibility to live a happy life can be shared. That already brings so much more peace. Love makes us whole, as part of a team. The *leela* or game of love thus manifests as the spice of life and of all other happy feelings. When feeling really connected in love, the illusion of separation is lifted and the Ego enjoys living in union, even from the depths of the individual subconscious.

As we can get in trouble with our own Ego, we may equally suffer from our expectations towards the Egos of those with whom we feel connected, and vice versa. Just as love can be found as the primary source of happiness, the dominant cause of unhappy feelings is equally found as trouble in our heart connections. Unconditional love towards all is the logical answer of any spiritual tradition. This is one of those things that are easy to understand, but hard to practice.

2.5.1. UNCONDITIONAL LOVE

Everyone is definitely worthy of love, independently of who they are in particular. All human and other beings are ever growing beyond their imperfections and limitations. There is no need to be perfect to deserve our love. The people that are the most difficult to love are those that no longer believe in their own potential, but even that we can just see as a passing phase of depression→4.1.5.

It is so much easier to adore a child than an adult, because the very image of youth indicates potentiality. Meanwhile, we are all children, as we all grow and are thus not yet fully grown, even when old and grey. To be alive means to grow and thus to be lovable, like any puppy. As in the beauty of a tree reaching for the sky, everyone without exception is lovable for basically trying to live a good life.

That trying and growing, that reaching upward, can be said to be the main power of the life force. We all share it as *prana* in our breath. We are all siblings as children of nature, born and fed from the same matter. We all struggle with that same Ego illusion, participate in very similar suffering. In a way, we are each only as different as sunflowers in a field.

The unconditional love that is experienced when meeting ourselves behind the eyes of another goes quite beyond. Then there is no more other. As our spiritual growth allows more and more identification with the universal Self, unconditional love becomes Self-evident. And even for the mistakes of the individual we can then feel love, as an adult feels for a child, or better even, as a child may feel for a child.

Parents usually experience a rather unconditional love for their children, ceasing to consider themselves as number one→4.10.1. In thus serving our children, our own needs and desires are usually easily set aside. We might feel the same way towards other people as well. Nevertheless, all personal love holds the trap of attachment.

2.5.2. LOVE & ATTACHMENT

Personal love always brings both pleasure and pain. The attachment that happens from the Ego produces the pain of temporary, permanent or even imagined separation. To avoid that pain, we may try to capture the object of our love, put it on a leash, keep it close, attach even more. As when we walk in nature and see a pretty flower. Can we just enjoy it and move on or will we take it with us?

All which is personal belongs to what naturally must come and go, so over time nothing is personal. Attachment means resistance to the natural impermanence of anything with form, to any kind of undesired yet naturally occurring detachment.

However much we may feel connected to someone or something special, it is an illusion, temporary make-belief. We assume a perfect match with some form or other, which is by nature ever imperfect, changing and growing. Love is not necessarily blind, but it does cast a rosy light.

Nevertheless, this is one of the most precious games of life. It is how love is practiced and many people thus perform the yoga of love within their communities. While feelings of love for everyone can be felt, proclaiming universal love remains rather theoretical without being practiced.

The action of love and thus the *karma* or destiny of love is to be actually lived on a scale that is smaller than the universe. The love that we can 'do' is limited in every moment to whatever or whomever we meet, or maybe invite in our mind. Thus love in practice is always personal, yet to meet its potential, it must feel as absolute as our more universal love, and thus romance is born. The practice of love requires faith and romance is the religion of love.

If we are everyone's friend, then we will have no real friends. While the feeling of love needs not to depend on anything, the action of love is an exchange of love. It means to be there for each other, comfort each other, give each other a good time. Living in love requires time, energy, attention. It is very logical that we mostly spend these limited resources on a few others that are both sufficiently similar and reasonably complementary. That is more a practical question on how to make a good team.

The feeling of personal love itself does not need to depend on compatibility and can thus be truly unconditional. We can freely love everyone we meet, as unconditional love is also without obligations from our side. Obligations are themselves conditions and they belong only to being part of a team. Our love for the members of our team can remain unconditional, even while our membership must be conditional by its very nature.

Lovingly believing in the divine in someone, both as the impersonal Self as in the Ego hero←1.7.2, we allow that Ego to reach for its divine potential. Boundless love then extends from the impersonal to the personal. So the illusion of love is also the truth of love.

What is said here about love and attachment is basically true for all kinds of love, whether more romantic, or between friends and family, or with animals, for art and music, etc. We are free to attach, to love, to enact the *karma* of love. Yet we can refrain from complaining about the pain of attachment, which is actually the pain of detachment.

It is our freedom to love with more or less attachment. Love always requires some sacrifice, as the needs and desires of others mingle with our own. Yet the more fundamental pain of love originates in our attachment and manifests upon forced detachment. What comes has to go. We can be grateful for what we can get, stop grasping for what isn't coming our way. We can suffer the pain of love without making the object of our love suffer for it. We are fully attached to the loving, yet fully detached from being loved.

The pain of separation is beautiful also, as without love it cannot be experienced, which is why many love a tear-jerker movie. We can accept to bear the pain of love and in the end we will even let go of our tears. Life has to move on people often say, and so does love. Moving on is truly what the life force is always doing.

Whatever we love, we love it fully, yet we are aware of the price tag of attachment. We love in detached attachment, which is not just some attachment mixed with some detachment. When living from the Self, there is nobody available who can attach or detach, nor is there anything to attach to or detach from. Yet love is not even a question. As our meditation practice grows, we will more naturally come to love that way, which is the way of the Self.

2.5.3. BHAKTI YOGA

Unconditional love of the divine Self is free of the problem of attachment. We might also say it is a clever attachment to something which is eternally present and available. Hence the attachment needs never to be followed by detachment and the pain of separation is absent.

The divine lover and beloved is ever nearby, never has a headache, nor anything else but us on its mind. To attach to something which is impermanent, ever changing, is an illusion, bringing both pleasure and pain. To attach to that which is permanent, never changing, is truth, free of any pain and known as divine love or *bhakti*.

To practice love for the divine is *Bhakti Yoga*, the yoga of devotion. This divine is the unmanifested source of the manifested universe, making everything one and divine←1.7.3. In *bhakti* practice however, we first differentiate between the eternal unmanifested divine and the timebound, manifested divine, including ourselves. It also means to mentally separate the divine Self from the individual Ego, even if that separation is the basic balloon that we are trying to pop.

It must be noted here that in the relatively recent development of the philosophy of *Dvaita Vedanta* in India, the ultimate divine is seen as eternally separate from the individual Self, just like in the Monotheistic religions→2.8.3. The Cosmic Self is then usually regarded as having the form(SAGUNA) of the Hindu deity Vishnu, like we find it in Iskcon, also known as the Hare Krishna movement. I personally do not adhere to this idea, which I perceive as fundamentally illogical, taking what is essentially a method→2.5.5 for its final objective. Yet no one can say that some form cannot exist beyond the unknowable absolute nondual reality.

Anyhow, mentally separating our Ego from the Self allows that Ego to fearlessly love the eternally perfect Self without any restraint, truly unconditionally and undisturbed by our more personal feelings of imperfection. In *Bhakti Yoga* we choose to love that which is eternally ours, so that the true power of love can be unleashed without any fear holding us back.

That love will become all-encompassing, so that even the timebound will become utterly lovable. Love is such a great practice for the Ego. When lovestruck, we become somewhat crazily obsessed, so entirely focused on something outside of us, that we forget ourselves. Whatever we want or need becomes entirely irrelevant compared to the needs and desires of the object of our love. The Ego thus loses itself in love.

Usually we are a little more wise and hold our loving back, rightfully fearful to get hurt. Imagine how in *bhakti* we can be really crazy in our love without needing to be careful at all. In the words of Harish Johari: 'To find the truth we need to be wise, yet to hold on to it, we must be crazy.'. Most modern minds are not able to be that crazy. The true *bhaktas* or devotees dance, sing, eat, clean, walk, talk, breathe and live only for the divine. And many people believe they are crazy, while the feeling is mutual. Advanced *bhaktas* are known for making miracles happen merely by their suggestion to the divine→Story3.

Bhakti Yoga is known as one of the most direct ways[15] to reach the divine. The Ego can entirely lose itself in this love, time and again surrender its individuality, to

---

[15] See field 55 in 'The Yoga of Snakes and Arrows: The Leela of Self-Knowledge' by Harish Johari, Destiny Books 2007.

Story 3 The Power of an Egoless Wish

Once upon a time, I met A.B.D. Kathia Baba, a Krishna devotee of the Nimbarka tradition. He usually did not stay long in one place, because rapidly miracles would start happening around him. People would become so excited and eager to get his blessing, queuing up and honestly making life quite impossible. So he used to travel with just one student from here to there. I have witnessed some of these miracles myself, impossible things becoming reality. And the only thing he really did when people would bring their problems, was to say 'Krishna will help you'. He taught me the principles of healing through divine love, the power of an entirely egoless wish. He was the sweetest person I ever met and also had great impact on my understanding of the Ego and in my deep meditation practice, which he would occasionally visit.

finally totally identify with the divine. The subject so much loves the object, becomes so full of it, that it becomes the object, which is an essential step to enter deep meditation. Then in turn, the object becomes the subject and the goal is reached.

The Ego thus merges in the divine and in that union a great transformation takes place. Afterwards, the desire to return to that embrace will also be there, bringing more love-bouts with the divine, that ultimately lead to the final state. There should be no doubt that what we are talking about here is a state of deep absorption inside, the only place where such full merging can happen.

Yet equally in life, love brings bliss and bliss brings love. Both can be practiced, simultaneously, as they are so closely linked. The ecstasy of worship through singing, dancing and praying is the more outer form of *Bhakti Yoga*, preparing the Ego for the journey inside. And also that journey through the different phases of meditation will be totally planned in favor of feeling love for the divine.

2.5.4. FORMS OF THE DIVINE

Spiritual traditions worldwide offer hundreds of thousands of forms of the divine for the practice of devotional meditation. To many modern minds they are limited to merely being symbols. Yet these divine energies actually exist as the infinite and omnipresent most direct manifestations of the Self in the various energies of the universe. Upon closer study, they are revealed as universal spiritual essences, whatever the name or form given to them in various cultures and traditions.

It is a mysterious subject, while there is a basic understanding which can easily be accepted by all that at least 'believe' in the Self. Our own experiences when trying to manifest the Self in our attitudes may definitely resonate with it. The supreme Self is that unwavering awareness that never changes and is essentially formless, without attributes or attitudes. Yet, when we live from the Self, its indirect role is not limited to that peaceful observation of everything. The truth of love that it inspires so beautifully affects our every attitude in thought, feeling and action. Living from the endless bliss of the Self, how not to feel courage for example?

We can thus distinguish a multitude of expressions of the Self into particular attitudes such as generosity, wisdom, courage, love, detachment, fearlessness, inspiration, concentration, lightness, selflessness, righteousness, cheerfulness, compassion, kindness, fortitude, acceptance, and so many more. And as the essences of courage or kindness are the same in everyone, they can be recognized as essential universal energies, ever manifested from the light of the divine, universal Self. We cannot see these many different trees within the seed that is the Self and yet they are so clearly inspired by it that they seemingly emerge from it.

Those deities or divine qualities are not the supreme, even though not existing separate from it. Like the *vedic* fire god(AGNI) is the divine essence of fire, all deities represent some essential energy that originates with the Self, but is not the Self. Hence they are named heavenly energies, which is the true meaning of the words *deva* and *devi*, usually translated as 'gods' and 'goddesses'.

These gods and goddesses are not the unmanifested Self. Yet as they manifest from the Self, they are eternal, unchanging, omnipresent, etc. In *vedic* lore, these divine energies are said to represent the first wave of manifestation, whether seen as happening at the moment of the creation of the universe, or as continuously emerging from the Self as principal manifestations in everyone.

In both cases, whether we see them inside or outside, these attitudes exist as divine energies which can be symbolized by naming them, maybe also painting a picture of them, and writing stories about them. Names, pictures and stories are a means for the mind to concentrate on those essential energies and thereby stimulating their manifestation in ourselves.

In Table 4 are a few examples of the energies or attitudes that some main Hindu deities represent, even though that is just my personal interpretation. As these energies became known in particular forms created by human culture, we can also communicate and interact with them, from our own culture or personal form. It is thus said that the Self will not answer our prayers, as it never does anything, yet those divine energies might very well do so→2.7.3.

Buddha	Compassionate intellect
Ganesha	Insightful lightness
Gayatri	Radiant Self-awareness
Hanuman	Selfless courage
Kali	Passionate fearlessness
Krishna	Playful love
Lakshmi	Generous beauty
Radhe	Divine Ego
Ram	Natural righteousness
Saraswati	Creative inspiration
Shiva	Ascetic goodness

Table 4 - Expression of the Self in some Hindu deities.

When the monk or *sadhu* worships the ascetic form of lord Shiva, the objective is to be an ascetic. When we pray for help to the goddess of art and music known as Saraswati, we want to become divinely inspired artists ourselves. When we look up to the brave monkey lord Hanuman, we want to courageously serve selflessly like he does, be a true hero.

These forms or symbols of the divine thus actually exist, whether we see them in our own lives, in particularly inspiring people of present or past, or within even more subtle dimensions→2.7.2. In the history of Hinduism, we can see the names and forms of these divine energies change over time, evolve, adapt and often literally being incarnated as specific personalities whose existence can also be historically proven, like Ram or Buddha.

We may thus very concretely aspire to merge with that object of our love in meditation. That object may be a man-made illusion, just a picture, name or story, while what it represents is not. The word for love in all languages may be different, yet the meaning is independent of it. We can worship love in Krishna, Jesus, our teacher or a rose, it matters not.

In the search for our main meditation object→10, we are entirely free to go for more abstract or more concrete forms to focus on. Many will however naturally go for a name, form, picture and story that they can identify with. It is how we ultimately imagine our own particular manifestation of the unmanifest Self, our personal form of the divine→10.1.2. It thus represents the divine Ego, which is that 'individual' manifested Self.

When an apple tree walks the spiritual path, it does not need to become a mango tree. It just means to produce the most divine apples. So while we can see the unique value of all manifestations of Self-awareness, we can still focus on the one that most resonates with us. That indeed is our divine Ego, the purest form of our individuality. Thus in our journey of spiritual growth, we may move for a while from one to the other, finding different heavenly energies to balance ourselves with. From that balance then, we may finally discover our true purpose and divine connection.

Some deities will incarnate more than one particular expression of the Self, and the more the *bhakta* or devotee associates that deity with the Self, the more its unlimited diversified expression will become apparent, as in the 'thousand names' prayers that exist for many deities such as Shiva, Kali, Vishnu, Lakshmi, etc. Comparing those lists, they are largely overlapping.

2.5.5. MEDITATION IN BHAKTI YOGA

Bhakti offers a rather fundamental solution to two basic meditation problems: concentration and surrender. Western minds usually struggle quite long to overcome these obstacles, while youngsters raised with stories of Hindu deities often more rapidly move through the meditation process. Their sincere and doubtless devotion to the meditation object makes it easy to focus. They also more naturally trust the divine and let go of control, when deep meditation sets in.

The wise man so often wonders why he is meditating, like he always has to first remember some reasoning to become motivated. The crazy worshipper on the contrary has so much desire for the divine that hardly any effort is needed to meditate. Only love is on a *Bhakta's* mind, so he flies straight as an arrow, with the power of a love rocket. Equally when so lost in love, the sense of doership is simply forgotten. All individuality is joyfully surrendered in the merging with the Self.

To stimulate this love game, we can use the power of romance to make our devotion grow. As we would buy flowers for our beloved, we offer them to the object of our meditation. As our prayers become poetry, our worship happens from the heart, not the head. Blissful smells, tingling bells, refreshing colors, the purity of water, some sweet fruits and scents of nature, they all contribute to the soothing sensory input that warms our mood and lightens our mind. The very act of giving has a profound impact on the subconscious and especially the reptile brain, so that the Ego may truly sacrifice itself to the practice as to the divine.

In *Bhakti Yoga*, the intention phase thus typically starts the meditation practice with some rituals and prayers that confirm our love and express our wish for divine union→6.4. Centering in the heart *chakra*→9.4.2 helps to fuel our love, as does the technique of heart breathing→8.1.

The Ego naturally feels insignificant when faced with the divine object of our meditation. This feeling has of course been used in religious oppression, preying on low self-esteem. However, we are freely making that choice for ourselves here, so religion has nothing to do with it→2.8.3. To the one who accepts the vastness of cosmic consciousness, the Ego is simply recognized as a rather trivial illusion. As the Ego looks up to the stars, it feels small. As the Ego bows down to the above, it forgets itself and all its troubles.

To play this game well, it requires a bit of illusion, make-belief, just like a personal love is supported by it←2.5.2. The divine obviously exists inside of us, yet to make the practice work, we take it out of ourselves so to speak and place it in front of us as our beloved meditation object. This can happen physically as an image or statue that we worship, or mentally as the *mantra*, image or idea that we focus upon in meditation.

We thus create a duality between duality and nonduality, so that from duality we can focus on nonduality. We gaze into the eye of the divine as lovers would, connecting to the essence of our meditation object. Our Ego thus faces itself with the divine throughout all phases of the meditation process. Once action turns to inaction in *Samadhi*, we merge inside and find our true divine nature back→13.2.4, division dissolved.

The need for a meditation object has been discussed before←2.1.3 and we will study a variety of more concrete and more abstract options in Chapter 10. Mind needs something to work with and it is first of all the mind that needs to concentrate and meditate. In *Bhakti Yoga*, our meditation object is the carrot on a stick that lures our lovestruck mind forward into the practice. The carrot is not the destination, while it leads us there. Both the mind and the Ego are quite child-like and need some lovely toy to play with, in order to go along with the game.

Our meditation object is only a symbol for the formless divine that we are trying to reach. Yet as every thing, it also holds that divine. We just focus on the divine within that object, as we have to concentrate somewhere anyhow. The existence of the divine itself is a matter of definition rather than faith, while faith is needed in the chosen object of the divine, seeing the divine in it.

For sure, in that goal and center of our practice we may also then recognize ourselves, as in the many Hindu deities with quite human characters, who may be angry or worry just like us. Some *bhakti* schools even work with a double object, one representing the Self and the other

Story 4 — Wordless Teaching

Painting by Pieter Weltevrede →A9

Once upon a time, Harish Johari was in the West, while I was in the East. He connected me to one of his own teachers named Baba Dwarka Das, a Sita-Ram devotee. For several months I passed a lot of time in his small temple courtyard. He could not speak English, yet he taught me what real bliss is. We would use sign language for simple tasks and some visitors occasionally translated my questions. He made it clear that my teaching would not be in words, even though he clearly taught others that way. He knew very well that Harish Johari had already imprinted many of those upon my mind. There was not much more to do than raking up some leaves and dusting some statues, as well as preparing our daily meal. I learned to do nothing there and not feel bored. Rather, blissful beingness became a little addictive and I joined in the repetition of 'Sita-Ram' to keep the mind focused in love. The main weekly event was the washing of his 2-meter-long dreadlocks(JATAS) under the pump, being honorably invited even to pound the hair floating in a gutter with my feet.

the divine form of the Ego. The Ego is then seen as the beloved of the Self, for example with Krishna or Shiva as the divine Self and their spouses Radhe or Shakti as the equally divine Ego.

The more modern insistence of our Ego to only focus on the experience of the formless divine within→10.6 - our very own divinity so to speak - is limited by our ability to love ourselves. Our individual freedom is of course something to treasure and protect, but who will free us from our Ego? That is what we are trying to do here, so why not freely set the Ego aside for starters?

As we love our object of the divine, we identify with it. As we meet the divine inside, we find it outside. Until everyone we meet is recognized as that and we greet each other as a god or goddess. Then the love of the *bhakta*, which before was maybe entirely focused on a statue or a river, becomes truly universal.

When the practice ends, the heart easily overflows with boundless gratitude, a powerful and durable feeling of a love matured into sweet tears. For the *bhakta*, blissful living thus becomes an uninterrupted ecstatic experience of love←Story4.

2.6. Thinking in Jnana Yoga

We have been thinking about thinking quite a lot earlier←1.3. Since meditation is about not thinking and the ultimate truth is only found in silence, some teachings seem to conclude that all thinking is useless, which it really is not. Even relative truth can be useful in reaching absolute truth. We should simply avoid taking one for the other.

Before being able to move beyond thought, we better first get our story relatively straight, even while words can never be perfect. Wrong understanding supports enduring unhappiness and easily produces ineffective practice. Moreover, as it will be at least incomplete, it will just lead to more thinking.

Even as not thinking must get a place in our lives, most of us are anyhow naturally going to think most of the time. Thinking is an inner dialogue between different aspects of ourselves and through our thought processes we may balance and satisfy these.

To always be aware of the underlying feeling behind our thoughts is advisable, so that instead of worrying about something, we are able to constructively think about some issue we actually do care about. Most of the time our thinking will be supportive as long as it originates in a good mood, a positive attitude.

Thinking means trying to make sense of the miracle of life in which we find ourselves. Far out most of us are born with quite absolute amnesia about who we are, where we come from, what we are supposed to do here and where we might be going afterwards. Trying to find some workable ideas about all of this is logical in order to make the best of the unexpected adventure of life.

Thinking provides the understanding on which we largely base our most appropriate actions, feelings and even the practice of nondoing. Thinking always consists of answering questions that come to our mind and when the answers are not satisfying, the questioning just continues. While knowing that all answers are just concepts, mere symbols of the truth, we can still try to settle for some of those that feel relatively real. We can equally accept that not all questions can be answered today, if ever.

At all times, we must be aware of the subconscious content on which our high-speed thought trains are based. Without any doubt, our attachments color our ideas. Conclusions may appear as axioms, not needing any proof. Yet the proof is in the pudding, so as long as our thoughts rather lead to habitual unhappiness, their original direction or underlying concept must at least be incomplete. The understanding that we are truly looking for is to point us in the right direction, towards durable happiness and anything that might support it.

Thinking should follow common sense and any conclusions that we cannot actually feel to be true should be avoided. Otherwise we are just parroting empty ideas and all too complex words borrowed from others, even if to those others they make sense. Some people will have a little more experience in solving the particular riddles that we are trying to decipher. Listening and reading, the being-together-in-truth[(SATSANG)] and the study of ancient scriptures obviously can make our understanding move forward more rapidly.

The age-old concepts available in *yogic* science have the big advantage of being confirmed in practice by a large number of very different people that have walked the path before us. If useless, these ideas would not have survived. We will still have to bring them into our own experience to actually get them, yet they are a good place to start from.

The ideas expressed here are all based in ancient *yogic* lore→3.4.1 and I have added my own experiences with these concepts mainly to inspire the readers to have their own. At some point however, the questioning slows down and we more and more turn to silence to find our answers.

2.6.1. SILENT SEEING

As discussed before, if the thinker can move beyond thinking←1.3., the voice of the cosmic intellect can be heard from the innermost layer of the subconscious←1.5.. Later on, we will discuss the actual techniques of using intuition, so that superior insight can play its role in developing our spiritual practice→3.5.. Yet first we need to see what is this intuition, so very required for developing real wisdom.

This knowing beyond words is often called a seeing, because when we see something with our eyes, we feel that it is real because we can see it. Even while dreaming we usually believe in what we see with our inner eyes, odd or not. To take a sensory experience as truth is incorrect of course→9.1, while the use of the word "seeing" corresponds quite well to the actual experience of intuition.

Compared to all thought-based knowledge, intuition is not a story told about an experience, it is the actual experience of knowing. This knowing is revealed as an almost sensory experience, hence named our sixth sense. In *yogic* science, the light with which the inner eye thus sees is named *tejas* and conserving its basis is an important *yogic* practice→4.2.3. It also relates to the third eye *chakra*, where the solar and lunar energy channels can be joined in the neutrality needed for inner seeing→9.4.2.

Inner silence is the basis upon which this seeing rests. As long as the conscious mind is still active, our subconscious impulses and opinions cannot be trusted. Only when the subconscious is no longer triggered from the outside through mind and the senses, messages from the inner layer of the cosmic intellect←1.5 can come through untainted by personal attachments. For real intuition to emerge, we have to stop thought for at least one long second.

As our meditation practice evolves, intuition will grow. From the most mundane to the most elevated questions, our inner voice may bring answers that we will know to be true, even if we have no idea why. Things are what they are and we see them as they are. We have no proof for this knowing, yet it is also not needed. Having faith in our true inner voice, we do not question the answers and convert them into actions. And even if the results of those actions may not always be what we expect, we know that their truth will probably reveal itself in time. And if not, we accept that all of it anyhow will in part remain beyond the limitations of what we think to understand. We trust the car to do the driving and relax in the back seat.

2.6.2. SELF-STUDY

There are plenty of things to think about in life, yet spiritual study will be most fruitful if the subject is ourselves. To study our own existence in a variety of ways and aspects is the superior thinking path (VICHARA), because it is based in direct experience, whether sensory or intuitive. As above so below, if we can come to know ourselves, we will know the universe and vice versa. Yet even while observing what we find outside of us has a role to play, without knowing the observer, the observed cannot be known.

Self-study always seeks to answer the principal question 'Who am I?'. It thus primarily means to study the Self, which is the wordless observer. It is the nondual understanding known as *Advaita Vedanta*. The moment we open our mouth there is this and that, duality. This knowledge in duality is *Dvaita Vedanta*. The Self is thus mainly known for what it is not. It is then revealed as unchanging, uncaused, unborn, untouchable, unknowable, unbreakable, unfathomable, unseen, unaffected, fearless, nameless, desireless, soundless, formless, thoughtless, colorless, nondual, etc.

In our thinking, the Self can thus only be known through the non-Self, while that non-Self has no existence separate from it. As such, the Self is also recognized as all pervading, all creating, all knowing, all empowering, all experiencing, all being. In other words, it is omnipresent, omniscient and omnipotent. Yet all these words ultimately reveal to us that the Self can only be known by stopping our mind from engaging with the non-Self, which gives us the direct experience.

Self-study may start with the Self and end in the silence of the Self, yet self-inquiry is not limited to the Self. Other advisable non-Self subjects are the bodymind, the Ego, the universe, the paths and the practices. The complex bodymind can be reasonably understood through the sheaths of consciousness←1.5. The Ego is found as an ever-evolving cluster of false but both natural and more unnatural ideas that manifest as identifications and attachments. The vast universe is discovered to be similar to our atomic inner space. The five paths can be seen as one path by discovering their complementary nature→2.8. Practicing the available practices, they are revealed to be as varied as the number of individual practitioners←2.2.1.

Self-study means that we are going through life while always holding up a mirror. Contrary to the more egoic state of being, where we seek some kind of value in that constant stream of selfies, we avoid any judgement and only seek understanding in the mirror of self-study. Whatever thought or feeling comes to our mind, we accept and observe it for what it is, until its origin becomes clear. Whether that insight leads to some action or not is secondary. The primary objective is always the ability to disidentify from what happens inside of us, see it as 'not-me'. Knowing that 'this is just by the nature of the body' or 'that is only a game of the conscious mind', gives us the power to withdraw. Peaceful inner silence, an end to all questioning, is the intended result.

2.6.3. JNANA YOGA

The path of true knowledge or *Jnana Yoga* starts with intense and repeated self-study. *Jnana* teachers thus chiefly answer similar existential questions over and over again. Yet they are also known for lengthy periods of silence, which is the real teaching.

The main task in *Jnana Yoga* is to be ever identified with the Self and disidentified from the non-Self. Unbroken awareness of the Self is the key to achieve this, as identification with that awareness will naturally follow. While the Self also has a pure unchanging energy, it is through its never changing pure consciousness that its eternal quality is principally attained. Aware of our awareness, the subject no longer loses itself in the object. As a standing stone unaffected by the seasons, any changes in our experience fail to change us. Pure being(SAT), pure knowing(CHIT) and pure bliss(ANANDA) are ours.

True *jnanis* are known for being able to answer any question, whether about the Self or the non-Self. They may be proficient in scripture or not, while their answers are always direct and neither scholarly nor intellectual. They are regarded as emanations of cosmic intelligence and seem to have access to past, present and future.

Without being questioned, they will not speak. Love shines in their eyes, while they are unconcerned about anything or anyone. Still, they usually live relatively normal lives, often as householder *yogis*. For example, Nisargadatta Maharaj was a shopkeeper and Papaji, famous student of Ramana, worked in a variety of businesses. People often feel that *jnanis* are contradictory, yet they live the undivided truth as they see it with a truly naked eye.

2.6.4. MEDITATION IN JNANA YOGA

While that awareness of our awareness can be practiced under any conditions and fits very well as a practice 'in life'→Story5, *jnana* teachers do advocate to regularly stop thinking altogether and withdraw in meditation. *Samadhi* is clearly the objective, so that the Self can be

Story 5 Crash Course to Enlightenment

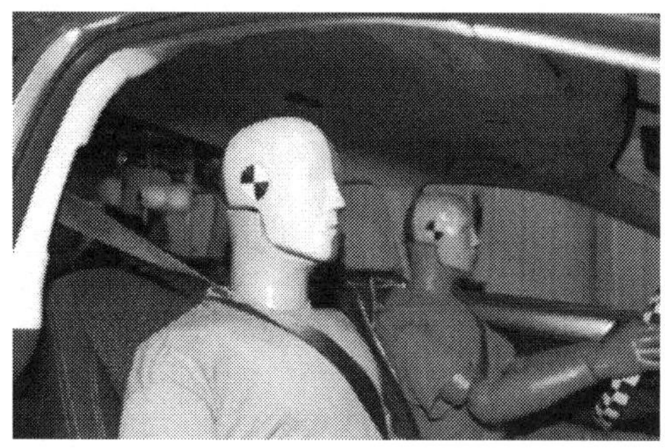

Once upon a time, in my mid-twenties, I was in a severe car crash. No other cars were hit and I was not injured, while my car was a total loss after rolling over several times. I got out of the wreck and other cars stopped to look if I was alright. Yet I laughed and laughed as I had never laughed before. People attributed it to me not being hurt, which was indeed quite a miracle, but my joy had nothing to do with that. It was because of the experience that I had during those few seconds, which felt like an eternity. While I was probably screaming my heart out, still trying to control my steering wheel, I was completely separate from it. Probably as a mechanism designed to stay sane, I had totally withdrawn in the Self. There was just this rather peaceful feeling, maybe thinking 'okay I might die', yet I was having no problem at all. So when I crawled out of the car, remembering the teachings of Harish Johari, for the first time in this life I fully experienced not being this body, not being this Peter, and life truly appeared as a gigantic joke. No need to organize spiritual crash courses though, as meditation may also bring us there.

experienced fully, without any distractions. The identification with the Self that follows such deep experience reveals the illusion of the Ego as self-evident, a somewhat amateuristic reflection of the Self within the bodymind and actually nothing very special.

The most essential *Jnana* meditation is very different from other types of meditation, as the subject becomes the abstract object of itself→10.6. The principal task is to observe the observer while we are observing things, thoughts and feelings. Meanwhile, we are minimally involved with that observed stuff and maximally focused on being the observer.

Normally in meditation there are only two players: the subject and the object. Here there seems to be a third, watching the Self as if from behind. Yet this third player is then revealed itself as the Self, making the observer that is being observed somehow a more individual Self, known as the Ego→10.6.2. It only seems able to observe stuff from within the body and seems more attached to that body as well. When we ask who is this Ego, we receive no answer, as just like the Self, the Ego has no form, except in the moment.

Here the Ego is truly experienced as a reflection of the Self, not different and not the same. The drop cannot be distinguished from the ocean and still it feels like just a drop. The water in a wave is the water of the ocean, and the wave only rises up from the ocean to fall back into it. The observer of the observer can then be experienced as the cosmic Self, the ocean, but that is still just an idea in the mind of a wave.

Image 6 - Self and Ego as wave and ocean.

Such practice in fact easily leads to replacing meditation by contemplation, which is not the same thing. We will discuss more about it→10.2, but while it is very good to sit and calmly think about our existence, it cannot replace real meditation. Are we looking for reality or do we settle for another good story? Only in silence our self-study becomes real.

Those who have tried these mind games know that we easily get caught. And as long as this process is still producing thoughts, we have not even reached the phase of concentration, let alone real meditation. Repeat, repeat, repeat, that is all we can do.

Again and again we redirect our focus to the awareness of our awareness, cease any commenting on the experience, until true silence draws us inside and the mind falls asleep. This technique heavily relies on the ability to really stop thinking for longer periods of time and hence it must be seen as an advanced practice. For the one who can do it however, it is the most simple and direct path→10.6.1. Repeat, repeat, repeat.

The technique can be made easier if the objects of our primary observation are selected more appropriately. In *Jnana Yoga*, these typically will be rather abstract, having similar qualities as the Self in being relatively formless, timeless, never changing, etc. Examples are the void beingness→10.5.1, the silent consciousness→10.5.2, the blissful now→10.5.3, up to even a motionless mountain like Ramana's famous Arunachala, or an ever flowing holy river like Ganga. Most *jnana* teachers offer their students at least one of these more or less abstract objects as an aid in meditation.

In any case, meditation cannot be performed without some awareness of the Self, hence all meditation practice includes some form of *jnana* meditation. In this way, it does not matter much if our meditation object is an apple, the light, the now, a mountain or a *mantra*. In any case, the object will allow us to focus our mind on it. It keeps the thoughts down, while we may try to maintain awareness of our awareness at all times. The only remaining differences between meditation objects are found in their energetic effects on the bodymind, all else being just a matter of our Ego's opinions, as explained before←2.2.2.

2.7. Magic in Tantra Yoga

If doing, thinking and feeling can be holistically combined with nondoing, our power to change things becomes truly magical. Note that this combination is actually always present in daily life, yet most people are not aware of it and whatever potential it produces lies beyond their grasp. Conscious use of this method in *Tantra Yoga* gives us the mysterious ability to change some of the more fundamental energetic patterns that rule our lives through the subconscious.

2.7.1. SUBTLE ENERGIES

In the Indian tradition, this practice of 'magic' is known as *tantra*, a mysterious 'weaving' of energetic patterns, vibrations and connections[(NADIS)]. While also potentially useful for rather mundane purposes such as enhancing crop growth, it mostly serves healing and divination, alongside *Tantra Yoga* as the fifth main *yogic* path. In a way, all paths are attempts to bypass some of the essential obstructions caused by the Ego. *Tantra Yoga* has the same objective, realized by magically 'reweaving' the subconscious Ego programming, unblocking the spiritual path.

In *Tantra Yoga*, the *tantric* magic is used for achieving the objective of yoga, which is endless bliss. That goal is obtained by unlocking the subtle dimension of our souls, in which both the deepest happiness and the deepest unhappiness originate. Hence it also includes cooperation with beings from more subtle dimensions of the universe, see below.

Tantra Yoga combines the principles of *Jnana, Bhakti, Karma* and *Ashtanga Yoga*, which are practiced simultaneously. It is the doing of something selfless and without any expectation of a result[(KARMA YOGA)], motivated by the feeling of unconditional love[(BHAKTI YOGA)], while seeing and thus accepting the truth of what is and simultaneously being effortlessly identified with the Self[(JNANA YOGA)], all happening in a natural trance of nondoing [(ASHTANGA YOGA)]. It represents a loving connection to nature, whether inside or outside. As the subtle empowers the gross, advanced practitioners can achieve many things that are usually considered impossible.

Tantra Yoga has many branches and practices, which all work by changing the energetic vibrations within one or more of our sheaths of consciousness. As such, many of the usual *yogic* practices with postures, breath or even food and home remedies, can be seen as *tantric* in essence. They harmonize the energies of the more gross bodies. These more physical approaches are usually present in any *yogic* tradition, thus practices are mostly seen as *tantric* if they are aimed at changing the more subtle energy body of the subconscious. The *tantric* qualities of mental objects such as *mantras* and *yantras* similarly affect the conscious mind and the subconscious. The *tantric Kundalini Yoga*→4.2.5 starts in the *pranic* body, but ends in the subtle body of the subconscious and the body of bliss. The specialty of *Tantra Yoga* mostly lies where it affects our more subtle programming.

In the West, the perception of *tantra* is often reduced to some kind of spiritual sexuality, also named *neotantra*. The use of sexual energy in *tantric* practice is not new however, as it has always been a rather minor branch of *tantra*. As Harish Johari used to say, if we cannot avoid something, we can make it truly spiritual, since everything anyhow is spiritual.

The Western approach mostly appears as some kind of sexual therapy, which may definitely help people in removing some related blockages. The original *tantric* idea however is to rouse sexual energy and then offer it to the divine by using *mantra* and ritual. We do not consume that energy ourselves in an orgasm, so that it can be transformed into a more subtle energy. It is an advanced practice, requiring extreme control over the bodymind, genuine spiritual devotion and an earlier developed strong relationship with some higher being of another dimension, to whom the sexual energy is offered. Thus it is not just some kind of light spiritual entertainment.

2.7.2. SPIRITUAL DIMENSIONS

As *tantra* affects not just our gross bodies, but also the more subtle bodies, it very much relates to the more subtle dimensions and our spiritual journeys in deep meditation→13.3.4. There we can harmonize our spiritual public relations, which is a practice that is very much associated with *tantra*. In *Tantra Yoga*, these relationships principally serve our spiritual growth rather than the more mundane purposes, even if that distinction is not always clear-cut. *Tantric* principals for efficient interdimensional communication are often less consciously used in *Bhakti Yoga*, with the same results, even if the objective is love only.

The seers have not only brought us the beautiful and totally essential understanding of the Self and cosmic consciousness. The same ones have also brought us the equally inspiring story of many lives, allowing us to walk our path towards enlightenment without needing to run. When we truly get an insight into the natural evolution of our desires←1.7.1, as well as in the many steps to take towards our goal→3.8.4, how can we actually imagine succeeding in just this one life? The perspective of many lives to joyfully walk our talk thus protects us against spiritual frustration, but it is not just a feel-good story.

Contrary to the story of the Self, the issue of reincarnation and different lives is a lot more difficult to experience, so naturally we all have some doubt. Yet those seers were not expressing some opinion or philosophy when talking about reincarnation. This understanding came to them through direct experience in deep meditation, where they could witness their former lives.

This understanding is the *vedic* and *tantric* knowledge on how the universe manifests from the Self and how this manifestation extends well beyond our limited sensory perception into different dimensions. As the Self manifests itself into the universe, it does so gradually, as a wave or waves. The manifested energies that emerge from it thus evolve from the most subtle *prana* to the most gross, material world. This is a process of densification from the most subtle element of space over air, fire and water to the densest element of earth→9.1.4.

Likewise, pure consciousness manifests as more subtle entities of beingness whose bodies are purely energetic, up to the more gross manifestation in a physical body such as ours. Those more subtle beings are usually called spirits, even though the term hides a lot of variety, which is in part again related to the subtlety of different types of energy bodies.

A funny thing is that many people believe in reincarnation, but not in spirits. Yet the process of reincarnation cannot happen without spirits existing somewhere, in between lives. When the body dies, something called the soul or spirit moves out and then after a while enters the fetus in the womb of the new mother. Where is that soul in the meantime and how long may it reside in that place?

We are multidimensional beings. The soul is not something that can be found inside of the physical body. It is attached to it through energetic channels, while it exists on another level of beingness, in a more subtle dimension. Deep meditation truly means that we withdraw to our more subtle beingness, to the subconscious, to our individual soul. It means that we withdraw to our more subtle kind of existence within another dimension.

I have discussed this subject more at length in the book on "Tantric Advaita"[16]. To show what these dimensions are like, very often one refers to the world-famous Russian dolls, where inside one doll there is a smaller doll, and again inside that one there is another doll, etc.

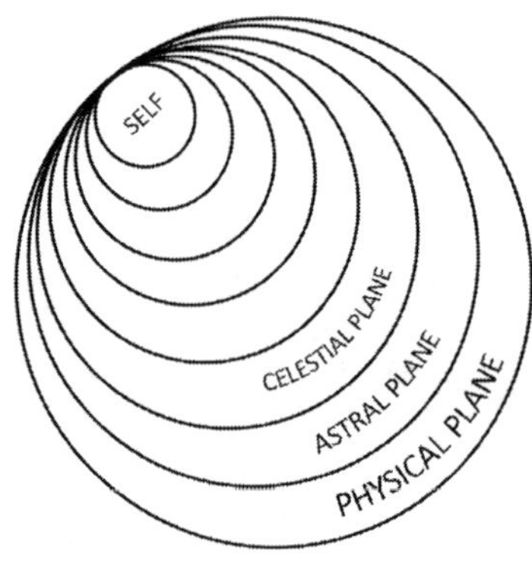

Image 7 - The experience of the spiritual dimensions.

The physical dimension is what we experience through the senses. Inside that dimension is the more subtle astral dimension, where most souls remain in between lives. Yet within that dimension, there is the even more subtle celestial dimension, where luminous beings live. And it goes on, layer after layer→13.3.4, up to the absolute dimension of the Self, which

[16] See Chapter 9 of 'Tantric Advaita, Energizing Nonduality', by Peter Marchand, self-published at Amazon 2021.

is beyond dimension.

The significance of this is twofold, as it relates to the deep meditation practice, but also to our lives, feelings and understanding. On all these levels, divine support is available.

2.7.3. DIVINE SUPPORT

Through my healing practice, I work with support from the spiritual dimensions on a daily basis. That obviously gives me quite a different perspective than most people. To me, the notion of divine support is not an idea or a belief, it is a fact of life. I have long doubted the wisdom of sharing that knowing here, as I have resisted it myself for decades. Yet how could I not tell this truth as I have come to experience it?

The spiritual dimensions have anyhow pervaded spiritual practice throughout history. There is no other way to understand the totality of spiritual traditions related to deep meditation practice. It is the weird side of the story, but it cannot be excluded.

That more magical side of the practice will actually not suit most seekers most of the time. That is totally fine and natural, as we are living primarily in this physical dimension. Yet at least sometimes, it pays to be more open-minded to the unseen.

I totally accept if the reader has doubts about all of this, while I also feel it is necessary to be clear that I have no doubt left about that magical aspect of our existence. There is simply no other explanation available for what I have learned to do, for example in changing the physical condition of a person living on the other side of the globe, through long-distance healing→A3. I hope the reader can forgive me when I bring this story forward as a matter of fact, even while remaining mysterious.

When in deep meditation we withdraw inside, up to the point where we no longer experience the physical body, we are withdrawing to the more subtle dimensions. Thus in all spiritual traditions we find different practices to ensure that someone is picking us up from the airport, so to speak.

The other part of this story is that these same seers are telling us that beings in the spiritual dimensions may also have quite an impact on our lives here in the physical dimension. All spiritual traditions of the world thus developed certain rituals, which are a kind of language, a communication with those other dimensions. They may help to solve or avoid problems and attain our objectives here, whether more worldly or more spiritual.

Spiritual healing is but one example, where we can actually rely on the spiritual connections of the healer. To gain individual support and guidance for our meditation practices, subtle feelings, insights and *karmic* issues, for our spiritual growth, is definitely also an option. We are free to go for this kind of connection or not, meaning it is not a requirement. But to my experience, it can really boost our progress, especially whenever we feel somehow blocked.

Some people have a talent for connecting to the subtle dimensions, resting upon certain energy channels(NADIS) generated already in past lives or in this life. Such talents may remain dormant unless used, but in some people they are so naturally active that they have to be positively used in order to remain productive in nature. Advanced *tantric* practices are the natural *karma* and *dharma* for those people, a destiny of spiritual servitude→A3.

We might equally see the more occult *tantric* practices for divine support as a kind of trading between dimensions. There are things that only we can do, with the five elements that constitute the physical dimension. And there are things that only spiritual beings can do, from the more subtle planes of existence. It is in truth a simple exchange, offering something from the abundance of physical nature and getting more subtle energy shifts in return, whether from our ancestors(PITR) or from even more subtle yet powerful beings.

Help from the spiritual realms is anyhow often asked from the ancestors. More information on ancestor rituals can be found in the 'Tantric Advaita' book[17] as well as online[18]. They logically help us with family issues and may also make our *karma* lighter to bear→3.6.3. These rituals may also be used to reduce some negative impact from unhappy ancestors. There may also be similar interactions with friends who passed away or other souls that we have known in past lives.

For help in spiritual growth and meditation, we logically ask those spiritual beings that are masters of yoga. This is the true meaning of the words *yogi* and *yogini*. These are often addressed directly, by concentrating on the pictures of teachers that passed on→3.7.7. Many meditators will start their practice simply by asking help from one or more spiritual teachers. It can be particularly motivating and true help is definitely available from that direction.

These masters are however also often 'contacted' indirectly, by asking help from the particular divine energies and *yogic* paths that they adhere to. This is very much the practice within the ancient spiritual schools, yet it also relates to the worship of more universal divine energies, where *Tantra Yoga* becomes *Bhakti Yoga*

[17] See Chapter 9 of 'Tantric Advaita, Energizing Nonduality', by Peter Marchand, self-published at Amazon 2021.

[18] See 'How and Why to do an Ancestor Ritual ? at youtube.com/youyoga.

towards specific forms of the divine, as discussed before←2.5.3.

Story 6 My Spiritual Teacher

Painting by Pieter Weltevrede → A9

Once upon a time, my teacher in the healing arts of Nepal announced that it was time to start a new practice in order to gain my own healing energy. Until then I had merely borrowed some of his healing connections in the spiritual world. After 3 years of sustained practice with a particular Kali mantra, that new connection was established, which one might say made me a healer in my own right. This yogini energy related to Kali thus became my literal spiritual teacher and supporting energy for the healings. Through this connection, also my meditation practice and spiritual understanding have been brought to another level. She is not an easy teacher, yet so protective, compassionate and peaceful, teaching mostly on the feeling level as a mother would. Together we have done well over 1000 healings.

So when Hindus pray to the elephant headed lord Ganesha for help in removing some obstacles, it is not that essential divine energy of lightness, which we name Ganesha, that will help us. The *yogic* masters that relate to the energy and the path of Ganesha, and themselves worship Ganesha, may however answer our call. Even spiritual beings that are maybe less evolved yet equally devoted to Ganesha will help us. As they see how we are trying to bring that Ganesha energy to life, they will support it. One might say that Ganesha, just like any other essential spiritual energy, has an 'army' of devotees [(GANAS)] in the spiritual world, that will act in support of what Ganesha stands for. Such groups of devotees exist in the spiritual world in the same variety as they exist in the physical realm.

Likewise in my healing practice, which is based around the goddess Kali, it is not Kali 'herself' that comes to help me. What I call my 'healing energy' is a *yogini* from another dimension, which is associated with Kali←Story6. Ok, this is all very mysterious for most and we also need to keep our feet on the ground and solve problems of the physical world first of all through physical means. Nevertheless, sometimes divine support comes in handy and it is available to every sincere seeker.

2.7.4. SPECIAL POWERS

Special powers(SIDDHIS) only appear as miraculous to the ones who do not understand them. Those who have such powers, know them to be magical in the sense of ever remaining beyond understanding, and yet they know them.

Special *tantric* powers depend on association with other beings living in the subtle dimensions. The even more advanced *yogic* powers rest only upon ourselves and may naturally manifest through any of the five paths for the Ego. They basically depend upon our egolessness→13.4.2. Whatever we can observe from a truly Egoless state becomes ours to know and change, whether that object is our life force, the mind of another, the past or future or some deep-seated attachment.

Only the genuine desire to help, to do something beneficial, may be the motivation to use these powers, as personal desire should not be involved. Hence, both *tantric* and *yogic* powers represent a potential trap, luring the Ego into believing itself to be above others and in misusing these powers for personal gain and status→13.4.3. A reset will take place, in which such powers are again lost and sooner than later a *karmic* reckoning will follow. This way it can be said that any desire to develop *yogic* or *tantric* powers is best avoided, except maybe where it can be used in *Karma Yoga*, such as in healing.

Such powers can never be seen as proof of our spiritual evolution. They offer some kind of proof of the magical nature of reality, something to be explored just as the magical wonders of the universe researched by science. Curiosity in the spiritual mysteries may thus be a motivation to practice for some, yet it must be combined with a firm hold on the Ego.

2.7.5. MEDITATION IN TANTRA YOGA

Cooperation with beings in other dimensions is surely not needed for every meditation practitioner. Support of meditation and spiritual development from the other dimensions will anyhow naturally grow. That is in part also why spiritual lineages and communities are so useful. They have not only accumulated the knowledge of those who went before, as they also offer ancient connections to these others in the subtle realms.

When help can be prayed for in a more energetically efficient manner, it may certainly boost our progress. Spiritual beings that like to help in moving our energy upward will always be very careful when interfering with our personal freedom without being asked for it. Only the more naughty spiritual beings might interfere in our lives without being given permission.

Therefore, for those who are naturally interested in these things, some very basic *tantric* rituals are explained later→6.4. The effect will usually be subtle but fundamental and can mostly be recognized through increased inner peace, deeper meditation and an increase in occasional fortunate yet strange 'coincidences'. The more advanced *tantric* practices, such as fire rituals, healing rituals, *karmic* rituals, etc. that I also practice myself in support of meditation, are not taught in this book. They largely have to be trained in person.

While spiritual support may very positively affect meditation, advanced *tantric* practice can also lead to distraction. When *Samadhi* is reached, connection to the Self and all that it brings may be reduced. Interactions of the subconscious mind with the other dimensions tend to dominate the experience. The energy of *Samadhi* may become more active rather than peaceful→13.2.6. As such, it is a choice to make, as much as it is a destiny to follow.

This chapter on *tantra* remains largely limited to the often disregarded subject of affecting the more subconscious energy bodies and dimensions. However, *tantra* can affect every area of life. Even without anything otherworldly happening, always remember that we live in a magical world and not everything is what it seems. Respect for everyone, for every place and everything we meet, is the logical answer.

The typical Indian calendar of spiritual festivals→9.2.3 actually produces the habit in society of regularly offering respect to the spiritual dimensions. Meanwhile, it protects most people from the need to remain aware at all times of the somewhat frightening subtlety of our existence, which is really clever.

2.8. One Yoga

How could we seek union if that seeking is not in tune with everything that we are trying to unify? How can we exclude anything from the path? All paths, practices, ideas and opinions are complementary. There is but one Yoga. It is no use even to talk about the fastest path, since it cannot be the same for everyone.

There is a yoga for every *yogi* in every moment. We are all different and the same. We are composed of exactly the same ingredients, albeit in entirely unique proportions. The recipe we all seek will also contain similar ingredients, but mixed for each of us in a very personal way.

Thus, the path of yoga and meditation

must include all paths and practices, mixed in unique proportions that are ever evolving. Many practices are of course overlapping in nature, harmonizing our various energies in the bodymind. We only need those that work for us, yet that might still be any of them.

Meanwhile, there is no escape from the five main *yogic* paths for the Ego, as no path can entirely avoid thinking, feeling, doing, nondoing and the occasional magic. Ironically, the pathless path includes all paths. It's about living in truth, love, selflessness, peace and energetic harmony. As long as the Ego remains involved with either untruth, a feeling of separation, selfish actions, restlessness or imbalanced energies, our personality will be troublesome.

So please, we must feel 100% free to follow our own path. It is not a straight highway. There are many crossroads, too many signboards, far too many seemingly attractive commercials on the way. Sometimes we may need to retrace our steps. Sometimes it may be wise to sit down for a while, studying a fork in the road. We might think about it, feel our way forward or flip a coin. Yet we've got to keep doing, keep walking, as every path brings some kind of growth. We can select a steep path sometimes, or a pleasant walk down along the river. Some roads look good until we round the corner and it gets bumpy anyhow. Our vehicle might get stuck, need servicing by a specialist. Sometimes we may seem to move away from the goal, but that may be temporarily necessary. Sometimes we thread the same path twice, while there is a reason. The way up goes up and down. Singing greatly enhances the feeling of adventure.

Unity in diversity is the nature of reality. And thus all yogas must unite in each of us differently, being in truth only one Yoga, the great *Maha Yoga*. Yoga means union, so it must happen in union. This book is all about empowering the readers in making clear individual choices. It is not about telling them what to do.

2.8.1. TRANSFORMING THE EGO

For the Ego to reprogram itself, the five *yogic* paths thus show the way. In *Karma Yoga*, the Ego forgets its selfish objectives. In *Bhakti*, it loses itself in love. In *Jnana Yoga*, the truth of the Self will show our individual existence to be irrelevant. In *Ashtanga*, the Ego stops thinking about itself and in *Tantra Yoga* it transforms more directly its subconscious attachments.

Our need and desire for any of the paths will anyhow evolve. As long as mainly the three lower *chakras* are active, we will practice only in support of the Ego, seeking a business opportunity, a source of fun or some popularity. *Karma Yoga* may help to move the energy upwards, as our feeling of public image naturally matures in the navel *chakra*. Upon the opening of the heart *chakra*, the *Bhakti Yoga* of devotion will support the feeling of connection. When the throat *chakra* is activated, we will be ready for the *Jnana Yoga* of truth and help ourselves forward through fundamental understanding.

Only when the third eye starts opening will our sixth *chakra* desire for nondoing be real and meditation may bring something more than mere relaxation of the bodymind, real *Ashtanga Yoga*. On the level of every *chakra*, the more occult approaches of *Tantra Yoga* may be useful to remove particularly tight attachments in the subconscious. And as our energy anyhow will move up and down on the *chakra* ladder of our spine→4.2.5, all 5 paths must ever be combined.

So, we let our opinions on all of this rest. Those who identify as thinkers are often too much 'in the head' and in need of connecting to their feelings and doing something about it. The more emotional type for sure also needs some rationality to detach from emotional imbalances and thus reach the decisions needed on what to do. The one who tends to act before thinking, or without listening to the heart, all too often responds from shortsighted subconscious instincts and feels sorry afterwards.

2.8.2. ENERGETIC PRACTICES

Ashtanga, Jnana, Karma, Bhakti and *Tantra Yoga* are thus principally practices for the Ego. The many more energetic practices that are typical in yoga serve the feeling of harmony in the bodymind. They are applied in all paths, even while they dominate only in some limbs of Ashtanga Yoga. As the Ego thus always tries to think truth, feel love, act selflessly and remain connected inside and beyond, we simultaneously maintain an energetic balance in the bodymind that will make all of that a lot easier.

Since the energies of the bodymind naturally always change, these practices can only bring a kind of dynamic balance. So while the ever-changing results of our energetic practices are an illusion, it is certainly possible with regular practice to keep our feeling always close to the bliss of the Self. This way, we may achieve the kind of emotional balance required for successful meditation, which ultimately results in a deep relaxation of the Ego.

These energetic practices are based in the three main universal powers of sound, space and time, which directly relate to the seeds of the universe that reside within the Self: the void beingness(SAT), the silent consciousness(CHIT) and the eternal bliss (ANANDA). These seeds may also be used as abstract objects in meditation, along with their primary manifestations→10.5.

The silent witness thus holds the seed of sound, the void beingness holds the seed of space, and the blissful eternal now holds the seed of time. To increase Self-awareness, we may change these energies. We produce sacred sounds to create silence. We balance our energy in gross matter and form to generate the lightness of formless space or *akash*. And we change the energy of our *prana* to the neutral vibration that produces blissful timelessness.

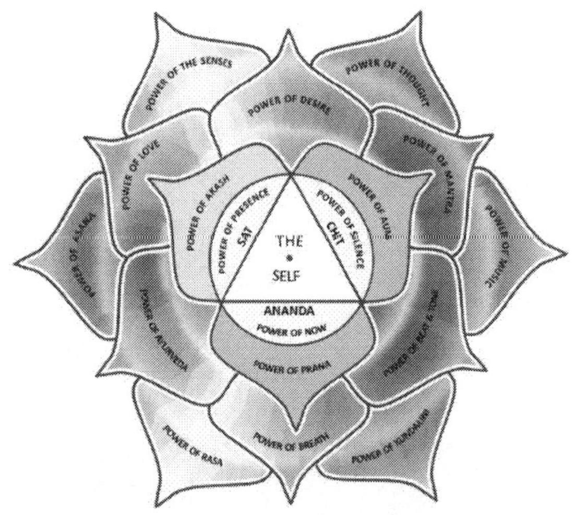

Image 8 - Powers of yoga emerging from the Self.

It is from these most essential practices that the entire *yogic* tradition emerged to help in bringing our energy and feeling more close to the bliss of the Self, as shown in Image 8, of which a larger image can be found online→A11. Each of the 3 original powers of Self-manifestation thus diversifies in a multitude of optional *yogic* powers. As this is the main subject of my earlier book on 'Tantric Advaita', I will not expand on the source, manifestation and utilization of these universal powers here. These energetic practices are anyhow included throughout this book and they all serve the five main paths for the Ego, as shown in Image 9.

Image 9 - Energetic practices in support of the 5 paths for the Ego.

2.8.3. TRAPS ON ALL PATHS

While it is just a reflection of the Self in the mind, the root of the Ego's problem is existential fear, creating attachment and separation. The illusion of separation is so powerful that when we use the five paths to relax the Ego, that fear will repeatedly seek new expressions. It is the problem of the spiritual Ego, grasping for shiny pearls with which to adorn a pig that is still just a pig.

Thus we find clever Ego traps on all paths, where the Ego can be witnessed to corrupt the practice in seeking some kind of personal validation. We so much like to pat our own backs, as an alternative for being overly self-critical. We fluctuate between the 'look at me!' Ego and the 'poor me' Ego. That is only natural, yet it can produce highly enduring blockages on all paths. It may even disrupt harmony in society and has caused many wars.

Traps in Bhakti Yoga

Bhakti Yoga is seen as the main culprit by many. The love for one's object of the formless divine may create a blind faith in the form of that object, placing it above all others. Any lover can make that error, yet if a group does, we get to our serious issues with the group-Egos of various religions.

The original latin *religare*, which means to unify, is actually a synonym of the word yoga itself. While religion should thus unite, it separates between Hindu, Muslim, Christian, etc. Aligning with the more worldly powers of commerce and politics, *Bhakti Yoga* may serve as opium for the masses in times of peace and as doping for times of war. Yet, all that is needed is the recognition of the formless divine and of the freedom to attach any form to it. The ideal belief system for society thus lies in the supreme formless being (Monism) to be recognized in each and every form

Story 7 A Survey of Polytheism in India

Painting by Pieter Weltevrede →A9

Once upon a time, I was traveling through India with a holy man from Finland and we did an impromptu survey with over 100 Indian people that we were meeting along the way, like taxi drivers, hotel people, etc. Our first question was 'Which of the Hindu deities is your favorite?' and we got a multitude of answers. Our second question was 'How does this favorite relate to the other deities?'. The truly remarkable result was that we could not find one among 100 who did not in some way respond as in 'Oh they are all the same, because in essence the divine is without form'. While they were all very fond of their favorite, they were also entirely aware of the formless reality behind it. And thus our journey turned into a wonderful experience of 'unity in diversity', of that so truly open-minded spiritual democracy known as Sanatan Dharm→A1.

(Polytheism). Even if one name is enough to work with for every practitioner→10.1.2, it leaves no room for Monotheism, a belief system allowing people only one form of the divine, whether they like it or not. In the *vedic* tradition that dilemma is solved by choosing a personal form of the divine(ISHTADEVA) to work with→10.1.2, without losing awareness of the essentially formless nature of divine reality, found in every object of devotion←Story7.

Traps in Karma Yoga

In *Karma Yoga* the Ego may corrupt the practice by claiming the results of our service. The main error is in seeing suffering as an ultimate reality→3.6.2, with too much seriousness as a result. True selflessness is liberation from individual responsibility, joyfully functioning as part of the whole, embracing any pain as an opportunity to let go, gladly offering our actions in return.

Again, when practiced in a group, there is a danger that our selfless efforts mainly serve the Egos of those in charge. Or that we may feel forced to so much give up on any personal needs we may have, also for the practice of other yogas, that it creates unhealthy inner tensions. How much time we spend in *Karma Yoga* should always be a free personal choice that usually needs adaptation now and then. We should not get stuck in some of the responsibilities we have assumed and no-one should use some moral highground from where to tell us what to do.

Traps in Jnana Yoga

In *Jnana Yoga*, the principal trap lies in overestimating the limited power of our understanding and underestimating the depth from which our individual feelings arise. The practice of detachment from any Ego game thus becomes an Ego game in itself.

In a group, the ridiculing of the Ego's natural limitations, also known as 'Ego-bashing', may become unnecessarily discouraging. The lack of compassion for the Ego, which is the only one deserving that often-praised compassion, produces a negative self-image in many. If we can only see the Ego as a villain, then how will it behave?

Jnana Yoga may be so obsessed with the ultimate practice of Self-awareness that any other practices are discarded as distractions created by the Ego, even if they may unblock our path. Many modern *advaita* teachers claim that there is no practice, that nothing can be done, that to give up doership is the only way forward. Indeed nothing can be done about the Self. All practice is for the non-Self, even if we only try to be aware of our awareness.

Of course simple Self-awareness always works very well for the rare one who can do it. Yet for most people, first some more energetic practices will be

Story 8 Maybe You Need a Holiday?

Once upon a time, I realized that the emphasis among modern nonduality teachers that 'there is no practice' does not fully correspond to the teachings of Ramana Maharishi. Many are the conversations that go like this: 'Oh Master, I have tried to sit and not think, but I just can't. Thoughts keep coming and I cannot find that peace & bliss.'. Then Ramana may answer 'Maybe you have to do some breathing exercises to calm your mind and then it will work.'. When people then come back and say 'I have tried using breath and still it doesn't work.'. Then he will usually say 'First you try some mantra to pacify your Ego and then you try focusing on the Self and not thinking.'. And when people complain it still doesn't work for them, there is one hilarious moment where he says 'Maybe you need a holiday?'. Upon finding that jewel, I took my first holiday retreat with Gayatri mantra→5.6.

needed to be able to stop doing and thinking for more than a few seconds. This is also confirmed by Ramana Maharishi←Story8, the best-known Jnani. This question is also a main subject in my book on "Tantric Advaita"[19].

When we maintain that there is only nonduality, we start with a 'no' and end in 'duality'. That 'no' creates in itself a duality between no-duality and duality. All is one under the sun, unity in diversity. If we can embrace duality and nonduality equally, which cannot be a paradox, we will feel the truth more clearly than we can ever understand it.

This riddle cannot be solved by the ever-separating mind, only in true beingness. For the ones who fail to stop mind, the Ego's games continue and there is no way out, leading to stagnation and spiritual depression. While indeed the Ego needs to stop trying anything, first our mind probably needs the more energetic practices→3.1.2.

Power traps

Both *Ashtanga* as *Tantra Yoga* bring the danger of too much identification with the powers they may generate. Whether we can stand on one leg for an hour, easily reach the trance state, affect the minds of others or even the weather, the

[19] See 'Tantric Advaita, Energizing Nonduality', by Peter Marchand, self-published at Amazon 2021.

Ego is still in danger of attaching to its achievements. These universal powers are not proof of our spiritual growth and should not be placed in service of the Ego.

The delusion of being someone more special than others is the ultimate spiritual Ego trap→13.4.3. As any true hero, the Ego must remain humble on the path, feel grateful for the grace of whatever divine power is granted and especially here also dissolve the illusion of separation. We are one and the power is one. Simple sharing should come easily.

On the paths for the Ego, the Ego is the only trap, not the paths. So the traps on each path are not reasons to stop walking, as they belong to each path. People naturally try to jump from lack of self-esteem to some inflated personal self-image. There is no need. Let it go, let it go, let it go.

2.8.4. MEDITATION PHASES & PATHS

Looking at how we could implement the 5 *yogic* paths within the meditation phases, it is clear from the following examples that these do not exclude each other at all:

INTENTION	*To meditate*
Karma Yoga	To serve all
Bhakti Yoga	To love the divine
Jnana Yoga	To merge in truth
Ashtanga Yoga	To silence the mind
Tantra Yoga.	To connect beyond
RELAXATION	*Body, breath & senses*
Karma Yoga	Without expectation
Bhakti Yoga	With love for our temple
Jnana Yoga	With detachment
Ashtanga Yoga	With the goal to let go
Tantra Yoga	With help from beyond
CONCENTRATION	*Upon the object*
Karma Yoga	Without expectation
Bhakti Yoga	Which I love
Jnana Yoga	Which represents truth
Ashtanga Yoga	Which holds the mind
Tantra Yoga	Balancing my energy
MEDITATION	*Relaxing into focus*
Karma Yoga	To let go of the doer
Bhakti Yoga	To forget myself in love
Jnana Yoga.	To observe the observer
Ashtanga Yoga	To remain in silence
Tantra Yoga	To transform my soul

Deep meditation is beyond all opinions, actions and paths. In order to get there, we are free to cook our own recipes. Throughout this learning process, we can only easily move forward if we do not get stuck in any fixed ideas about the path. We can go crazy onto one of the paths or practices for a while sure, yet we fix our understanding into flexibility→3.4.

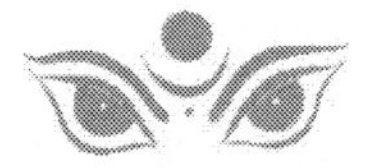

3

THE LEARNING PROCESS

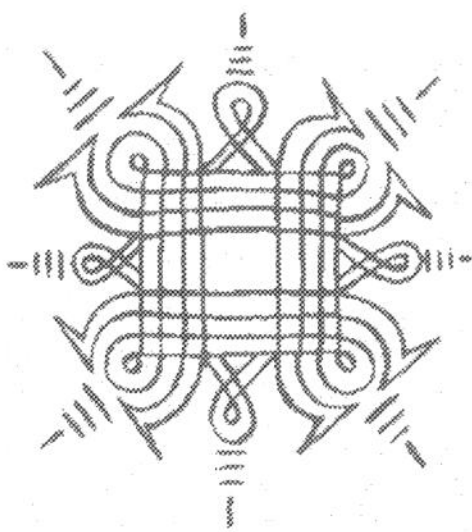

Spiritual growth is a learning process that is mostly energetic in nature. Walking the path with confidence, gradually our inner vibration will change, gaining peace, bliss and also strength. We have 6 treasures to pick up along the way and 9 mental traps to avoid. Our understanding, practice and also karma show us where to focus. The outer teacher pushes us to the inner teacher. Some milestones mark our progress and point to the path ahead.

3.1. Confidence

Nothing can be done without the confidence that we can do it. Especially if we aspire to reach some spiritual heights through our deep meditation practice, confidence is key. We enter uncertain terrain. It means we have to look for confidence in a different place than we did before. Most people seek confidence in their past, based on whatever they have achieved or not. That only somewhat works when doing something similar as before, while when we start the game of deep meditation we have no previous experiences to draw courage from. When trying something entirely new, our previous achievements are meaningless.

Still, repeatedly people will fabricate some story about who they are and what they have achieved, in order to feel confident on the spiritual path. Yet that kind of confidence will always be shaky, as we are well aware that all things change. We might not even be able to do the exact same thing today, which we were quite fine doing yesterday. So whatever steps we have already taken in the direction of *Samadhi*, they have little meaning whenever we again sit down to meditate. Whatever spiritual growth we may feel to have gained in the past means little if today we are not feeling up to life.

3.1.1. THE ENERGY OF CONFIDENCE

Confidence is a feeling, an energy derived from our very life force[(PRANA)]. To have confidence, we just need confidence. As long as we are breathing that life force, confidence is something we take. It does not depend on anything except itself. If we take it we have it, if not we don't. Confidence is actually not at all based in the individual's achievements, only in the energy of the moment and the ability to go for it.

So while that also means that we can make it so much easier by managing our energy well→4.2, in any moment we can generate the energy of confidence by willpower alone. Through unconditional faith in ourselves, we can draw up that power from inside. That is the secret of the so-called 'strong people'. Applying that secret will be essential for doing our practice, which anyhow mostly happens on our own, where we can rely only on ourselves.

That faith is again not based on our personal abilities. Meditation and spiritual growth are processes that essentially work the same for everyone, even if the how, the when and the what are entirely personal. If we follow the path with confidence and do not attach to any result, there is no question whether we can do it or not. If we feel little faith in ourselves, then we can still have faith in the path. The *yogic* process cannot fail and we can only fail if we decide to have failed and stop practicing. We may thus gain the confidence that there is not one aspect of our being that cannot to some degree be affected by some practice or other.

Confidence is thus a choice as well as an energy. Confidence is a state of mind, a positive energy and attitude. Yet before people start jumping of roofs, let it be clear that there is also a thing called overconfidence. We cannot just expect to be able to do anything without some learning process. However, in the long run, we can be confident that we can learn to do anything.

On the one hand, the energy of the bodymind has a feeling of strength or weakness. On the other hand, the Ego is the one to overrule this feeling or not and if we do, the energy changes. Lack of confidence is often a matter of habitual doubtful thinking, a negative self-image, which keeps the energy down. A confident person ignores all doubts and this also protects the energetic feeling of strength in the bodymind.

To move from doubt to confidence is a decision we make. It might include a plan to change the energy of the bodymind through breathing practices and other means, further strengthening our resolve. Yet that key moment is where we say 'Yes we can'. Even if our energy feels totally depleted, we are still entirely free to smile in acceptance and defiance and make that choice. And the more we then see ourselves move forward, the more confident we get. So whenever we hesitate to meditate, which happens to all, we can still meditate. Whenever we feel blocked somewhere in the meditation process, we can persevere. There is really nothing to doubt when it comes to progress through practice.

Doubt is an expression of the emotional essence of fear→4.1.5. Fear comes when we imagine that in an unknown future something to which we feel attached might get lost. To remove all doubt means having nothing to lose. Yet losing doubt not only happens by being less attached.

It also comes from clearly understanding that the fear of lack of confidence is a fear of fear, a self-fulfilling prophecy. Just like we will have confidence if we take it, we will have fear if we embrace it. We laugh at the absurdity of it, transform our uncertainty into curiosity, love our little Ego hero, bring up our courage and act with peace of mind. Every warrior that survived some war, testifies to have been sometimes terrified when running into battle, laughing or not, but the fear was overcome. To generate confidence, we go in warrior mode.

3.1.2. BUILDING MENTAL STRENGTH

Too many people involved with spirituality have plenty of sweetness, but lack mental strength and are easily hurt or imbalanced by others. In other words, they need more power over their mind. Most importantly, unless we are in control of our mind, we cannot let go of the Ego too much. Otherwise, the mind will dominate the Ego, but it is a lousy, erratic ruler. It will amplify all attachments of the Ego, stimulating unpleasant emotions, ill-timed desires and fruitless actions.

Mind easily tends to panic whenever some disturbance or lack of energy is experienced in the bodymind, thus aggravating nervousness. On the path of the *yogi*, first the Ego must be made strong, determined, focused, which means in control of mind. This is symbolized by the Hindu god Shiva sitting on a tiger skin. The tiger represents our powerful mind, which is both controlled by being sat upon, as it has been skinned to reveal its true nature.

When the mind is one-pointed by the Ego, confidence is ours. When we are firmly in charge of the mind, we can relax our will power. This is true in life as it is true when moving from the phase of forceful concentration to effortless meditation←2.1.4. Thus we are able to reduce stress in the Ego, merge the form into our formless beingness, play the game of life lightly. First the Ego takes on mind, then it can take on itself.

The power of confidence is nevertheless not equally distributed in everyone. It is easily depleted by a lower vibration of energy→4.2.1. It readily comes to people born with a more solar energy→4.2.4 or a more fiery biochemistry→4.3.2. Those who somewhat more rapidly lose confidence by being more lunar and cool have other advantages, such as more capacity for empathy and intuition. It all matters little, as in all cases confidence remains a choice that anyone can make.

When somehow the energy of confidence is low, we can change it, both on short as on long term. For a short boost, we can increase fire in the body for example by drinking some hot ginger tea→4.3.3. This can be followed by a push into physical action, doing whatever needs doing, so that our energy becomes less inert→4.2.1. In case of a more long-term lack of mental endurance, regulating the digestive fire may be a major issue→4.5.1.

Balancing poses as well as martial arts will particularly help to ground us into the body, away from that ever-doubting mind. Any concentration exercises as well as any controlled work with pain→7.6.5 will increase mental strength. Since fear and doubt are largely a mental problem, getting our mind under control is key to generate confidence. *Mantra* meditation with an appropriate *mantra*→10.3.3 is very powerful in this respect, especially when combined with fire rituals→5.4.6. There is also the main practice of gazing without blinking→11.3.4.

Natural confidence can also very well be exercised through all kinds of physical sports, where it is often called 'flow'. Naturally graceful and perfectly timed movements reveal a person in control without stressfully holding on to it. Tennis matches provide excellent spectacles of this practice. Suppose a player is winning many points quite easily for a while. Then suddenly, a few small mistakes are made, yet with great consequence in the score. The player is filled with self-doubt and as a result grasps for more control. Natural grace is lost, the playing becomes too mental and now even simple shots fly wide off the line. Until maybe near the end of the match, the player feels there is nothing more to lose and just lets the game happen. Some wonderful points follow and before you know it, confidence is back and the match might still be won. I so love tennis!

For people who have experienced low confidence over longer periods of time, natural flow must be built up step by step. A variety of disciplines, a healthy daily schedule and diet, concentration, meditation, they all must work together. This is all part of our mental reprogramming, which is the purpose of all our endeavors, particularly in the subconscious.

We should never identify with our weakness as this is mainly an energetic issue, which can be remedied for everyone, given that sufficient discipline is maintained. As confidence may then fluctuate, some coaching, some help by others may be needed, lest one becomes caught in a lack of confidence that makes any action towards more confidence impossible→A3.

Let it also be clear that sometimes we need to accept ourselves to be weak. Sometimes we are just not up to some tasks, that are expected from us by others or ourselves. Other people might even misuse and waste whatever strength we have gained. Also here we need a balance and should make sure to always keep some energy in reserve. Once the energy is depleted, that will itself lead to an increased consumption of energy, so we better watch our strength. Always holding some strength back is equally part of the warrior mode.

The process of spiritual growth anyhow has its ups and downs, and confidence may vary accordingly. We better not take the ups and downs seriously. There will be periods of relative peace, where not too much trouble stirs in the subconscious, nor manifests in our lives. To move forward it is necessary for such periods to be followed by more restless and challenging ones, where there is a little too much going on and our confidence is easily lost.

We may sit somewhere meditating and suddenly feel so very insignificant in that vastness of the universe. How can we ever aspire to something as great and mysterious, while simultaneously struggling with seemingly absurdly small problems? We should then reconnect inside and reinforce our awareness that nothing essential really changes. It is an old saying that what doesn't kill us makes us stronger and this is very true→3.6.2. During hard times, let our confidence rest in that self-fulfilling prophecy.

3.2. The Six Treasures

The 6 jewels, wealths or treasures of the *yogi* are particular attitudes(SATSAMPAT) that are practiced to ensure control over our mind and replace doubt with confidence. They make a person strong of character, are useful in facing any challenge life brings, while essential in the practice of deep meditation.

Mind needs to obey the following six rules in order to help the Ego to be detached, wise, disciplined, longing to move forward and not be destabilized by conflicting emotions. We might say they are simple to understand and yet as all wealths they do not come for free. These jewels adorn the invisible crown of any *yogi* and while they are essential for practice, they are also earned through the practice.

3.2.1. EQUANIMITY

To have equanimity(SHAMA) means to react calmly upon what happens. This ability originates in the deep insight that whatever happens, it does not matter. Some things may seem less desirable or pleasurable than others, yet that is an illusion. Whatever happens will have a positive and a negative effect both. Even if one of those remains hidden at first, one day it will reveal itself.

To be born in a wealthy family might spoil us as kids, or create a lonely person. To be exceptionally pretty might mean we never encounter anyone who truly sees into our heart. Whatever suffering we experience might give us the power of compassion and we will never be alone again. To lose ones eyes might produce perfect pitch or even clairvoyance, need I continue? Every little thing always carries both what we may call a blessing and a curse, while the curse is also a blessing and vice versa.

So whatever happens, we respond naturally, yet in tranquility, equanimity. There is absolutely no reason to lose our mind over anything. We avoid what is natural to avoid, as we also do not need to seek out suffering. We enjoy the enjoyable without getting overly attached, as enjoyments come and go. We thus acquire emotional stability, which is a practice in itself→4.1. Thus avoiding the drunkenness of being overly emotional, equanimity allows us to think straight and drive confidently.

Throughout the meditation process equanimity must be equally present. Whatever happens, it does not matter. To let some little trick of the bodymind create any strong emotion, agreeable or not, is detrimental to our progress towards peace. Whatever happened needed to happen, is part of the path. It only turns into a blockage if we lose our calm, our equanimity, as that will destroy the results of any practice.

3.2.2. RESTRAINT

To have restraint(DAMA) means that if we like to have chocolate, we can have it, at the right time and in the right amount. So while training restraint may require regular abstention, it only means that we have our sense buds under control. When we are fighting our desire for chocolate, we are not just fighting ourselves, even while many feel that way. According to *yogic* science, every cell and organ of our body has some Ego, some mind, some desire. We are thus also fighting our entire bodymind, which yearns for that taste. Yet it truly can learn that no is no, if taught that way.

It is of course principally the mind that enjoys the senses, so weakness in restraint is fear of the power of mind. Our eyes might not agree with our decision and focus again and again on that cupboard that hides the chocolate. Ever felt that sudden fleeting taste of chocolate on the tongue, while it is still awaiting our decision in the cupboard? That imaginative power of the mind to unrelentlessly bring up painfully tempting ideas on chocolate is what we fear.

So wherever we feel lack of control, we exercise, free ourselves of it, fast from whatever for a while. Chocolate isn't bad, the desire for it isn't bad, only our lack of restraint must be remedied. Restraint is not an ascetic philosophy that ends all sensory enjoyment. It is only a matter of being in charge of ourselves, rather than becoming a slave of the bodymind.

When meditating, restraint is mostly needed in the phase of sensory withdrawal→9.2.1. When moving inside, we need to restrain mind and the senses from distracting us from the object of our meditation. This is really fairly easy if we are used to having control over the senses, while they are used to times of enjoyment and restraint both.

3.2.3. DISPASSION

Various schools have quite different opinions about dispassion(UPARATI), as well as rather diverging translations such as desirelessness, withdrawal, satiety or detachment. Yet, this quality is quite simply to be understood as being patient in passion. The Sanskrit word can be literally translated as moving towards(UPA) enjoyment(RATI), as the opposite of wanting that enjoyment right now, or when meditating.

Nobody can deny desire to be the main attribute of the life force and the power that creates and sustains life. And nobody can deny that desire can lead to both constructive and destructive actions. Dispassion simply means that we approach the fulfilment of our desires with patience, whether for chocolate or enlightenment. Passion is great if at the same time contained.

As a *tantric*, I do love myself a good desire. Yet even a hedonist by nature should never force things. No sensory enjoyment is worth a broken heart. So we enjoy what comes our way and for sure we might take an excited turn in the direction of the object of our desire. Still, we are not children to immediately want what we want, never mind the consequences of our actions. Living from the heart means not to become so obsessed with our desires that we lose our patience. Dispassionate meditation means that we patiently produce more and more peace inside.

3.2.4. TOLERANCE

Things do not always happen to our liking, yet we can exercise tolerance (TITIKSHA). While with dispassion we manage our desires, tolerance deals with our aversions. Whether some person is annoying, the weather is terrible or some rocks under our meditation mat make the sitting difficult, we can take it. Whatever unpleasantness we cannot avoid, we see it as an opportunity for strengthening our endurance, forbearance, tolerance. When we have tolerance, we stop complaining to ourselves at least.

When meditating, sometimes outside disturbances cannot be avoided or maybe the body is not well and causes pain. Many people are disturbed by the sounds of neighbors or birds, yet they can still tolerate and meditate. If the disturbance is strong, we might not even be able to reach very deeply inside. It matters not, as our investment in tolerance will serve us well some other time. It means that while we should avoid disturbance whenever we can, it should never disturb us.

3.2.5. FAITH

Faith (SHRADDHA) is what we need when we are uncertain if and how to move forward. When it is clear what to do, then faith is not needed. When nothing else works, then faith works. Sometimes we just do not know, right? Then all we have is faith. Faith in ourselves, in the divine, in the path, in those that have preceded us and encountered similar difficulties.

As the meditation process always remains some unclear way of messing with our own mind and heart, we need faith. Without faith, we will only half-heartedly move into some new practice. So, we know what we believe in and go for it→Story9. Then the power of our faith will work for us.

Story 9 What do You Believe In ?

Once upon a time, one of the first things Harish Johari ever asked me was about my faith, what did I believe in? And since I had a hard time answering, he asked me to think about it and write it down. It is good to be sure about our faith, even if faith is for those things that we are unsure about. But we can still feel from deep inside that we believe in it. So faith is not a story, an argumentation that will always allow doubt to exist. It is a feeling that points us in the right direction, even against all odds. The discussion with Harish Johari about my later written down faith has given direction to my entire journey, against quite a few odds. And obviously, my faith also evolved.

3.2.6. PERSEVERANCE

The Sanskrit word for perseverance (SAMADHANA) is usually translated as focus, concentration. It basically means that all that we are becomes one-pointed towards our objective with determination, perseverance. While the ever distracted and doubting mind needs it, it is principally a quality of the Ego not to give up and exert its willpower over mind.

In any practice, we cannot give up too soon. Many practices need time to bring results. So we should persevere and train ourselves to persevere. Many people like to be quite free and changeable in their practices and do not regularly train themselves so.

It is advised, especially in the beginning of learning how to meditate, to set certain targets, such as in the duration of our practice→6.2.3. We do not expect any results, yet we do expect some effort. With a clearly set target, the Ego will not allow us to give up easily.

This is especially true in the phase of concentration and in the related chapter→11 we will discuss many creative ways in which to set our concentration targets. Likewise, on longer term we must train ourselves to stick to the promises we made with regard to daily practice→5.4, even if only to strengthen our power of determination.

3.3. The Nine Impediments

While the mind itself can be seen as pure and innocent, still its particular nature and very function produces a number of obstacles when the Ego gets involved with it. The 9 impediments of mind(ANTARYAS) 'stand in the way' of progress, a classical approach to the mental obstacles in reaching the higher states of meditation and spiritual growth. Whenever we feel blocked in the meditation process, we return here for better understanding of the underlying mental imbalances and traps. With some persistence, they can be resolved, even if the first of these may require a lot of patience sometimes.

3.3.1. SICKNESS

When we are sick(VYADHI), it may be quite a bit harder to feel good. The body itself may continuously produce a variety of stress signals such as pain, nausea, temperature fluctuations, etc. that produce distress and take away our peace. Sitting in meditation may become particularly difficult and it may feel too hard to stop our mind from reporting on our discomfort.

We first of all need to accept to be in this condition, otherwise our resistance may further aggravate the dis-ease. That does not mean we cannot try to get out of this condition, which can go as it came. And it also does not mean we cannot try to feel good regardless→Story10.

Even though modern medical science knows so much about our body, still the origin of most chronic diseases remains surprisingly unknown. Risk factors aside, scientists remain incapable to point out a clear cause for most forms of arthritis, asthma, diabetes, Lupus, cancer, psoriasis, Alzheimer's, ALS, MS, chronic fatigue, Crohn's disease, endometriosis, RSD Syndrome, fibromyalgia, low immunity and many of today's other major health issues.

The commonly named risk factors are unhealthy habits and environments, as well as emotional stress. These are not regarded as causes in the West. Medical science will mostly point to inflammations and other malfunctions of our auto-immune systems, without offering an actual explanation. Hence modern medicine is rather limited to dealing with the symptoms.

Emotional stress however is the one risk factor which has been found to clearly stimulate all of these diseases. Also our natural resistance against bacteria, viruses and pollution largely depends on it. Unhealthy habits are themselves most often a response to unhappy feelings. Ancient medicine sees unhappiness thus

Story 10 The Art of Never Giving Up

Once upon a time, when in early puberty I got involved with spiritual pursuits, I met Pierrot. He became my best friend and we enjoyed great times together. As he was 4 years older than me and had a huge spiritual library and plenty of knowledge on various spiritual paths, he was also like a teacher-friend. Together we became students of Harish Johari. The most precious gift that I received from Pierrot was the power to never give up, whatever the challenge. From childhood he was severely disabled, and most of his life he was very dependent on others, in an electrical wheelchair, on rather permanent breathing aid. And yet he was so strong in his desire to live life to the fullest that he inspired many people around him. We also toured India together, where his attitude astonished many. Having outlived medical predictions by over 25 years, he finally passed away and I surrendered his ashes to Ganga, as per his request.

as the main cause of all disease. As also Candace Perth, the Nobel prize winner for chemistry once said, every disease has its origin in our emotions.

Body and mind are entirely interrelated. It is actually quite strange that modern science often fails to see that, even while it so much limits mind to the body, in the workings of brain and nerve cells, hormones and neurotransmitters. If the mind is unhappy and stressed, then the body will weaken and suffer, which is the origin of all sickness from a *yogic* perspective. As we can all easily agree that an unhappy, unhealthy body produces a more unhappy mind, why would it not work both ways?

To feel ill is not just hard for the mind to manage, it is an impediment of the mind itself. It is a state of the bodymind. The expression of emotion is not particularly unhealthy, it depends. The suppression of emotion→4.1.6 on the other hand is the main cause of disease, when both mind and Ego resist letting go of some emotional attachment.

Contrary to its own findings, medical science still tends to disregard most psychosomatic origins of disease. As unfortunately the modern medical approach is still largely inspired by the pharmaceutical industry, even mental issues are mostly countered with pills.

Emotions as a source of disease are a sensitive subject for people that are really ill, as it may produce a feeling of guilt, which is counterproductive. While we must assume some responsibility for our sickness, we should never blame ourselves, as it is quite natural to go through phases of emotional turmoil→4.1.4, which may in turn negatively affect the body. The outer symptoms of disease are nothing but *karmic* expressions of some unhealthy yet natural *karmic* impressions in the subconscious→3.6.1. These pains are pains of spiritual growth and ultimately it is through this growth that we will be freed from them.

This understanding often makes people believe that they are all alone in solving their health issues, that looking to others for help is proof of not having fully accepted their own responsibility. But even if we see unpleasant emotions as the original cause of our disease, it does not mean that happiness is the only solution needed.

We should look beyond the typical symptomatic approach towards a more holistic understanding of such issue, working on all levels of our being simultaneously. Once the body is destabilized, some more physical and energetic remedies or therapies may well be required to unblock it. The people who have specialized in such techniques have so much more understanding and experience. If we want to assume all responsibility, we must also see it as our task to find those that can truly help us. Similarly, while the health of our car needs our maintenance and gentleness, we will still ask a mechanic to fix it if damaged. To make these techniques work in the best possible way, we may maximally avoid further unhappiness.

In order to remove this impediment from our practice, the *yogic* lifestyle traditionally involves the entirety of *Ayurvedic* knowledge, the Indian science of a healthy life. Here we learn how our body functions and how we can balance it with proper food, exercise, etc. Of course this knowledge also comes from other cultures and through personal experience.

Fixing our body will thus include achieving that physical→4.3, energetic→4.2 and emotional balance→4.1 that is so essential on the path. Sickness thus forces us to do what anyhow needs to be done, for which we can be grateful.

We mainly need some home remedies→4.6, so that whenever some imbalance develops, we can easily fix it ourselves. That way we will not need to wait until we can have an appointment with a doctor, while the imbalance aggravates. Thus, we can often avoid the more drastic cures that often have undesirable side effects.

As a spiritual healer myself, it is very clear that when a disease is present over a longer period of time, it will affect all layers of our existence. It will manifest in the physical body, in the life force, in the conscious mind and also in the subconscious. All these layers are ever connected and in part responsible for maintaining the disease, regardless of its original cause. The spiritual aspect relates to the energetic blockages in our very soul and its relations within the spiritual dimensions. If all else fails, the remaining blocking factor may be spiritual in nature and can be dealt with through shamanic rituals and other healing approaches of a more subtle *tantric* nature→A3.

Whatever increase in peace and happiness we can create through our own spiritual practices will be the most deeply helpful in keeping us more healthy. The inside job of meditation remains our most essential tool for happiness and to reduce stress.

We are thus advised to simply take our physical limitations into account when meditating, assuring that some meditative practice continues in relative comfort and can have its healing effect even if we are ill. Even in case of severe physical discomfort, a meditation pose with props can be developed that is suitable for most practices→7.6.4. We may then need to forego the more intensive concentration exercises and focus more on wellness meditation, fully and repeatedly relaxing body, breath, mind and senses.

3.3.2. DULLNESS

Dullness(STYANA) is a condition in which the lower vibration of the energy body→4.2.1 has become unnaturally dominant. Most heavier energy is produced by the physical body. After action, the body needs some rest, which is also true for example following the action of digestion. It is quite natural to feel a little dull when tired, while if the feeling persists it points to an instability in the bodymind. Dull people lack the clarity of mind to understand, as well as the energy to put the theory into practice.

When either the body or the emotions are imbalanced, lots of energy is wasted and dullness is easily produced. It may also be caused by excessive indulgence in gratification of the senses. We will discuss this aspect at length in the chapter on energetic balance→4.2. Excessive dullness, which seems hard to overcome even though one really tries, may also be due to an excess of waste products in the body, needing purification. Related also may be a lack of digestive fire→4.5.3.

3.3.3. DOUBT

We already discussed doubt(SAMSHAYA) in the chapter on confidence←3.1 and there really is not much more to say about it. Some thinkers have made a big philosophy of doubt, which has its merits. Every question is literally an expression of doubt, so should we then not question? Truly, we cannot just take any understanding for granted. We have to doubt everything we think we know, and especially all knowledge that comes as words, which will always at most be relatively true.

Yet if we have to doubt everything, then we also have to doubt the doubt. At some point we have to set it aside. We may not have full certainty, but we can have faith←3.2.5 in the path, so we walk confidently. Since we are walking, we will arrive somewhere. The people who are truly blocked in lack of confidence cannot reach any decisions, as they keep doubting each one of them, as much as they doubt themselves.

As long as we rely on our thinking alone, doubt will be our companion. Better we move beyond the two-edged sword of mind←1.3.1 and live from the certainties abundantly present as faith in our heart.

3.3.4. INCOMPETENCE

Incompetence(PRAMADA) does not mean that we do not have the knowledge or the skills needed to do a certain job. It does not even mean that we do not want to do a good job. It means that we are too much distracted to apply our knowledge and make good use of our skills. To then improve our concentration power is essential and it will not only help us in our meditation practice, but in all aspects of life.

Some distraction is not wrong in this funny game of life, yet if it blocks us from reaching our goals, we must get a little more serious. Exercising concentration is the yoga of being serious, which only requires some attention every day. It allows us to practice the most important yoga of being not too serious the remainder of the time, while still competent.

It is nothing personal. Everyone's mind will be distracted if it is not regularly concentrated by the Ego. Especially if unhappy, our mind tends to be all over the place, unable to concentrate. So this quite directly relates to the earlier chapters on restraint, concentration, perseverance. It is about being in the here and now, and what we are doing there.

3.3.5. LAZINESS

Repeated reluctance to put in an effort may produce a condition of sloth or laziness(ALASYA). Dullness in the bodymind may be at the source of it, yet laziness is more like a mental habit and a philosophy even, a choice we make. As modern society has so much forced people into endless activity, some have rightfully claimed the right to be lazy. And to some degree, laziness sometimes just comes to everyone.

Sure it should not all be work and no play. Every day some time should be reserved for wasting time without much purpose, and enjoy relaxing our willpower and Ego→Story11. The most ideal time for some lazy entertainment is in the evening, when the energy is naturally more lazy→4.2.1. Giving ourselves a break from all ambition is a logical prelude to sleep.

Habitual laziness may also be produced when sleep is disturbed, which is itself indicative of a serious mental and/or spiritual imbalance that should be urgently addressed→5.3.12.

The habit to be lazy often develops as a defense mechanism and sometimes it is the result of improper parenting. Sustained unhappy feelings may lead to a pattern of escapism, when every effort is shunned out of principle. Some people thus really make a profession out of not doing their job. It demonstrates a disbelief in their ability to make their efforts bring them something worthwhile, making their laziness essentially a matter of negative self-image.

Laziness also comes as a generally bored attitude, an 'I couldn't be bothered', which is most often the result of excessive

Story 11 — 007 Spirituality

Once upon a time, I had my first one-on-one meeting with Harish Johari. I arrived at the house of the artist and guru brother Pieter Weltevrede. Everyone was busy in the kitchen, so I was told to seek Harish Johari out in the living room. Imagine my excitement to have him all to myself, as I had hereto only enjoyed his teachings in a group setting. When I entered he had just started watching a James Bond movie and enthusiastically invited me to enjoy it together. It was a very revealing experience to see such a wise person so childlike in his adoration of the many 007 stunts and special plots. We laughed a lot and sure afterwards there was room for some questions. Yet the main message already was clear, to enjoy life without prejudice and too much seriousness. He never needed much of an excuse to make fun of us, or of himself. He always loved to play with children and even though he did not speak their language, children easily felt so comfortable around him, like my little niece in this picture.

mental activity, whether in sensory and mental distraction, or in unhappiness. Some people are bored and lazy because there are so many things that are too painful to think about, that there is nothing left to think about, except time-filling nonsense.

Laziness can be a major obstruction in sustaining a daily meditation practice→5.4. Especially when we are not feeling emotionally balanced, our mind will naturally resist any plans for concentrated action, as there is that general feeling of needing a break. Yet we are advised to ignore that signal especially when it comes to actions that are particularly helpful in making us feel better. When the feeling is however so persistent that it is also very much felt in the body, our practices should again be more aimed at mental wellness rather than towards a mental workout.

It is always funny when someone starts snoring during group meditation. In corpse pose sessions→7.3.1 it is even more common, when as a result of mental relaxation people cannot help falling into blissful sleep, which is probably exactly what they need at that time. Moving into deeper meditation, some people will feel as if they are falling asleep as well. That subject is discussed at length later→12.3.3 and is in fact not a matter of laziness or tiredness, contrary to what people tend to believe.

In any case, we should never identify with our laziness, never think that we are born to be a lazy person. While some body types are somewhat less ambitious than others, laziness is essentially a temporary energetic habit of the bodymind, which can always be changed. Even the subconscious programming of our Ego will produce a more or less lazy character, while this is just the same matter of reprogramming, which means to go against our programming. We are only predestined to be lazy if we think we are.

3.3.6. NON-ABSTENTION

Non-abstention[(AVIRATI)] is related to the earlier chapters on restraint and dispassion, yet it is also quite different. While restraint and dispassion deal with avoiding unhealthy imbalances in our lifestyle, abstention is needed when some habit is particularly blocking a phase of spiritual growth. The impediment of mind in non-abstention is a matter of mental addiction, which stops us from moving forward in the practice.

There are too many examples found also in many of the other chapters. Like in drinking too much coffee→4.6.3 before morning meditation or in an addiction to in-between snacks, which may often disturb *Asana* practice→7.2.2. For the deepest meditation practices, some abstention from sensory and sexual gratification is a requirement, which may be difficult→13.3.1.

Through the system of various neurotransmitters, the body may also be very involved in our addictions, yet like the mind, the body can be weaned from them. Fighting some addictions may be a significant challenge and it may be advised to first build more positive energy. At least as much effort as we spend on getting rid of things that bring our energy down→4.9, we should invest in those that lift us up→4.8.

3.3.7. WRONG UNDERSTANDING

Erroneous understanding(BHRANTI) is like a nonsensical idea that really does not correspond to reality. It can be caused by wrong information obtained from others. For sure in this age of ignorance(KALI YUGA), wrong understanding is everywhere. This problem is most often a matter of delusion(MOHA), related to the fantasizing quality of mind. Wrong teachings themselves are products of fantasy, usually inspired by the stress related to comparing our level of spiritual evolution with that of others. We can say the same about wrongly understanding correct teachings, even while that may also be caused by lack of actual experience in practice→3.5.

Wrong understanding usually draws us to inappropriate practices, which are either too ambitious or not aiming high enough. One example is the wrong idea that since we will never be able to stop thinking, we should be content to just observe our thoughts→9.3. Another misunderstanding is that since reaching the Self is essentially a nondoing, we should never engage in any spiritual activities←2.8.3.

Fantasy is the great power to imagine a reality that is at least in part unrelated to reality. It has produced great stories and helps us to imagine our future. Like we may desire to become a chef and opening a great restaurant. We already see ourselves cooking the tastiest food there, with people queuing for a bite. It is a natural part of creating something for ourselves in the future, but we do not know the future. If our plan holds too much imagination and too little fact checking, then it will probably fail. Delusion is created by the Ego, yet through the imaginative power of the mind such a good story is created, that the Ego itself believes it to be true.

In spiritual growth and practice, the main delusions are about ourselves, again a matter of handling our spiritual Ego. Maybe something good happens, some progress is made, yet we are not only overthinking it. We are blowing it out of proportion, imagining it to be a lot more than it is.

I hear this a little too often when people describe their meditation experiences and have firmly made themselves believe to have opened their 7th *chakra*, ascended to some other dimension or met God in person. It is somewhat difficult to handle, since it is hard to judge another's experiences. Most of it makes me smile though, in the knowledge that it may be just a passing phase, a beginner's mistake. Some of it may nevertheless be truly a unique spiritual experience, as some really miraculous things can happen, which we will discuss later→13.4.1.

The higher we fly, the bigger the fall. Entertaining such delusions about ourselves means playing a rather dangerous game with our self-confidence. As fantasy ultimately crashes into reality, the Ego will feel to have lost all power. It might also make people feel extremely lonely and leads to narcissism.

Spiritual progress is not about flying and there are no true shortcuts to the final destination. To grow, we need roots and patience. There is no need to know how high our branches are already reaching, as long as we keep making the effort to grow. The destination is certain, the arrival time is not. We can take all the time we need, as long as we are practicing. All too often such delusions serve as an excuse for not making any real effort.

Obviously, most wrong understanding is the result of a negative self-image, which people try to escape from. Yet those negative ideas are delusions in themselves, where we identify with our past limitations. Wrong understanding is definitely not only about people that overestimate their achievements. Some people are underachievers, caught in the delusion that they are somehow different from others in being unworthy of the hope that 'normal' people feel for any work in progress.

Much of this kind of understanding is based in habitual thinking. Whenever we recognize such wrong understanding and want to go against it, we may nevertheless see the old thought patterns repeat themselves easily. We can change them by recognizing whatever triggers them and then very consciously and repeatedly attaching a new kind of thought pattern to that trigger, for example by replacing it with a *mantra*→4.1.7.

To know reality, we have to face it. There is no need of fairy tales or horror stories about past, present or future. We neither give the positive nor the negative too much importance, as all leads to the same glorious end. Always remember that those who have reached there usually describe it as the most ordinary thing in the world. The role of understanding is actually quite limited anyhow and will be discussed below→3.4.

3.3.8. NOT ATTAINING A YOGIC STATE

The inability to attain a *yogic* state (ALABDHABHUMIKATVA) means the inability to reach *Samadhi*, as well as any of the meditative phases that precede it. So, it must be clear that this is quite a natural impediment of mind in everyone. In each meditation phase some failures must be overcome, such as the inability to sit motionless, to hold the breath, to stop listening, to halt the trains of thoughts, to let go of control, etc. The process of meditation means to learn how to stop everything. It is the ultimate exercise in full control of the bodymind.

The ability to reach a *yogic* state is affected by all other impediments of mind. Often our failures in practice are themselves the cause of laziness and doubt, generate delusions about our progress, leading to incompetence, non-abstention, dullness and even sickness. All these basically mental problems are then often encountered together, blocking us from moving further. The only healthy way to move into the practice is without expectation.

If we have reasonably mastered all meditation phases yet *Samadhi* is still not happening, it can be highly frustrating. We should accept that the main blockage lies in the subconscious, whose restlessness may stop us from letting go of control→12.3.2.

3.3.9. NOT STAYING IN A YOGIC STATE

The inability to stay in *Samadhi* (ANAVASTHITATVA) is even more predominantly a difficulty of the subconscious mind→13.3. The more unstable our deep programming is, the faster it will draw us out, away from the Self. Yet this problem solves itself. Every time the real trance happens, the particular unrest in the subconscious will be at least partially healed in the process. It is a gradual purification and successive sessions will draw us ever deeper. When in the deeper trance states also breath starts to stop, the body may break off the *Samadhi* due to lack of *ojas*→13.3.1, which is a different issue.

3.4. The Role of Understanding

Under-standing means 'that upon which we stand', the thoughts that support us, guide us in moving further. It is the knowledge base from which to decide upon our actions. We anyhow mostly think about what we are to do. The role of spiritual understanding is thus to support our practice, nothing more or less. The purpose of this book is to solve the little problem of understanding about *Samadhi*, so that we can effectively meet the real challenge of changing our deeper energetic vibration through *Samadhi* practice. Yet the understanding will not lead us there, only the practice will.

Understanding is always conceptual in nature, an intellectual construction that may be related to reality, allows us to work with it, yet is not a reality. Even though so many books have been written about it, the Self can never be understood purely as a thought construct. It can only be known in silence and even though that knowing can be shared in inspiring words, they will always somehow limit the unlimited. The most enlightened thoughts will not make a person enlightened.

With some guidance, even children can get an idea and experience of the Self, so it is really not needing an intellectual approach. Many illiterate *yogis* have demonstrated that given some good symbol of the goal, which becomes their object of meditation, the highest levels can be reached without needing lots of words 'to stand upon'.

The one who needs all these words is the Ego. While the truth of the Self is easy to get, it is hard to accept, because it seems to go against all that we stand for as individuals. So all words are only needed to help us accept this truth in order to motivate us into action. Practice will only feel like a good idea if it seems like an appropriate response to some clearly defined issue. Before putting in the effort, we want reassurance that it all makes sense.

In the traditional seven steps towards enlightenment, understanding mostly belongs to the 2nd phase of study, which is logically followed by the 3rd phase of practice→3.8.4. As the practice leads to the knowing beyond words, which also comes as a great feeling, the need for understanding to motivate us becomes less. Practice becomes natural, no questions asked, no more reassurance needed.

Yet still, as the practice evolves, new issues are encountered, which may need some new concepts in order to be solved. These concepts are thus all related to the changes in the non-Self, to the practice on the path, rather than to the goal.

There is a variety of stories on how the ever-wandering saint Narada Muni - symbolizing full understanding - can only stay in the same place for a limited time, lest that place perish. One can have only as much understanding as one can put into practice, which is also true when reading this book.

3.4.1. TIME-TESTED CONCEPTS

This book is largely based upon the initially rather overwhelming number of ancient *yogic* and *tantric* concepts that are shown in Table 5. All of these concepts have proven to be very useful in overcoming blockages in the practice, whether on the mat or in the spiritual practice called life. We do not however need to know them in Sanskrit. The Sanskrit terms are mentioned for further reference, so that my translation or interpretation can be checked in the original scriptures. They are thus clearly not my own inventions, even if the writing about them will always be subjective.

CONCEPT	SUBJECT	CH.
5 Koshas	Layers of the non-Self	1.5
7 Chakras	Centers of desire	1.7.1
5 Margas	Paths for the Ego	2.
8 Ashtangas	Phases of practice	2.3
3 Bijas	Manifested seeds	2.8.2
6 Sampattis	Treasures of the Yogi	3.2
9 Antaryas	Impediments of mind	3.3
7 Bhumikas	Stairway to heaven	3.8.4
9 Rasas	Emotional essences	4.1.5
3 Gunas	Vibration of energy	4.2.1
5 Pranas	Movement of energy	4.2.2
3 Pranas	Storage of energy	4.2.3
3 Pranas	Polarity of energy	4.2.4
3 Doshas	Physical imbalances	4.3.
5 Tanmatras	Sense Perceptions	9.1.2
5 Bhutas	Manifested elements	9.1.4

Table 5 - The ancient vedic concepts used in this book.

If too much effort seems needed to get acquainted with these concepts, remember that we are being quite ambitious here. To stop all modifications in the non-Self, which is the essential practice of yoga according to Patanjali, we need to understand them. How many years do we spend in regular education to prepare for life and our profession? To intellectually understand these *yogic* concepts, which will also be really helpful in our lives and jobs, maybe just a few weeks of 'college' are needed. The over 150 hours of free teaching offered on my Youtube channel likewise are not truly that excessive to watch.

Let it be clear that while we can make good use of these ancient concepts, they are also partially untrue. Some people may then see them as useless, relative and irrelevant in seeking the wordless reality of the Self. They indeed represent the stories and obstructions produced within the non-Self. To work with the non-Self, they must nevertheless be known, otherwise their changing natures can too easily fool us, take our attention away from the Self.

These concepts are also incorrect in their inability to grasp the infinite variety of changes within the non-Self. Like when we study the seven *chakras*←1.7.1, we may forget that the body has many more energy centers. Yet those seven allow a workable step by step process, that may guide our practice→4.4.2. Likewise, the incredible wealth of different emotions

Story 12 Mister Understanding

Once upon a time, when I eagerly asked Harish Johari one of many questions, his answer was that the issue was not a matter of 'miss-understanding', rather a problem of Mister Understanding. It became my nickname for a while, again and again making fun of my tendency to conceptualize everything. Fortunately for me, Harish Johari did like to talk and had such vast knowledge that he could also very well satisfy my thirst. And yet some things I was not ready to understand, as I saw later. Many years after he passed away I met another teacher→Story22, who actually does not like to explain the why and how of anything. He only clearly tells me what to do and whatever story I then distill out of that experience he may confirm it if correct. If incorrect, he just points me back to the practice.

that a human being may experience, is not given much credit by being reduced to only nine emotional essences or *rasas*. Yet again, this knowledge may be key to achieving emotional balance→4.1.

The age-old concepts on which this book is based are mere symbols of relative reality, like when we see light shine through some crystal - as we find it on a famous album cover of Pink Floyd. While we observe how it produces the rainbow colors, it may get the deeper meaning of the diversity of personalities produced by the light of the same Self, depending on the crystal, which is the bodymind. Thus that image can summarize a book load of knowledge. If we can equally see our words as symbols, with broad and flexible definitions, we are on the right track.

One might say we mostly need 'right' understanding to counter 'wrong' understanding, which anyhow tends to come. Wrong understanding, as discussed before←3.3.7, is mostly Ego-inspired and based in imaginative delusions about ourselves and the world, leading to inappropriate actions and practice. Right understanding[SUVIDYA] may not be absolutely true, but it leads to the truth through practices that step by step bring us closer to the goal. We just put one foot in front of the other until we can walk beyond understanding.

3.4.2. BEYOND UNDERSTANDING

Many more concepts than the ones named above have been developed by the *yogic* traditions over the ages. To my personal experience however, with the above list of concepts I got quite beyond the need for concepts. By all means we keep studying, yet somehow this intellectual searching also must end.

For the one who has mastered this kind of understanding, no more books may be required→Story13. Sure there is always something more to learn about the infinite changes in the energy of things, yet if that does not lead to fruitful practice, what is the use? And how many different practices can one be seriously involved with? It is a question that may likely pop up when reading this book. Sure, all that is offered here are mere opportunities for practice, allowing different readers to make different choices. As the role is to bring us to the practice, the search for more understanding should end there, at least for as long as the practice is fulfilling its purpose.

All sciences ever redefine and refine their concepts. Within this book, including in this chapter on the role of understanding, how can everything be truly covered? Like an artist has to decide on the final brush stroke, the author has to write the last word somehow. And the reader also has to end the reading. The endless story has to end somewhere. Some people are just addicted to little tidbits of wisdom in the same way as being addicted to sweets, just seeking some momentary pleasure in the taste.

Everyone has the right and the freedom to taste of all different schools and traditions. That is nevertheless a rather new and fairly unnatural option created by airplanes and the internet. What is the use to study many different points of view, if we fail to heed the first wise words we meet? And how useless and potentially confusing is it to learn different sets of concepts from very different traditions? Sure we can zap around for a while until we find some tradition with which we particularly seem to connect, especially if we do not feel a connection to our own. From then onwards it is advisable to stick to one body of knowledge only, one set of concepts that fit nicely together. Like I really adore the principles of Buddhism, but largely stay away from it in order to avoid confusion within my original Hindu concepts, which cover the same grounds.

Some ignorance we have to accept, as we cannot know everything, let alone practice it. New understanding will come at the right time, when we are ready. After my original teacher Harish Johari passed away, I discovered many things he surely could have taught me, but did not. The knowledge would have been useless to me, as I could not yet apply it. First I needed to work with the understanding already provided, putting it into practice and gain the abilities needed to do that. Fortunately other teachers came at the right time later←Story12.

3.4.3. SUBCONSCIOUS KNOWING

The learning process is essentially energetic and subconscious. It cannot be forced, however many books we devour→Story13. And that process mostly requires practice, not some new wise words. Imagine if every blockage in the subconscious would want an answer all at once? We would just explode. There is a spiral learning motion in which we move forward, gain understanding, benefit from putting it into action until a new issue emerges from deep down, which requires new understanding. That new knowing may start in the conscious mind, yet is only really going to work for us if it is accepted in the subconscious.

Words are concepts based on concepts and if we start analyzing them to the bottom, nothing is left. Even while it is wonderful to embrace our ignorance in exploring new views and ideas, the real seeker is destined to increasingly look inside. Developing our connection to the cosmic intellect→13.4.2 is essential on the

Story 13 *From Rubbish to Bible*

Once upon a time, at a rather young age, I started reading 'I am That', with the Jnani teachings of Nisargadatta Maharaj. I really felt it was rubbish, as the straightforward teachings too much clashed with my beliefs. I did not finish reading it, which was unusual. 7 years later it was the only book that was available during some retreat, so I gave it and myself another chance. It totally struck home and became like my bible, which I reread many times over the years, while also connecting to Maharaj very much in the heart. So spiritual books are definitely a way forward and I have read a few of them every week for decades. About a dozen years ago it was enough and I stopped reading spiritual books, in order to let the understanding come out of the practice and from the source. Few years ago I also got rid of the over 1000 books I had gathered on spiritual subjects, keeping only those of Harish Johari for reference.

path of meditation, because the deeper we go, the more we move beyond the rationality of the conscious mind towards subconscious intuition.

As the light of the Self triggers our cosmic intelligence in the subconscious, it still uses the words that we have stored there. If our inner concepts are incoherent and too personal, even the Self will be unable to efficiently communicate. If our concepts are sufficiently coherent and universal, our intuition will bring us messages that can easily lead to deeper insights and highly fruitful actions.

We can then apply our concepts to a wide variety of phenomena found in ourselves as well as in our relationships and the universe. In this way our understanding of just about anything can become quite complete, based on a rather limited number of essentially subconscious concepts, used by our cosmic intelligence. Thus it is the objective for our understanding to evolve from book loads of stories to just a few dozen words.

This learning process is stimulated by repetition, as it takes a while for not only our intellectual understanding to adapt, but also for the subconscious to accept these innovative ideas. Repeatedly reciting scriptures and learning them by heart is how tradition has ensured that engraving of our understanding upon our very soul.

Overwriting our inner encyclopedia needs to happen again and again, so that our Ego's objections are fully countered and we may practice with confidence. For example, many years ago, I listened over a dozen times to the 15 tapes of *rasa* lectures by Harish Johari, a total of over 24 hours of teachings. If one ever imagines to do some intensive study of a particularly relevant subject, one should not doubt what it can bring about.

This book is all about bringing this more subconscious understanding. There is so much to be learned that one cannot expect to remember all that one has understood while reading. That is only a minor problem, as the concepts will anyhow be stored deep down and emerge when needed. The source of it will then often not be clear, yet who cares?

And if somehow one fails to sufficiently recall what has been read, we can always reread the related chapter. A handbook is a book to keep at hand. Maybe we feel unusually lazy, blocked somewhere with a *mantra*, encountering some sitting issue or a new emotional challenge, etc. It will pay off to again get the understanding about that aspect more clear. So we read, absorb, store and then move forward in the practice, which will bring the deep, true understanding that we will never again forget.

3.5. The Role of Practice

While the Self as the prime observer is the first teacher→3.7.1, practice(ABHYASA) is the second most important *guru*, which we should always revere, through our practice. We will discuss further on how anyone can create space for practice→5.1, so let not our struggles with time and effort obscure our appreciation of the role of practice. We can teach people from a country which knows no chocolate all about the taste of it, yet it cannot beat giving them a taste of it. Knowledge and practice are one.

Whatever we have learned in words will only become ours through practice. The story will become a knowing, as that seeing is allowed but not created by the practice. So we learn by doing and the practice gradually will affect everything that we do. When we try to remain aware at all times, it does not signify that we think very deep thoughts about everything all the time. It mostly means that whatever comes to us, we use it to practice. That is what always being in the observer mode is really about.

3.5.1. THE 2 BASIC MOVEMENTS

As explained before←1.7.1, the process of spiritual growth is essentially energetic and subconscious. Increased conscious understanding is thus also not the primary objective of the practice. Practice aims at changing our energy, both temporarily as permanently. Temporary changes in the energies of the bodymind are useful to not be bothered by them for a while, so that we can let go and move inside. From inside then, the more durable changes in the energetic vibrations of our subconscious programming can happen, especially if also manifested when moving again outside.

The first half of the practice is to learn to go inside, closing out everything which is outside. To go inside means to connect to the Self and experience who we truly are. This is called the finding of heaven inside. The second half is that we come out again from the inside, but we bring heaven with us. We bring this feeling with us, this true seeing, this love, this universal connection. And we try not to lose it, while we manifest it in our lives.

It is a circular movement from inside to outside and back inside, etc. This is traditionally named the paths of the Hindu gods Shiva and Vishnu. The image of HariHara, half Vishnu and half Shiva, represents the ultimate *yogi*, in which both movements happen simultaneously, being outside without ever losing connection to the inside→13.5.

People who are rather new at this

game must first learn to go inside, the path of Shiva, the one who destroys the illusion of the Ego. More advanced practitioners easily find their way inside and may then need to be more focused on bringing the inside outside. That is the path of Vishnu, which is the preserver of the illusion(MAYA) for the sake of the divine game(LEELA). Yet also for them, regularly going inside is still required to reconnect to our divine nature and further deepen that connection. This is why there is the practice on the mat and the practice of life. One cannot succeed without the other, which is why this meditation book includes so many pointers about life.

Image 10 – The yogi as HariHara, one half practicing like Shiva and the other half as Vishnu.

Those who are more familiar with the Hindu pantheon will recognize that Shiva always appears in the stories as Shiva, even if some people recognize some more incognito appearances as Hanuman for example. Vishnu on the contrary openly manifests in many very different incarnations, of which Krishna, Ram and Buddha are the best known. This symbolizes that the path of going inside is always ultimately the same. It is about finding the Self, which is then also represented by Shiva. And it shows how the path of making the Self come truly alive in life is highly varied and to some degree personal, as Vishnu manifests as love in Krishna, as righteousness in Ram, compassion in Buddha, etc←2.5.3. As the game of life offers endless variety, a wealth of specific divine energies or abilities emerges from the Self, allowing us to play with maximum satisfaction.

3.5.2. A WORK IN PROGRESS

Regular practice is essential to remain at peace with ourselves. Once we get involved with the spiritual story, we all desire to be like the Buddha, never get angry or worried, always keep the bliss. Yet all this can only be gained through practice.

As we practice, we can accept not to be perfect. As long as there is no practice, it is all just stories going on in our mind. Then very easily we become dissatisfied with ourselves, maybe even turn away from the whole idea, because it just creates too much frustration. If we are unwilling to put in some effort, better we refrain from entertaining such lofty spiritual ideas altogether.

To practice, we accept ourselves as practitioners, a work in progress. Whatever imbalances we find in ourselves, we know we can change them like everyone can. There have been phases in my life when I thought I no longer needed any practice. In all these years, the longest that I have been able to stand myself without practicing was about three months. Then the need became all too urgent at first, a natural duty further on.

From own experience I can testify that an overload of understanding which is not sustained by practice, leads to spiritual depression. Those great teachers that have inspired me actually always taught by example that the practice never stops. Even if in my eyes they truly no longer needed it, they would still make time for it every single day.

3.5.3. THE NEED TO FOCUS

For our practice to have real value, it must be appropriate, which means adapted to where we are in the process. We will discuss how to evaluate our progress later on→3.8. While our Ego should not get involved with any results, we need

Story 14 The Success of Failure

Once upon a time, Harish Johari was getting ready to leave us after a nine-day workshop in Belgium. Usually he would give me some technique to practice for the year to come, yet this time he asked me what I wanted to learn. I answered that I aspired to build more will power and he then told me to daily practice Tratak, gazing into a flame→11.3.4. 'It is described in my book Dhanwantari' he concluded, while already waving goodbye to everyone. I looked in the book and found the technique explained in full detail. For one year however I couldn't succeed in it, the eyes always blinking too soon. The next year I told him that maybe this technique was not for me, as I could not do it. He asked me to demonstrate how I was doing it and I just put a candle in front of me when he already concluded that I had not correctly read the book. 'The candle should be only 30 cm distance from the eyes and it should be on eye level, not on the floor. I did it as he told me and it worked! He laughed and concluded that for sure trying something for a year, even though it did not work, must have boosted my will power very well.

to know where we are to decide where we are going. Why try to learn inner *mantra* recitation if we cannot yet sit comfortably? Sure we can have some nice experience with *mantra*, but to taste the cherry on that cake, we may first need to digest some others.

Once we have found an appropriate practice that seems to work for us - which is personal and often temporary - we should really focus on it. Harish Johari would usually give me only one practice to concentrate on for a year, like making one breathing cycle last for two minutes→8.6 or the practice of gazing at a flame←Story14. We have to really master our practice and be patient. In the old school way, some teachers would give their students only one practice to last them a lifetime.

Too many people are continuously changing practices and never master any of them. The first time we try something new, it might yield quite a nice result. So we try more of it, while often the result is then not very spectacular and most people move on to something else. That first experience is often stronger because every new practice somewhat relaxes some new part of us and that effect is easily felt. Yet the true feeling, when that part of us is actually fully relaxed through this practice, we will only get by mastering it. That usually doesn't happen in just a few sessions.

The practices in life are as varied as life itself. Also in the meditation phase of relaxation, many different techniques can work for us, even without being fully mastered. However, once we start the concentration phase→11 and move towards real meditation→12, only one practice is needed. That especially is the one we must find and then master, for years on end.

3.6. The Role of Karma

When some past impression in the subconscious is active, it will bring a period of related thoughts and feelings, supported also by some events occurring in our lives. This can be experienced as positive and negative both, like as in good luck and bad luck, producing happiness or unhappiness, yet always making us grow.

As discussed before←2.4.1 our *karma* is first of all our work, needed to support our needs and desires. Our spiritual aspirations thus produce our *karma* as practice. And all action also produces *karma* as our destiny, which is a strange, magical phenomenon that plays a central role in our spiritual evolution.

Karma as destiny originates in our

actions or *karmas* of the past, and still we so much tend to seek in what happens to us some validation about our current actions and spiritual endeavors. I am doing the right things, so why does this suffering come to me? Do I deserve all this bad *karma* for my wrong behavior? Don't I already have enough trouble for all these problems to come my way today? All these questions rest upon a giant and rather naive misunderstanding of how *karma* works.

Some actions produce instant reactions of the universe sure, like if we are careless we might drop something and it breaks when meeting the floor. Many more natural laws like gravity will ensure our *karma* thus, even those that are highly mysterious, too subtle for our mind and science to grasp. Yet what happens to us now may have been generated long before. How we react to it now, may create *karmic* ripples expanding over many lifetimes. What happens to us today is simply no judgement on our current actions, intentions, thoughts, feelings and behavior.

Within *karma*, also thoughts are seen as actions that affect our destiny. The more they are repeated, the more creative *karmic* power they will gain. Habitual negative thinking thus has short- and long-term consequences. Positive thoughts will produce a more positive future, yet again not instantly, maybe only in the next life. The more emotional and passionate these wish fulfilling thoughts are, the more power they will have. We just cannot judge ourselves through what happens to us in the now.

We can only judge ourselves, to some degree, in our thoughts, feelings and actions. The natural *karmic* laws - that support the preservation of harmony in the universe - will only bring us what we have produced ourselves. *Dharma* in *karma* is the great teaching of the Hindu god Ram, as the incarnation of Vishnu, the preserving principle.

The law of abundance is a related delusion that has been particularly selling well, such as in the famous book 'The Secret'. Of course it is no secret in *yogic* science that whatever ideas we have about the future will have some *karmic* power to materialize in our lives→Story15. So if we imagine abundance to come our way, it will come. Yet there is no saying when, as the *karmic* effects of all that we have thought, felt and done before are also at play. We might actually at a particular time be better served by poverty than by abundant wealth.

The delusion that just by having great fantasies of the future will shortly make us healthy, wealthy and wise, has thus created many casualties in spiritual circles. And if these people then complain about it to the authors of abundance theories, they are blamed for lack of confidence in creating their visions of the future. Such circular theories are an extreme example of the delusions to avoid on the path. Just keep walking forward.

Story 15 The Healing Hands Wish

Once upon a time, I had a wish to use my hands in healing. Since from a very young age I was immersed in the teachings of Harish Johari, I became quite the alien to my fellow citizens. I actually lost many friends during that time, for example when responding to someone's anger by indicating that we are also free not to be angry. It created a kind of loneliness for a while and it is there that again and again came this wish to be able to just put my hands on people's heads and let them feel how I felt. It seemed far-fetched at the time, but I even dreamed I could do it. Ironically, decades later I am now in my healing practice somewhat able to do that indeed. With the added power of a Rudraksh mala, my hands are now able to purify the energy field of my patients. It was a serious illness that practically led me to become a healer, while only much later I realized that maybe this over 20 year old desire was also karmically involved.

3.6.1. KARMIC EVOLUTION

When asking ourselves what is the role of *karma* in the process of spiritual evolution, we should realize that our *karma* represents our spiritual evolution. *Karma* starts with the *karmic* impressions in the subconscious. They produce our *karmic* expressions in thoughts, feelings and actions. The universal response to those expressions manifests as our *karmic* destiny, maybe immediately, maybe later.

Whatever comes to us is thus a response to some subconscious vibration inside of us. It will allow or even force this energy to be brought to the conscious mind. Spiritual growth then happens whenever we are able to let go and express that vibration in peace, love, understanding and total acceptance. If we can respect *dharma* in response to our *karma*←2.4.3, then that very shaking in the subconscious will be neutralized, satisfied, pacified, deep inside.

Key to that spiritual reprogramming will be the ability to observe that vibration from the Self, whether in life or in deep meditation→13.4.4. The main role of meditation lies exactly in its impact on our *karmic* evolution. *Samadhi* is thus always seen as the main way in which to reprogram our *karmic* impressions or vibrations, yet the same must also happen in the practice of life.

We need not to worry about which *karmic* impressions to work with first, as life will lead us there. Our destiny will literally show us the way. Every problem and every solution will come exactly at the right time. Our only task is to accept the solution and let go of the problem.

If we do not feel particularly challenged during some period of our life, we can maximally enjoy it by working more with the Self itself. Maybe we also clean up some residues of past inner battles of the non-Self, finetune and express any newly emerged abilities. If on the other hand we feel a lot of pressure has come our way, whether as outer disturbances or as inner turmoil, that non-Self is showing us what part of it needs reprogramming, so that we may lighten up again for a while.

Sometimes we feel strong and then again we feel weak, challenged. We should attach to neither. It is all part of the same process. Every problem is an opportunity for more transformation, essentially a letting go of some related attachment.

3.6.2. THE JOY OF SUFFERING

Enjoying the pleasures that our *karma* may bring does not lead to many questions, except maybe in our attachment to them. It is the more unpleasant *karmas* that seem so often on our mind, whether of past, present or future.

Yet we can accept that as a rose bush needs pruning lest it falls apart, we need to be regularly cut to prevent weakness. Our challenges make us grow more durably, like snakes again and again shed old skins for an improved version of ourselves. Our suffering is thus a blessing in disguise, yet that is not its purpose, since suffering is an entirely natural thing.

There is this old saying that the taste is in the tongue, not in whatever it tastes→Story16. Something can only taste good or bad if those distinctions are present in the tongue. So both pleasure and pain are just natural fluctuations within our perception. There can be no tongue that only tastes good things, as taste can only be experienced in a zillion varieties from truly delicious to utterly disgusting. The same goes for all senses, where no enjoyment is possible without at least the potential of some suffering.

Our ultimate tongue, with which we taste our very lives, lies beyond the sense organs in the subconscious. It is through all attachments present in the Ego that we experience life as agreeable or disagreeable. That duality principally exists in ourselves and only there it can be dissolved.

For the one who understands *karma*, there is thus no more reason for tears,

Story 16 The Taste is in the Tongue

Once upon a time, Harish Johari's father taught him an essential lesson. He first gave him his favorite sweet, which he enjoyed very much. Then he let him chew on some leaf, and then again gave him the same sweet. It now tasted like sand and he spit it out. That herb must have had some numbing effect on the tongue. Then his father asked whether the taste is in the sweet or in the tongue? And since he could not taste that second sweet, he had to conclude that the taste is in the tongue, since if the tongue is not working, the taste is not experienced. His father then concluded that whenever he desired to taste something which was not available, he could just bring the taste out by sucking his tongue, enjoy the taste from memory and by the inner senses only.

there is only joy. That suffering is a liberation, so our sour tears become sweet. We then see beauty also in any death, as the *karmic* opportunity for renewal that it is. What came has to go, life follows death.

As the Self, we never suffer. While suffering is thus actually unreal, an illusion, the feeling of suffering is experienced and must be respected. It is good to cry, because it means that we are letting go. Even many great masters are known to occasionally shed some tears.

The *yogi* will expand any personal sadness into universal compassion. It is the kindness originating in the recognition that we are all on the same boat, carry the same cross. In that way, our own *karma* is definitely not only personal. It is a universal *karma* or action of attachment and detachment. As it signifies the spiritual evolution and expression of the whole, it is a source of great mystery as well as joy. Ultimately all suffering teaches us love.

3.6.3. MASSAGING KARMA

Karma as destiny is often seen as an arrow that we have shot ourselves and comes back to us like a boomerang. Our *karmic* expressions as thoughts, feelings and actions are the arrows that we are shooting in a certain direction, with a certain power and intention. The active *karmic* impressions in the subconscious are like arrows that we keep ready in our quiver. The passive *karmic* impressions are the potential arrows that we still need to assemble from the feathers, sticks and arrow points we have gathered deep inside.

Every second our thoughts, feelings and actions thus have some power to change our destiny. We can decide which arrows to shoot where, which ones to store, assemble or disassemble. However, the arrows that have been shot before and are already coming back to us cannot be stopped.

Yet that *karma* can be massaged, the impact of these arrows softened, so that we can keep moving forward regardless. For those that believe in astrology, a *vedic* horoscope usually shows multiple possible death days. Which day will be the final one largely depends on how we live. It demonstrates how our *karma* is not a fixed thing.

Softening *karma* already happens in a way beyond our doing, as if the universe somehow only brings us the troubles we can handle. Not everyone may always agree with that anyhow mysterious assessment of nature. Especially if we become unable to practice, blocked from producing the best possible reaction to some difficult *karma*, we can try to reduce the *karmic* pressure. That is where the path may also include helping ourselves to overcome some very challenging *karmas*. Not in order to avoid learning that lesson we need to learn, letting go of what needs to go. It is only to maintain a productive balance, so that we can keep moving forward.

Massaging *karma* involves every kind of spiritual practice, and especially meditation. Whenever we make the extra effort to stimulate our growth, the universe will see less need in enforcing growth upon us. So the more we feel challenged, we challenge ourselves, practice discipline, go in warrior mode.

Acceptance of our present situation, with its opportunities and limitations, is often the key to change our *karma* and that very situation. It will not always work, as there may be other *karmic* powers involved, while the opposite for sure is true. As long as we so much resist our situation, *karmically* it will probably not change until we accept. Nevertheless, unpleasant *karma* also comes and goes, as shown in the science of astrology. Yet when it goes without being accepted, it will be back with the same message later.

Image 11 – Ritual for the 9 planetary energies.

Story 17 *God or the Helicopter*

Once upon a time, a flood was threatening a valley and everyone fled to higher grounds. Yet one pious man refused to leave his house, saying 'God will save me'. When everyone left, he fervently prayed to the Lord to be saved. The water came and it was already knee deep when a man on a horse offered to bring him to safety. But he answered 'only God can save me' and kept praying. The water rose and he had to move to the first floor of his house when a man in a rowboat came and offered to take him, but to no avail. More water came and he was sitting on the roof of his house when a helicopter flew over, lowering a rope ladder for him to climb aboard. However, still he refused, sure that his Lord would save him. So then he drowned and when he came to heaven before God he complained 'How is it possible that you could not save a faithful devotee like me?'. And the Lord replied 'Well, I heard your call, so first I found you a man on a horse, but you did not want that. Then I got the boat, but that was not good enough for you. Then I even managed to send a helicopter and still you did not want to be saved. So maybe next time you should have more faith in me being present in everything.'

In the Indian tradition there exists a wide range of *tantric* practices directly aimed at softening some particular *karmic* challenge, such as the ritual shown in Image 11. As the other dimensions are involved with the more magical workings of *karma*, particular colors, sounds, minerals, metals, herbs, patterns and rituals are advised to deal with general 'bad luck' as well as for removing severe physical and mental blockages. My spiritual healings are of a similar nature and I can testify that this 'mumbo jumbo' very often does work→A3.

It is also true that some people are too much involved in trying to magically avoid their *karmic* responsibilities. *Tantric karmic* healing is mostly to be used when people are truly blocked and can no longer get out of it in the usual ways. It should not be the answer to every problem. We are our *karma*, as individuals, so we better play the part, even while as the Self, we have no *karma* at all.

As we see the divine in everything, we also recognize the opportunities offered in everything←Story17. In the same way, if we want to increase the divine in ourselves and our lives, tools like meditation are available to all.

3.7. The Role of the Teacher

3.7.1. THE INNER TEACHER

The ultimate teacher(GURU) is the Self. That pure beingness is the truth and nothing but the truth. In that way sure, it is inside that the learning has to happen, which also means it is all about practice. And that practice primarily is meditation, the process of withdrawing to the inner teacher. The Self is the only knower and the little problem that we have is to manifest that wordless knowing into our more 'wordly' knowledge. Then we will clearly understand our desires and feelings and plan our actions and practices accordingly.

First of all, the Self holds all answers about itself. And since it is our primary goal, we first and foremost study the Self. As discussed earlier←2.6.2, that includes the study of the non-Self. Even there, the Self holds all the answers through the intermediate of our cosmic intelligence ←3.4.3, which basically clarifies how the unmanifest manifests. It is also primarily through Self-awareness that we may come to really understand the phases, paths and practices of meditation.

The moment we feel confused, whenever there is a question and we do not find the answer in our thoughts, the smile of silence is the only answer that we can give. In silence, the Self will observe, the subconscious will see and then when thoughts come back or things happen, they will hold the answer. This is the main way to work with the inner teacher.

Even things we have never heard about or never been taught, will come to us that way, through our silence. Of course this is also something to learn, and from this attitude of learning, then everything we meet will be like our teaching or our teacher. It does not matter whether it is a person, a thing occurring, a child or a mouse or whatever. Through the observer mode, everything will bring us messages, provide the answers and this can happen in quite a miraculous way. Yet it only works if we can keep our own mental texting down.

The methods may vary a little, as discussed also earlier←3.4.3, but the basic process is simple. First probably we use whatever works for us to produce some durable silence inside. When we have found that silence, we pop the question in our mind and return to silence. Then suddenly the answer comes out as a simple thought and if not, yet thoughts return, we let it go for the moment. We then wait until something happens either inside or outside and we maybe do not immediately see a connection, but five minutes or five days later we may recognize the answer provided. And we will know that it is the answer, because it comes as a doubtless knowing, not as a complicated narrative that we fabricated in our mind.

This is even more true if it is the result of a conscious choice to find some answer in the deepest states of *Samadhi*. Hence many spiritual traditions advocate to regularly retreat inside and receive some vision that answers our questions →13.4.1, a process often supported by food fasting→4.7.1.

This way of seeing represents a somewhat strange advice, difficult to believe in, but we can always give it a try. The result will depend of course on how good we already are in finding and holding our inner silence. To work with the inner teacher is thus a learning process. We will get better at it, until from that stillness words, ideas and insights will flow, like an unstoppable river, even without asking a question. That is when we truly become our own teacher.

Anyhow, whatever we can learn wherever, only by working with it, we will truly come to understand it. Only when we can bring it into our own experience, translate it in our own words, practice it and feel the truth of it in our lives, it becomes ours.

So when silence leads to a new idea, we try it out until again we feel a need for silence. Then again a new idea comes and we let it manifest. Words or thoughts can never be perfect and ideas never cover the full answer. Each successful session of letting our innermost voice speak in words will only compliment, not contradict, whatever ideas came before from that same source. So slowly slowly our concepts will become rather satisfying altogether, useful complementary guidelines on the path.

We then turn more and more to the real learning beyond words, to the clearest voice of the inner teacher. The Self is the true teacher of truth^(SATGURU)^, leading us from the darkness^(GU)^ to the light^(RU)^, from untruth^(ASAT)^ to truth^(SAT)^.

3.7.2. THE OUTER TEACHER

We all love the idea of being our own teacher. While we can maybe somewhat reluctantly accept that practice is required for that inner voice to be heard, we often resist the need for an outer teacher.

Obviously, most people first need to master inner silence to clearly hear the inner teacher, which is more easily said than done. And whatever we may feel to emerge from it may still be quite colored by our subconscious Ego programming. Our experiments in life with some truth found inside may equally be corrupted. It is then hard to make sense of, and that also means we have no idea how to move forward with it. We keep listening to the inner teacher of course, yet why not experiment also with some of the experiences shared by others that preceded us? Is that not also a way to move forward?

Traditionally, there is thus an outer teacher and the inner teacher. And the inner teacher is absolutely number one and will also attract the outer teacher. As we desire to work with the inner teacher, the outer teacher *karmically* manifests. And the outer teacher will do nothing more or less than push us back to the inner teacher. As our quest is for the Self, the outer teacher can only point towards it. And to the practice of course, as the second teacher←3.5, the outer teacher only being third in line.

Many of the questions that the student just discovered have nevertheless already been digested many times over by the teacher. It is just our Ego that may have an issue with listening to somebody, of having to accept maybe someone else has a better idea, more experience. Yet who wants to learn Chinese without any Chinese teachers, books or apps? Especially with the objective of writing some real poetry in Chinese?

The rather absurd desire of wanting to somehow find all this understanding and develop all these techniques ourselves, is only coming from the spiritual Ego←2.8.3. We relax, as we are the Self. There is nothing to prove. We relax that Ego and just listen for a while. We let ourselves be inspired.

What is of course true is that the teacher can do nothing if we are not doing our part. The spiritual teacher is not somebody who tells a story that we memorize and then we are there. Hearing about the Self must lead to a better experience of it, which brings the real knowing. Remaining dependent on the experience of the outer teacher means to stop moving forward.

The teacher is just somebody like us, who has already gone some way on a path that we also intend to follow. So the outer teacher kind of knows the way, like a guide in some strange country. He figured out many details and the process is also in part about many details, like how to sit painlessly→7.4. So at least for these details, it is very good to have a teacher. I have experienced this so often along the way←Story14. And as we will see when studying the teaching lineages, tradition sets us free to have one or more teachers, depending also on the details we need.

There are many other ways in which teachers can be very helpful. They are inspiring examples of who we want to become. They may not even be enlightened or anything like that, but at least they have gone part of the way. They have achieved some progress, mastered at least some things and are willing to share that experience.

Both the inner as the outer teachers will support our faith in ourselves. If some teaching does not provide that, we are listening in the wrong corner. The path of meditation and spiritual growth is not easy, so faith usually gets lost now and then. As the inner teacher is impossible to reach without faith, the outer teacher may help to restore the connection.

The experience of the outer teacher is mostly about practice. So the outer teacher gives us both the faith and the practical guidelines to turn faith into productive action. The closer the relationship is, the better the outer teacher will be able to point us towards the practices that may deal with some particular state of disconnection from ourselves. I have been really fortunate to encounter so many teachers that really took the time to get to know me and guide me accordingly.

3.7.3. SPIRITUAL ENERGY TRANSFER

The most important power of the outer teacher is not in the teachings. A person who has attained a certain *yogic* balance has a very particular energy field. This brings us to one of the best things that we can do upon meeting a new teacher. We can let others do the talking, just sit nearby, close our eyes and try to meditate. And if that teacher can be really helpful to us, then more easily than usual we will reach inner peace. It depends of course on whether the situation is suitable for practice. It takes a reasonably good student to thus recognize a good teacher.

To practice postures together with a teacher is logical since there is something to see. To practice meditation together with a teacher may more fundamentally pull us forward, even though there is nothing to see. To share in such teacher's energy is the biggest blessing→Story18, because it can make Self-awareness so easy. The mere taste of it may fuel our meditation progress for months.

Many people experience being at a loss for words when meeting a master. Even when they are not particularly awed by whoever is in front of them, still they seem to forget their questions. This happens because their energy has been temporarily changed by the radiation of the teacher. With some teachers one has to be really close by to have such experiences, yet others seem to affect people in a very wide radius. One may wonder, if all real meditators in the world would stop meditating, what would the state of the world be like?

Many spiritual Westerners these days believe that there is actually no reason to visit those countries where deep meditation has been practiced by many over thousands of years. They feel that we

Story 18 *A Bubble of Love*

Once upon a time, I met Narayan Rishi, who was a main teacher of Harish Johari in various yogic practices and especially in numerology and astrology. He was known as an extremely powerful yogi. Even in his 70's he did many yogic performances, attended by the late Prime Minister Nehru, of which some video is available. That included shooting blindfolded, letting a jeep drive over him, stopping a driving jeep with one hand, etc. I stayed with him for a while, 105 years old at the time, which was simply great. However, I did not fully realize what was actually happening. Only when driving away and leaving that village, I suddenly felt as if coming out of a love bubble, bursting out in tears. I was missing that love, which I had so taken for granted. It felt so terrible that all I wanted was just to go back, but my flight was waiting. One year later, he left that body.

now have all the knowledge we need and can find everything else by ourselves. Yet the moment we get off the plane in India and start to meditate, it is just different. Newcomers may need to go through some culture shock first, but then after a while, new experiences start happening, even if only the same effort is made as at home. Not to forget that some teachers may be found there that have evolved way beyond what I have ever experienced with our Western teachers, however devoted and genuine. That is also true for myself.

To have a connection to a person with a more advanced energetic balance is very helpful for our progress, which is primarily energetic in nature, a retuning of the songs of our inner programming. That energetic transformation produced by connecting to the energy field of the teacher also works in quite magical ways, producing unexpected results, change the course of our life even. And once we have that connection with the teacher, we may benefit from it even long-distance.

Aside of the natural energetic blessing included in meeting a saintly person, some traditions also have more formal ways of transferring spiritual energy (SHAKTIPAT). Maybe through a pat on the back, a gazing, a touching of foreheads, a guided meditation or some other method, the teacher consciously pushes the energy of the student upward.

This produces mostly a temporary

change, where we experience a more subtle level of being and some temporary detachment from our usual stories. As the energy of it goes, even our memory of it will fade. But it may definitely teach us something, motivate us to move forward and unblock particular subconscious blockages in the student.

It all depends on who is giving what and who is receiving it. Some teachers are even able to artificially induce *Samadhi* in some students. In this way it is as every more forceful method: it can give us a push, but are we ready to be pushed? The same is true in my spiritual healing practice, where a similar kind of energy transfer is the primary tool.

We can use whatever help we can get. It is all part of the divine program. But better we do not depend on another's energy too much. Some people tend to keep chasing that one energetic exchange with a teacher, which they believe may solve all of their issues at once. Bringing the inside to the outside, we can pat ourselves on the back, as that power resides in each of us. Yet if we feel blocked somehow, we can ask our questions elsewhere and find more than answers to help us in letting go.

3.7.4. HOW TO BE A STUDENT

The first requirement in the student is the willingness to bring the theory into practice, not just to be satisfied with some wise words or a borrowed good feeling. Just listening is not enough. And practice needs not consume time→5.1.1, so there is no excuse. Only through practice the teachings become truth.

For example, in my lengthy online class on anger[20], I explain how anger always emerges from unfulfilled expectation. The question of 'What did I expect?' may thus be sufficient to defuse the anger. I can explain that in just these two lines or write a book about it, yet if nobody tries to have the experience of it, nothing is learned. The teaching, all that talking, this reading as well, are only an introduction.

Becoming a student means to really start observing truth and be dedicated to transforming ourselves. Teachers sometimes give students a new name to symbolize this change. Originally this tradition belongs to the initiation of renunciates, when they break all connections to their family and the past. Harish Johari never wanted to hand out names, arguing that one name is one problem, two names are two problems. Only if we are truly ready to let the entire

[20] See 'How to Stop getting Angry ? (edited)' on youtube.com/youyoga.

past go, our 'past' name can go along with it. Yet still, a new name is a new problem, maybe even bigger, with more expectation. So, I am still just Peter.

Students can listen to the teacher in two ways. Some will listen to the teacher while continuously talking to themselves in their mind. Whatever is being said, they will compare it to what they already think to know. They immediately try to formulate an opinion on what is right or wrong in the teaching. With one ear they listen to the teacher and with the other they listen to their own commentaries. People then even ask questions which already have been clearly answered, but these answers were somehow not heard because of their inner dialogues. It is quite a natural way to listen, while it means we may miss out on a lot of truth.

The alternative is to eat first and digest later. We just listen from inner silence, absorbing the teaching without judging it. It is anyhow just a story, so it may be partly right for us and partly wrong. It may be right for others and wrong for us, or vice versa. If we can receive it with an open mind, the better we will understand the full story. And then afterwards we can go back to it, practice with it, find out our own truth about it, make the story come alive.

One might say that many people these days read far too many books, listen to far too many different teachers. They no longer take the time to digest and thus often end up intellectually indigested. I remember the time when a really good book was hard to find and thus cherished, on our mind for months on end.

If we ask the teacher to fill our cup, that cup will be filled. If we bring a bucket, then it will be full also. Same for a bathtub. And if we can open the bottomless well of our heart, it will overflow. What a real teacher can teach does not depend on their personal experience alone. The moment the teacher opens up to the teaching, the answers will come, through that same cosmic intellect that we ourselves try to reach.

3.7.5. LOVING THE TEACHER

The above title probably feels controversial to many. It shows that this rather confusing subject must be discussed. Love between teacher and student is natural, yet it is not a romantic love, because of the roles that both actors are playing. Romantic love is an equal partnership between two Egos, while in teaching the Ego of the teacher should not be involved. The student need not know the individual personality of the teacher to understand the basically impersonal teachings. All that is thus needed is to become a lover of the teachings.

The typical love the student may feel towards the teacher is therefore a love of the Self, not for the person. Also the love the teacher feels for the student has nothing to do with the person of the student, as it is unconditional. Yet these love connections can produce very powerful feelings and all of it tends to become quite personal anyhow.

It is understandable that the student's Ego gets involved. Upon meeting a person who not only answers our every question, but also seems to produce in us such a good feeling to go along with the understanding, we easily attach. And when we express our gratitude thus, even the teacher's Ego might take that personally.

It can be very confusing and then of course especially if some more personal or romantic attraction becomes involved. Lovers do not make good teachers of truth. For the student, feeling personally attracted to the teacher may be a novel and overwhelming experience, yet the teacher should know better already. As long as the student does not know the teacher as an individual, the love cannot be personal. The love for the teachings is then confused with love for the unknown and often idealized person.

I disagree that a teacher cannot get romantically involved with a student, if both clearly desire it. But then a choice must be made and the teacher-student relationship must end. So that as lovers these two people may meet as equal individuals and the love and the attraction can be balanced, untainted by the charisma and typical behavior attached to the role of the teacher.

Many of these problems are related to the teacher that declares to be celibate but cannot do it, which is another problem altogether→4.9.5. That is a matter of trust and honesty, with some teachers misusing whatever power they may have over the student. Unfortunately there are too many really terrible examples. The principal responsibility resides with the teacher.

Even without romantic involvement, the teacher-student theatre can be quite dramatic, even highly entertaining, especially for others. Like with a lover, some students become too possessive of the teacher, push their 'guru brothers and -sisters' aside, steal the attention. Others may doubt the teacher's love for them or feel ashamed to admit to a lack of progress. Some become jealous of the attention or abilities gained by others. A few cannot stop crying when absent from the teacher. People who have never experienced such love for a saintly person cannot understand it→Story19.

To get some information, we do not need to love the teacher, only pay the teaching fee. Yet love is just another word for the connection which is required for the teaching to happen on a more subtle, energetic level. If the teaching is real, love will be felt, yet it should never be taken

Story 19 I thought I must be Gay

Once upon a time, Harish Johari was leaving us and I felt so much pain in my heart. That was not unusual, but this time it felt a lot more dramatic. The feeling stayed for days, in which I became quite unable to function. All I could think of was him and whether I would think of him or very much try not to do so, I was feeling totally alone and miserable, missing him so much. It troubled my sleep and disrupted my digestion. I remember even thinking 'Maybe I am gay after all and have fallen in love with Dada'. Yet that was a strange thought, as my best friend was gay. If I would be gay, I would have long ago fallen in love with him, since I loved him dearly anyhow. That is when I recognized this love for Harish Johari as a different kind of love and attraction. It is the love of the student for the teacher, which is actually the love for the Self and the truth of the teachings. Thus remembering that truth being always available, I finally laughed and was very happy to have found this love through Harish Johari, while not depending on his presence any longer.

personally. Equally, to surrender to the teacher only means to surrender to the teachings and ultimately to the Self.

Of course, we have to be choosy in this love just like we are in romantic love. We do not put flowers at the feet of just anyone. It is not enough that someone takes on the role of a teacher to be our teacher. Yet when the student feels such love, it will be as potentially powerful as when falling in love with someone the more usual way.

Obviously, some people fall into the trap of a narcissistic teacher, which rightly explains many people's reluctance to accept loving a teacher. We cannot expect all teachers to be fully enlightened beings, as these are rare and usually keep a low profile. So the teacher commonly has some Ego left, but it should disappear when teaching. A narcissist cannot teach anybody, because the true knowledge only comes to the one who at least temporarily is able to drop whatever Ego is left→13.4.2.

To be a spiritual teacher is really one of the greatest challenges on the path. Many truly advanced masters have fallen in this trap. We have to be able to withstand the wrong ideas of our loving students, especially when they place us high above them. We are all on an infinite path→13.5.3, so who is ahead and who is behind? We are one and if the teacher forgets that, the teaching enters into untruth.

And the student must always remember it as well, lest it becomes basically discouraging, creating the illusion of an unbridgeable gap between student and teacher. Whenever we start thinking in terms of 'our teacher', we must remain vigilant for any attempt of our Ego to make that teacher into more than just a normal person with good, universal, timeless, fairly impersonal teachings, which are also being applied. This equally means that we are able to cross that gap by applying the teachings ourselves. Thus the egoless teacher will not rob us of our basic self-confidence, our faith in our own spiritual potential.

In some schools, love for the teacher is practiced as devotion or *Bhakti Yoga*←2.5 and while this is not wrong, it holds plenty of danger. We find that phenomenon in every tradition in Hinduism, quite literally in Buddhism and Sikkhism, very strongly also in Islamic Sufism and obviously equally in Christianity. Jesus is only the son of God who calls everyone his brothers and sisters, so he is not the only divine child for sure.

In *bhakti* some craziness is needed←2.5.3, when an object that holds the formless divine as much as anything else, is equaled with it→10.1.2. As we love the teacher as the divine, we can fully absorb the teachings and will not question any advice on practice. Bringing so much confidence, this devotional method has obviously worked out well for many over the ages, yet just as clearly it has left room for lots of abuse.

Still, the most common *guru mantra* of *vedic* culture combines total veneration of the teacher with the clear recognition of the divine as the ultimate source of all teachings. The full text is in the chapter on contemplative objects→10.2.3, among many other chants of a less religious nature, but the meaning is very revealing. The teacher is first seen as being present in all three main gods of Hinduism and then literally equaled to the Self. That is the teacher which is honored, without any mention of the person of the outer teacher. And that impersonal teacher then becomes the object of all meditation and devotion, while the teachings are repeated as *mantras* and the final liberation happens through the blessing of that teacher, that 'Unity Beyond Diversity'.

3.7.6. THE TEACHING THEATER

Teaching is not different from life in that it is just a game, a theater. The two principal actors are the teacher and the student. By its very purpose it is just a temporary arrangement, a learning format. And yet it can feel very complicated, love aside. First of all, the student has to respect the teacher in fulfilling the duty of teaching, which means students listen before they speak.

There is no real way for the student to evaluate the teacher, except in honesty. If a teacher basically starts lying about his own level of discipline, then trust cannot be given. If a teacher declares to be celibate, then that is what we should see. If he claims to be a full vegetarian, then no meat should pass his mouth. Bottles of alcohol should not be found hidden on purpose. To lie means to become unreliable as a source of truth.

However, that does not mean that a teacher who tells some students to avoid caffeine cannot drink coffee, since those rules are personal, as needed. It does not even mean that a teacher cannot have any unhealthy habits left. We cannot judge the state the teacher is in. We find that wisdom in the story of the teacher drinking wine, as well as boiling lead→Story20.

As long as the Ego is there in some form, *karma* will be there for the teacher as well. If it is our experience that the teacher can truly teach us, then we cannot judge the level the teacher is playing from, nor the rules of the teacher's own game. Once we recognize the teacher, we connect and this love must be unconditional, even if the teacher-student theatre-playing relationship must retain the condition of honesty, which applies to both. Yet neither the teacher nor the

Story 20 *Drinking Boiling Lead*

Once upon a time, someone criticized Harish Johari about his smoking and he answered with a story. It is available in one of his story books[21] and what follows is my own short version. Once upon a time, the famous teacher Shankara was traveling in the desert with his disciples. When they finally arrived at an oasis, the people there could only offer some wine to quench their thirst, which Shankara graciously accepted. That confused the students who thought that drinking alcohol was not allowed. Since their teacher anyhow drank it, they enjoyed a great party that night. The next day, Shankara took them again on a long hot walk through the desert, with many students suffering from a hangover. That evening they arrived at a place where craftsmen were boiling lead. Shankara approached the kettle and immediately drank the boiling lead, inviting his thirsty students to do the same. I would never answer similar questions with this story, yet in Harish Johari's case it was really very clear that there was no way to judge him.

21 'The Monkeys and the Mango Tree' by Harish Johari, Inner Traditions, 1998.

student need to be perfect.

The teacher-student drama is usually more the problem of the student. I have been fortunate to meet many advanced souls who knew so well how to play this game, that my own little struggles with this theater easily subsided. Plenty of true laughter also did that. The teacher must tickle the student a little, tease us into relaxation and let us bask in the love of full acceptance. Truth is the best comedy and our Ego illusion is always the best subject of any joke.

Sometimes the teacher is not available, maybe busy or far away. One day somehow, the teacher may have to leave the body behind, along with the dear students. There are also many stories in scripture where the teacher refuses to teach a student, for a variety of reasons. They give us the main answer as to what to do when the teacher is unavailable.

First of course, we practice and connect to our inner teacher to find the answers we need. Yet if unconditional love and true surrender towards the outer teacher are present, then that teaching will anyhow happen also in absence of the teacher. Any genuine inner request for help to the outer teacher will bring an answer. The conscious mind of the teacher may not be aware at all of what happens, but the soul of the teacher will have no choice but to comply.

Some students may experience that in

Story 21 — The Eyes of Sivananda

Once upon a time, I sat waiting in the boathouse of the Sivananda Ashram in the Bahamas. A boat was to take me to the airport on the main island, after teaching for a fortnight. I stared at a large picture of Sivananda, whom I had never met, and thanked him for letting me teach there. Suddenly, looking into his eyes, I had an experience which I cannot describe, yet I can explain what followed. When I stepped into the boat, I was in one of the most spiritual states ever in my life. I could so much see the Self behind the eyes of everyone, starting with the boatman, that I was completely overwhelmed by it. For over 24 hours I was totally in bliss, making beautiful connections with all kinds of people. I missed my connecting flight in Atlanta, even though I had 3 hours. I did not hear my name being called over the loudspeakers, so totally distracted by everyone I met. I remember that all people responded very nicely to my state of being. The feeling was finally lost after falling asleep on the last plane home. Yet somehow that connection to everyone has stayed, albeit in a less overwhelming fashion. Thanks Sivananda.

writing their questions to their teacher, the answer already comes before the question can be finalized. Then again they come up with a new question and again they delete it once written, feeling the answer already quite clearly. In the ancient stories, students that had never met a particular teacher still gained extreme mastery of the specific skills that this teacher was teaching, just by praying to their picture←Story21.

In the spiritual sense, the distance between souls is not measured in miles. It is only a matter of love, which generates the energy needed to create and maintain the somewhat electrical cord(NADI) between the hearts of teacher and student. In this way at least, it is advisable for the student to keep a picture of the teacher or teachers nearby, so that we are invited to regularly reconnect. Quite naturally, we might express our love by offering some flower or incense. Whenever missing the teacher, feel unending presence rather than temporary absence, which is an illusion anyhow.

To my experience also, this works very well, even with teachers that I have only met through their books←Story13. It is the love and trust that makes this work, as it gives the pure permission to be helped. So for those who feel that they have not yet met an outer teacher to whom they can surrender, all the past teachers of the great, historic teaching lineages are actually quite available. Through them, a living teacher might anyhow manifest, allowing a more direct kind of learning.

All these games between student and teacher rest upon trust and a true teacher will always be very aware of the law of *karma*. The subconscious soul anyhow is totally aware of it. In any help given by the teacher, the freedom of the student must be respected to avoid any negative *karma*. Some tickling aside, if the student is unhappy and not asking for help, the teacher cannot interfere, as the student has a right to be unhappy. So asking for answers or help is very wise.

If the relationship may deepen, the surrender to the teacher provides a continued permission to interfere, free reign to help, a 'carte blanche'. Such relationships are often older than just this life, when a teacher may *karmically* attract a new student, which is actually already known from before.

Many students will fail to see the logic behind all this theatre. Many will just get some information, hope for some wisdom even, but leave all else to their own efforts and abilities. They are free in that also. The only advice to then give would be not to resist such love when it is felt.

All of the above has mostly to do with the student, who first has to accept the teacher. Whether this is already a very emotional connection from the start or not is irrelevant. It means that the student decides to really listen, which includes a willingness to follow the teacher's advice on the appropriate practice. So the student first has to accept the teacher for the theatre to start, but then also the teacher has to accept, which is part of the theatre.

Whether the teacher will accept the student or not does not really depend on loving the student. And yet the student may very much feel that it does. The teacher is entirely free in the way of teaching, to how many students and what are the requirements. Whether he is open to teach only one or everyone is the teacher's choice, while it is based upon his particular spiritual approach. The more this approach requires the teacher to narrow his efforts, the more he will naturally need to be strict in selecting those that seem able enough to not only practice the teachings, but also pass them on. I have had teachers that indeed first have put me to the test→Story22, while others have accepted my request without further ado. Usually, the teacher-student relationship just becomes clear within the first exchanges, without any formal question. Nevertheless, such question may be a requirement to permit the real teaching to also happen on the level of our souls.

Once acceptance of the relationship is complete, the game can truly start. In my fortunately rather old-school experiences,

Story 22 — 24,000 Gayatri Mantras

Once upon a time, after actually hesitating for over a year, I decided that I wanted to learn to become a healer from Kedar Upreti of the Tantric & Ayurvedic Healing Center of Kathmandu. He only had one other student at the time, since his job was just being a healer. When I formally asked to become his student, he answered that now that I had made up my mind, he had to test me to see if I was worth the effort. He told me that I needed to meditate on 24,000 Gayatri mantras in the following 10 days. He made it very clear that my mind would be watched at all times, so if there was not enough concentration, I would anyhow fail his test. I accepted the challenge and without warning he completely shaved my head and told me to start. It was a wild roller coaster, as I had never done something like that. 10 days later he confirmed that I had passed the test, even 'if barely' he smiled. This Sadhana→5.4 was concluded with a fire ritual, as would the many old school Sadhanas that came later.

the teacher will then do everything in his or her power to help, guide and protect the student. The love of the teacher for the student then acquires a rather absolute unconditionality, which means the student must no longer worry about meeting any requirements for this love. Of course, the teacher will coach the student into more efficient practice. Yet one may then benefit forever from the permission to fail. Thus through doubtless practice we really become one with the teacher→Story23.

In the old school way, the student would not only live with the teacher. Students would live the life the teacher decided upon. The teacher might define the entire daily schedule. With such a 100% personalized approach, progress could be perfectly coached. The usual doubts and struggles of the student then disappear, as the student has handed the keys of his spiritual journey to the teacher. We no longer have to think about our own progress, trusting the teacher to bring us on the teacher's own level, if not beyond.

These days, most students as well as most teachers are not at all willing to accept such breach of privacy and individuality. It means that the students must take full charge of their own endeavors, start thinking about it like the teacher would. One is still free to ask the teacher's advice on practice and try to live up to it, accepting the truth of it as a matter of principle. Much of my coaching work→A3

Story 23 The Search for Harish Johari

Once upon a time, Harish Johari left his body, far away, with his family in India. When I received the unexpected news, I was quite unable to function for about a week. I was literally stunned by the loss of someone who went far beyond being like a father or mother. Then somehow I realized deep inside that what I was missing was not this body, creating this person. I was lacking that blissful feeling which he so easily produced in me, as in others. That energy being so contagious also indicated that it equally existed inside of me. To bring that out, which is a practice, became the way to no longer feel his absence. The search to thus 'find him back' became the greatest motivator for meditation of my life. Every memory that I have of him became a joy to cherish, a smile of love, beyond action. And still it was so essential to support my perseverance in the practice. To that person then who we called Dada or 'elder brother', I feel nothing but gratitude, also for regularly visiting my dreams for all those years, joyful reminders. Whenever I teach or write, I ask him to speak through me, as if it could be otherwise.

consists of finding out how to adapt practices to the particular needs, desires, schedules and abilities of the student.

Another source of confusion regards the learning process itself, which principally rests upon getting certain experiences in practice, rather than upon the transfer of information. Many teachers will apply the 90% rule, which means the student will have to discover the remaining 10% of the understanding on their own, through the practice.

I have often felt confused as a result, as both a student and a teacher. Anyhow, without the practice the student has little chance of fully understanding the words of the teacher, so this problem also takes care of itself. Therefore, I am trying to be as complete as possible in this book, while naturally the 100% understanding can only come through the practice.

One of the most confusing teaching techniques that contributes to the teaching theatre is when the teacher starts talking from Self-identification. On the one hand this technique can be very revealing, beautifully showing what it means to live and think from the Self. On the other hand, it can be disorienting and not only because it sort of negates the teacher having an Ego, which is only risky if intended.

When a teacher for example then says that he has the power to remove the unpleasant *karmas* of the student, he is principally pointing to a power of the Self→13.4.4. As the teacher using this technique equals himself to the Self, and as the path to the Self, that is of course true. To however see this as a power that the teacher has as an individual is false. Whenever this teaching format is used, the true message should at least be made clear to everyone, which basically means the marketing department should not exploit it.

3.7.7. TEACHING LINEAGES

Every teacher is also a student. So every teacher has a teacher, who has a teacher and so on. Nobody should take these roles personally. These are the teaching lineages and they are very much alive while teachers also die. Long gone teachers that support our learning from the other dimensions are very much what these lineages are about←Story6.

Hence all these lineages will promote specific age-old rituals that connect the students to the lineage through the process of initiation. Teaching lineages thus aim at preserving and sharing whatever we have learned as a group, throughout the ages. This work is truly invaluable, while it has its downsides like everything.

The ancient debt to the teacher is a holy duty to pass on the teachings. It is the final *dharma* of the student and often leads to really beautiful opportunities for *Karma Yoga* as well. The main problems arise when the lineage becomes an institution that needs to sustain itself. The current head teacher may be less popular than some of the predecessors. The institute may thus start to corrupt the teachings with the sole objective to reach more students and pay the salaries. One of the main and most confusing results is that many of these organizations claim to offer the best approach for everyone, while what is best is always personal, as already pointed out at length in Chapter 2.

Whether one has only one or more teachers largely depends on the teaching lineage, as it is principally a choice first made by the teachers. Some teachers may not be interested in students that also listen to other teachers, tired of having to explain different approaches, instead of being able to truly coach undoubting students. Some may prefer if other teachers take care of part of the job, which is also my position.

It is of course equally a choice that the student has to make. And contrary to widely held belief, there are many less institutionalized teaching lineages that do not require adhering to only one teaching or teacher. These are especially found among householder *yogis*, while renunciates tend to stick more to one-on-one relationships.

Renunciates usually belong to a particular school of thought(AKHARA), while few choose a more personal path. Within such schools, students can nevertheless also benefit from a variety of inspiring people and teachers with complementary views. Being in a school does not mean that we cannot agree to disagree, otherwise what is there to talk about?

From a more historic perspective, with the limitation of traveling no further than the nearest village for many seekers, one was happy enough to meet an advanced teacher just once in a lifetime. So then naturally, people tended to stick to one *guru* only. Travel did exist of course and especially in youth some spiritual seekers would undertake long journeys and meet many inspiring teachers.

Harish Johari was one of those, studying for about 15 years with over 30 teachers, before getting married and taking up the responsibilities of a householder. Yet once I met him, I ceased being interested in any other teachers, even though he never required such exclusivity. But after he left his body, very easily I bowed down to the many other great teachers that I have been very fortunate to meet.

In modern society, traveling and long-distance communication are so much easier and the preservation of scriptures, audio and video of the teachers of the past happens quite by itself on the internet.

Only if one wants to make these teachings popular, it does require a lot of marketing effort. Then we are back to the typical problem of expensive organizations that sell misleading, overhyped and overpriced teachings just to support themselves.

Revealing in this respect is the original name of Hinduism, which is *Sanatan Dharma*. The name 'Hindu' was only given by outsiders to the culture that existed along the 'Indus' River valley. The word *sanatan* has three meanings: universal, original and eternal, pointing to the Self. *Dharma*←2.4.3 here means the truth of the teachings as they apply as rules of conduct, understanding and practice. So the *dharma* of the spiritual aspirant is ever the same and always changing, from beginningless beginning to endless end.

Sanatan Dharma is eternal only as it adapts to various times and places, while the essence of it is timeless. We are all children of this time and of different places, which are looking more and more alike through this so-called globalization. So we can find our path together, yet each in our own way. This is also very practical, like for example in the rule to get up before sunrise, which is very essential in most Indian schools→5.2.4. For a practitioner in Scandinavia however, where the sun may not rise or set for many weeks of the year, that is impossible.

This book might in a more modern way also produce like a branch of teaching on working with *Samadhi*, maximally adapted to the life that most of us are living these days. Yet while all teachers who would be a part of this must make their own choices, it is of great service to the students to link the teachings to the lineage, as I myself try to do.

The reader may already have wondered why this chapter on teaching is quite long. Here is the answer, as it can only be through the readers that this volume of knowledge becomes part of *Sanatan Dharma*, the eternally evolving yet same teaching of truth.

3.7.8. HOW TO BE A TEACHER

In absence of the teacher, the student becomes the teacher. I like to quote here from a talk by Harish Johari on the debt to the teacher[22], which has guided my entire teaching game:

> *'Whatever you learn, you owe a debt to the teacher, which cannot be paid by paying him money. This debt can only be paid by teaching somebody what you have learned, so that the knowledge also continues and it does not stop with the teacher. You add to it your own experience, how you have*

[22] See youtube.com/youyoga.

improved your life and how you have improved your understanding. Then you pass that on. Thus you pay that debt and that gives you a satisfaction which brings peace.'

At some point, everyone thus becomes a teacher, whether in a more formal way or not. Maybe as poets or artists and musicians, as doctors or healers, as schoolteachers, craftsmen or even businesspeople, we share what we have learned. As long as we keep these treasures to ourselves, we will not be at peace with the teachings. At the very least, we can teach others by example.

Teaching is an essential evolution in the throat *chakra*, which greatly enhances our own understanding. It helps us to realize more consciously what we have understood. Understanding starts in the conscious mind, yet it is then accepted and stored in the subconscious. By explaining this largely subconscious knowledge to others, we complete the cycle by bringing the understanding back to the conscious mind, in our own words. Then we understand what we understand, any doubt is removed and practice comes easily.

The One-Eyed King

In the land of the blind, the one-eyed is king. Many would-be teachers tend to disregard the fact that some people have three eyes open. Our spiritual Ego games must be well anticipated, for example in not trying to answer every question our students might have. There is also a substantial difference between the sharing of knowledge about practice, originating in our own direct experience, and the expression of more general ideas that we might have on the spiritual nature of the game. Maybe first of all, spiritual teaching means to inspire people towards fruitful practice, not to tell them what to do with their lives or enforce our world view upon them.

We should teach only the practices with which we have sufficient experience. Even if many of the practices described in this book are no longer included in my current practice, none of them are without long-term personal experience. Only then the details can be correct. And when we teach for example *Asana*, we should definitely know more than a thing or two about anatomy and people's limitations.

Let's face it, some people open a yoga studio or become spiritual teachers and even healers after just a few weekend workshops. Some people have learned a few things because they desperately needed to. They must however be extremely careful to not let their Ego jump from a negative self-image to the pretty picture of being the teacher. The old lineages did have the quality advantage of not just letting anyone play at being the teacher, while usually offering many high-quality teachers.

We should only teach when being invited and not bother people that are not open to our teachings. It is generally not advisable to teach people with whom we have another kind of relationship, like friends or family. However great, our role as a teacher is less important than our roles as parents, partners, siblings, buddies or children. Each child has only two parents, while teachers there are many.

While our great words can never cover the whole truth, whatever people can achieve in practice should not define their overall perception of that truth. Again there is something natural about this trap. When we tell people that they will ultimately have to go far away over there, yet for starters can only aim a lot more nearby their current state, they resist. It is part of how the Ego fights the truth.

The Teacher-Student

It is best anyhow if we only take up the role of the teacher temporarily, not 24 hours a day. Thus we can keep learning and not stop our own progress and process from the idea that as we became teachers, nobody can teach us anything anymore. To listen to a teacher, the teacher must once more become a student. No one should identify with the teacher role all the time, unless they have truly moved beyond all identification.

Even if the most essential story of the Self holds no more secrets, still in the energy of things, new insights are endless. The wisest people I have met have also been the most curious ones, ever excited for something new and refreshing.

Teaching from the Heart

'Dear teacher' is a common nickname for children[(GURUJI)], as they easily speak very wise words without thinking, straight from the heart. To think means to believe that we already have the knowledge, which our thought process may then bring forward. Yet when we thus think we already know, the voice of the cosmic intellect will not speak. True knowing requires not knowing.

Every teacher will have a particular way to prepare for a class. However, as long as we need to create a very detailed story in advance, we are not really teaching. Only when it comes out naturally from inside, we are going to reach inside our students. If the story is only intellectual, we will merely teach their minds. We have to speak from a state of not knowing, except in sharing practical experiences. That is also when we will not need to use complex words to explain difficult subjects, and our students will easily understand us.

One of the ways in which to ensure this, is to start each class with a request for help. We can ask our teacher or teachers, or divine energies of other dimensions, as well as our very Self, to teach through us. Whether that happens with a *mantra*→10.2.3, as a ritual or purely mentally, it will create a fundamental shift. It will clarify that ourselves as individuals, we carry no responsibilities for what comes out of our mouth, except of course in keeping that Ego in check. Also in a child, if the Ego is involved, the words that come out may be very far from wise.

Teaching from egolessness, we will not feel restrained or shy and whatever we say will be nuanced enough to be open to interpretation. Anyhow everyone is connected in the common mind field, so if we teach from there, we should never for a second believe to be the teacher. Only then will we have the confidence and the energy needed to make people see. This teaching is not related to the Ego and what it thinks to know. It requires nothing more than stepping aside, whatever is our personal background.

Sharing Energy

Understand also that our sharing is most importantly a matter of energy. Even if our knowledge does not become less by sharing, rather the opposite, our energy can be depleted. The more we engage with people and their relaxation, the more we will have to practice in order to maintain our energy balance. Sometimes we may take people's problems on our shoulders, yet there are limits.

We can never substitute our own practice with the teaching of that same practice, as the effect will be entirely different. Yet, this error is all too often made.

A major way to conserve energy is in not expecting any progress from the students. Whether the practice brings the intended result does not depend on the practice, only on the practitioner. There is nothing to expect, as progress through practice is as natural as it is unpredictable. Not expecting any results of our performance as a teacher means to create the peace associated with *Karma Yoga*. We accept our students and the results of their practice as they are and just maybe try to see what would be the next step they might take. Towards our students, practicing patience and tolerance is essential.

We best assume that only say 5 % of the result will depend on our beautiful words, our great energy, whatever powers we have in our arsenal as teachers. 95 % will depend on the student, even if the 5 % may tip the balance in the right direction. So sometimes it will work and sometimes not. If we teach in this way, also the students will feel more comfortable.

Nevertheless, the teacher sometimes has to point out some inconvenient truths and even some convenient untruths, cherished by the student. We should then always play the ball, not the player. We can criticize the way something is done, but never the one doing it. It is all not personal, a natural process of transforming the energy of the student.

Commercialization

In ancient times, spiritual teaching mostly happened as *Karma Yoga*. It was either a hobby of householder *yogis* who had other ways to provide for their families or it came from renunciates who lived on a bare minimum. Since students would usually live and eat with the teacher for a while, some donation(DAKSHINA) was made to cover those costs. The professional commercialization of spiritual teaching is a fairly recent phenomenon, even if obviously the great ancient schools and temples of Hinduism have not materialized out of thin air.

The objective of the spiritual teacher is always to bring the students to the point where they no longer need the teaching, nor the teacher. Sometimes just the answer to one question might suffice to generate a few years of steady spiritual growth. Yet if teaching follows a traditional business model, we need people to return to the teacher again and again, forever. Whichever is our system, it must be clear whether we want to lead people to the light or to our payment app? Do we want to free them or bind them to our services? And how are these choices affecting our teaching stories?

Just as the pharmaceutical industry does not benefit from bringing people true health, spiritual 'industries' often seem unwilling to provide more than fleeting glimpses of eternal happiness, while hiding the keys. In the words of Jesus as found in the Gospel of Thomas, 'The Pharisees and the scholars have taken the keys of knowledge and have hidden them. They have not entered nor have they allowed those who want to enter to do so.'. And yet, the same has been done in his name.

In today's world nearly every value has become monetary and *Sanatan Dharma* has also needed to adapt. In modern society people have become quite uncomfortable with a system of free donations, ever uncertain if they paid enough or too much. Especially in the West it is so common that everything has a price tag that many forgot how to handle getting something for free or freely giving something. They don't like to owe anybody anything, which often leads to feelings of guilt or the suspicion that the teacher must have some hidden agenda.

All of this I have experienced while

teaching for free for over a decade, until just a few years ago. I had a good and interesting career as an environmental engineer and earning a living for my family this way seemed easier and more relaxed. I have always been somewhat of a reluctant teacher, fearing the spiritual Ego trap that it represents. This danger seemed all the higher should my teachings need to provide food on the table.

Involving the powerful first *chakra* desire for survival into the teaching game thus seemed too much of a risk. What would it do to the quality of the teachings? How would I need to market myself to survive? What would come out of my mouth when talking to clients rather than souls? For about a decade, my answer was to give a free teaching every week and put over 150 hours of teaching videos on Youtube. It did not leave any time for marketing though, meaning that my contribution to universal understanding did not reach that many people.

It is up to everyone to decide how to handle our teaching role in respect to the first *chakra*. My personal story just provides some insights into what is at stake. Meanwhile, I have no more financial responsibility towards family and my living costs have been reduced to the bare minimum. I earn most of what I need by providing coaching and healing to individuals who do not mind paying for my time. Teaching larger numbers of people mostly happens for free online and is supported by donations[23]. Books also help me to survive, especially as some generous people have crowdfunded their creation, which is true for this book as well.

We can try not to be too damned commercial, yet if we want to survive in this age of greed and competition(KALI YUGA), we will have to be commercial enough. The main thing to watch out for is in marketing. I really prefer people not to have some inflated image of who I am, lest I feel forced to live up to it, which never works.

These days, words are so cheap. The main danger in our stories about our own spiritual level is that we may believe in them ourselves. Remaining truthful is advisable and there is definitely also a market for teachers who do not seem so full of themselves. It usually attracts a higher level of students.

The quality of a teacher cannot be measured by the number of followers. The success of the teachings lies not in how well they sell, only in how helpful they are in transforming the students. Reaching many people is of course great, while as teachers we are truly many, so the burden is also shared.

[23] See youtube.com/youyoga.

3.8. Evaluating Progress

While we should not attach to the results of our efforts, we still need to know where we stand to see where to go next. We need to determine where we are in the process of spiritual evolution, so that we do not resist the changes that are due, nor try to enforce those that are not. We need to equally monitor ourselves in the meditation phases, to know what to try next or to retrace our steps to where more work is needed first. Yet there is no true opposition between knowing where we are and not attaching to it, even if that attachment comes easily.

To know our phases of the moment is still quite possible without overly judging. Wherever we find ourselves, we neither get cocky nor desperate about it. We trust the path, which leads to the same destination for everyone. As we keep walking, we can have faith. We have actually already discussed how to overcome that attitude by practicing equanimity, dispassion and faith←3.2 and by avoiding doubt, laziness and delusions about ourselves←3.3.

Anyhow, the main spiritual progress is energetic and subconscious and there is no way for us to evaluate that, even if some advanced *yogis* can, just by looking at us. While we may feel to be in a period of real natural connection and balanced energy, we do not know what new issue might still be lurking down there, waiting for the *karmic* opportunity to manifest. So the best answer to where we stand is in our silence, acceptance, smile. We best remember all that, when for the sake of advancing progress through appropriate practice, we need to somewhat measure our progress.

When it comes to our skills in the actual practice on the mat, we will discuss how to evaluate those in the appropriate chapters. They relate to lots of details that first must be properly clarified. They are also quite straightforward and less confusing. Why would we identify with how long we can hold our breath or stand on our head, as we can always improve ourselves through more practice? Whenever we feel blocked in the meditation phase we are working on, we might need to spend more time first in the earlier stages. If in doubt, each related chapter will offer us some targets with which to measure our progress.

Our main concerns are thus not about practice. They chiefly regard the progress of our dear little Ego in being happy whatever happens←1.1. Since we are anyhow going to think about it whenever unhappy, the *vedic* tradition has provided some conceptual frameworks that may tell us where we are and where to go from there.

3.8.1. LIKE A HOT AIR BALLOON

The most principal understanding is that spiritual progress is not about acquiring something. Yes, we need to develop understanding, skills and all that, yet the essence is to let go of things. To reach outer space in a hot air balloon, we throw out every last sandbag.

We do not need to reach for the Self as we are that Self. We only need to let go of our Ego's attachments, so that they no longer obscure the light of the Self. We need to become more light, both in the sense of carrying less luggage from the past, as in letting the light of the Self shine through. So we play this game well, but we play it lightly, never forgetting that it is principally unreal, part of the theatre of life and of a natural evolution.

3.8.2. SNAKES & ARROWS

We have already discussed the natural evolution of our desires as related to the *chakras*←1.7.1. As the desire for enlightenment of the 6th *chakra* increasingly gains importance, it pushes us further on the path of yoga and meditation. Thus all readers of this book are involved to some degree with the first six *chakras*.

Yet while we thus bring our energy upwards and inwards to our more subtle dimensions, we also often need to return to our more dense manifestations and the related desires. This is quite visibly clarified in the snakes and arrows seen in the ancient *Leela* gameboard of life and spiritual evolution shown in Image 12.

Image 12 - The Leela gameboard

This *Jnana* gameboard[24] shows our evolution through the *chakras*, with each row representing a *chakra*, lowest below. Each arrow brings the energy upward to a higher *chakra*. Every snake swallows us up and deposits our energy on a lower *chakra* level, because we still have some work there. Examples of the arrows are purification, selfless service, doing our duty, having right knowledge, spiritual

[24] See 'The Yoga of Snakes and Arrows: The Leela of Self-Knowledge', by Harish Johari, Destiny Books 2007.

devotion, etc. Examples of the snakes are envy, dullness, jealousy, impurity, laziness, ignorance, violence, etc.

Many problems in the lower *chakras* can be solved by moving into the higher *chakras*, while to apply the solution we need to again descend to the lower energy centers. Those changes in the lower *chakras* then in turn create new opportunities in the higher centers. It is in fact one big puzzle and it all hangs together. Throughout the entire process it is thus very useful to know which arrows tend to bring us up and which snakes often take us down. Experience can teach us, yet also playing this game might bring some insight.

The main thing to remember is that however high we fly, it may be needed to descend to the Earth plane again and do our work there. For example, there are two snakes that may bring us down all the way from the 7th *chakra* level to the 1st *chakra* level, called Ego and inertia or *tamas*→4.2.1. Most importantly in terms of self-esteem, whatever more gross desires we have in the lower *chakras* should never be seen as a negation of the more subtle spiritual aspirations that we have in the higher *chakras*. High or low, our desires are natural and we are free to pursue them and thus also exhaust them.

Needless to say that, while the upward evolution of our desires is natural, many people choose to limit themselves to the desires of the lower *chakras*. Mesmerized by the 1st *chakra* illusion of physical security, they do not dare to endanger any of their material achievements and block any 'dangerous' ideas that there may be more to life than to just survive for as long as possible. They are content to numb their higher aspirations with sensory and mental enjoyments in the 2nd *chakra* or limit themselves to acquiring some position in society that provides them with false feelings of popularity, success and security in 3rd *chakra*. They often remain in this lower vibration for a long period of time, even spanning many lifetimes. Yet the yearning of their soul for more will always put a damper on their hearts. Out of boredom or other suffering, one day their energy will really move upward.

We are free to enjoy the game of life as we desire. There is no moral obligation in any choice of desires to pursue, even if there are *karmic* consequences in how we choose to pursue them. As we will discuss further on→4.4, there is nevertheless a certain way to handle our desires, so that they fit within a more *yogic* lifestyle. That is also our freedom.

3.8.3. THE 3 KNOTS

Another traditional way to look at our spiritual evolution is through the 3 knots (GRANTHIS). As the energy ascends in the *chakras*, the Ego encounters these main knots, among a multitude of smaller knots. Each requires a major transformation of the Ego.

First is the knot of selfishness, the so-called knot of Brahma, the creator of the phenomenal world. It is located in the third *chakra* and concerns the 3 lower *chakras*. To cut the knot of Brahma the Ego has to let go of unnecessarily selfish attachment to the material world of names and forms. Only then the heart *chakra* can really open.

Second is the knot of suffering which relates to Vishnu, the preserver of the phenomenal world. This knot is located in the heart *chakra*, where our love and empathy for others bring us the feeling of suffering. The solution to untie this knot is found in the higher *chakras* and in practices that produce emotional balance, such as alternate nostril breathing→8.5.2. To cut the knot of Vishnu, the Ego has to let go of the feeling of suffering in the ever-changing world of names and forms, where suffering is as natural as enjoyment is←3.6.2. Only then we become ready to truly move inside, where the real issue is found.

Third and last is the knot of enlightenment, known as the knot of Rudra-Shiva, the destroyer of the phenomenal world. This knot is located in the 6th *chakra*, where our desire for enlightenment becomes so powerful that we want to destroy any cause of unrest and attachment in ourselves and in our lives. The solution to untie this knot is found through the practice of deep meditation, as both *Samadhi* and enlightenment cannot be done. We can only allow them to happen. To cut the knot of Rudra, the Ego has to let go of the very desire for the escape of enlightenment and accept every single thing as it is, achieve total equanimity←3.2.1.

All readers of this book can be expected to have cut the knot of Brahma to some degree, to desire to nurture and open the heart *chakra* more wide into Vishnu's compassion and to have at least attempted to tinker with that 3rd knot.

3.8.4 THE STAIRWAY TO HEAVEN

Image 13 - 7 steps towards enlightenment.

This 7-steps concept is somewhat of a joke of course, as there may be a zillion steps towards the illustrious end of the game and side-stepping is allowed and quite natural. Yet the seven steps towards enlightenment(BHUMIKAS) is an ancient understanding[25], a jewel I found with Ramana Maharishi. It represents a very logical insight into our spiritual evolution and allows us to efficiently direct it towards the next phases.

The rather annoying yet main question now for the reader is which step on this stairway to heaven is currently the most important. We may be dancing on other steps as well, but this one will still represent quite a challenge, while those below are already a lot more familiar. This understanding of our position will tell us where our focus should be.

Everyone who is on the spiritual path, will walk on the first six steps in some way or another. Only the level of having mastered these steps differs. The 7th non-step can only be taken at the very end.

Step 1 - The Question

As the 6th *chakra* activates, our uplifting desire for enlightenment(SUBHECCHA) brings the game of spiritual growth on a more conscious level. Seeking an answer to unavoidable suffering, we ask ourselves the most essential question if happiness can be found independent of what happens.

There can still be a lot of doubt in this phase on whether this is a valid question and if we can afford to ask it. Strong attachments to the desires of the lower *chakras* often muddle any attempts to answer. These people may thus awkwardly attend a yoga class and still very much wonder how the hell they got there. Hopefully it will bring them some good experience that helps them to somewhat move beyond doubt.

Aside of visiting those that seem more close to the truth(SATSANG), they are advised to more clearly analyze the results of pursuing a variety of other desires in the past, that happiness which depends on the outside. The desire to be happy from inside should anyhow only be seen as complementary to all other desires, which we remain just as free to pursue. Even whenever we become enlightened, we will still be free to play→13.5.3.

Often as a result of more suffering, triggering an overload of unpleasant feelings from the subconscious, people finally seek the answer more seriously in the next phase.

[25] From the 'Varaha Upanishads' by the ancient saint Brigu.

Step 2 - Study

In the second phase of self-study [(VICHARA)], understanding attains its master role and we become eager to get it. So we read books and listen to lectures, until both the essential question as the many answers, the goal and the paths, are somewhat clear. That knowledge will support us in moving confidently into the next phase of practice. The main obstacle lies in thinking it is enough to have understood and there is no need to walk the talk. It often manifests as expecting a lot from a little practice. We cannot talk our way towards enlightenment and still many people keep trying.

People in this phase have thus become really enthused and curious about the story of enlightenment. They mostly like to spend time thinking about it. They also try out a variety of practices here and there, but have not yet made a clear choice as to their main meditative practice. They seem like the most obvious group that would be attracted to this book, so probably a majority of readers find themselves in this phase.

The advice is straightforward here: keep studying, both in theory as in practice. Some book worming is usually useful, while the pure scholar never attains any real understanding←3.5. That only comes when putting the theory into practice, into our own experience. It will allow our concepts to become our own, so that they may support our resolve to move beyond.

Step 3 - Practice

In the third and most relevant phase, we start the sustained practice of thinning the veils of the bodymind[(TANUMANASI)], so that we can move beyond ever-changing illusion and truly find the Self. That practice may be quite varied and irregular at first. It is destined to evolve into a daily meditation exercise that aims at attaining some kind of *Samadhi*, where we can have the unobstructed experience of the Self.

People in this phase may still read and listen, yet their main effort is in the doing, rather than the thinking. They have found a way that really seems to lead inside and they are repeating more or less the same approach over and over again, on a regular basis. They really go for a sustained practice or *sadhana*→5.4.

This perseverance already changes them, creating a more durable calmness that affects their personality and lifestyle. Ups and downs are still present, both emotionally as in the practice. All in all, they manage to keep going until they start having their first deep meditation experiences→13.2.3, that may also have led them to this book.

The overall advice is to keep grinding

that stone and not fall into the trap that is included with every true experience of the Self, to believe one has arrived. However great our trance, we only had a temporary taste of enlightenment and there is still a lot of purification and reprogramming needed before we can claim anything, which anyhow we cannot.

We keep going at it, until our identification with the Self has become so strong that we no longer need any techniques to have the power of the Self with us. More and more, we rely on the cosmic intellect→13.4.2 to guide us.

As distraction is the main stumbling block, this is the only phase which really requires some forceful but temporary detachment from the pleasures of life→4.9.5. This is needed both to create time for practice, as to make the going inside more smoothly→9.2.1. We may also need quite some time to change our lifestyle, generating the more harmonious energy that is needed in moving further. Still, some landmark experiences of the Self during practice will lift us up to the next level.

Step 4 - Connection

In this phase we become the ruler of our own happiness[(SATTVAPATTI)], having gained sufficient connection to the Self to effortlessly return to it at will. It is the phase of true, nonintellectual Self-realization, which allows for rather permanent emotional stability. Being really free to be happy or unhappy, we can pursue whatever desires remain, yet in harmony with all other beings. In this phase also, *Samadhi* regularly occurs and assures the hold on our inner connection.

It is still natural to encounter more unpleasant feelings, as attachments and desires are still present. What separates people in this phase is that any unhappiness is really short-lived. It may need to be allowed to stay for a little while, in order to discover its origin and thus better be able to deal with it→4.1.9. But then we simply connect inside, smile and move forward. We know we have that power and we also use it.

For everyone on the *yogic* path, the main exercise is to stay happy whatever happens→4.1.3. While everyone has that power, illusion, doubt and attachment usually stand in the way, yet in this phase that is truly no longer the case.

The yearning for enlightenment thus becomes much less. It can wait, since anyhow we are fine and life becomes quite enjoyable. That may create a tendency to let go of practice, which is felt as no longer needed, which is untrue. The subconscious still holds potential for more severe unhappiness and our *karma* may provide the triggers. Whenever some little more persistent unhappiness seems to threaten our state of connection, we take a step down to phase 3.

As we quite easily let go into the effortless state of actual meditation and have regular occurrences of deep meditation, practice no longer feels like a workout, rather like a holiday. We also hold less expectation towards our practice, which becomes as natural as eating or sleeping. We more and more meditate for everyone.

People in this phase may still read a book like this one, but they will less and less seek understanding outside of them. Scriptures become mere entertainment and confirmation, while they basically rely on the cosmic intellect to guide their choices. There is a strong feeling of knowing, of destiny, of under-standing.

While in the third phase the advice is very much to be minimally involved with other desires, here we are again invited to play the games of life. We thus respect the elements and the life force, which are their primary source. However, we are not running after our desires, not yearning for what we do not have.

From observing ourselves, we are aware of our more essential desires, such as the desires to create a family or to become a master artist. We can clearly distinguish them from the more fleeting suggestions of mind, such as the desires for ice cream or another movie, which are easily ignored when ill timed. Yet when we see an opportunity to fulfill our more important desires in *dharma*, we go for it and don't hold back.

We allow ourselves thus to play the divine game, while we also always honor the divine within the game. If we would go against *dharma*, hurting others in the pursuit of our desires, it would immediately threaten our presence in this state. To go against the law of love, which is *dharma*←2.4.3, will literally cut the connection to the heart and the Self. That is also immediately experienced whenever even just contemplating such actions. Thus these people usually can hold themselves back and patiently wait for a better opportunity to get what they desire.

As our *karma* brings our *dharma* or duty towards the whole, we play our role. Just as every single tree species fulfills a task within the divine ecological theater, so does every one of us. Next to the debt to the teacher already discussed←3.7.8, there are also the debts to the ancestors and to the universe to consider. As we were taken care of as kids, we take care of our kids→4.10.1. The debt to the ancestors is usually paid by having kids, though also other kinds of services can replace it. The debt to the universe is paid through whichever activity sustains the preservation of harmony in the universe. It can involve social or environmental work, arts and music, good cooking, sharing resources or taking on some other valuable role within society, be a rebel why not, the path of Vishnu←3.5. Whoever really desires to plant a million trees should not hesitate.

Everyone actually wants to be in this state, where life can be enjoyed without much trouble at all. Yet if we still experience more enduring unhappiness now and then, we have not arrived and serious practice is the only answer.

The best news in this understanding of the 7 steps is that this phase is attainable for most people in this life, as long as they are not too disturbed to even practice. Enlightenment may require many more lifetimes, depending on what is still rumbling in the depths of the subconscious. On the contrary, to have the power to be happy most of the time is considered to be there for all. This faith lies at the basis of *dharma* in culture.

For many people living as householders, just a few years in phase 3 may suffice to enter the 4th as rulers of our own happiness. As fulltime practicing renunciates, it may be just a matter of months. Harish Johari called this becoming a real human being. It is the phase I mostly seem to identify with for myself, no more nor less.

Step 5 – Non-Attachment

Non-attachment(ASAMSAKTI), which is also named desirelessness, is the result of fulfilling all remaining desires in the former phase. The Self is then the only place left where we seek happiness as well as understanding. There is no desire to read any spiritual books, as no problems or questions remain. The only task left is to pay off any remaining *karmic* debts through some *Karma Yoga*. These are true *yogis* that serve as great examples and spiritual teachers. If they have already done quite a lot of selfless service in the previous phases, this one can be short.

Step 6 – Non-Perception

When not only all desires are fulfilled, but also all *karmic* debts are paid, we stop perceiving the outside world(PADARTHA BHAVANA), even with eyes open. The attention remains now fully with the Self, all action becomes automatic reaction, free of desire or even intention and *karma* is no longer created. These people generally live in natural *Samadhi*→13.5.

Step 7 – Enlightenment

Then after a while follows the final liberation of all individuality and the full merging in Cosmic Consciousness. Enlightenment(MOKSHA) is a difficult concept, which we will somewhat pursue later→13.5.3.

We are anyhow going to dance quite a bit up and down these stairs, so to know where we are is not very relevant. Whenever we doubt, we practice and whenever we do not doubt, we practice. If we can live by this rule, then it does not matter much where we find ourselves. Believing in practice means believing in ourselves, in our unlimited impersonal potential. Negative thinking regarding practice should truly be frowned upon, as it questions an absolutely self-fulfilling prophecy.

3.8.5. NATURAL STAGES OF LIFE

A main *vedic* understanding on our spiritual evolution is that of the 4 natural stages of life[(ASHRAMAS)], which are somewhat age dependent. Every stage is estimated to take about 25 years, while that number is of course highly flexible. This traditional view of Indian culture does not very much correspond to the Western model. How it works out is also quite personal and dependent on *karma*, even in India This understanding mostly teaches us to be patient, as there is a time for everything.

Stage 1 – The Student

Youngsters[(BRAHMACHARI)] are naturally in a learning phase, preparing for life as independent adults. In the ancient *vedic* education system, much emphasis was laid upon spiritual practice and understanding. The objective was to lift the students already up to step 4 of the 7 steps towards enlightenment←3.8.4. Through some early *Samadhi* experiences as young adults, they will thus be enabled to start the next stage with sufficient connection to the Self. To that purpose, distractive enjoyments of mind and the senses are relatively restrained during the second half of this stage→4.9.5. Without pampering, youngsters are also protected from any unnecessary burdens and suffering, so that they can fully focus on their studies. This stage is symbolized by the musk deer, intoxicated by its own seductive scent.

Stage 2 – The Householder

When as householders[(GRIHASTA)] we start a family, we thus already know how to practice. Less time for practice on the mat is available as we shoulder many responsibilities, yet less time is needed to get good results. The main practice is now that of life→4, meeting our *karma* in perfect *dharma*←2.4.3. We are free to fulfill the natural desires of all *chakras*←1.7.1, as we desire it. This stage is symbolized by the bull, ever pulling hard on the plow to provide for the family and our desires.

Stage 3 – The Elder

As elders(VANPRASTA) we somewhat withdraw from the business of life, leaving most responsibilities to the next generation, which in the old way would take over the family trade. We are still available with good advice from own experience to support our grown-up kids and grandchildren, yet we turn more towards our spiritual goals. We spend more time in nature and visit holy places and saints. We study the scriptures and apply them in lengthy practices again aiming at the deeper meditative states. This stage is symbolized by the dog, lying around, keeping an eye on everything, producing the occasional authoritative bark and spending lots of time playing with the next generation of puppies.

Stage 4 – The Renunciate

In the last stage(SANNYAS) we naturally become renunciates, as we feel to have neither worldly desires nor duties left. Many people in India then leave their home and families. They live in spiritual communities or in nature, or they go on endless pilgrimages from which to never return. Meditation is the main pastime, avoiding most other activities. This stage is symbolized by the owl, half asleep during the day, awake at night, yet hardly moving.

The Ages of the Chakras

A complementary understanding to the 4 stages of life are the ages of the *chakras*. If our spiritual evolution happens in an ideal fashion, then the maturing of every desire related to the *chakras* is said to take seven years. The following ages are purely indicative of course and much depends on the experiences in past lives.

- A young child up to 7 years old cannot easily handle feeling insecure, so this first *chakra* desire must be sufficiently assured in normal, human conditions.
- From 8 to 14 years old, the teenager will much more freely and daringly explore the enjoyment of mind and the senses in the second *chakra*, which must also be brought under control.
- In puberty then, the third *chakra* desire to be somebody is established and we slowly develop a more fixed personality.
- Around age 21 the desire naturally comes forward to connect in a family of our own, meaning where we can be ourselves and thus live from the heart.
- Wanting to keep everyone happy in our inner circle, which is difficult, we may start around 28 years old to sincerely ask the more essential questions of the fifth *chakra* about the meaning of life and how real harmony can be achieved.
- This ultimately leads us to the desire to

profoundly transform ourselves through the path of yoga and meditation of the 3rd eye *chakra*, which means most people only really start to meditate seriously from age 35 onward. Many younger exceptions nevertheless prove them wrong in waiting that long.

Timely Renunciation

Whatever the age, the logical moment to become a renunciate is when the fifth step on the ladder towards heaven is solidly reached←3.8.4. When we have become truly nonattached to worldly pleasures and pursuits, then our renunciation is a fact, not a desire.

We all can have the desire to renounce, especially when we feel that life is not very kind to us. Yet if we still experience to have plenty of other desires, to become a renunciate is premature wishful thinking and another Ego game.

Rarely people become renunciates at a young age, truly feeling no interest in a more normal lifestyle. That usually means that their soul has already experienced enough in past lives. And if in doubt, most schools for renunciates require to spend a few years as some kind of novice, before any lofty promises are made. Thus we can always give it a try if really the Self is all we want. To then maybe come to the conclusion not to be ready to leave the

Story 24 — I Want to Go to India

Once upon a time, my grandfather on my mother's side arrived in India, around 1925. He traveled the entire globe, working on freight ships. Somehow India particularly attracted him, so he found a job and stayed for some time. All we have left of it are pictures of sadhus and places, and the first Ganesha statue I ever saw. He passed away when I was 2 months old, but somehow also passed on some teaching to my grandmother. She often took care of me as a child and thus she was like a first teacher, even if that role belongs to our mother and father. Her understanding just came in her own simple words. When faced with our troubles, she would often say 'everything ever changes'. It mostly showed in her way of being, the most compassionate and wise grandmom one could ever wish for. She passed away at 101 years old, entirely sound of mind and heart. One day at 7 years old I arrived home from her place and proudly announced that I wanted to go to India, a desire that I could only realize 10 years later.

world is no real issue. It does not mean at all that those novice years were spent in vain. It may be tricky nevertheless to detach from the social status of being a renunciate.

Spiritual Bulls

The reality of modern society is of course that most of us get involved with spirituality when already adults. Having to work like bulls, people become stressed for some spiritual release, while the how is still largely unclear.

I was lucky to start the search at a young age, thanks to my first teacher, which in a way was my grandmother ←Story24. Already in puberty, I was reading spiritual books and attended my first yoga class. Yet these days, most people become students and practitioners when adults, as a hobby for which their busy jobs leave little time and energy. Patience is needed.

As we get older we might have less faith, especially upon understanding the lengthy process of spiritual growth. When feeling to have insufficient time left to get anywhere, we should develop faith in the fact that death is not the end. We will always benefit from our efforts sometime, if not today.

However long it takes to become quite durably happy, we will anyhow see our happiness increase as we move forward. Once we reach the 4th step on the stairway to heaven←3.8.4, everything will happen by itself, fall into place. As explained, given sufficient practice, that only takes a few months or years→13.2.3. Thus our age truly matters little.

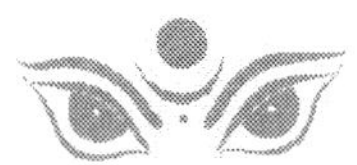

4

THE PRACTICE CALLED LIFE

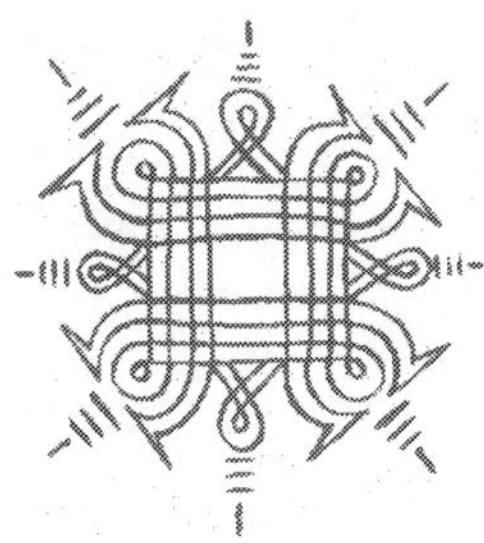

Deep meditation cannot work if we do not get involved with the practice of life. The main keyword is balance: emotional, energetic and physical. It is maintained with good food, home remedies, exercise and fasting. A variety of activities and restraints will support our practice on the meditation mat, which then no longer needs to compensate so much for the stress of life. Some changes in our relationships may equally be needed.

4.1. Emotional Balance

As the central objective of all yoga and meditation practice is to become happy independent of what happens, this entire book is also about emotional balance. Whatever spiritual practice we do, the ultimate result will be an increase in happiness, even if the path may be quite challenging for a while. The art of happiness is thus learned through the many arts of yoga, yet it is also logical to look more closely at what it means to be emotionally balanced and how such balance can be achieved more directly.

If we can step onto our mat with a genuine smile, then our meditation practice has the best chance of succeeding. On the contrary, when our day is dominated by unpleasant emotions, the objective of our practice may be limited to changing our mood.

Beginners are anyhow mostly interested in meditation to make them more peaceful and happy, which goes together. Advanced practitioners see happiness as a continued activity→4.8.1. that supports their deeper meditation practice.

Deep meditation experiences may lead us to a happiness that is truly unbroken, yet there is no need to wait till we can generate those trances to already experience a much-improved emotional balance. Better understanding of our feelings, applied in a more *yogic* lifestyle, can do that for us.

My original teacher Harish Johari attached much importance to directly working with happiness and so it has been for myself a main practice. I wrote my very first book - on the subject of the nine emotions - nearly 2 decades ago →Story25. It is still a valuable read for those who want to learn more about their happiness.

4.1.1. EMOTIONAL FEEDBACK LOOPS

Interestingly, there is no scientific consensus on a definition for emotions. In *vedic* lore, emotions are considered to be qualities of energy that are primarily experienced in the *pranic* body. Yet, they are also 'felt' in all other sheaths of consciousness, which respond to the central feelings in our energy body

Story 25 — *How I Became an Author*

Once upon a time, I wrote a synthesis of a class Harish Johari gave on the subject of disgust and depression, wanting to see what I had understood. I presented it to him the next morning, on the day of his departure. He had no time to read it, yet touched it to his forehead and then seemingly out of the blue asked me if I would like to help him in writing a book on the rasas. Seeing me hesitate in front of such a big question, he just said 'every student becomes a teacher' and 'writing is clearly in your destiny'. How could I not accept? So I did and less than a year later he left the body and also left me with the sacred task of writing this book on my own. Nevertheless, as he is showing here with that picture of his teacher Baba Dwarka Das←Story4, I am not feeling very responsible. Equally all other books, including this one, mostly just happened, paying that debt to the teacher←3.7.8.

through a variety of feedback loops. This complexity makes it hard indeed to define what an emotion really is. We might understand e-motion as an energy-motion, an outward movement or expression of the feeling of the life force, essentially an energetic response to both inner as outer experiences.

There are too many of these interactions to describe here, yet the main feedback loops can be easily understood:

- The central feelings in the *pranic* body, such as love, sadness or anger, are experienced in the nerves and in all parts of the physical body through the intermediate of hormones and other neurotransmitters.
- Strong emotions may even create physical sensations such as goosebumps, shivering, redness, sweating, nausea, as well as lovely butterflies in the stomach.
- Sensory input→9.1.2 through the sense organs of the physical body has a clear effect on our feelings, experienced as neutral, pleasant or unpleasant.
- Neurotransmitters that communicate feelings in the physical body may also block or stimulate neural pathways in the brain, directly affecting our thinking in the conscious mind. Also the more energetic feeling that we have will color our thoughts and stories.
- The most important, durable feelings emerge from the subconscious mind, generating thoughts in the conscious mind as well as feelings in the *pranic* and physical bodies.

The entirety of these interactions can be seen as one gigantic feedback loop between the subconscious programming in our soul and our outer environment, a continued impression and expression of emotional energy, as shown in Image 14.

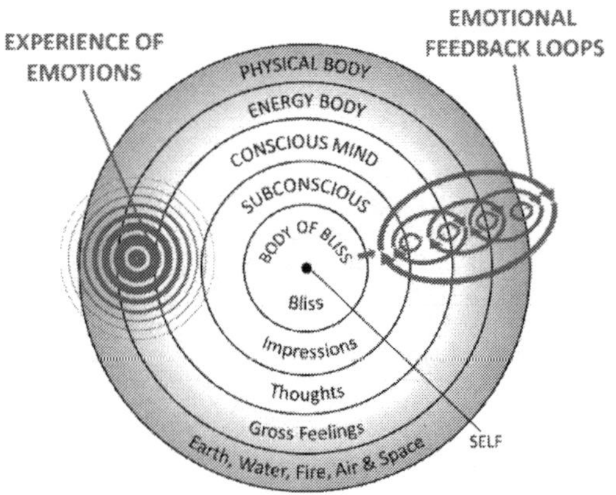

Image 14 - Emotions in the sheaths of consciousness.

The interaction between the body of bliss and the subconscious is only a one-way ticket, as the subconscious fortunately cannot affect the dimension of the body of bliss, which is unchanging. Usually the body of bliss also has no noticeable effect on the other layers, because that subtle bliss is not 'heard' within the usual emotional noise found there. But if the subconscious and all other layers can be brought to a rather neutral energy vibration, great bliss will spread everywhere from inside. That is the process of meditation, bringing us the ever available, eternal happiness of Self-awareness.

The impact of our environment cannot be underestimated when trying to achieve emotional balance. Sensory input has a strong influence on our feelings and other people are often very much involved in changing or maintaining our particular emotional state. It may very well be needed to create a more soothing environment→6.1, as well as to clear out our relationships to the universe→4.10. There can also be a strong influence from the other dimensions→4.1.9, as well as through a variety of cyclical cosmic patterns, such as the moon phases→5.4.4.

Our dear Ego attaches extreme importance to our emotions. Whether we feel happy or unhappy very much defines our self-image of the moment. Feelings are also responsible for creating like and dislike and thus the primary programming of the subconscious.

The feedback loops between different layers of consciousness do not always function in the same way. A rather heated physical body will much more easily go along with an angry feeling. A *pranic* body calmed by slow breathing will not. Thoughts already agitated by stressful computer work will more rapidly get irritated. A subconscious that is gnawing on some ancient insult, may be ready for an anger party anytime.

4.1.2. MASTERING OUR EMOTIONS

Our emotional feedback loops can be controlled to quite some degree by maintaining some physical and energetic balances, which we will discuss in the following chapters that relate to the physical and *pranic* bodies. Here we will focus more on understanding the conscious and subconscious spiritual processes and approaches that affect our emotions. Key will be the more *tantric* understanding of the 9 emotional essences(RASAS)→4.1.5.

For the one who can easily connect to the Self, happiness is a conscious choice. Yet that is actually true for everyone and we can certainly make it true given some understanding and practice. In *Jnana Yoga* especially, people easily get frustrated when told they have nothing to do but to stop trying, in order to obtain the peace and bliss they want. They 'get it' alright, while they are continuously proven wrong by their ever-changing emotions. So how to also 'feel it' and make that feeling permanent? We can wait for some ultimate understanding to fall out of the sky, or we can learn to truly master our emotions, quite methodically. From dynamic emotional balance it is only a small step to the feeling of the Self.

To change our emotions we need an integrated effort on all levels of our being, including of course increasing Self-awareness. The emotional quality of the physical body is slow to change, so whatever we do elsewhere will have to be maintained for some time to have a durable effect. The *pranic* body on the contrary can jump from anger to love in just a second for example, or vice versa. How fast the conscious mind will respond largely depends on how habitual the related thought patterns→4.1.7 are, meaning usually quite fast. The subconscious then is like the proverbial elephant memory, never forgetting anything. Often years will be needed to change some old emotional patterns programmed in brain and soul.

Thus 'manipulating' our emotions is however still largely a taboo in modern society. Meditating people are often looked upon as 'just sitting there, imagining to be happy'. People generally believe that we should deserve our emotions, otherwise they are regarded as unreal. As they feel that their happiness depends on what happens, they hate it when people smile 'for no good reason'. And likewise they do not mind negative emotions, even if very unpleasant to others, given a good enough excuse.

The truth is of course that we are actually always managing our emotions. We are just not doing that very consciously and many people are thus not very good at it. While logically running from unhappiness to happiness we often find ourselves strangely moving in the opposite direction. We should neither overthink our emotions, nor remain ignorant about them.

The idea is of course not to fake our emotions, which just means to hide how we really feel. It also does not mean that we are so much in control of our feelings that we become emotionless, 'like a plant', quite the contrary. When in dynamic control of our emotions, we will be much more in touch with them and our happiness may be allowed to flourish beyond usual levels.

So we drink a glass of water to cool down our anger. Or we let go of some disturbing attachment, that is anyhow no longer ours. Whatever we do, we use it to durably produce a happy energy, until it extends to all layers of our being and just needs to be maintained and enjoyed. Our lives then become happy symphonies filled with the music of our emotions, allowing to express our human heart to the fullest. Emotional balance is a musical, energetic art especially suited for the householder *yogi*, who is usually more regularly emotionally affected from interaction with others.

4.1.3. CHOOSING HAPPINESS

Happiness is a choice, yet one has to be quick in responding to any unhappiness that develops. We're fine and then suddenly a small thing happens, whether outside or inside of us, and our energy barometer changes from happy to unhappy. That is where we need to react quickly, which is a matter of attitude and technique.

If we are not alert, that little bit of unhappiness, which often comes quite by chance, will attract more and more unhappiness. That little feeling may result in more unhappy interactions with the world and our own thought patterns, which will further aggravate it. When then from deep down old painful stories are awakened, they may flood our feeling and we feel truly miserable. The entire process may take less than a minute, or it could happen over the span of a day.

Happiness as well as unhappiness thus manifest as chain reactions in our energetic vibration, often starting from rather insignificant triggers. We need to nip our unhappiness in the bud and the longer we wait to consciously respond, the more difficult it will get.

This attitude is no tool for trying to ignore our problems. Sometimes we need to really dive into our unhappiness, find out what is really there and in that way be able to more fundamentally work with it, a process which we will explore at length→4.1.9. The danger of unhealthy emotional suppression will equally be discussed below→4.1.6. It does not mean however that every little unhappy feeling must receive our full attention, lest we turn a mouse into an elephant and become increasingly unstable.

The required attitude is that really at some point somehow, we no longer believe in unhappiness. We are continuously observing our emotional barometer and whenever we feel something unpleasant emerging, returning to happiness has our top priority. So we drop everything if we can and fix our mood first.

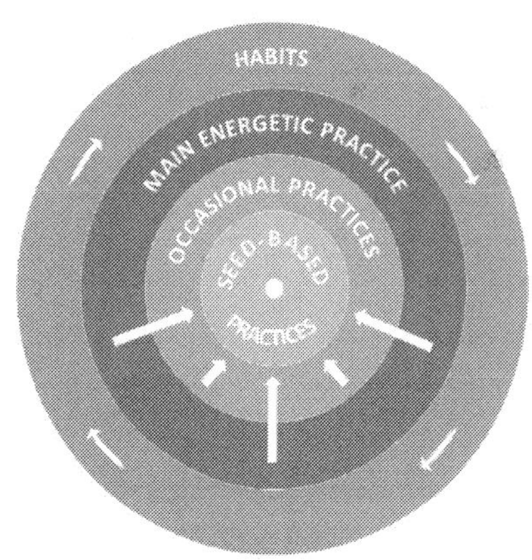

Image 15 - The combination of practices

It is highly advisable to have mastered at least one energetic technique, with which to rapidly alter our mood. It will produce a neutral feeling in our energy, that stops unhappy energy from increasing, while more happy feelings may easily emerge from it. We will have invested quite a lot of time in practicing this technique. Preferably it should be something which works relatively fast. It is most practical if we can use this technique without anyone noticing.

The importance of that main energetic practice in our overall effort is to always ensure emotional stability. Combined with healthy habits→5.3 and some occasionally needed exercises, it will allow us to easily maintain the more essential seed-based practices←2.8.2 of generally being calm, present and blissful, see Image 15.

As main energetic practices, breathing exercises have the big advantage of speed, as they directly affect the *pranic* body, where our feelings are experienced. There are so many breathing options, which we will discuss in the related chapter→8. Personally, I mostly use heart breathing, which means to focus on our breath in the area of the heart *chakra*→8.1. And since I have been doing this a lot, it immediately produces a very good energy and easily my heart starts smiling.

Our primary tool might definitely also be our preferred *mantra*, which does not work so fast on our gross energy body, but has great power over the subconscious. In a secondary phase, if the unpleasant emotion is a little more persistent when applying the heart breath, that is definitely my next move. Some *mantras* are particularly powerful in beating negative emotion→12.3.2.

There are many other options found in this book and they all have a power, so they all can be used, including of course basic awareness of the observer. The main thing is that we make a choice and stick to it.

People tend to use a mix of techniques instead. One time we will make a cup of tea and the next we take our guitar. At yet another unhappy occasion we start some breathing, go for a walk or we chant some *mantra*. All these techniques are very good to develop and can be part of our daily program. But we really need to choose at least one technique in which we will excel and which will give us a very concrete power over mind and our emotions.

Thus we can develop the attitude of simply not identifying with any unhappiness and immediately decide to throw our master technique at it. And the more we do so, the more confident we get, which means the fear of unhappiness sees its power evaporate. That represents a main change in who we are. For many, that fear of emotionally 'losing it' is even more relevant than the primary fear of death. To let go of it is actually a lot easier, since there is this simple solution, while we all have to die.

The technique that people most often use to change their energy is to change their thinking. They feel that by understanding what is happening, we can more easily let go of it, which is of course true. But unless the answer is immediately apparent, it is quite a weak technique, because it does not directly affect our energy. If the process of thinking is going to take some time, then during that time there will be a negative feeling, which will also affect our thoughts. Whatever positive thoughts we are trying to produce may be corrupted by that feeling, making us doubt their power. Sometimes we start thinking about some problem and through the thinking it just becomes a bigger problem. Sure, thinking differently about some issue may be extremely important, as it guides our actions, but it is not the first thing to do. First, we change our energy, then we can think properly.

It might feel somewhat premature to decide to stay happy at all times. And sure, it is all about confidence, so that doubt has power. Many are even afraid to see happiness as a spiritual objective, having been hurt all too often when believing to have found happiness somewhere. However, here we are searching for happiness only within, where we are in charge. Still sometimes it may be hard to do and we might take that personally. For people caught in habitual unhappiness it is probably no option. To come to the point where we say 'I no longer accept unhappiness' and 'I will fight it whichever

Story 26 The Robber King of Heaven

Once upon a time, some robbers attacked a village. However, all robbers were killed, except for the leader. Hiding in the forest, he heard a woman crying. She had delivered a baby but was in terrible pain. Having never seen a birth, it made him remember his mother, the only person he ever loved. Feeling that same love now for this mother, he feared for her life and that of the baby, so he carried them to the village. He knew very well that the vengeful villagers might kill him on sight and so they did. He then came before Yama, Hindu lord of death, who looked at his karmic records. Yama announced that because of all his crimes, he was sentenced to 1000 years of hell. Yet because of that last great deed, he was also allowed one day as King of Heaven. He had to choose which to do first. He decided to first become king of heaven and used all powers available in his palace to do good, asking everyone in heaven the same. Yama then again looked at the records and concluded that the robber had one day in hell left, and earned 1000 years in heaven. Again, he had to choose which to do first. This story originates with the lineage of Swami Rama (picture).

way possible', is not a light thing.

I still believe that to always keep at least a little inner smile is our main power to develop. And to decide that we are going to fight our unhappiness from the very moment it manifests, does not mean that we immediately have to win this fight. But our smile can be generated immediately, in the knowing that we will be victorious anyhow. Ultimately, what came has to go, which is true for unhappiness just as well.

Yet when we have that attitude to respond really fast, we will experience that it is relatively easy to live up to that promise, especially when involving our master technique. That master practice might not solve anything about the particular cause of some unhappiness, but it will allow us to work on it with the lightness that spirituality has to offer. A main understanding on the importance of living and responding from happiness is in the ancient story of the robber who became king of heaven←Story26. The one who has understood the story knows how to stay happy, always choosing heaven over hell. So often people condemn themselves to hell by remaining unhappy.

Of course, if something really touches us deeply, if some powerful attachment is really triggered, if someone has done something really bad to us, then there are other ways in which we have to respond→4.1.9. Yet in normal life, most of the things that change our energy towards unhappiness are actually not very important or unexpected. They are not the things that require so much special attention, while still so many people get caught in unhappiness because of them.

It may be just a little message someone is texting to us and which we feel is rather dishonest or disrespecting. Maybe random association triggered some painful memory. Or we make a small mistake and there is some cost attached to it. Having the attitude of *yogis*, these things should not affect us.

4.1.4. CAUSES OF UNHAPPINESS

Patanjali gives us the following understanding regarding the principle causes of unhappiness(KLESAS), in my own rather free and simple translation[26]:

> *'The essential causes of unhappiness are a lack of insight in reality, the feeling of being an individual, the attraction and aversion towards things, and also the desire to stay alive.*
>
> *The lack of insight into reality is the source of all causes of unhappiness, whether the unhappiness is present in pure potentiality, mild, changing or strongly active. The lack of insight in*

[26] Yoga Sutras of Patanjali, verses 2.3 to 2.17.

reality means to confuse the perishable, impure, negative and unconscious with the eternal, pure and positive consciousness.

The feeling of being an individual originates in identification of pure consciousness with the knowledge in the subconscious. The attraction to things is produced by the pleasure they provide. The aversion towards things is caused by the pain they bring. The desire to stay alive is so natural that even the learned ones cannot escape from it.

The more active causes of unhappiness can be reduced to their most subtle, dormant form in the subconscious through meditation.

When the causes of unhappiness are reduced to their most subtle subconscious form, they can be removed by absorption into their origin, which is the only reality.'

While this text is rather straightforward, there is one essential consequence that is maybe less obvious. As the cause of causes is the lack of seeing reality exactly as it is, we have to accept some unhappiness to exist till the end of ends. Even at one breath from enlightenment, unhappiness can still manifest. The same goes for the Ego illusion of being an individual, as well as for the natural fear of death, which we can only expect to disappear at our destination.

The only issue that can be somewhat gradually resolved along the way, is in having less fixed ideas on our desires and aversions, which is another subject related to the *chakras*→4.4. As long as we can avoid attaching our happiness to the presence or absence of things, if we can let go of our fixed ideas on what we want or not, we can attain relative emotional balance. Such a state of sustained emotional stability is fortunately attainable to all, that 4th step on the ladder towards heaven←3.8.4.

As we thus handle our desires and attachments with dispassion←3.2.3, our deeper unhappiness may remain quite mild instead of very active, which will allow the ultimate solution brought forward by Patanjali. As we stay out of too much unhappiness, our meditation practice may sufficiently calm the bodymind, so that our issues are reduced to mere potentials in the subconscious, hardly disturbing. From there they can be finally dissolved in the Self within the state of absorption called *Samadhi*→13.4.4.

After all, we can each easily find many good reasons to feel lonely, hurt, disrespected, mistreated, etc. Yet that is not what we came here to find. We came in hope of happiness.

4.1.5. THE 9 EMOTIONAL ESSENCES

In the past decades, emphasis in the Western sciences on emotional wellbeing has dramatically shifted towards the study of emotionally active molecules in the body. Initially I have been very enthused about this research as well, but I stopped following it long ago. While some interesting stuff can be found there, the complexity of the thousands of such different molecules active within the body does not allow for much clarity. It does not seem to lead towards workable practices, rather to feeding people's feelings with pills. While it demonstrated for example how a hug could produce really pleasant and healthy neurotransmitters, we're at a far cry from the memorable 'Hugs not Drugs' slogan.

On the contrary, I have more and more experienced how the ancient *vedic* science on the nine emotional essences (RASAS) provides us with a clear path towards emotional stability. Not only do we find there many natural therapies for the body that support pleasant emotions. The understanding equally offers us the ability to change our less emotionally intelligent attitudes.

The 9 *rasas* are emotional essences that appear as essential emotions. They belong to the *pranic* body and are energetic in nature, yet almost liquefied, as they relate to the water element. They indeed express themselves in the physical body as emotionally active molecules such as neurotransmitters and hormones, present in blood plasma and cell waters. In thoughts and feelings, the *rasas* produce an unlimited variety of emotional states (BHAVAS) that each fit within these nine categories, as shown in Table 6.

RASA	RELATED EMOTIONS
Love	Friendship, adoration, devotion
Joy	Humor, laughter, sarcasm
Wonder	Curiosity, astonishment, mystery
Peace	Calmness, relaxation, rest
Anger	Hate, irritation, stress
Courage	Heroism, confidence, focus
Sadness	Compassion, pity, empathy
Fear	Anxiety, nervousness, worry
Disgust	Depression, negativity, self-pity

Table 6 - The nine rasas or emotional essences

Very often when we ask if someone is angry, the response may be 'I am not angry, only irritated'. And while that distinction is relevant, it may be very important for that person to realize to be essentially angry, even if only a little. Because then whatever we know about dealing with the anger *rasa* can be used to reduce or remove that irritated feeling.

The art of *rasa* very much applies to life, offering the ability to reduce our thousands of emotional issues to only nine essential energies to be mastered.

This ancient knowledge on our essential emotions is still very much part of the art scene in India[27]. The central objective of all Indian arts and music is to produce *rasas* in the spectators. These essential emotional energies are seen as infectious, producing and allowing emotional communication between people. They are linked for example to colors, shapes, postures, facial expressions and musical notes[28].

How we deal with these emotional essences is often an expression of our culture. Like in some countries we find lots of public crying when someone dies, while in other places people will largely hide their sadness.

Image 16 - The 9 rasas as masks of the yogi.

For the *yogi*, the nine *rasas* are often seen as masks that we may put on our faces to communicate on a more emotional level in this theatre of life. They are part of the act of life, like the costumes of the actor. We are free to play-act these *rasas* with a detached feeling and yet an actor must always somewhat feel the emotion that needs to be expressed.

The relationships between the *rasas* and the physical body→4.3.1 or gross energy body→4.2.1 will be discussed later. This knowledge will provide many powerful practical means to counter some emotion, like in understanding that all flavors of anger can be reduced by physically cooling down. In this chapter however, we will come to understand our feelings better on the mental level.

The *tantric* knowledge on the *rasas* defines each *rasa* as having particular causes, giving dominance to specific sheaths of consciousness and producing typical behaviors. They have a unique changeability, which can be used to either increase or decrease a particular *rasa* energy.

While we might simultaneously experience a variety of subtle feelings emerging from the subconscious, our main emotional energy or *rasa* can only have one flavor in every moment. Some

[27] A primary subject in the 'Natya Shastra' the ancient scripture and central doctrine on Indian art and theatre.

[28] See 'The Yoga of the Nine Emotions: The Tantric Practice of Rasa Sadhana', Peter Marchand, Destiny Books 2006.

emotional states may show a fluctuation between *rasas*, which cannot actually be mixed in the uniform energy that pervades the sheath of *prana*. In stress for example, the *rasas* of anger and fear are alternating rather than co-existing. One moment we may feel irritated by the expectations of others, while in the next we worry about not being able to meet these expectations.

Love

The emotional essence of love(SHRINGARA) manifests when we experience some agreeable attachment or connection. We feel personally at one with the object of our love, which usually makes our mind dominant, reveling in a feeling of beauty, seeing perfection in imperfection.

Love is the most original *rasa*, the source of all other emotions and the spice of life. Love can also be for some art or music that we resonate with, as the aesthetic sentiment is also classified as belonging to this *rasa*. The feeling of love easily leads to more attachment, which produces the pain of love in separation.

To master love, we need to see beauty without discrimination and love in detached attachment.

Joy

The emotional essence of joy(HASYA) manifests when we enjoy a feeling of connection, whether to something or someone, or to life in general. Thus it is regarded as a direct result of the experience of love. We feel that we are personally lucky and that life is funny. Our mind will be dominant, playfully teasing the Ego's loves or attachments.

Joy is the *rasa* of youth and play, when we easily laugh at the illusion and theatre of life. As the main subject of our jokes is the Ego, our humor may become more painful in satire or sarcasm.

To master joy, we need to meet every problem with the sacred *mantra* 'Aum No Problem" and if we can make others laugh at our own Ego, we will experience joy to the fullest, as laughter is so infectious.

Wonder

The emotional essence of wonder (ADBHUTA) manifests when we surrender to a feeling of total ignorance and let go of all attachment. We feel to witness some miracle of life, which will make our mind very dominant, being totally surprised by our inability to fit our experience within our understanding.

Wonder is the lightest of all *rasas*, in which our Ego becomes extremely small, feeling positively insignificant when faced with a higher power. The feeling may easily turn to fear however, our other response to ignorance.

To master wonder, we must accept our

basic cluelessness, stop trying to control everything by naming it and recognize that our ignorance when faced with the divine truly frees us from the responsibility to understand. When nothing particularly miraculous is witnessed, we are ever invited to feel the divine miracle of our very existence.

Courage

The emotional essence of courage (VEERA) manifests when we feel able to support and maintain our attachments. We feel personally in charge of ourselves and our life, which will make our Ego quite dominant, aware how confidence is primarily a mental issue, something that we have if we take it←3.1.1.

Courage is the *rasa* of the hero and we are all heroes in our own lives, usually overcoming one challenge after another. The feeling easily leads to overconfidence, attachment to past achievements and misuse of our power over others.

To master courage, we need to increase our abilities step by step through continued exercise. Placing our courage in service to others, we can avoid the related Ego traps.

Peace

The emotional essence of peace(SHANTA) manifests when we experience non-attachment. We feel personally pacified, connected to the body of bliss of the Self, being at least temporarily without desire.

Peace is the *rasa* without much *rasa* or emotional energy, popular yet scarce. It is a feeling of calmness that also easily makes others feel more peaceful. It is the only *rasa* that can be mixed with other *rasas*, allowing to pacify them. Attachment to the feeling of peace easily leads to seeing others or our jobs as the source of essentially inner disturbances.

To master peace, we need to get mind under control, stop resisting our natural *karmic* debts and remain connected inside.

Anger

The emotional essence of anger(RAUDRA) manifests when we believe that some attachment has been disrespected. We feel personally insulted, which will make our Ego very dominant, seeking to defend its own importance.

Anger is the most destructive *rasa*, hurting our relationships and the Egos of others. The feeling easily leads to overly dramatic expressions, attacking the person rather than maybe rightfully criticizing its mistakes.

To master anger, we need to be assertive enough to effectively defend our boundaries, while avoiding to expect things from others or to intentionally hurt another in revenge. We forgive ignorance and lack of control, seeing innocence even in the biggest of errors and we trust in karmic justice←3.6.

Sadness

The emotional essence of sadness (KARUNA) manifests when we believe that some attachment is lost. As that attachment was like a part of us, we feel personally torn apart. It may make the Ego rather dominant, crying in self-pity, centered around its pain.

Sadness is the *rasa* of detachment, our tears allowing us to let go of what naturally goes. The feeling easily leads to a lack of vitality, a withdrawal from the joys and responsibilities of life. The 'poor me' Ego may become just another form of the 'look at me' Ego.

To master sadness, we need to use the feeling of detachment to withdraw inside and expand our sadness to the natural suffering←3.6.2 of everyone. Thus we cry the sweet tears of compassion as opposed to the sour tears of self-pity, being kind and helpful to the many others that are suffering as well.

Fear

The emotional essence of fear(BHAYANAK) manifests when we imagine that some attachment might get lost in the future. We frantically search in our thoughts for a solution, which will make our mind very dominant and quite erratic, unable to think straight or even take decisions.

Fear is the *rasa* that causes us to protect ourselves from harm. The feeling easily leads to the mental imbalance of endless worrying and an increased sensitivity to all kinds of stress.

To master fear, we need to gain control over the fantasies of mind, develop equanimity←3.2.1 to whatever happens and keep focused on our next logical task, rather than waste time in imagining all potential disasters upon our path.

Disgust

The emotional essence of disgust (VIBHATSYA) manifests when we believe to have neglected some attachment, which is thus lost, threatened or disrespected. We feel to have personally failed, our Ego loses all self-confidence and leaves mind in charge, which will mostly seek to distract us from our depressed feelings in empty entertainment.

Disgust is the most ugly *rasa*, utterly useless, based on identification with past mistakes. It may bring us to increased discipline only if we let it go. The feeling easily leads to more negativity, losing all faith in ourselves and life, producing acts of self-sabotage. It may end in total disrespect of duties and social norms, acting in ways that are disgusting to others. The development of severe addictions may further aggravate our assumed identity of a loser.

To master disgust, we need to let go of the past, stop cultivating a negative self-image, believe that we can change and step by step build up more discipline, with special attention to the purification of body and mind.

Relationships Between Rasas

The science of the *rasas* also shows how our emotions naturally tend to evolve from one to the other, as shown in Image 17. While we are free to jump from whatever *rasa* to another, this is the most likely path to take, ultimately all naturally leading to joy.

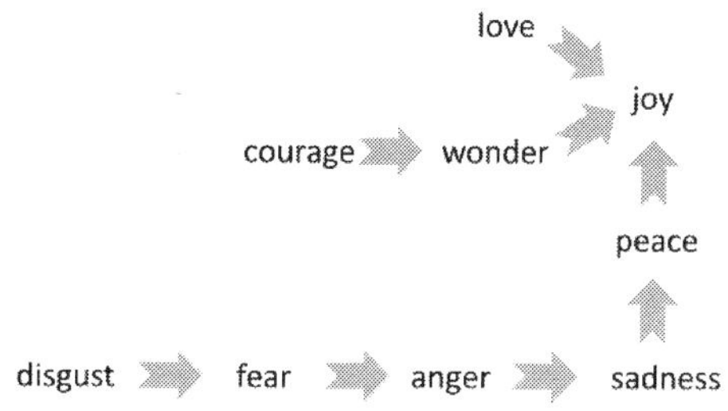

Image 17 - Natural evolution in the rasas.

The courage *rasa* easily produces wonder, both in others as in ourselves. Both love as wonder typically produce joy. On the side of more unpleasant emotions, our negativity in the disgust *rasa* leads to the fear of being unable to properly take care of our life. This fear creates much stress energy, which seeks to point outwards in anger. As anger is destructive and hurtful, the tears of sadness often follow. If sadness can become compassion, it leads to peace and from there to the more pleasant *rasas*. These anyhow all stimulate each other.

	FRIEND	ENEMY	NEUTRAL
LOVE	joy wonder	all other rasas	peace
JOY	love wonder	sadness disgust fear	peace courage anger
WONDER	fear sadness	anger	all other rasas
PEACE	sadness	all other rasas	disgust wonder
ANGER	fear	joy, love wonder	all other rasas
COURAGE	anger	fear, love peace	all other rasas
SADNESS	peace	joy, love	all others
FEAR	wonder anger	all other rasas	disgust sadness
DISGUST	wonder anger	love courage	all other rasas

Table 7 - Relationships between the nine rasas.

The nine *rasas* have particular relationships, as shown in Table 7. Some are friends, which means they support each other. Some are enemies, which will counter each other. And some have a more or less neutral relationship.

There are many exceptions to this overview. Some of these are discussed below, but as our emotions know endless variety, there are many more. Hence what follows may always be doubted. Yet in most cases these relationships prove true. They can be very useful in supporting the agreeable *rasas* by inviting their friends, while countering the unpleasant *rasas* with their enemies.

It works somewhat differently when we apply this understanding on ourselves or try to affect other people's emotions. When we feel irritated, laughing about it may work very well. Both *rasas* are fire dominated, so the energy of the body needs not to change, only the mind. But when we answer an angry person with a joke, it might backfire. These and other nuances will be learned through practicing with these relationships. Like when a musician plays a song from a musical notes sheet at first, but is later able to reproduce it with real finesse from inside. We should always work with our emotions as artists, not like scientists.

When love is lacking, it can be supported by the friendly *rasas* of joy and wonder, laughter and mystery being essential ingredients of romance. All non-agreeable *rasas* are enemies that will damage the feeling of love. The peace *rasa* will neither reduce nor stimulate it. Also the *rasa* of courage is considered an enemy of love, which mostly points to the idea that to fall in love with a hero is not very wise. They are not afraid to die, while they are easy to fall in love with. On the other hand, courage can support love, as lovers may support each other's confidence.

Joy is supported by the friendly *rasas* of love and wonder, being an expression of both. All non-agreeable *rasas* are enemies that will reduce our laughter, with the exception of anger. This is because both are fire dominated→4.3.1 and often then anger expresses itself as sarcasm, a laughter designed to hurt. The peace and courage *rasas* will neither reduce nor stimulate our joy. One major exception here is in meditation, when our peace reaches the bliss of the Self and laughter comes so easily. Another is when we courageously achieve something great and we feel very happy about ourselves and released from the stress of our effort.

Wonder is supported by the friendly *rasas* of fear and sadness. When caught by anxiety or great loss, we no longer see a solution to our problems and are basically forced to give up responsibility, trying to have faith←3.2.5 in the divine game. Anger is the enemy *rasa* since it is so dominated by the Ego, while the feeling of wonder requires a tiny Ego. All other *rasas* hardly affect the feeling of wonder, unless they make us experience something wonderful.

Courage may be boosted by the fire of anger, the Ego being dominant in both. Its enemy *rasas* are fear, love and peace. Fear is the opposite of courage and courage the will to overcome fear. The relationship with love is somewhat more flexible. If the hero has too much love, the fear of loss may weaken our resolve. Great courage can nevertheless be produced in defense of our loved ones. While calmness in a warrior may be very helpful, ultimately peace so much reduces the Ego that it may remove the energy of courage, which is very much based in doership.

Peace only has one friendly *rasa*, which is sadness. While sadness can shortly be very intense and active, it usually leads to withdrawal from the universe, as the desire to party is much reduced. Hence sadness can become really peaceful and may be transformed into universal compassion, which is very peace giving. Anger, fear, courage, joy and love all produce a lot of desire and action, hence they are enemies of real peace. Disgust and wonder are more neutral towards the peace *rasa*, as the Ego feels powerless in both, leading to inactivity. On the other hand we can also see how disgust is the ultimate killer of our inner peace, since if we have no trust in ourselves, peace becomes impossible to get.

Anger is a dear friend of fear, known in Western psychology as the fight/flight response. A lot of anger is preventive, born out of the fear to be hurt again, rather than just retaliating because of feeling hurt. Love is the main enemy *rasa*, as an angry person feels disrespected and unloved. As explained for joy already, to see the joke of anger can reduce the anger mostly in ourselves. Experiencing something wonderfully incomprehensible reduces the Ego and hence the anger. Courage, peace, sadness and disgust will not much affect our anger. It still takes courage to express anger and occasionally the deep unhappiness felt in disgust may lead to some ugly angry responses. They are short-lived as anger needs the Ego, while disgust is essentially a lack of confidence. Expressions of sadness can still counter the anger of another person, as it is basically proof of our love. Peacefully responding to an angry person may help to calm them, but the anger will still need to be satisfied.

Sadness and peace have a rather strange friendship. As peace allows some sadness, it may be increased. Like when we reach the safety of home, we might cry. In peace also however, the tears can dry up as we accept our suffering within the whole. Having released them along with our attachment nevertheless also produces peace. Knowing how to cry is an essential emotional skill, as is knowing how to stop crying. Joy and love are the main enemy *rasas* of sadness, bringing our attention to what we still love and have, and the joy they bring us. All other *rasas* are fairly neutral to sadness. A sad person might be angry for a moment if the occasion demands it, yet afterwards the sadness will return unaffected.

Fear can be temporarily replaced by its friendly *rasa* of anger, but that fire will further fan the winds of fear. While disgust and sadness will neither stimulate nor reduce our fears, all other *rasas* counter it. Courage is its opposite and feeling loved and believed in equally supports our confidence. When peace of mind is established, fear disappears. If we can laugh at the attachments that produce our fears, peace will be the result.

Disgust can lead to foul language as well as pointless accusations and projections. That can be so disgusting that it produces great anger in others. When met with some incomprehensible thing, the Ego is further reduced, so the wonder *rasa* often just stimulates disgust by removing the last shreds of confidence. Depressed people thus have great difficulty in meeting with very happy and peaceful people or teachers, yet they should try to meet them anyhow. Depression may increase when another person is showing courage, which may further stimulate the feeling of our own incompetence. However, courage and its exercise in discipline can definitely help to overcome disgust and depression. The best way to help a depressed person is by showering them with love, since they lack love for themselves. That does not mean however that we should support any of their destructive behaviors or let them abuse our love. Peace, joy, fear or sadness are neither helpful nor aggravating.

4.1.6. SUPPRESSED EMOTIONS

Unpleasant emotions can be seen as soldiers guarding our borders, sending us warning messages as emotional frequencies. In the business of life, we often do not have the time to think about all that is happening. However, our emotions function as a sixth sense→9.1.1 that alerts us to something worth looking into or thinking about.

Some colleague has said something which we have not yet been able to fully process, while our irritation shows us some boundary of ours has been crossed. This can be seen also for example in the functioning of the Amygdala area of the brain, which can bypass the conscious mind in generating an instant subconscious response to some potential danger. Emotions will often prepare the body for an eventual reaction, for example by increasing heartbeat and breathing rate.

Emotional suppression is what happens when we do not listen to these messages. There is a very basic and rather sad confusion about this subject. Should we ignore unpleasant emotions or should we dive deep into them? It is once more the two-edged sword of mind that creates a separation between these two approaches, while they are truly complementary.

Ignoring an unpleasant feeling is the natural response that most people will apply, turning away from what is disagreeable. Why would we keep our hand in the fire? Yet there is a difference between letting go and pushing aside. If we can let go, why not? However, forcefully pushing it away means suppressing the emotion, which will then require attention later on.

People quite naturally postpone their emotional processing. We then think in the evening about what really happened with that dominating colleague during the day, analyzing why it caused such a strong unpleasant emotion. But if we keep ignoring that unpleasant feeling and refuse to face it, we are suppressing it in a very unhealthy way.

Very often people use addictions to TV, alcohol and other drugs, social media, sweets, etc. to allow them to keep up their level of emotional suppression. Many people do not see how weird it is that they need to check their phone every single time life and work give them a break for a few minutes. Given how stressed many of them are, they could use that time to actually relax, breathe and maybe process something which happened. They are thus not so much addicted to this media input, as they are addicted to running from themselves and their emotions.

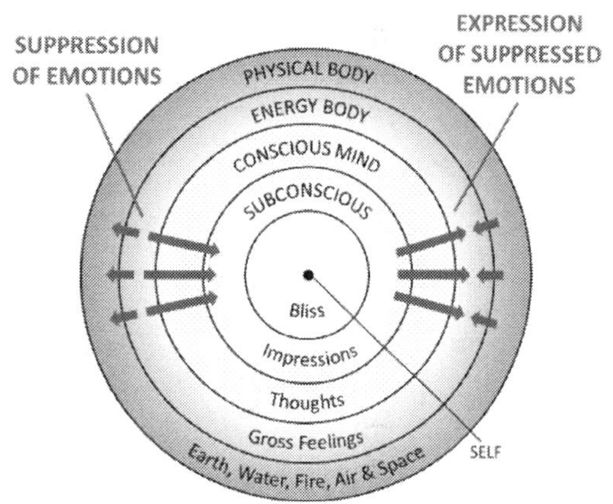

Image 18 - The suppression of emotions.

When we thus suppress an emotion, we basically push the gross emotional energy felt in the *pranic* body towards the physical body, while the more subtle negative energy will be stored in the subconscious mind, as shown in Image 18. Both movements are very unhealthy.

We already discussed before how most chronic sickness is ultimately emotional in origin←3.3.1. Yet expressing our emotions is not particularly unhealthy, only their suppression is. The impact on the physical body basically happens through the five elements that it is made of. These disturbances called *doshas* in Ayurveda will be discussed later→4.3.1.

As in our *yogic* practices we will develop many tools that give us more control over mind, we will have to be very careful not to use them for emotional suppression. There is real danger here, as is demonstrated in Table 8, showing the principal unpleasant *rasas* and their relationship to a variety of main health problems affected by emotional suppression, often called psychosomatic.

EMOTION	RELATED HEALTH ISSUES
Anger	Inflammations, cardiovascular diseases, liver malfunctions, skin issues, acid reflux & stomach ulcers, nerve pains...
Fear	Immunity & stamina issues, hypersensitivity, respiratory problems, intestinal problems, bladder cramps, chronic fatigue, burnout...
Disgust	Cysts and cancers, skin issues, constipation, dullness...
Sadness	Immunity & stamina issues, eye and other mucus issues, chronic cold & cough...

Table 8 - Health risks of emotional suppression.

People that suffer from chronic illness can use this overview to see if indeed there may be a relationship with their more chronic emotional issues, currently or in the past. If some emotional issue lies in the past and no longer triggers much emotion, then we mostly need to work on the physical and energetic levels to rebalance. If that old story however still easily triggers unpleasant feelings, then we have to deal with the suppression of emotional energy that has been pushed towards the subconscious→4.1.9. Only then may our more physical therapies bring the desired result in the body. It is not much use to mop up the floor without first closing the water tap.

Suppression of emotion is often confused with the suppression of memories, which therapists often find in people that suffered from severe traumatic experiences. When a highly emotional memory is suppressed because it is too painful to face, we do not remember what happened, yet the subconscious will keep generating the associated emotion. Therapy will then be needed to recover that lost memory, so that the emotion can be properly digested. Usually we just suppress an emotion without creating any kind of memory loss, yet the result will be the same. Regularly that emotion will seek expression and digestion.

On the emotional level, we thus really

cannot durably forget, while we can let go of our emotional attachment. If we feel happy most of the time, we should not worry to have suppressed a lot of unpleasant emotions, which unlike a memory will always be experienced by the conscious mind. If on the contrary it is hard to feel happy even when life is not creating much trouble for us, then probably the source of our unhappiness lies in the past. Suppressed emotions can be more active or more dormant in the subconscious. Advanced self-observation will reveal that even if quite happy, we all have suppressed some issues in the past, waiting for the opportunity to emerge.

Emotional suppression thus also means that we may not be very aware that we are angry for example, but it will be very clear once we start observing ourselves. Some may then realize to be grumbling inside most of the time. Many people are however so little in touch with their underlying emotions, that a friend or therapist may need to make them aware of that part of their very personality that they have suppressed as well.

Emotions always seek and find expression and thus suppression actually never works for truly challenging issues. Many fleeting emotions we can just let fly by. Yet if unhappiness becomes chronic, then there is work to be done. Further on we will discuss more about diving into our underlying emotional issues→4.1.9.

4.1.7. FRESH THOUGHT PATTERNS

Much like the algorithms of online video platforms, suggesting us the same and similar stories as we have been looking at before, the algorithms of our mind will also regularly come back to old thought patterns. Whatever we have done to let go of our subconscious emotional blockages, we may still need to also reprogram the related neural thinking patterns in our brain.

Our thought patterns quite literally follow the connections between the nerve cells in the brain, called neurons. The typical connections that we use between neurons in our thinking thus create our neural patterns, which are thought patterns, but also produce various response patterns, which are mostly biochemical, energetic and behavioral.

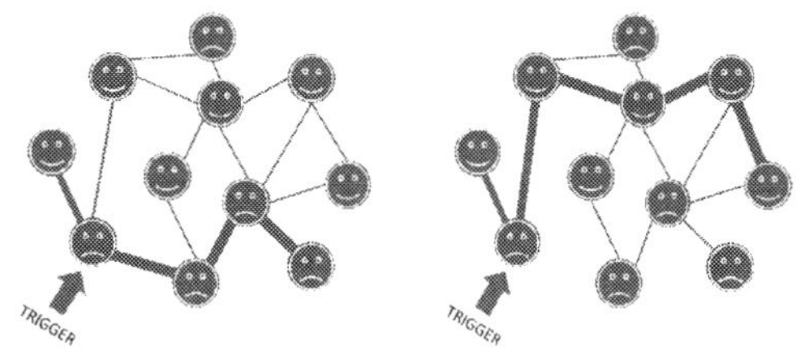

Image 19 - Happy & unhappy thought patterns.

The more we think certain thoughts, the thicker the connections between the related nerve cells will become. On the left side of Image 19 we see a more dominant negative thought pattern and on the right a more positive one. They involve the same neurons and are different only in the strength of the connections between particular cells or thoughts. The thicker the connection, the easier the thought energy will pass through. The thinner the connection, the more difficult for the thought to develop.

This is such an inspiring story of modern science, because it proves very clearly that we can change our thought patterns, while at the same time revealing why thought patterns tend to become habitual. If we want to change how we think, we have to recognize our thought patterns first, including an understanding of what triggers them.

Once we know the trigger, we can force ourselves into a more positive response and strengthen that fresh thought pattern by repeating it whenever that trigger reappears. If the old thought pattern is thus no longer used, the connections between the related nerve cells will gradually but literally fall apart and that neural pattern will then no longer bother us. This way we can directly reprogram ourselves, rewrite the code in our brain.

Suppose we are in the aftermath of a broken love relationship. We have worked hard with the related emotions, have let go what was there to let go. When we now think about it, we are quite fine with it. Yet still some related negative thought patterns may bother us sometimes, through an automated process of association with certain triggers, such as particular activities or objects that remind us of that past relationship. The error which we then easily make is to attach too much importance to it, feeling that the thought proves we are still not over it, have not really let go. That may be the wrong idea altogether, as the repetition of old thought patterns is natural and will only stop when repeatedly we turn them into new thought patterns. This process will need to be continued until the nerve connections that relate to that old thought pattern disintegrate. That is just part of the job, somewhat tedious yes.

Whatever comes to our mind, we thus should remember not to take it seriously. We so much tend to believe in our thoughts, while they may be just a repetition of outdated thoughts. They may also come through rather random association and may be affected by some food we ate, someone we met, some ancestral influence, the moon or whatever. Whenever we think something, it only means that it is up to us to decide to go along with it or not. Is it true, important, useful? Or is it untrue, irrelevant, useless? Once we have released some emotional issue, we need to recognize the related thought patterns and decide that they are useless, as we have repeated them so often without much further result. Then we change them, repeatedly replacing them with fresh ones.

4.1.8. EMOTIONAL FASTING

For those eager to move forward more rapidly, fasting from unpleasant *rasas* and fasting on pleasant *rasas* increases the level of spiritual entertainment. The tradition of emotional fasting^(RASA SADHANA) is quite basic in *Tantra Yoga*, as the more advanced *tantric* practices are not advisable unless emotional balance is well established. In milder forms it is also well known among householder *yogis*, who often practice to stay happy without much ado. For most people, life naturally and *karmically* provides enough emotional exercise. Many people may first need to learn how to express their emotions, both negative and positive. To become truly silent, we need the courage to shout or cry if needed.

In emotional fasting we first learn to avoid the unpleasant *rasas*. That is required to durably generate the pleasant *rasas*, which will become ever more intense as a result. If staying happy is too difficult altogether, we exercise ourselves in staying out of one particular unhappy flavor for a certain period of time. For example, we promise ourselves that whenever anger develops, we will stay out of it and go against it, using all means available.

Emotional fasting thus means that we consciously choose to suppress that emotion for a while, so we should be really careful. I remember one excited *rasa* student who decided out of the blue to suppress all anger for a month. Within three weeks, he hit someone really hard, which he had never done in his life. I very strongly advise to start this practice one day at a time, leaving at least a few days in between. Slowly we may move on to two days, three days, one week, etc. Usually after years of such periodical practices we may end up in a more permanent practice.

The great power that this practice can bring the people that can handle it, is the confidence of being in charge of our own happiness. After making such a promise, whenever that unpleasant feeling manifests, we will remember our pledge. That will immediately create a distance between ourselves and that initial feeling, allowing us to make a more conscious choice to follow it or not. Instead of letting it overwhelm us as emotions usually do, we can then decide not to go along with it, respecting our promise. This practice gives us the actual experience that if we can be quick about it, we really can decide to stay happy, as explained earlier←4.1.3.

Emotional fasting will allow us to fully

understand what is written above on the mastering of every individual *rasa*. We usually start with the unpleasant *rasa* that bothers us most, unless we feel that may be too hard. The main effort will be in the mastering of a first unpleasant *rasa*. Once we have mastered one, the others will be a lot easier. Yet each *rasa* has its peculiarities when fasting from it.

Anger fasts

In fasting from anger, we temporarily postpone any response to any reason for anger. Whatever happens, we can be angry about it tomorrow, but not today. The longer the practice lasts, the more we will need to develop peaceful assertiveness, straightforwardness→4.9.2, in clarifying our truth and opinions to others. It should never become a practice of not communicating our objections. And if some people cannot respect our boundaries, we may respectfully keep them at a distance. If that is impossible, the fast will force the relationship to change or break.

Disgust fasts

If a persistent feeling of disgust and a negative self-image are present, this will be the *rasa* to start fasting from, as the feeling renders all other practices impotent. Fasting from disgust is fairly straightforward, going against any identification with failures of the past, not allowing a negative self-image to exist. Often it is easiest to just say no to any thoughts about the past and look only at the present or eventually a better future. And also there we avoid any stigmatizing of ourselves. This practice will need to be supported well, maybe also by others, producing a step-by-step increase in discipline. It may include the fasting from a particular addiction, which must first be overcome in order to restore a minimal level of self-esteem. If that seems too hard at first, still fasting from disgust can be helpful, temporarily then even leave dealing with the addiction issue for later.

Fear fasts

While we can usually afford to stop thinking about the anyhow unchangeable past, some planning for the future is part of life. When fasting from fear, we cannot avoid planning some things, especially as the duration of the practice increases. Yet we can closely guard our feeling against actual worrying. Once we have a plan, we stick to it and stop ourselves from repeatedly revisiting it. In case of rather relevant worries about health or finances for example, it is advised to limit our thinking about it to a particular day of the week and stay away from the subject the rest of the time. In my case for example,

Friday is 'paying invoices day' and the remainder of the week I just stack all incoming envelopes without opening them. Another kind of emotional fasting from fear is to consciously take calculated risks, thus working for example on our most basic fears of death and injury with daring activities such as Bungee jumping. Particular phobias, such as fear of spiders or heights, can be fasted from by very slowly increasing our exposure to the object of our fear.

Sadness fasts

To cry for some time is a healthy way of letting go. As sadness is potentially the most positive of all unpleasant *rasas*, to fast from sadness is only important if the crying just continues. Fasting from sadness mostly means to stop thinking about our pain of the past, which happens most easily if we can share our suffering with others in kind *Karma Yoga*←2.4.4. If an overwhelming feeling of sadness persists long after a loved one has left the body, spiritual healing may be in order→A3.

Love fasts

Fasting on the agreeable *rasas* means to fast on them, not from them. To fast on the *rasa* of love, we love everyone we meet, see the beauty in everything. It does not just mean we are kind. The feeling of connection must be truly experienced and never waver. All unpleasant enemy *rasas* must be mastered first, before attempting this practice for any prolonged duration. We have to be careful with our promise here, lest we lose self-confidence, as it is not so easy to just love without discrimination. One might start this fasting towards one person only, which is the essential practice of a love relationship. Ultimately, to fast on love becomes *Bhakti Yoga*, seeing and loving the divine in something and everything←2.5.4.

Courage fasts

To fast on courage means to always remain confident, whatever the challenge. We have already discussed this in many other chapters and it obviously must include fasting from fear and disgust. We avoid all uncertainty in meeting our *karma* and *dharma*, accepting once and for all that we can learn to do anything. Extreme sports and spiritual practices that are hard on the body→4.8.3 directly force us to fast on courage, as doubt cannot be afforded in such conditions. The best courage fasts are done in *Karma Yoga*←2.4.4, giving some project our doubtless best, while actually all spiritual practice requires to persist in staying focused.

Story 27 *Laughing for Days*

Once upon a time, about 2 decades ago, I experienced my very first Samadhi in the Vashistha Cave, about one hour drive above Rishikesh in Northern India. Saint Vashistha, one of the original 7 seers(RISHIS), is supposed to have lived and meditated there. The cave looks like nothing special, just two small chambers and one hidden chamber. Apparently some yogis locked themselves in there to meditate till the end. I visited that place with some friends mostly because of the nearby splendid beach on Ganga. We decided to meditate in the cave for a while and then meet each other on the beach. Most came out after half an hour or so, while I stayed for over 3 hours without being aware of it at all. One cannot describe what happens, but when finally coming out I basically laughed for 3 days. Some people were worried about me being on drugs or something, yet that just produced more laughter. As real craziness seems not like a happy state, I must have been extremely sane. I thank the energies that helped me in that cave and have also seen others having similar experiences there, while one should not expect it.

Wonder fasts

To fast on wonder means to give up all feeling of understanding. Even the simplest thing feels like a miracle and we neither think to understand it, nor know what to do with it. This is actually a very advanced practice, since it stops all purposeful action, except that which comes naturally. Only saints can truly perform this miracle of giving up all direction and trusting the divine universe to guide us every step of the way. Ever visited a new city by flipping a coin at every intersection? Imagine living like that. It can be part of our *Karma Yoga*, letting go of all results of our actions, which are anyhow unpredictable.

Joy fasts

To fast on joy and humor means we cannot take anything seriously, laugh at everything and everyone, especially ourselves. Again, this is an advanced practice and Harish Johari said that in his life he had only met one person who performed this practice permanently. While most people thought he was crazy, it was apparent to the more attentive observer that this was a conscious choice. I myself experienced this state for about 3 days following my first deep meditation experience←Story27, yet that did not happen on purpose.

Peace fasts

To fast on peace means we literally let nothing disturb it, including ourselves. To actually develop a real peace fast for a longer period of time is said to require at least one *Samadhi* experience, as peace can only be maintained in continued full Self-awareness. This entire book is about regular fasting on peace, which is the practice of meditation. Retreats→5.6 may be our best shot at a real peace fast.

4.1.9. PERSISTENT UNHAPPINESS

Even while we can see that the ultimate purification of our *karmic* impressions can only happen in *Samadhi*, we still need to deal with them in life. As long as our unhappiness remains so persistent that we feel unable to reach inner peace, it must be faced more directly.

When people hardly experience happiness anymore, they usually move in circles from one unpleasant *rasa* to another. A negative self-image, disgust and depression are often the most central feeling, which is nevertheless not true in all cases of persistent unhappiness. It may regularly produce fear of the consequences of not doing our duty or of performing below our abilities. When the fear becomes too stressful, one might lash out in anger at others, wrongly identifying the problem, projecting our own negativity. The result is usually sadness and pain, as we feel to have further damaged our relationships and situation. That may again be taken personally, producing even more disgust, despair and depression.

Such a negative emotional spiral will easily produce extreme subconscious resistance against spiritual wisdom. When met with questions of this nature, Harish Johari often answered that the path of yoga and meditation is for relatively healthy people. The spiritual insights, practices and rules may not apply to people that are particularly imbalanced, needing special therapy instead. It is an inconvenient truth, yet very logical. Just as it is no use to force the Lotus Pose on a person with a recent hip injury, it is definitely not advisable for people with strong mental imbalances to try emotional fasting. The same can be said for the more concentrated meditation practices→11, even if wellness meditation, using body→7, breath→8 and the senses→9, can be very helpful.

How to deal with persistent unhappiness is anyhow case-specific and beyond the scope of this book. For that individual approach to work, we usually need help. As chronic unpleasant *rasas* often attract support from the unseen world, spiritual healing is highly advisable→A3. One might also consult the rather complete videos that I have created on all *rasas*[29].

It has become popular to practice something called 'the dark night of the soul', also known as 'shadow work'. I can only say that if we want to see something useful in the dark, better we bring the light with us. The one who goes down that dark cave without a flashlight will only get hurt and come out none the wiser, but maybe more weak, more injured even.

Some people believe that they have to get comfortable in the dark before getting access to their light, yet the exact opposite is true, which is no joke. The Ego can only get comfortable with itself as it knows to be the Self. Meditation essentially means to get comfortable in our own light. And of course, truly accepting the dark is complementary to lighting our light. To embrace our dark side does not mean however that we believe it to be an eternal truth, as our light so clearly demonstrates.

Whenever we feel the need to dig deep inside some emotional issue, we are advised to prepare ourselves through all kinds of spiritual practices that will equip us with a little more pure seeing from the Self. If we fail to do that, this becomes a dark night of masochism, with far too much attention to the 'poor me' Ego. It may further aggravate the negative identification and condition. For sure it may be needed to face our demons and as such there are no 'negative' emotions, as they are all on to something and can teach us. Yet, we face them with our gods.

Many suffer thus mostly because of some problems of the past, which created like a pain body in the subconscious. Too many people unfortunately have no choice but to try to recover from a variety of childhood traumas, which have produced some very unhealthy programming in the subconscious. This may be a tough journey indeed, with people often needing to relive those times in order to better understand them. Knowing why we tend to feel and respond in a certain way, allows us to change our patterns. It will thus be very important to see what really happened and why, in order to let go of the past. And what we cannot remember, we have to imagine as well we can.

This may lead us to accept some deep spiritual insights, depending on which *rasa* is involved:

- In case of persistent anger, the main insight to gain is that everyone, whatever they have done, is innocent of lack of understanding and control.
- In case of seemingly endless depression, we have to accept that the Ego does not exist except in this moment and that we thus cannot

[29] See youtube.com/youyoga.

stigmatize ourselves, as we can ever change.

- In case of enduring anxiety, we have to see the positive and negative side of every attachment and be thus established in equanimity←3.2.1 towards whatever the future holds.
- In case of prolonged sadness, we need to accept the nature of suffering ←3.6.2, see the impermanence of every form, as well as the permanence of the life force, ever producing new forms that we can love.

We then need to see these insights to be true in whatever happened to us to bring about such severe unhappiness. Just reading them here will not do the trick. We need to really work with them. These thus more personal insights need to be expressed repeatedly so that also our feeling about whatever happened can truly change. Using journaling, arts, music, ritual, theatre, etc. we bring out that emotion, including our understanding of what happened, as well as the related spiritual insights.

We may have to repeat these exercises of emotional expression for a while, in a variety of ways, combined with correcting our related habitual thought patterns←4.1.7. We might then become more ready to start fasting from that unpleasant emotion for limited amounts of time. We will know to have truly let go, if we can look that old issue straight in the eye without losing our smile, not for one second.

4.2. Energetic Balance

As explained above, our feelings are primarily experienced as energies in the *pranic* body. We can work in all sheaths of consciousness to achieve emotional balance, yet most directly, we can affect the energy of the life force itself. Our *prana* is the primordial energy originating in the bliss of the Self and responsible for all changes in the universe and thus the creation of time[30]. Our breath of immortality is the main source of *prana* and breathing is also the primary tool with which to regulate the life force→8.1.

Understanding *prana* relates to its vibration, movement, storage and polarity. While this provides us with many exercises throughout the meditation phases, which we will discuss in other chapters, we first here need to understand how to generally create and maintain more energetic balance in our lives.

[30] See Chapter 4 of 'Tantric Advaita, Energizing Nonduality', by Peter Marchand, self-published at Amazon 2021.

4.2.1. VIBRATION OF THE LIFE FORCE

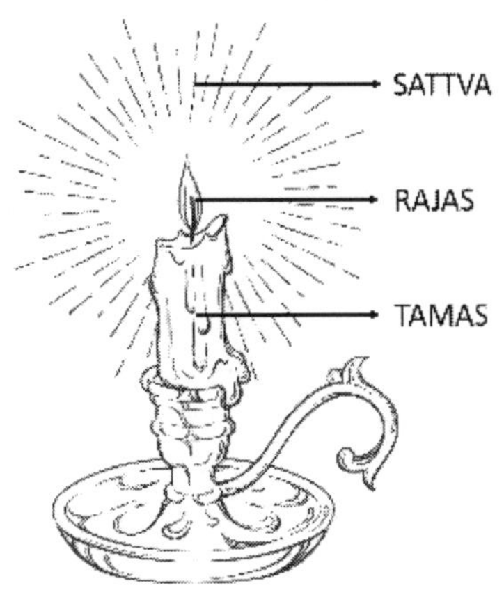

Image 20 - The gunas in the candle.

The 3 *gunas* represent the essential vibrations in the life force. Our *prana* can be inactive, active or neither active nor inactive. This directly relates to feeling either dull, agitated or peaceful. A great symbol through which to understand the *gunas* is that of the candle.

Tamas is the inactive energy, represented by the hard wax of the candle. This energy is not vibrating, unchanging, inert, pure potentiality. When this feeling dominates the life force, we experience a lack of energy, a dullness, which usually means it is time to rest and recharge. The feeling often produces unpleasant emotions, so it is predominantly regarded as a dark and heavy energy. This tiredness also easily leads to lack of understanding.

	TAMAS	RAJAS	SATTVA
Candle	Wax	Flame	Light
Change	Unchanging	Changing	Beyond
Activity	Inactive	Active	Beyond
Color	Dark	Rainbow	Light
Density	Heavy	Changing	Light
Nature	Potentiality	Manifestation	Being
Seeing	Ignorance	Knowledge	Wisdom
Feeling	Dull	Excited	Blissful

Table 9 - Properties of the gunas.

Rajas is the active energy, represented by the melted and burning wax of the candle flame. This energy is strongly vibrating, ever changing, busy, manifesting. When this feeling dominates the life force, we experience an excess of energy, an excitement, which usually means it is time for action. The feeling can produce pleasant and unpleasant emotions both, so it is seen as an energy that pulsates in varying colors of the rainbow. It leads both to right as well as to wrong understanding, supporting our actions.

Sattva is the energy that is neither active nor inactive, represented by the light of the candle. This energy is gently vibrating, beyond changing or unchanging, balanced, pure being. When this feeling dominates the life force, we experience neither lack nor excess of energy, an alert peacefulness, which is ideal for the more spiritual activities. The feeling produces pleasant emotions, infused by the bliss of the Self, so it is predominantly regarded as a sun-bright or feather light energy. It easily leads to wisdom.

One might say that, as the light of the candle is also its essential purpose, the light of *sattva* is the purpose of life. Yet the light game of life requires all colors of the rainbow, and even black, the absence of light. How else could we see anything? The 3 *gunas* each have their proper place in life and only when they are present in the wrong proportions at the wrong time will they promote unhappiness. Still, there is quite a direct relationship between the *gunas* and our essential emotions, even if exceptions exist.

When in Table 10 it says that the *rasa* of love is *rajasic*, it does not mean it cannot be *tamasic* or *sattvic*, only that the typical *guna* associated with love is *rajas*.

TAMAS	RAJAS	SATTVA
Sadness	Love	Peace
Fear	Joy	
Disgust	Wonder	
	Courage	
	Anger	

Table 10 - Relationship between the rasas & the main related gunas.

When the *tamasic* energy is present and it is time to sleep, we can totally enjoy resting in peace. Yet if we feel tired and dull when some action is needed, easily the *rasas* of sadness, fear and disgust will manifest, which are all emotional expressions of energetic weakness. While sometimes they may lead to lots of mental activity and maybe also to dramatic expressions of emotion, they produce inaction or actions that are unproductive and thus *tamasic*.

When the *rajasic* energy is present and it is time to act, we will usually easily generate the excited *rasas* of love, joy, courage and wonder. They readily bring desires for positive action, which may be fruitful or not. If our actions are blocked somehow, not leading to some expected results, easily the frustrated *rasa* of anger will manifest. This may also happen if the *rajasic* energy dominates when it is time to sleep or if we want to find peace and bliss in more spiritual activities.

When the *sattvic* energy is present at an appropriate time, we will easily generate an alert kind of peace and this energy may also manifest in peaceful forms of all pleasant *rasas*. If however it is time to act more forcefully, we have to replace it with a more *rajasic* energy. One of the main objectives in spiritual growth is the ability to combine *rajasic* activities with a rather *sattvic* energy and feeling, which mostly relies on connection to the Self. And even if the body feels *tamasic*, like when sick, we can still try to remain *sattvic* in thoughts and feelings.

Changing our Guna

The truth thus does not lie in any of the 3 *gunas*, even if the *sattvic* energy can be seen as the most spiritual energy vibration. Correct understanding lies in balancing the *gunas*, so that they meet the requirements of the moment and our intention. If possible, we can adapt our activities to the energy present. If not, then we need to change the *guna* so that it better suits our needs and unpleasant emotion does not develop.

The change from *sattva* to *rajas* and then from *rajas* to *tamas* happens naturally everywhere in the universe, as well as in ourselves. It is the gradual densification of the original subtle *sattvic* energy of inspiration, over the gross *rajasic* energy of change and creation, to the more dense manifestation of the *tamasic* energy in all kinds of matter. When the *sattvic* energy is present, it will generally inspire us towards some activity or other. Thus the available *rajasic* energy will be used and when it is depleted, the *tamasic* energy naturally emerges and it is time to rest. After rest, again both the *sattvic* and the *rajasic* energy will be naturally available.

When we want to change from a more *rajasic* energy towards a more *sattvic* energy, we just need to let go of action and calm down, which is also the principal method of meditation. The more agitated we are, the more difficult this will be. Sometimes the *sattvic* energy that we can generate may still be somewhat *rajasic*. Yet if we persevere in inaction, also on the mental level, true *sattva* can be ultimately attained in all conditions.

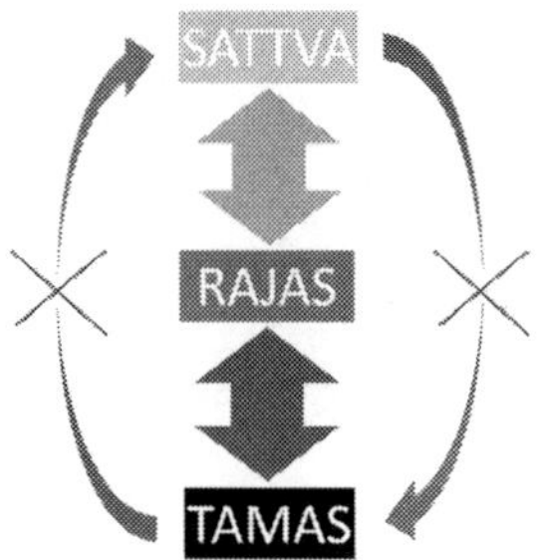

Image 21 - From tamas over rajas to sattva and back the same way.

To change a *tamasic* energy directly into a true *sattvic* energy is near impossible, which is a major error spiritual people often make. When we feel really dull, heavy and negative, we cannot use inaction to become more alert, light and neutral. Some physical or mental action will be needed to convert the inert *tamasic* energy first into an active and positive *rajasic* energy. Like a person with a hangover will be better first served by jogging than by meditation. Only when all *tamas* is thus activated into *rajas*, we can use inaction to move from *rajas* to *sattva*, as explained before. The only way to easily move from *tamas* to *sattva* is when we rest long enough in *tamas*, so that this energy becomes exhausted by itself.

In conclusion, when we come out refreshed from a *tamasic* state like sleep, we can move through action into *rajas* or through inaction into *sattva*. From *rajas* we can move into *sattva* through inaction. From *tamas* we can move over *rajas* towards *sattva*, through action followed by inaction.

The above understanding will be valid in all meditation phases that we will discuss in the chapters on body→7, breath→8, senses→9, concentration→11 and meditation→12. It will also be the basis on which to understand how to plan our daily rhythm→5.2.1. The *gunas* are equally very much affected by our food→4.5, the use of home remedies→4.6, fasting→4.7, activities→4.8 and restraints→4.9. They will be the primary force that determines the quality of our desires→4.4.1, as well as of our meditative efforts.

The *gunas* are thus largely created by our breathing, our practices and lifestyle, while they are also present in some proportion in the energy with which we are born. All will have the 3 *gunas* present, but some people are by nature more *tamasic, rajasic* or *sattvic*.

Since some action is always needed in life, most people are either *rajasic-tamasic* or *rajasic-sattvic*. *Tamasic-sattvic* is not an available option, yet some people can be truly quite balanced in *sattva-rajas-tamas* while others may be really *sattvic* from birth. All this will not only affect our desires in life, but also our relationships, where some compatibility in the original *gunas* is required→4.10.2.

4.2.2. MOVEMENT OF THE LIFE FORCE

The *rajasic pranic* energy is moving through the physical body along with the air element. If these natural movements of *prana* become disturbed, all elements of the physical body→4.3.1 will get out of balance. As a result, it will be hard to remain emotionally stable in life, as well as concentrated in meditation.

There are five main *pranic* movements, that are thus also 5 basic movements of the air element, or *pranic* winds(PRANA VAYUS).

PRANA

Pure *prana* enters the body through the inhale, as well as through the senses, food, water, etc. It is the origin of all other forms of *prana* and provides direct energy to the brain and the nerves, to the *pranic* body and the more subtle bodies. The speed and depth of our breathing largely determines the *pranic guna* that we experience in our general feeling. It also depends on the freshness of the food we assimilate→4.5.3, bringing more or less *prana* to the intestinal flora.

Apana represents the energy that usually leaves the body through the exhale and in the passing of wind, urination, defecation, menstruation, etc. *Apana* is the most impure, polluted form of *prana*, which is usually why it is outgoing[31]. The impact of *apana* on the life force will be *tamasic* if digestion is disturbed and *apana* is recirculated in the body rather than being expelled from it. It is mainly released by regular bowel movements. Deep or shallow exhalation is another factor that affects it. Menstrual disorders can have powerful polluting effects on women's *pranic* energy as well, increasing *tamas*, which usually means rest is essential.

APANA

Vyana is the energy that is distributed to the entire body through the oxygen in the blood stream and other bodily fluids. The primary center of *vyana* is the area of lungs and heart. Movement is the essential activity needed to support *vyana* and the *gunas* will be destabilized by the malfunctioning of *vyana* in case of lack of physical exercise. The energy will then either be too *rajasic* or too *tamasic*, while *sattva* will be hard to produce.

VYANA

Udana is the life force that is used to do all kinds of things, like moving, speaking and growing. It is associated with the throat area, dominating our will power, actions and expression. When *udana* is weak, a *tamasic* feeling will easily develop. Its power largely depends on the balance within the other *pranas* and especially *samana*. Particular breathing exercises →8.7.1 can temporarily stimulate *udana*.

UDANA

Samana is a churning, 'cooking' form of *prana*, centered around the navel. It digests food, water and air, as well as all kinds of mental impressions. It requires a healthy digestive fire→4.5.3, which is affected both by the quality of our food as by all kinds of physical and mental activities. Suppressed anger may particularly disturb it. When *samana* is weak, it will be hard not to become stressed by our environment and the actions of others. This may create a fluctuation between the *rajasic* and *tamasic* energies, known in Western psychology as manic-depressive behavior, which of course also has other causes.

SAMANA

The proper functioning of the 5 *pranas*

[31] Ejaculation and childbirth are also outgoing functions of *Apana*, though obviously for other reasons than 'impurity'.

is thus mainly affected by breathing→8, exercise→7 and food→4.5. Emotional imbalances generally also produce disturbances in the movements of the life force←4.1. Mastering *apana* is in part related to getting up before sunrise→5.2.4. *Prana* visualization is another way to affect the flows of energy→9.5. Thus we will encounter the 5 *pranas* often in many chapters of this book.

4.2.3. STORAGE OF THE LIFE FORCE

While disturbances in the vibrations and movement of the life force are quite immediately felt, the proper storage of *prana* mostly has long-term effects. Improper storage of *prana* can happen for years before its effects are noticed. Restoring depleted *prana* reserves likewise takes a long time and much sustained effort. Especially as we grow older, this issue becomes more important, even if improper storage of the life force often starts in youth.

Ojas

Prana is not stored in the physical body, but in the *pranic* body. The storehouse of *prana* is an energy called *ojas*, a word which means 'luster'. If we have *ojas* aplenty, our skin shows a kind of brilliance, even without makeup, which actually tries to mimic this effect. The skin of people that are near death usually shows an extreme dullness instead. *Ojas* is a more dense, 'oily' form of *pranic* energy, grounded in the water element, while active *prana* is connected to the air element in the 5 *pranic* winds←4.2.2.

Lack of *ojas* produces a long-term lack of vitality, since it is like an elixir of the life force. Our immunity goes down, as well as the quality of all bodily functions. Everything experiences a kind of dryness, a lack of lubrification, especially in the joints. The naturally ongoing rejuvenation of all tissues is stalled, producing premature aging. Physical stamina will thus be severely affected and that may bring our energy of confidence←3.1.1 down, on long term. It will particularly impact the endocrine system, digestion, fertility, the nervous system, etc.

Also the emotions will experience a kind of dryness, becoming overly mental and airy, with the occasional flaring up of fires. The emotional essences or *rasas* are directly related to *ojas*, both belonging to the energy body where it connects in the water element. Perhaps the main consequence is in the difficulty to sense more subtle feelings, such as love and compassion, and including the bliss of the Self.

All of these difficulties typically increase as we 'dry up' in old age, while they can also be overcome. This is well proven by so many kind, peaceful and balanced grandmas and grandpas, as well as by a great many sweet elderly *yogis*.

Yet why make the final phase of life more hard, as we aspire to put it to proper use in spiritual development←3.8.5? Lack of *ojas* is already showing its effects in too many young and middle-aged people with lowered immunity and vitality.

Moreover, *ojas* is also needed to supply the body with *pranic* energy when breath stops in the deeper stages of *Samadhi*. Sufficient *ojas* is required for our deeper trances not to be prematurely ended by lack of it→13.3.1.

Ojas is produced from *prana* during the exhale, when the inhale has absorbed more *prana* than is immediately needed. Also in this regard, it pays to have sufficient time for rest and *ojas* production. Both the depth and length of the inhale and exhale very much affect the generation of *ojas*. Many people basically suffer from lack of *ojas* through a habit of shallow breathing. Emotional stress often causes impaired breathing, through a cramped posture and by blocking the diaphragm muscle in the area of the heart, further reducing ojas production. Another factor is a lack of physical efforts, which help to open up the lungs.

Another requirement for the creation of *ojas* is that the water element in the body should not be disturbed. Proper balance of the related mucus *dosha*→4.3.1 is needed, which depends on the intake of fluids, proper nutrition and digestion. Premature aging was often in the past caused by lack of food, while these days most people that suffer from lack of *ojas* have enough to eat. Junk foods and disturbed digestion may still lead, amongst other things, to the depletion of *ojas*.

Last but definitely not least important is the consumption of *ojas*. It is mainly consumed by the mind through excessive sensory, sexual and mental/emotional activity. Burnouts are typical examples of how prolonged emotional and mental stress can literally deplete our *ojas* reserves. *Ojas* is also consumed by the body's natural rejuvenation and healing, as well as by its conversion into *tejas,* see below.

The restoration of *ojas* may require profound changes in diet→4.5, the use of home remedies→4.6, achieving emotional balance←4.1, control of sensory, sexual and mental exhaustion→9.2, as well as of course deeper breathing→8.4. The practice of deep breathing builds *ojas*, especially through long exhales→8.6.2. Feelings of love and devotion, of whichever kind, equally help to create *ojas*. This happens because love supports our rejuvenation processes, which are linked to our reproductive system.

One of the main aspects of restoring our *ojas* reserves is in managing our energy well and avoiding any exhaustion.

As in most burnouts, or when recovering from serious disease or injury, too rapidly starting to use the limited amount of energy that one has stored easily leads to another episode of chronic fatigue, low stress resistance and blocked natural healing processes.

Tejas

Image 22 - Storage of prana.

When *prana* is again liberated from *ojas*, it first becomes *tejas*, which literally means brightness. It is attached to the flames of the fire element and brings mental and intellectual clarity. It is the light with which we see through our inner eye→9.1.3. It thus digests impressions, feelings and thoughts by allowing the proper seeing of them. Intellectual understanding as well as intuitive insights very much depend on the presence of *tejas*.

Many of the earlier mentioned consequences of the lack of *ojas* are related also to a lack of *tejas*. Such shortage of *tejas* is principally caused by depletion at the source, which is *ojas*. Proper balance of the fire element is however required for producing *tejas*, which principally depends on the digestive fire→4.5.1.

4.2.4. POLARITY OF THE LIFE FORCE

The life force is basically electromagnetic, even if it is a lot more subtle than what we usually encounter as electrical energy. All changes within *prana* are produced by a basic polarity, similar to the positive and negative poles present in electrical currents and magnetic fields. All changes in the life force happen because of a similar polarity between the so-called solar(PINGALA) and lunar(IDA) energies and are *rajasic* in nature.

While the solar energy is electrical and heating, the lunar energy is magnetic and cooling. Funny enough, many of the more essential identifications of our Ego are with either the solar or the lunar energy. The solar energy manifests as more rational, extravert and verbal, while the lunar energy is rather emotional, introvert and visual. The solar energy thus relates more to thinking and doing, while the lunar energy is more into feeling and experiencing. Our Ego indeed very typically identifies with all these aspects of the solar and lunar energies, which are often regarded as masculine and feminine characteristics.

Masculine & Feminine

The opposition between solar and lunar energies sounds familiar to what is usually called a more male or female energy. While both men and women have both, the solar energy on average tends to dominate in men and the lunar energy is more found in women. Thus seeing the solar/lunar polarity as male/female may be both revealing and confusing. Comparing solar with lunar is quite straightforward, while comparing men to women will never be simple, leading to endlessly hilarious discussions.

Some women are of course more solar and masculine than some men, who may be quite lunar and feminine. This is not a gender issue, just a generally different attitude towards life and its problems, either more rational or more emotional. In gay couples we usually find a similar kind of role play, because that solar/lunar polarity creates the dynamic of change and progress. The naturally inherent complementarity of solar and lunar also causes love and attraction between people.

To be male or female is an illusion as we all have masculine and feminine energy, albeit in different proportions. This is explained in the Hindu story of Ardhnarishwara, while there exists a similar story in the Thomas Gospel with Jesus and Mary Magdalene. The Hindu god Shiva was traveling with some of his devotees and his spouse Shakti decided to join them. This caused the all male aspirant *yogis* to complain about her distracting presence and ask if she must not be excluded from the path? Then Shiva transformed himself into this figure of Ardhnarishwara, which is half Shiva, half Shakti. He told them that we all have both sides and that the very purpose of the practice is to bring these in balance.

Image 23 - Solar & lunar in Ardhnarishwara, half Shiva, half Shakti.

The solar way of dealing with a problem is to rationally analyze and solve it. The lunar way is to emotionally experience and digest our problems. Both ways are obviously complementary, even though many discussions between men and women are about which approach is the most important or even correct. And certainly the same discussions may occur between two men or two women, one being more rational and the other more emotional.

The solar approach is to largely ignore our emotions and use our rationality to address any problem. The lunar approach is to ignore reasoning about that problem to some degree and use emotional processing to deal with our issues. If a solution can be easily found, the solar approach is more suitable, while if a solution comes less easily, the lunar approach allows to accept it. Seen as one approach, neutral in energy, we accept a problem as we try to solve it. Solar and lunar are part of the same dance.

A too solar approach will lead to emotional suppression←4.1.6, while an all too lunar approach tends to overly dramatize what happens. It is thus natural that the communication between more masculine or feminine people touches upon all these subjects. That communication will be fruitful if both parties see through the illusion of that somewhat needed identification with the solar or the lunar approach in the dance of life. Then both the male and the female approach will be equally respected in reaching some conclusion.

To the man who dares to ask the question where else he could find that which makes women so attractive, the answer is in his own emotional lunar energy, and all related activities such as nice food, art and music, wellness and meditation, the typical relaxation games. To the woman the opposite is true and when no man is around, they are invited to more develop their rational, solar side, alongside activities such as sports, martial arts, writing and teaching, the typical concentration games.

The Solar or Lunar Ego

One of the most fundamental attachments of the Ego is in being a man or a woman. And while most people base this identification on some features of the body, the more essential identification is with the solar or lunar character. A majority of men will think and act quite rationally and believe that this is the right way. A majority of women will think and act more emotionally and believe that this is what makes them a woman.

The roles attached to the masculine and feminine viewpoints are part of the conscious and subconscious conditioning in society, already from a young age. It usually begins with being raised by a father and a mother, each playing a different role. Some of it definitely lies within the body, genetics and the related biochemicals such as hormones. Even the soul has its own original gender or solar/lunar dominance, which may differ from the gender of the physical body. Fortunately, more lunar men and more solar women are increasingly accepted to be free to be who they are.

Transgender people have difficulty in accepting the body they are born in. Yet their struggle also relates to identification with the solar or lunar energies, which are unrelated to the features of the body. Nevertheless, other aspects may play an important role, such as having had a different gender in the preceding life.

Half of the typical archetypes that our Ego identifies with belong more to the solar and masculine role, such as that of fathers, leaders, scientists, players, philosophers or warriors. Others identify with the more lunar and feminine roles as mothers, hedonists, artists, caretakers, healers and servants. And every man and woman should feel free to do so and find their rightful place in the whole. The complementarity of all these roles in society is what works. For example, while we need leaders to make group decisions, we also need rebels to keep our leaders in check.

In trying to make our Ego more flexible, we can detach from these roles sufficiently to be able to choose which role to play at any given moment. One moment we are leaders, the next maybe rebels, or mothers. Thus we can balance the solar and lunar energy in a flexible attitude that is most effective and peace giving.

The Patriarchal Society

Just like our Egos, society's culture always expresses the desire to find harmony within the solar/lunar polarity, which we find in infinite variety within politics, art, music, fashion, architecture, etc. Modern, western-style society shows a clear dominance of the solar energy.

Some thousands of years ago, as far as historians can see, there may have been more of a dominance of the lunar, feminine energy, or at least more of a balance between solar and lunar. With population growth the fighting over the available land increased. Thus gradually leadership appears to have been transferred from the wisest women to the strongest men, while the worship of goddesses was largely replaced by that of gods.

In any case, Western society has long given preference to rationality over emotion, along with giving men dominance over women. In both cases, we can see a gradual weakening of this imbalance. The rationalization and suppression of emotions is however still strongly promoted by patriarchal culture, such as in the expression 'Be a man!'.

In politics, the solar argument of endlessly stimulating economic growth usually beats the lunar argument of caring more for the poor, the weak and nature. That is why we live in this strange world where some people have obesity while others starve to death. Or how mankind has landed on the moon yet also nearly destroyed nature on earth→Story32.

Balancing Solar & Lunar Energy

When dealing with our own emotions and thoughts, we must be aware that most of us are unreasonably conditioned by patriarchal society to suppress our emotions. That is true for many women also. Some emotions merit letting go of, while others certainly need more attention. To find that balance means to balance solar and lunar energies. This strongly pertains to our relationships with others→4.10, but also very much defines how we relate to ourselves.

Balanced solar and lunar approaches are very much what characterizes a saintly person. They are neither forceful nor weak, give answers that are rationally and emotionally balanced, clear but poetic. They solve people's problems both practically as in their feelings and are neither indifferently detached from nor particularly attached to their feelings.

The principal dialogue between the conscious mind and the subconscious happens between the frontal lobes on one side and the midbrain and hindbrain on the other side. Yet the most essential conversation in the thinking processes of the conscious mind is between the left and right hemispheres of the forebrain.

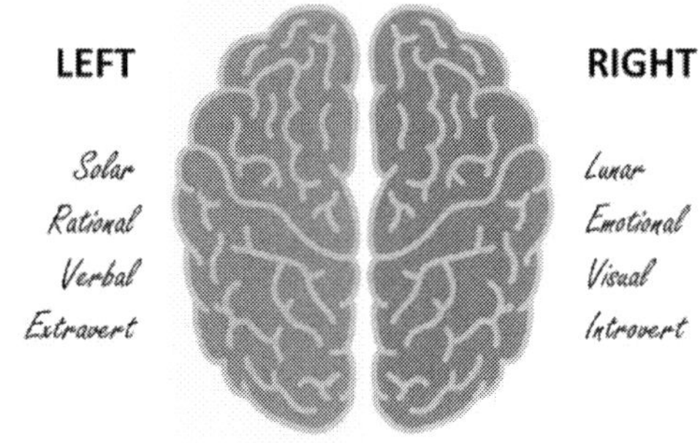

Image 24 - Solar & lunar thinking in the brain.

One side of our brain is classified by modern science as more rational and verbal, while the other is seen as more emotional and visual. Through all kinds of experiments with our brain, scientists have come to this general conclusion, which is already known since thousands of years in *vedic* science.

Image 25 - Ancient-style depiction of the solar and lunar brain hemispheres, as well as the reptile brain.

It is not a clear-cut division, as the reality of our brain is infinitely more complex. Both hemispheres have more rational or emotional, visual or verbal aspects. Yet it very clearly shows how our thinking is dominated by the solar/lunar polarity, by some disagreement between reason and emotion, between what we think and how we feel. To stop our internal dialogue in meditation will thus work most easily if already in life we practice this balance, which chiefly regards our Ego's identifications.

Solar & Lunar in Practice

The solar versus lunar identifications in the Ego may thus be overcome through better understanding, which is the solar way. The lunar way is to start working more seriously with our feeling nature, which is why so many more women than men are involved with wellness, yoga and meditation. This is of course also related to the fact that women on average are suffering more from the lack of attention for the lunar approach in this patriarchal society. For sure also many men suffer from the same, but they are less likely to be aware of it, or to admit it.

All of us can ask ourselves if we are either more solar or more lunar in character. The inside might nevertheless be different from the outside, and this not just in the body. A rather lunar person might be seen as quite solar by others, when the Ego seeks to compensate for tender inner feelings with outer organization and determination, if not a black leather jacket. In all people there will be a mix of both, while on the inside one will usually dominate. This rather intimate understanding will help us to determine which practices are the most suited for us, as we will see throughout this book.

Solar/lunar can also be found in the duality between concentration and relaxation. Meditation itself requires that fluctuation between phases where our focus is more forceful or solar and others where our focus is more gentle or lunar, as discussed before←2.1. Yet they ultimately end in the phase of deep meditation, where the focus is firm but soft and the solar and lunar duality has been dissolved.

The more we attach to either the solar or the lunar approach, the more we will resist some necessary phases in the meditation process, and spend too much time in others. Ultimately meditation is a lunar practice because of the essential focus on silently experiencing everything as the observer, rather than analyzing everything in preparation of some doing, which is the solar way. Yet to get to that point, more solar and more lunar practices need to be alternated.

From an energetic or *tantric* point of view, the objective of meditation is ultimately seen as the union between the solar and lunar energies, the marriage of the man and woman present in each of us. Just as the complementarity between men and women is the basis of many productive love stories, the solar and lunar energies inside must complement each other harmoniously in order for us to be made whole.

Yoga means union and the principal duality in our identifications is between individual and cosmic consciousness, which must be ultimately unified←3.8.4. However, to bring balance to the energy of the life force, the principal duality to unify is the solar/lunar polarity. When the energy is thus neutralized, union with the Self is easy.

Essentially all changes in us are powered by this polarity, much like the polarity in an electrical wire keeps the currents going. Truly, they are the one energy of change that is the *pranic* life force. Yet in the meditation process we want to stop all change, so also for this simple reason the solar and lunar energies must be brought into balance.

One of the principal findings of *yogic* science is that aside from the solar and lunar energy, there also exists a neutral energy, which is generated when solar and lunar are in balance. Out of the thousands of string-like energy channels found within our system(NADIS), the three main channels are the lunar(IDA), solar(PINGALA) and neutral(SUSHUMNA) energy channels. When solar and lunar are balanced through a variety of practices, they exclude each other and the neutral energy that then manifests brings us the utterly peaceful feeling of the Self.

We will discuss the practical details in the appropriate chapters. All peace giving practices in fact will naturally restore balance between solar and lunar, so we do not need to do that so consciously. But if we feel blocked in either concentration or relaxation, we can use this understanding in more purposeful balancing exercises.

The best-known related practice is alternate nostril breathing→8.5.2, based in the relationship between nostril dominance and the activity of both brain hemispheres. That same knowledge is applied on a much more profound level in *Swar Yoga*, where ultimately all activities are synchronized with nostril dominance by will power alone→8.5.3.

Solar and lunar are however not only encountered in nostrils or brain hemispheres. The left side of the body is more lunar, while the right side is more solar. Bringing a balance between both is an essential objective of all *Asana* practice→7.2.2 and relevant also for our meditation posture→7.4. Regulating body temperature just by adjusting our environment or clothing→6.1.3 is another way to balance solar and lunar. Solar and lunar nostril breathing also correlate with bringing heat or cold in the body, producing respectively more acidic or more alkaline blood chemistry. Here we also find some special breathing techniques through the mouth that are particularly cooling→8.7.4 or heating→8.7.5.

The way we concentrate on our meditation object may be more solar or more lunar, not to say more male or female. The combination of visual and auditory meditation objects is particularly aimed at bringing about this balance and meditation objects will also have a more solar or lunar effect, while some may be more neutral→10.

How we balance our desires in the *chakras* is largely a matter of balancing solar and lunar approaches→4.4.3, expressing itself also in our daily balance of more solar and more lunar activities→5.2.1. Home remedies can be used to address an imbalance between the solar and lunar→4.6. In a way, every problem and every question can be answered by finding a balance between the lunar and the solar viewpoints.

4.2.5. KUNDALINI ENERGY

The Sanskrit word *nadi* for channel includes the gross energy channels of the physical body, such as nerves, meridians or blood vessels. Yet it mostly emphasizes the more subtle energy channels, which are connected to the physical body, but are purely energetic. The solar, lunar and neutral energy channels belong to the most subtle *yogic nadis* present in our most subtle bodies, where they activate the *chakras*.

When the solar or lunar channels are active, they literally provide the life force to all other channels. If they are truly inactive, all energy is withdrawn to the neutral channel, which is what happens in *Samadhi*. It is how we lose awareness of the physical body and ultimately withdraw our energy from all but our most subtle body. It explains how this state of deep meditation causes a kind of human hibernation→13.2.4.

Whichever way the balance between the lunar and solar energy is achieved, it will activate the neutral channel in our spine. It reaches from the first *chakra* all the way up to the crown *chakra* and when activated we feel increasingly peaceful. Either by reaching *Samadhi* or through more direct *kundalini* practices, this then allows the rising of the famous *kundalini* energy within the most central part of the neutral energy channel.

The Power of the Snake

The *kundalini* energy is the essence of the essence of the purest *pranic* energy. It normally lies dormant at our base, coiled like a spring or a snake in the first *chakra*. When in *Samadhi* the *kundalini* is awakened, which is also related to natural breath suspension→8.6.3, it moves up through the *chakras*. As the *chakras* relate to the elements and also the spiritual dimensions, the main result is a temporary disidentification from these elements and dimensions→13. Thus the veils of our different bodies are lifted, the Ego is temporarily lost and we may fully experience the Self. Important to note here is that an upward position in meditation is most suitable to allow *kundalini* to rise→7.4.

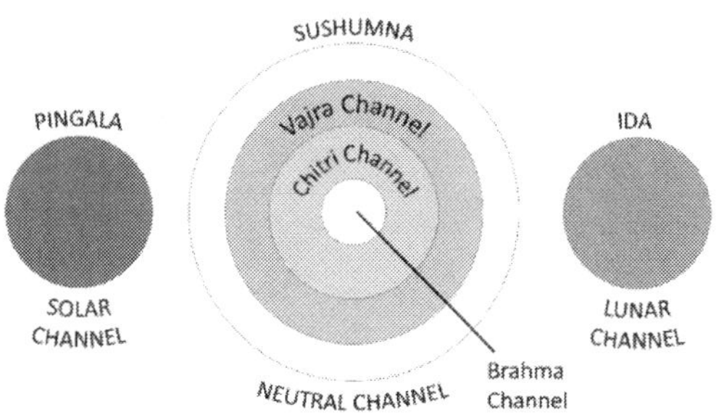

Image 26 - The essential yogic energy channels.

The rising of the *kundalini* snake happens within the most central *brahma* channel within the neutral channel. Even before that occurs, the increase of energy in the neutral channel may activate its other inner channels, creating all kinds of deep mystical behavior and experiences. The activation of the thunderbolt *vajra* channel is associated with the typical unforced shaking of the body during a *kundalini* experience. The activation of the supreme intelligence in the *chitri* channel produces spiritual insights and visions.

The science of *nadis* and *kundalini* is highly complex, as explained in more detail in Harish Johari's book on Chakras[32]. When we activate *kundalini* through the practice of *Samadhi*, we do not need this understanding. We are also advised to largely ignore any energetic experiences within the spine and refrain from drawing lofty conclusions about our achievements there. One may naturally experience hot and cold currents, or throbbing, pulsating, and radiating sensations. It is all quite irrelevant and the more we focus on it, the more experiences we will have, as energy follows our attention→9.5. Those games only distract us from the object of our meditation.

Kundalini Yoga

In *Kundalini Yoga*, the process of raising *kundalini* is approached directly. It involves highly advanced techniques of breath retention combined with physical locks→8.6. The resulting fusion of *prana* and *apana* produces a powerful energy surge that awakens the snake.

[32] *'Chakras, Energy Centers of Transformation', by Harish Johari, Destiny Books 2000.*

This shortcut requires not only a highly advanced ability to control body and breath. It also must be preceded by an intense purification of the energy channels and of the personality, lest these rather forceful techniques lead to physical and mental imbalances.

Harish Johari was taught *Kundalini Yoga* already from a young age by his father, who was a reputed *Kundalini Yogi*, as well as a judge. When students in the West asked Harish Johari to teach them *Kundalini Yoga*, he was always open to it. Yet enthusiasm rapidly dropped when people heard that it might take them a few years of intense purification and preliminary exercises under his guidance, to even come to the level where they could start practicing the actual *Kundalini Yoga*. I never went for that 'shortcut', trusting his confirmation that *kundalini* will rise also by the more 'normal' practice of *Samadhi*, if attained in a *yogic* fashion →13.2.6 through a combination of practices and paths. To experiment with *Kundalini Yoga* techniques and breathing locks is not advisable without proper guidance.

Natural breath suspension is however the driving force behind the process of awakening *kundalini*. Further on we will focus on how to slow down breath and practice breath retention→8.6. These abilities are quite essential not to block *kundalini* from rising when breath suspension happens naturally. By all means, we need to get used to stop breathing.

Purifying the Chakras

The *chakras* not only represent energy centers related to the elements and our desires←1.7.1. They also very much reflect our subconscious blockages and attachments, which are essentially energetic. While some of these blockages may be permanently removed when *kundalini* rises, their resistance also reduces the power of its ascendance.

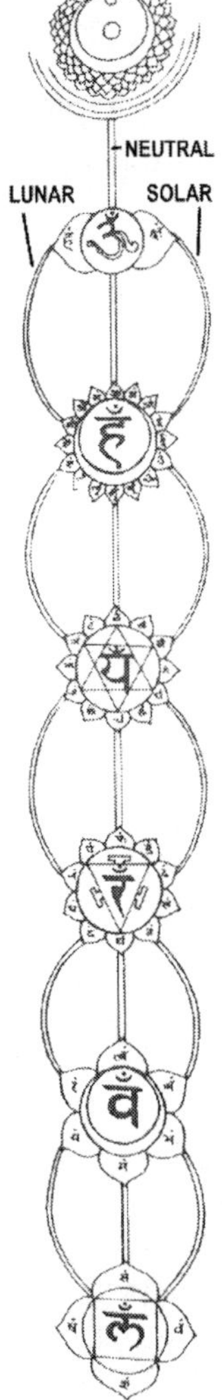

Image 27 - Chakra sounds

Hence it is advisable to purify the energy of each *chakra*, which is the main *kundalini* related practice that Harish Johari teaches in his book. It involves working with the colors, shapes and sounds of the *chakras*. It usually goes along with a gradual purification of the desires of the *chakras*→4.4.2.

Numerous traditions have brought forward highly varied practices that somehow or other relate to *kundalini*. One cannot help but ask how great must be the marketing power of the word *kundalini*? More often than not these techniques are however only related to *kundalini* simply because *kundalini* is a form of *prana* and these techniques work with *prana*.

Scriptures are very clear that the *kundalini* energy will only rise in some state of *Samadhi*, which means with total loss of any awareness of the body. All energetic experiences while awareness of the outside world and the body remains, are not considered to represent the actual rising of *kundalini*.

These techniques include all kinds of visualizations, breathing practices and rapid body movements, maybe used along with sounds, *mantras*, colors, gems, metals and other items. One can only judge them by practicing them. They usually help to relax, focus, rejuvenate and energize. They may be very useful, yet they do not make *kundalini* rise.

The main result of the *kundalini* energy moving just beyond the 1st *chakra* is the literal disappearance of the fear of death. If that would be the result of these quite easy techniques, then it would be frontpage news everywhere. So we try out what seems of interest with an open mind, keeping our fantasy in check.

Visualization techniques are definitely a great way to deal with a dull energy. It is a practice of *pranic* bathing that I have greatly benefitted from. It is very useful to ground and relax the body→7.3.1, calm the energy in the *chakras*→9.5.1, improve circulation of the 5 *pranas*→9.5.2 and to purify and pacify the senses→9.5.3. We will discuss it at length in the related chapters, including the need to avoid seeking the 'high' that these techniques might produce when used in excess. Anyhow, visualization is one of the '*kundalini* related' techniques that I have come to really appreciate.

Through the help of the healing energies, I have also experienced how highly evolved beings from other dimensions may help in the rising of *kundalini*. Some yet alive *yogis* are also able to similarly help their students, while once again these are more forced methods, which bring an experience that is rather impermanent.

The Kundalini Journey

When we leave the 1st *chakra* behind, then all insecurity will disappear from our mind. When the *kundalini* truly rises above the 2nd *chakra*, it brings a total disinterest in the enjoyments of mind and the senses. When the 3rd *chakra* is pierced, we no longer care at all what others think of us. When *kundalini* passes the 4th *chakra* we cannot help but love all unconditionally. Beyond 5th *chakra* words no longer hold meaning.

Beyond 6th *chakra* starts a mysterious journey of immortality in the *Soma Chakra*, including special powers offered by the wish fulfilling cow in the *Kamadhenu Chakra*, which are best ignored→13.4.3. It leads to the final union of consciousness and the *kundalini* energy in the *Kameshwari - Kameshwara Chakra*, where consciousness and the *kundalini* energy are seen as Shiva and Shakti in peaceful embrace.

Image 28 - The journey from 6th to 7th chakra.

This then finally brings us to the 7th *chakra* beyond any limitation, separation or qualification. In *Tantra Yoga*, the final objective of all *yogic* endeavors is thus seen as the union of the *kundalini* energy with pure consciousness.

Our primary awareness naturally resides in a *chakra* located within the heart *chakra*, our spiritual heart(HRIDAYA)→9.4.2. In meditation withdrawing inside thus means that our consciousness moves into the so-called *corpus callosum*, a neutral 'space' that connects the lunar and solar brain hemispheres, traditionally named the cave of the bumble bee(BHRAMARA GUFA). Through *yogic Samadhi* practice, the *kundalini* energy can move upwards, piercing the *chakra*s and finally unite with consciousness in that 'cave'→13.2.5.

Fortunately one might say, this entire journey through the *chakras* does not happen in just one *Samadhi* session. When before I mentioned that the true spiritual growth occurs through many *Samadhi's* over a longer period of time←1.6.2, this is why. One has to be able to digest that rising of the *kundalini* energy, which will gradually alter our entire perception of ourselves and the universe.

Herein also lies maybe the most important limitation of the more forceful methods to make *kundalini* rise. This is also the main reason why it is often said that the real spiritual growth only comes with the support of a real teacher. This protection is needed to overcome the many *chakra* related emotions that may be unleashed during this digestion process and might destabilize the practitioner even to such degree that their Ego entirely turns away from the path.

4.3. Physical Balance

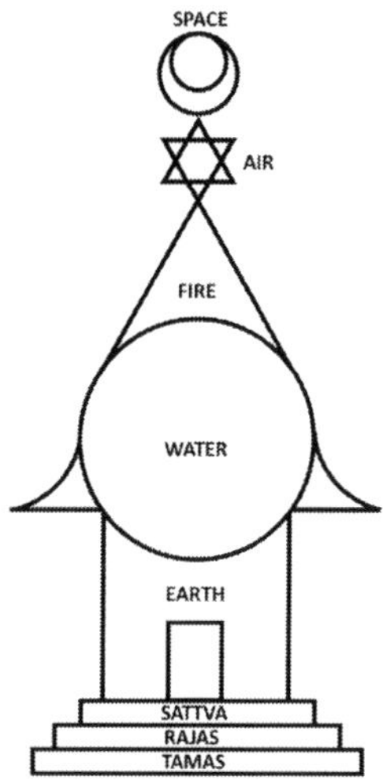

Image 29 - The temple(STUPA) of the body.

The shape of our physical body as well as of all tissues, bones and organs originates with the earth element. Earth is the densest of all elements, which are created by the densification of the space element, the most subtle of all, originating in the void of the Self[33]. The earth element thus also contains the elements of water, fire, air and space, which constitute the temple of our body. Earth is *tamasic*, while water, fire and air are *rajasic* and space is *sattvic*.

Each element has a variety of roles within the physical body and when they are in balance, our body feels healthy, happy, strong, painless and clearheaded. Imbalances between the elements are known as the *doshas*, which are central to understanding our physical balance.

4.3.1. THE 3 DOSHAS

	Earth	Water	Fire	Air	Space
Mucus	x	x			
Bile			x	x	
Wind				x	x

Table 11 - Elements involved in the doshas.

The mucus(KAPPHA) *dosha* consists of the earth and water elements and is *tamasic*. A running nose is a typical example of imbalanced mucus. Earth and water provide shape and stability to the body, which they nourish and lubricate. Mucus is essential to protect all mucous membranes that are exposed to the environment, as well as also those of the brain and nerves, the inner lining of the intestinal tract and the joints between our bones. The main diseases associated with an imbalanced mucus *dosha* are respiratory diseases, poor digestion, abnormal weight gain, joint pains and dullness.

The bile(PITTA) *dosha* combines the fire and air elements and is *rajasic*. Acid reflux is a typical example of imbalanced bile.

[33] See Chapter 6 of 'Tantric Advaita, Energizing Nonduality', by Peter Marchand, self-published at Amazon 2021.

Fire and air are responsible for all metabolic processes, providing the digestive fire that cooks the food in our biochemical factory. This energy is also used to maintain body temperature and fuel our physical efforts. The bile *dosha* also secretes sweat, powers our vision and burns toxins. The main diseases associated with an imbalanced bile *dosha* are disturbed digestion, skin issues, eye problems and blood pressure problems.

The wind[(VATA)] *dosha* is made of air and space and is *rajasic*. A bloated feeling is a typical example of imbalanced wind. Air and space are behind all movements of the body and responsible for the circulation of the life force, oxygen, nutrients and waste materials. It rules the nervous system, the sense organs, respiration, blood circulation and the work of all muscles. The main diseases associated with an imbalanced wind *dosha* are constipation, an inability to gain weight, chronic pains, nervousness and stiffness in joints and muscles. As the wind *dosha* is the primary mover, when it is disturbed it will also imbalance mucus and bile, which may produce the related diseases.

Next to the *gunas*←4.2.1, the *doshas* are the most important subject in the ancient science of health called *Ayurveda*. It is a highly evolved and naturally complex science, with each *dosha* displaying many varieties and playing different roles within all parts and processes of the physical body. This is not a book about health, so we do not need all these details. In case of real sickness, best consult a specialist.

Still, the basic understanding may take us a long way. To put down the fiery nature of the bile *dosha*, we use the cooling nature of the mucus *dosha*. Vice versa, we use the fiery nature of the bile *dosha* to heat the cold mucus *dosha*. To reduce the wind *dosha* we use the fiery bile *dosha*, in a mild fashion, to make the air expand and move out. This is the most basic and quite simplified way in which we can manage the *doshas*. In the chapter on food→4.5 we will look more into the details, which may be less straightforward.

4.3.2. THE 3 BODY TYPES

Imbalanced *doshas* are temporary problems, while we also each have a particular inborn *dosha* mixture, which is our original body type. We need all *doshas* to live, yet usually one or two of them will dominate in our body. The healthiest people are born with a perfect balance between them, while perfect health can equally be attained through a particular lifestyle adapted to the dominant *dosha(s)*. These body types also strongly affect our emotionality, mentality, character and meditation methods.

A wind dominated person is generally thin and tends to think a lot. A bile dominated person is more muscular and prefers some action. A mucus dominated body has a more rounded shape and lives from feeling rather than from thinking or doing. Various in-between types are obviously also present and our lifestyle affects these body types as well.

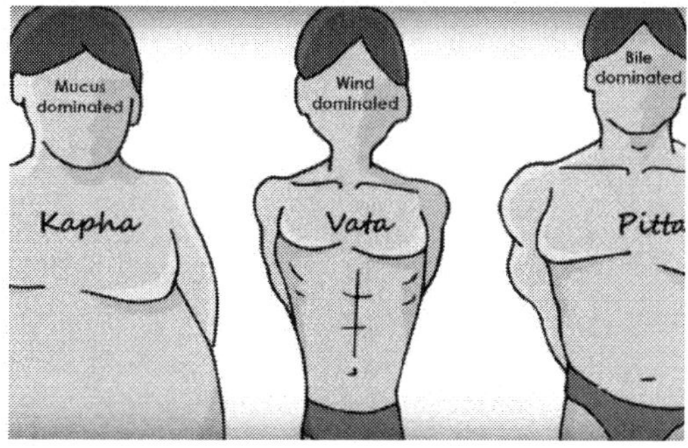

Image 30 - The 3 body types related to the doshas.

For example, a bile dominated individual may become less athletic and more rounded by overindulgence in sweets. It takes an *Ayurvedic* specialist just a minute to check our pulse and determine which is our original body type, usually the most clearly present in early puberty. It may then also become clear if lifestyle has changed that original body type, which can then be restored for better health through diet and other changes in behavior.

The *doshas* will also affect how we identify with certain physical characteristics, which the Ego perceives as part of its personality. Like a bile dominated person with lots of natural body heat may feel other people are too much complaining when the climate becomes colder. And they might feel the same if others cannot so easily summon the courage to overcome any emotional turmoil, which is just so much easier for them given the dominance of bile. So easily we mistake a property that is actually dependent on our personal body chemistry for a kind of universal quality that everyone needs to live up to.

4.3.3. DOSHAS & EMOTIONS

The *doshas* clearly affect our more spiritual objectives, and especially our emotional balance and ability to meditate. The emphasis here lies more on maintaining a dynamic balance between the *doshas*, rather than in dealing with any serious imbalance. Thus we can make sure that our vehicle is not blocking our spiritual evolution.

BILE	MUCUS	WIND
Anger	Sadness & Disgust	Fear

Table 12 – Unpleasant rasas supported by imbalanced doshas.

Imbalances in the body may aggravate particular unpleasant *rasas*←4.1.5, while these may in turn lead to disturbances in the *doshas*. The feedback loop between *doshas* and *rasas* can thus be positive or negative.

This works in quite physical ways, such as in nervousness being created by too much gas in the belly, which will irritate the nerves. If our digestive fire is too low, we will feel weak and lack confidence. If the stomach fire is in excess, just a spark is needed for anger to flare up. When the mucus *dosha* is depleted, it will dry our feelings and it may be hard to cry.

The inborn *doshas* also explain why we each have *rasas* that naturally trouble us more and others less:

- Bile dominated people more easily have an anger issue, while they generally do not worry much, nor do they often become sad or depressed.
- The mucus dominated body type more readily feels down, without experiencing much anxiety or anger.
- Wind dominated individuals may tend to worry all day. To feel irritated, sad or depressed is also quite possible for them, as the wind *dosha* may destabilize the other *doshas*.

Often the inborn *dosha* will indicate a prolonged need for some *sadhana* with the related *rasa*←4.1.8. Through proper food→4.5, exercise→7.2.2 and some home remedies→4.6 we can balance the *doshas* and maximally stay happy, healthy and wise.

4.4. Balancing Desires

When we fulfill our desires, we naturally expect some happiness as a result. We thus seek happiness outside of us, while it is also found for free inside of us. The logical conclusion is to at least seek happiness both inside and outside. It equally means to maximally balance our desires, so that each gets sufficient attention.

Carefully balancing desires and aversions is the main power we have over our happiness, while fully resolving the other essential causes of unhappiness requires no less than enlightenment←4.1.4. Managing our desires is thus essential in the process of spiritual growth.

The pursuit of desires is the main activity of life. They usually pop up in response to our emotional states. As shown in the lower half of Image 31, because of feeling happy or unhappy, we desire to get something, keep it or get rid of it. This choice is largely based in the *karmic* impressions of past experiences, stored in the subconscious. Then we develop a plan to fulfil our desire and whether the plan is good or not depends on our understanding. Next we put the plan into action and our ability to focus will determine how well we are able to follow the plan. Thus a certain result is obtained, which also very much depends on our *karma* as destiny. This result again produces an emotion and the cycle can restart.

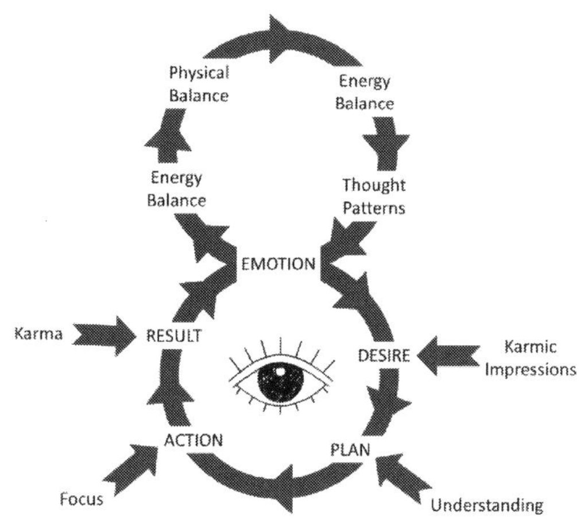

Image 31 - Desires in relation to our emotions.

As discussed before, our emotional balance also very much depends on our energetic and physical balance, as well as on our thought patterns, as shown in the upper half of the image. It is the unique approach of *yogic* philosophy to seek happiness more in ourselves, in keeping these balances, in controlling those thoughts and of course also in the Self. Yet even here, whatever change we desire will enter the carousel of emotion - desire - plan - action - result - emotion. The key element thus lies in how we deal with our desires, which largely depends on our emotional balance.

Desires & Needs

Actual needs are only present in the first *chakra* desire for security, a natural duty to stay alive. Buying that tenth house is not what one needs to survive, while that desire still belongs to the first *chakra*, as more of an addiction to the feeling of security, called greed.

Needs are relatively few, while desires mostly depend on our imagination. As shown in Image 32, our fantasies make a desire feel like a need, as they create the illusion of having it fulfilled and through this illusion produce attachment.

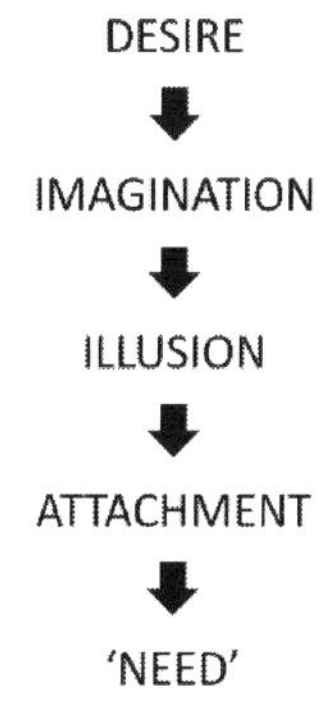

Image 32 - Taking a desire for a need

When we fulfill a desire, we mainly feel happy because we are temporarily desireless, until a new desire pops up. We feel satisfied for a while, until something triggers a less happy feeling and a new desire emerges. Even our happy excitement after fulfilling a desire may trigger the desire for more of the same or for something to add to the party. We then again feel that we cannot be happy unless that new desire is fulfilled, and thus we create unhappiness in the pursuit of happiness. So many people thereby endlessly postpone their happiness, in a state of wanting what they do not have, rather than enjoying what they have.

To understand that every desire serves our happiness at least means avoiding fixed ideas on what we want. So why be unhappy if a desire cannot be fulfilled? This feeling only comes because we have attached to a particular desire, but we simply do not need it to be fulfilled. If there is no ice cream, cake may be just as great, be flexible.

It is generally advisable to know which desires are really important to us and not push that knowledge away. At the right time, we may be ready to make the effort of fulfilling them. Yet we must keep our ideas about what we desire as flexible as possible. The more rigid our ideas, the more difficult it will be to feel fulfilled. Maybe a kitten might actually fulfill our desire for a puppy, and then maybe not. We can at least be open minded about it.

Natural desires

While we are thus advised to always remember that desires are not needs, still most of them are just natural. We have already discussed in the earlier chapters that our spiritual evolution includes a gradual maturing of the six natural desires for security, enjoyment, status, love, understanding and enlightenment, related to the first six *chakras*[34]. We have also seen that for our hot air balloon to move up towards the higher *chakras*, we have to lose excess luggage←3.8.1, yet also regularly come back down to the desires of the lower *chakras*←3.8.2.

Desires are seen as the driving force of the holy *leela* of life and the natural way in which the players give meaning to the game←1.7.3. They essentially belong to the elements of the physical body. They are triggered when the emotional energy of the life force interacts with the elements in the *chakras*. From the body they then manifest in our mind. It is up to the Ego to identify with them or not, guided by its own programming, based in past experiences with the nature of things.

The life force naturally travels up and

[34] Traditionally also seen in the 4 natural wealths or Purusharthas of the Self, wealth, enjoyment, harmony and enlightenment.

down the *chakra* ladder in a span of 1 to 2 hours or 900 breaths, highlighting each of the six main desires in turn and usually staying far longer in the lower *chakras*→8.5.3. Most people are so much caught in the desires of the lower *chakras* that they hardly allow the energy to move into the higher centers, let alone stay there.

In *vedic* philosophy it is said that when the universe is dissolved, the power of desire remains. Symbolized by the five- or seven-headed snake Shesha, it will lead to the natural creation of a new universe. Without desire nothing can happen, as it provides the power through which we do anything. *Shakti* means goddess, energy and power, but also desire. In *tantra* especially, *Shakti* as desire is worshipped as a source of liberation.

It is not because we have discovered the absolutely great reality of the Self that we must set the universe and our natural desires aside. Some people even believe that 'God' made a mistake when creating this world, not understanding that the Self never takes any decisions, which is the Ego's job. The universe is just a natural manifestation of the Self←1.7.3. Playing the game of life may hurt sometimes for sure, yet we are free to learn. It is up to us to not whine about it and ensure sufficient connection to the Self so that our pains of growth can even be enjoyed←3.6.2.

Exhausting desires

There is a lot of imagination involved in desiring. Often fulfilling a desire may turn out less juicy than imagined and the desire ceases being desired. The natural maturing of our desires thus depends in part on their fulfilment. A well fulfilled desire is a desire gone. Anyhow, the more we get of something, the less we want it, which is even known as the law of scarcity in economics. If all stones in the world were made of gold, nobody would want to wear golden jewelry.

As we mature in knowing what we really want, the desires of the higher *chakras* will start dominating. We will become more aware of the impact that the pursuit of our desires has on our general energy and feeling, and choose accordingly.

Some desires we have taken this very birth for and even the desire for the desireless peace and bliss of the Self may create many problems. Nobody knows when we will become truly non-attached, reaching that 5th step on the stairway to heaven←3.8.4.

There is thus no general morality or *dharma* in the kinds of natural desires that we can pursue, even if some darker desires can be seen as unnatural, originating in mental disease and extreme delusion. Within our personal *dharma*←2.4.3, some desires may simply be less suitable.

For example, the desire to party all night every night is generally not fitting the responsibilities of a mother or father.

For those on the path of yoga and meditation, there is certainly also no general morality with regard to the natural desires they want to pursue. Nevertheless, some restraints are needed so that 'higher and lower' desires remain sufficiently balanced against each other→4.9 and are fulfilled in a timely fashion. For example, scrolling on social media is not a good preparation for meditation, yet we can still be involved with it at other times, while respecting certain restraints in content and duration.

The main *dharma*, for everyone and for *yogis* in particular, lies not in what desires to pursue, but in how to pursue them. It is the difference between the natural, unforced fulfilment of a desire and the forceful grasping after desire. Whenever we use force, there may be consequences to ourselves or others that need to be avoided if we want to keep our heart connection intact. Needlessly hurting others or ourselves will severely increase our unhappiness and make it impossible to really meditate.

4.4.1. DESIRES & GUNAS

People that are mostly vibrating in the first two *chakras*, mainly desiring security and some enjoyment, are generally *tamasic* in nature. Even while they will need *rajas* to pursue their desires and might occasionally even feel somewhat *sattvic*, their underlying emotional energy will be rather dull and their vision clouded.

People that mostly go for the desires of the 3rd, 4th and 5th *chakras*, as in status, love and understanding, will be usually quite busy and *rajasic*. Their mood will very much depend on how successful they are in fulfilling those desires. They will also need more *tamasic* episodes to rest, but *sattva* will be mostly shortly felt when after fulfilling a desire they are temporarily desireless, maybe just for a few seconds.

People that also pursue the desire for peace, bliss and why not enlightenment, may truly experience more *sattva* in their lives. It depends on how active they still are in the *chakras* below, which may generate more *rajas* and *tamas*. Even the pursuit of the 6th *chakra* desire requires some action, some *rajas*, but they might be able to avoid untimely *tamasic* or *rajasic* episodes and maintain a deep emotional balance all the way.

It definitely pays off to analyze the hours spent on the various activities related to the desires of the chakras, as shown in Table 13. Most of us anyhow experience the need to work for a living, so naturally many hours will go to 1st *chakra* activities. That does not mean we cannot do this work from the energy of the higher *chakras*. The main question is how we spend our free time→5.1.3 and whether that reflects our preferences in the desires of the *chakras*.

CH.	ACTIVITIES	HRS.
1	working to pay the bills, householding, improving health...	O
2	partying, casual socializing, enjoying multimedia & the senses, creating good food, art & music, daydreaming...	O
3	working to improve status, self-promotion on social media...	O
4	caring for family, friends and whichever being is in need of help...	O
5	studying, reading, contemplation, spiritual learning and teaching...	O
6	meditation and all directly related practices...	O

Table 13 – Analyzing the hours of our waking time spent on the desires of the chakras.

4.4.2. THE DESIRE RIDDLE

The subject of desires causes much confusion in spiritual circles. They are seen as the cause of all our troubles and yet they are the very power of life and of all yoga. The truth is that we need some minimal level of involvement with the desires of each *chakra*. For the rest we are free to pursue any desire in *dharma*. That is the overall spiritual solution to solve the desire riddle.

However high we fly, we need to work in all *chakras* so that the related desires are satisfied to a degree that allows us to forget about them. If we do not take care of the first *chakra* desire for some income, then how to meditate in peace? Every creature has to work to survive. We cannot claim to be exempt from that rule just because of our spiritual pursuits. The same goes for the other *chakras*, so if we want to truly respect our desire for a more *sattvic* life, we need an answer for every one of them.

Security

The desire for security of the body in the first *chakra* can actually never be fulfilled, as we are all born to die. Even if we feel that our related desires for health and wealth are secured, it is an illusion. Whatever we have achieved there can so easily be lost, if that is our *karmic* destiny.

The only spiritual solution that we can depend upon to feel relatively secure on the physical plane is in being self-sufficient. Even the richest people should base their feeling of financial security on the willingness to do any job as needed. We just once and for all accept that some effort and pain are part of the game and we let the matter lie.

Thus we actually achieve the maximum security anyone can get, purely in the cheerful acceptance to do what is required, maybe nothing more but also no less.

Enjoyment

On the contrary, the desire for enjoyment of the second *chakra* can always be fulfilled. Mind and the senses can enjoy such a multitude of things that always some enjoyment is potentially available, maybe just in looking at a flower growing through a crack in the road.

Beauty is in the eye of the beholder→9.1.1, so we are ourselves the only ones who can block some enjoyment, as unhappiness spoils the taste of anything. The fear that we will not get exactly what we want stands in the way of enjoying every little thing that comes our way.

The only spiritual solution to meet our desire for enjoyment is thus found in flexibility, which is largely a matter of mental control. Flexibility in our sensory desires is needed for enjoyment to be always available and it also expresses itself as moderation.

Moderation allows us to avoid selfish behavior towards others. It also cures mental imbalance and exhaustion, or an inability to meditate→9.2.1. The high produced by excessive enjoyment of inner and outer senses is largely responsible for some lack of moderation. It leads to wanting more of the same, while that is less and less fulfilling. We best choose quality over quantity, in endless variation. Shared enjoyments are anyhow the most enjoyable and if we can be creative about it, most of it comes quite for free and can be very healthy and wealthy.

So we bake our cake and whistle that tune and have not a care in the world for securing our enjoyment of the endlessly diverse miracle of life.

Status

The desire for status in society, related to the third *chakra*, is another desire that cannot be fulfilled. No social position or power can ever be permanent, nor very fulfilling.

One needs just a few experiences of a more elevated status to realize that it is always under pressure. The one that seems to truly respect us today, might gladly take us down tomorrow. Even the king of a country must always fear for the throne. There is also the added disadvantage of never knowing whether people love our power or us, which is quite the recipe for loneliness, even in lots of company.

The spiritual solution to the desire of the third *chakra* is in simply being useful and dependable, which means we will always find some position within society. Especially through *Karma Yoga* we can achieve quite a nice and secure social status. Wherever we are or try to be on the social ladder, as we work for others, to some degree they will care for us.

Love

The desire for love in the fourth *chakra* is again a desire that can be easily fulfilled, even if many feel a lack of love. As beauty is in the eye of the beholder, so is love.

Then why is love so hard that it might break our heart? When we get love from another, easily we feel love for that other, yet love is not a business. The love that we feel as a result of being loved, is not a true feeling of love, only attachment to being loved. So for sure, that love which is not love will always bring pain, when we experience a lack of it and the illusion is shattered.

In love there can be no expectation, because when love becomes conditional it is not love, only a business exchange of words, feelings and actions. The desire for another person to love us, is only a desire of our Ego to be validated, while there is no need for it. Why would we need the love of others if we actually do love ourselves? However great it truly is to feel loved, it is only because it boosts self-love.

The key is that as we love ourselves, love will always be in our eyes as well. As explained above←2.5.1, we are all lovable not because we are perfect, but because we always try to attain perfection. True love must be unconditional as we cannot expect it to work for us. It may neither make another happy, nor be returned.

The spiritual attitude towards love is in surrendering any fruits of our love, to love everyone, ourselves included, without any expectation. To always keep love in our heart means to have love in our lives. That is how the fourth *chakra* desire can always be fulfilled. When that love is truly universal, as when practiced in *Bhakti Yoga*←2.5.4, at all times we can feel loved by the divine as well, especially as individuals.

The desire to find an endless exchange of unconditional love with someone special is nevertheless probably one of the most difficult desires to let go. We are quite programmed by nature that way, as the solar attracts the lunar. Nature thus assures our survival in being connected to complementary others and it obviously also powers reproduction and the survival of our species→4.9.5.

It is equally a divine desire to manifest the love of the unmanifested into the manifested universe of our life with another. If we see an opportunity to fulfill this desire, with someone that seems willing enough to do their part, we open our heart to it and do our part in loving unconditionally. And we surrender to the pain naturally produced by the ever-changing nature of the objects of love. It is a small price to pay, as that suffering holds its own treasure←3.6.2. And remember, there are conditions to being part of a team←2.5.2.

Understanding

The fifth *chakra* desire to understand is based in the illusion of understanding and thus can never be fulfilled. There are simply no words to correctly express reality. No scientific study of even the smallest thing happening can ever be considered complete. As all of our understanding is supposed to guide our actions towards more efficiency, it is a means by which we seek to control the results of our efforts.

Knowledge is power people say and in a more practical sense that certainly holds true more often than not. Yet so many of the most important things in life are entirely beyond our power to control or understand. Did we plan to find that perfect partner, job, house, teacher, book, flower?

The spiritual solution to the question of understanding is in the acceptance that there is no absolute answer. That is the truth which we always need to keep in mind. All difficulty in understanding is principally created by our resistance to accept our answers and especially their limitations in bringing us what we want.

So we accept that our understanding can guide us to move forward, but we know it to be relatively unreliable, a mere expression of our feeling of wonder at that very basic miracle of being somewhere, sometime, somehow, going somewhere, sometime, somehow. So we liberate ourselves from all ultimate responsibility, smile in silence, the practice of *Jnana Yoga*, which is anyhow the best way to see something of an answer through our cosmic intelligence←3.4.3.

Enlightenment

In sixth *chakra* we desire to become enlightened or something similar, which is a desire that we can always fulfill. We essentially are enlightened beings and all that is needed so to speak is to be aware of the cosmic light of our awareness, to always remember who we truly are.

The spiritual solution to this non-existing problem is to let go. Whatever we feel currently stands in the way of our enlightenment, we let go of it, disidentify. The only little bit of action needed to do that may be in changing our emotional energy about it, using breath or whatever. Yet changing our raw energy vibration is not the true task, only a little help.

And in learning all that, the desire for enlightenment may inspire us. We're on a road to nowhere, as we are seeking ourselves. Only in letting go there is a path, walking in a circle around ourselves. The breadcrumbs that show where we have walked are pieces of redundant luggage that we have dropped along the way. The desire for enlightenment is fulfilled by letting it go, laughing our heart out at the joke of unhappy individuality.

Tantra & Desire

So, we can solve the desire riddle by being self-sufficient, flexible in our tastes and useful to others, while keeping love in our heart, accepting the relativity of any answers and letting go of the desire to escape from ourselves. Only then we will be free to do anything more than that, pursue whatever desire we want, preferably in the right way.

When we work on readjusting our desires in a particular *chakra*, the *tantric* tradition offers a variety of energetic practices in support. How we deal with our desires is primarily an emotional issue as discussed before, yet our feelings can change as our energy changes.

Whenever we want to change how we deal with a desire, Harish Johari advises in his Chakras book[35] the purification of the related element through the use of shapes, colors and sounds→9.4.3. We can work directly with the elements also, for example by placing a small water fountain in our office, generating soothing lunar energy to balance our first and third *chakra* solar activity.

And if we want to get more support from above, Harish Johari proposes devotional practices towards a variety of higher beings associated with the *chakras*, among which are the famous female doorkeepers→9.4.3. All of this is useful only if we are prepared to also purify our attitude towards our dear desires, which mostly relates to balancing solar and lunar attitudes.

4.4.3. SOLAR & LUNAR DESIRES

The reader may have noticed that the desires of the first, third and fifth *chakras* can never be really fulfilled, while those of the second, fourth and sixth *chakras* can always be fulfilled. This is because the *chakras* with even numbers are dominated by the lunar energy, while those with uneven numbers are predominantly solar.

Remember how the solar energy is more into achieving something, while the lunar is more into experiencing←4.2.4? Logically, if we want to achieve something outside of us, such as security, status or understanding, we cannot control what happens. Thus we actually can never

[35] *'Chakras, Energy Centers of Transformation', by Harish Johari, Destiny Books 2000.*

really and durably get what we want, having to settle for less. The experiencing of something however, such as enjoyment, love and peace, fully depends on ourselves. In as far as we can control our own attitude, we can always get the experience that we seek. Still, both solar and lunar desires are natural and needed in the game of life.

The first *chakra* desire for security is predominantly solar as it seeks security outside of us. That also means that this desire must be largely fulfilled in the solar way, being practical and rational about it. Excessive lunar emotionality will not bring much and produces unnecessary stress which may be quite counterproductive. Yet a too solar approach may lead to workaholism, stress, greed and dishonesty, so still there must be a balance in solar and lunar. Thus also the more lunar relaxation of enjoyment in the second *chakra* will help to relax our obsession with survival in the first *chakra*.

The enjoyment of mind and the senses in the second *chakra* is principally lunar in nature, as it is found in the creativity of producing nice feelings. As we get high on them, our energy may become too lunar, leading to overindulgence and an inability to withstand unpleasant sensory input. Then we need some more solar discipline and the ability to ignore what is best ignored. Thus also the third *chakra* solar desire to be strong, in control and respected, may motivate us to overcome our dependency on sensual and mental gratification in the second *chakra*. Nobody likes the one who ate all the cake.

Pursuing the desire for social status in the third *chakra* is a largely solar matter, yet when the lunar energy is absent, the feelings of others will easily get hurt by our power struggles. As a result, whatever position we attain will be even under more pressure than usual. As a good king must love his subjects, opening the lunar fourth *chakra* will stop us from being heartless in our pursuit of status in the third *chakra*.

Love is obviously very much about feeling and thus the fourth *chakra* is lunar in nature. While love can never be approached too rationally, if we are too emotional about it, we cannot love in detached attachment. It leads to irrational jealousy, a tendency to capture the object of our love and an inability to function when it is absent. The solar understanding pursued in fifth *chakra* may then help us to see the beautiful reality of the impermanence of anything with form, helping us to live the true detached, unconditional nature of real love in the fourth *chakra*.

The search for understanding in fifth *chakra* is mostly solar, as it requires a logical approach with clarity in definitions and reasoning. When however it becomes too solar, it gets dry and intellectual, missing some understanding of the emotionality of things. As all understanding ultimately aims at increasing happiness, how its application will make people feel cannot be ignored. The development of inner peace associated with the lunar sixth *chakra* will allow us to be patient when applied understanding meets its limitations. It is not because we see how something can be achieved, that it can be achieved right now, like say world peace→4.10.3.

To find peace in the sixth *chakra* is predominantly a lunar activity of turning on the 'feeling' observer mode inside. The central task is to stop all that thinking, which is solar in nature. When we approach it as lunatics however, we become entangled in the fantasies of mind about all kinds of spiritual experiences. The neutral desirelessness of the seventh *chakra* allows us to stop all desire to achieve something when we try to meditate in 6th *chakra*.

Is it not wonderful how so much understanding can be brought about by analyzing the solar/lunar balance? The categories of problems discussed in this overview apply to the majority of the issues that people struggle with in life. So whenever we feel unsure about anything, we ask this question. Even in business I have used this knowledge for defining company strategy, solving team issues, creating marketing and developing products.

More important even is maintaining the balance between lunar and solar energy in ourselves. Then pursuing our desires will naturally balance both. The main way to rebalance is in creating a neutral energy, which is the practice of meditation←4.2.5, resting upon the practice of life.

4.5. Food

This is no cookbook and we can address the food issue in a zillion different ways. Anything can be balanced somehow. Having traveled over 30 times to India, I acquired quite a taste for Indian food, yet there is no intention to convert the reader to the same 'foodie religion'. Nevertheless, many of the traditional Indian recipes hide deep *Ayurvedic* understanding on how to balance our body chemistry. These principles can actually be applied to any food tradition.

Not all Indian food is balanced though, nor is it suitable in all places. The typical rather excessive use of salt compensates for lots of sweating in a hot climate. The emphasis on rice and coconut, especially in South India, equally rests upon their cooling properties. In North-India, more heating wheat largely replaces rice during the colder periods. Many Indian recipes are too spicy, as addiction to that taste has led to dosages that are unsuitable for tongues and stomachs that are not used to it. Good food is food that is adapted to us, as well as to the climate, the season, the time of the day and our activities.

When Harish Johari started traveling west, he rapidly began teaching people how to cook. He attributed many of our emotional issues to our imbalanced diet. Wherever he would be a guest, the deal was usually that he would take over the kitchen, much to every body's delight. He would never eat in a restaurant without first meeting the chef and usually preferred to fast rather than eating food along the way.

On a physical, mental and emotional level, we are what we eat. Food affects the *rasas*, *gunas* and *doshas* quite directly and many of its effects are rather long-term. As we grow older, our digestive system definitely needs a more refined approach. Especially if we want to spend more time in meditation, like on a retreat, the food we eat will be an essential factor contributing to our success. Special *sattvic* foods 'for meditation' will be discussed in the fasting on food chapter→4.7.1.

However, we cannot always live on a strictly balanced diet, as our digestive system would become overly sensitive. That means it is not a big problem if it anyhow gets challenged by less appropriate foods now and then, for example when traveling. Be conscious about food, not obsessed. We know what our digestion can take and what foods must be really avoided. I obviously totally recommend Harish Johari's cookbook[36], which contains lots of background information as well as so many great Indian vegetarian recipes.

In *Ayurvedic* cooking, the cook is an alchemist and the vibration of the cook is one of the most important ingredients of the food. The cook should be happy when cooking and food should be served cheerfully. Eating food made by a cook with a particularly low energy vibration can quite directly imbalance our bodymind. The vibrational quality of food already starts with the farmer. Large scale food manufacturing will produce lower quality food compared to small scale food production with a more spiritual attitude.

Cooking and eating are forms of worship of the bounty of divine nature. Offering a little of our food to the divine before eating is a typical practice.

We try to cook the most appropriate food for everyone. As not everyone needs the same, a typical Indian meal will offer plenty of optional sauces, chutneys,

[36] See 'Ayurvedic Healing Cuisine', by Harish Johari, Healing Arts Press 2000.

pickles and other additions, with which to fine-tune our own plate, not just for the taste, but also for its biochemical effect.

Harish Johari very much emphasized to cook without tasting. As every wine taster knows, the taste of one food will affect the taste of the next. Throughout the cooking, the taste of a dish will evolve. Tasting is thus not a way to cook tasty, balanced food.

The one who cooks without tasting, even preferably on an empty stomach, may develop more intuitive cooking. Whenever gathering ingredients for a dish or adding some spices to it, the neutral taste on the tongue allows to mentally pretaste the food, to intuitively dose and combine ingredients. I have been cooking without tasting for a few decades and all I can say is that people really seem to like my food.

4.5.1. DISTURBED DIGESTION

The main digestion disturbances are experienced as constipation, bloating, acid reflux, nausea and diarrhea, which may occur separately, but are often also related. According to *Ayurveda*, constipation is the most serious condition that can cause many physical and mental problems. Some call it the mother of all diseases. As incorrect ideas on the subject exist, I like to clarify that if people cannot pass stool on a daily basis, they are basically considered to be constipated.

Constipation causes stress and depletes energy, while stress and a lack of energy also aggravate constipation. It is a downward spiral. The one who understands this when faced with a serious constipation issue takes a holiday if possible or otherwise tries to maximally calm down using all means available. Nervous intestines are usually not a problem created by the intestines.

In any case of chronic constipation, one is advised to fundamentally deal with it. It should really stay away and not be reduced to some bearable condition, which I see all too often. As it relates to food, lifestyle, stress and movement, to truly get rid of constipation means to make some profound changes to our lifestyle and stick to them.

Lower back pains are most often caused by constipation, with many people not realizing that constipation is the underlying problem. If food does not move through our system sufficiently fast, it starts to truly rot, which produces many gases in the intestines. These create a bloated feeling and are very often also the cause of lower back pain, as blocked stool and gases push against the spine.

Sometimes constipation and diarrhea may alternate, the latter being an attempt of the body to treat the former by flushing out the system. It is not advisable at this time to use medication to stop the diarrhea, situation permitting.

Except for the last part of the intestines near the anus, stool is usually not the main blocking factor, gases are. Reducing gas production and improving gas elimination is a principal task when dealing with constipation, see below.

The main keys to treat constipation are to increase movement, to correct postures, to increase inner hydration, to facilitate easy passage, to reduce gas production and to calm down. How to deal with constipation is also somewhat personal, depending on many individual factors. Some tricks are provided in the chapter on home remedies, yet of course our daily meals are where to start.

4.5.2. EFFECTS OF FOOD

Effects of Tastes

The most immediate effect of food is through the six tastes: sweet, sour, salty, pungent, bitter and astringent. That last taste is maybe less known. It is found in many peels, pomegranates, red wine and many spices. Taste(RASA) obviously can be a major addiction, as each taste affects both the *gunas* and the *doshas*, and thus also our emotional energy, as shown in Table 14.

From this overview we can see that most strong tastes, such as we find them in spices, will make our energy more *rajasic*. Foods that thus strongly tickle our taste buds will stimulate an active, creative attitude and boost our confidence. On a meditation retreat however, where we mostly want the *sattvic* energy, better we get used to more subtle tastes.

TASTE	GUNA	DOSHA
Sweet	Sattva	Mucus
Sour	Rajas	Mucus & Bile
Salty	Rajas	Mucus & Bile
Pungent	Rajas-Tamas	Wind & Bile
Bitter	Rajas	Wind
Astringent	Rajas	Wind

Table 14 - Gunas and doshas stimulated by the taste of foods.

The sweet taste is very special as it will immediately produce a more *sattvic*, emotionally comforting feeling. It is why food offerings(PRASAD) used in rituals are most typically sweet. Sweets make us a little sweeter, if not taken in excess.

The *sattvic* power of the sweet taste explains why it is the most popular among people that are emotionally addicted to food. A related trick for chocolate addicts for example is to consume it only as hard candies, without allowing oneself to bite. Chocolate addicts usually can devour a lot of chocolate in just 10 minutes. When slowly melting in the mouth however, one chocolate candy can provide the desired taste for the same 10 minutes, with minimal chocolate consumption. Hence during digestion the *tamasic* effect on the liver and our confidence can be easily avoided. When overeating chocolate, the high produced by the taste will be followed by the low generated during digestion, which then may even lead to eating more chocolate.

In the *doshas* stimulated by specific tastes, we also see clear ways in which to subdue the other *doshas*. An example is in using bitter foods to reduce acid reflux caused by an aggravated bile *dosha*, while the bitter taste primarily stimulates the wind *dosha*. Honestly, one must study this overview in more detail and work with it in the kitchen, to effectively apply this understanding. All tastes also relate to particular effects during and after digestion.

In any case, the immediate effect of taste on both *gunas* and *doshas* is largely limited to the duration of the tasting, so not all that important.

Effects of Digestion - Doshas

Much more relevant is the effect of food during digestion(VIRYA), which can be felt for many hours after eating. If digestion is disturbed and we are eating several meals a day, that effect will be experienced quite permanently. These effects may also generally be correlated to certain tastes, but with many exceptions.

The effect of digestion on the *gunas* mostly depends on whether foods are heavy or light to digest, see below. The effect on the *doshas* depends primarily on how foods impact body temperature and moisture. Whether they produce an excess of gases during digestion is a separate issue, see below.

Foods are thus cooling or heating, and drying or hydrating. The *doshas* may be increased or decreased accordingly:

	BILE	MUCUS	WIND
TEMPERATURE	hot	cold	cold
MOISTURE	dry	moist	dry
INCREASE	He & D	C & Hy	C & D
DECREASE	C & Hy	He & D	He & Hy

Table 15 - Cooling (C), Heating (He), Drying (D) or Hydrating (Hy) effects of foods on the doshas.

This overview seems rather theoretical, yet it corresponds to effects that are usually quite well known. Many people are already taking them into account when adapting their food to the climate of the moment. Yet we can use that same knowledge to more deeply alter our body chemistry and mood.

If the weather is hot and dry, we mostly go for cooling and hydrating foods. When it is wet and cold, we need drying and heating foods. If the weather is cold but dry, we use heating and hydrating foods. And if the weather is hot and moist, like during the Indian monsoon, we need cooling and drying foods.

HEATING & DRYING	black pepper, walnuts, dried dates, chickpeas, lentils, onions...
COOLING & HYDRATING	butter, coconut, cucumber, limes, peaches, yoghurt, lychee, oranges, radishes, spinach, zucchini...
HEATING & HYDRATING	apples, almonds, beets, eggs, fish, ghee, kidney beans, peanuts, pistachios, sugar, sweet potatoes, wheat...
COOLING & DRYING	barley, berries, cauliflower, corn, pears, tamarind, vinegar...

Table 16 - Effects of foods during digestion.

So likewise, if we want to decrease mucus, like when having a running nose, we use foods that are heating and drying, as shown in Table 16. We thus increase the bile *dosha* and reduce the mucus *dosha*.

If we experience a bit of a hot temper or acid reflux, we use cooling and hydrating foods. They will reduce the bile *dosha* and increase the mucus *dosha*.

If we are nervous, which points to an imbalanced wind *dosha*, we use heating and hydrating foods. They will reduce the wind *dosha* and increase the bile and mucus *doshas*.

Last, cooling and drying foods are used to subdue the bile and mucus *doshas*, rather than to increase the wind *dosha*, which does not bring much advantage. These foods are mainly used to purify the blood, subdue skin issues and reduce depressive feelings.

Some foods are neutral in effect on the *doshas*, such as fresh cow milk, *mung* beans, tomatoes and turnips. Important to mention is that when foods are eaten cold or hot, this will also affect whether they are more heating or cooling. The effects on our *doshas* are also dependent on the *dosha* of a person, both the *dosha* one is born with, as the *dosha* which temporarily dominates←4.3.

As our aim here is not to treat real diseases or imbalances, which is the job of specialists, it is enough to learn only the basic principles. One cannot approach this in a very scientific way, as once more, there are too many data. The cook that uses the mental pretasting of foods explained before, will instinctively know what feels right. It also generally means that a meal should not be too drying, hydrating, cooling or heating. We can use each type in a mix of dishes and ingredients with complementary properties. That is what creating a balanced meal is first of all about.

Next to some book knowledge about

the effects of foods, we can thus definitely also use our intuition, as well as our own experience. Anyhow, the effects of food will be personal, so if we know coffee easily causes acid reflux in us, then we avoid it or add more milk for its cooling effect. It is about compensating a rather spicy dish by adding a cooling cucumber salad with a yoghurt dressing. Another example is in making Indian milk tea[(CHAI)], where ginger and black pepper usually compensate to some degree for the mucus producing milk.

Effects of Digestion - Gases

The biggest worry for the *yogi* when it comes to the *doshas* is when food produces lots of gases in the intestines. Not only are these a major cause of most digestion problems, they also increase nervousness. If we want to generate more peace in our lives and meditation, we cannot afford the wind *dosha* to become aggravated.

Many foods are quite well known by experience to produce lots of gases, such as onions, cabbages, lentils, pulses, beans, sprouts and leeks. We can avoid them when retreating in a rather warm climate for example, which is what many *sadhus* will do. In a colder climate however, these typical winter foods are needed. Below I will explain how they can be prepared with minimal gas production.

Most vegetables will produce lots of gases when eaten raw. Salads are thus best made with lettuce, cucumber, tomato, red beets, most fresh herbs, radish, etc., which are the main exceptions. Listen to the body for more details. A raw food diet is possible, yet should be light and very well balanced. Intensive breathing exercises will then be needed to convert the increased wind *dosha* to pure *prana*→8.4.

Effects of Digestion - Gunas

Whether food makes us feel heavy or light is also something which most people have some idea about, from own experience. And it is definitely not only about which foods we eat, yet also how they are prepared and consumed. Further on I provide some cooking and digestion guidelines that may be just as important as our food selection. Digestibility is largely personal and also very age dependent.

This effect is mostly produced by the stomach, depending on how much stomach acid is needed to process the food. The more digestive fire is needed, the more we will feel our energy go down. The heavier foods such as pulses will thus produce a more *tamasic* feeling. Some foods like rice contain lots of energy, but are rather easy to digest, so they will mostly produce a *rajasic* energy. Very light foods that hardly take any energy to digest, such as most fruits, allow the light of *sattva* to manifest.

Nevertheless, all these foods are needed by our system, depending largely on our activities. If we live quite active lives, we will need more heavy foods. In a sitting retreat however→5.6, we can survive on little food, which is easily digested. We will look more in detail what this means when discussing the digestive fire, the *gunas* of specific foods, as well as the methods of preparing and balancing.

In any case, if the *doshas* are disturbed as explained above, this may also produce either hyperactivity or laziness, *rajas* or *tamas* coming at the wrong time. Generating a *sattvic* feeling will then be more difficult, and all *sattvic* activities such as meditation will be disturbed by it.

Digestion in the stomach has the strongest immediate effect on the *gunas*, takes about two hours and will also very much affect the ease of digestion in the intestines. The intestines take at least half a day to process the food precooked by the stomach, while in many people it may take several days.

The longer the food stays in our system, the more it will putrefy, creating toxins that produce a more *tamasic* feeling. Easy passage is thus a major objective, which among others depends on the consistency of food. Low water consumption easily leads to constipation. Fibers should be sufficiently available as these non-digestible molecules stimulate intestine function. Vegetarians often absorb an excess of fibers, which makes their food heavier to digest and might aggravate already nervous intestines.

The freshness of foods has a major impact on the *gunas* through the intestinal flora. If the foods we eat still have lots of *prana*, then the main microbiological process of digestion in the intestines will be more of a fermentation. If the foods we eat are quite dead, putrefaction in the intestines will increase. As we naturally avoid eating rotten foods, we avoid foods that tend to rot inside our body. The effects are quite similar, even if more mild. Protein quality also very much determines whether putrefaction will increase our *tamasic* energy.

Effects after Digestion

The effect of foods after digestion(VIPAKA) depends on what happens when foods have been assimilated by the body. It largely relates to their nutritional value. As known in Western science, we need a balance between carbohydrates, fats, proteins, vitamins and minerals. Carbohydrates are generally *rajasic* in after-effect, while fats and proteins are more *tamasic*. Vitamins and minerals are more *sattvic* in the sense that when they are lacking, to feel peaceful will be very difficult. When used in excess as food supplements, they can also be *rajasic* or *tamasic*.

A major mineral is salt, which aids in predigesting foods while cooking and also plays a key role in cellular metabolism. The need depends on whether climate or work produce more perspiration, yet we all need some salt, whether added or naturally present in the selected foods.

In very general terms, we avoid the quite common overconsumption of rich proteins and fats in modern society, which will create a more *tamasic* energy. We also largely avoid carbohydrates that are so easily digestible that they will create fluctuations of *rajasic* energy, such as the insulin imbalances related to sugar consumption. Other carbohydrates, such as starch or molasses, provide the *rajasic* energy more evenly.

We make sure that the variety of foods we eat, including the wealth of herbs and spices that nature offers us, provide the nutritional basis from which to feel more *sattvic*, giving the body the more subtle nutrition that it needs. Long-term malnutrition, caused by lack of food or the consumption of low-quality junk foods, definitely negatively impacts people's mental, emotional and spiritual capabilities.

While we have thus discussed the most important food effects, there is quite a lot more to learn. Some foods have very specific effects on both *doshas* and *gunas*. Some are really incompatible with others, while healthy on their own. Some foods are good in winter, yet really imbalancing in summer, and vice versa.

The more we can learn the better, especially as we encounter seemingly food related imbalances through our observer mode, like when seeing negative thinking increase after eating. Cooking nevertheless must always remain an art rather than a science. We use our intuitive faculties, which are anyhow very naturally present in each of us when it comes to food, as the result of countless generations of experience.

Once we have developed our new cooking skills, healthy cooking does not need to take a lot of time. I can cook a tasty and healthy fresh meal in under 30 minutes. Too many people these days have kitchens without actual cooking equipment, except for a microwave oven. As food is the very essence of natural wealth, how can people sentence themselves to such poverty?

4.5.3. COOKING GUIDELINES

Choose Quality

Go for quality rather than quantity, preferably choosing naturally processed and organically grown foods. We let others cook whenever we feel particularly unhappy. We create meals that have all six tastes. This way we will not crave a missing taste after eating, which creates the unhealthy desire for in-between snacks. While junk foods often are limited to a few tastes, most real meals will have all five tastes except the astringent taste, which can most easily be added by using a variety of herbs and spices, such as basil, bay leaf, coriander, dill, fennel, marjoram, nutmeg, oregano, parsley, poppy seeds, rosemary, saffron and turmeric.

Digestive Fire

Cooking is a way of reducing the power needed by the digestive system in cooking our food inside. Whatever is hard to digest needs to be cooked well, even using a pressure cooker to prepare beans, pulses, etc. On the other hand, the more easily digestible foods should be cooked lightly, on a low flame, in order to keep the more *sattvic* energies intact.

Have at least one dish in each meal that is rather spicy, so that the digestive fire[(AGNI)] is sufficiently activated without being overly stimulated. The right spiciness is rather individual and cultural. Imbalances in the digestive fire can better be solved with some home remedies→4.6, rather than by cooking overly mild or extremely spicy foods. To avoid lack of digestive fire, we should never overload our stomach with too heavy foods.

Limiting cold foods in our meals is very important to cure weak digestive fire. Digestion processes will work better on foods eaten hot rather than cold. The digestive power of our stomach acid increases at higher temperatures, so that our digestion needs less acidity. Also much of the *sattvic* energy of cooked foods is lost when they cool down.

Fresh Foods

Fresh foods are a main way to reduce the *tamasic* energy and create a more *rajasic* or *sattvic* energy. We maximally avoid eating old, canned or frozen foods. The more a food is processed, the more dead energy it will provide. There is for example a huge difference between split pulses and whole pulses, which will still sprout when planted. Many cereals that are currently seen as quite healthy, such as muesli, are also quite dead.

Vegetarian Foods

As we want less *tamasic* energy in our lives, we need to rely more on vegetarian foods. Animal protein will putrefy more easily in the intestines, which can be directly experienced in the smells that we produce. Harish Johari used to say 'If you want to think and feel like a pig, eat it'.

Definitely foods from animals that have lived unhappy lives and died in extreme agony are emotionally toxic.

For some people not eating animals is a moral, ecological and emotional issue. That *dharma* aspect remains personal however, as it depends on availability like for the people living at high altitude in Tibet. Ecologically, avoiding animal foods clearly makes a whole lot of sense in terms of pollution and optimal use of the lands available for agriculture.

As for the moral and emotional issues, eating something anyhow means to kill it. Who can say how that carrot feels when chopped up and boiled alive? To believe that it does not matter, means not to understand how every being is alive with feeling just like us. Our most essential emotionally charged neurotransmitters are active even in single-cell organisms. 'Energy eating energy' is how nature works, yet for sure we can try to avoid unnecessary suffering.

Milk Products

Typical Indian vegetarians are lacto-vegetarians and a high variety of milk products are used in India as an important source of protein. Meanwhile in the West many people have become intolerant to cow milk, which is related to a large number of diseases. These problems are however mainly caused by the ultra-high temperature sterilization of milk, which is common in the West. It affects the milk proteins in a way that makes them very hard to digest. Because of its primary function to feed new digestive systems, unsterilized milk is easy to digest.

I have often demonstrated that lactose intolerant people can drink my *chai*, if made with raw or pasteurized milk. Consuming too much milk will produce an increase of the mucus *dosha*, so if that *dosha* becomes imbalanced, we better avoid milk. Obviously we are free to use milk or not and may certainly find sufficient proteins in a purely vegetarian diet.

Semi-Liquid Foods

Best we create meals that are sufficiently liquid, for easy passage through the system. Consumption of dry fried snacks is a major cause of blockages. While in the West soups are often consumed before the main meal, in the Indian way they are eaten along with other foods, to create proper consistency in what goes down. Exclusively turning to liquid foods is usually not a good idea, because it will too much extinguish the digestive fire.

Cold bread meals are a major cause of digestion issues in modern society and not just because bread can be quite constipating and gas producing. Bread meals are usually too dry to easily move through the system and these meals often are not spicy enough to sufficiently stimulate the acidity needed in the stomach. If we add some spicy soup to any bread meals, we probably will experience much better digestion overall. To always have some soup available at home is quite easy and often also an option when for example buying a sandwich along the road.

Intestinal Gases

Many foods are gas producing, namely onions, leeks, cabbages, pulses, lentils, as well as all heavy, greasy foods. We can try to avoid them altogether, but especially in colder climates they are needed, as they support our immunity.

Of everything I have learned from *Ayurveda*, I still consider this the most important one : proper use of *Asa Foetida* (HING) in cooking resolves many problems of gases in the intestines, as well as the related nervous problems, from general nervousness to actual nerve pains. It can be used with all gas-producing foods.

It gives a somewhat heavy, meaty taste to these foods, often well appreciated when non-vegetarians are served veggie foods. We can buy it in pure form, but then it is harder to use, because we need so little of it that dosage becomes difficult. More easy is to use a form which is diluted in some grain powder and even then for the average dish you don't need much. That form is readily available in an Indian grocery shop, since it is one of the most commonly used Indian spices.

For the average dish we only need a knife point of the diluted powder form. First heat some oil or clarified butter and add the *Asa Foetida* powder when hot. Stir in the particular gas producing foods and keep stirring while frying these foods for a few minutes. This way the herb can do its wonderful work. Only now we can add water as well as any additional foods that we like to have in this dish.

4.5.4. DIGESTION GUIDELINES

To avoid overeating is absolutely necessary in order not to create traffic jams in our system, which is a major cause of digestion problems. Harish Johari often declared that it is better to eat junk food than to overindulge in healthy food.

We have to eat consciously, especially assuring proper mastication, which very much improves digestibility because of the enzymes present in saliva. A good way not to overeat is to fill our plate with the amount of food needed and avoid second helpings mostly inspired by our taste buds. We also avoid in between snacks so that our intestines may empty and clean themselves properly in between meals.

Especially we avoid dry and fried snacks such as chips. If we need some snack, better we eat fruits. While fruits are generally helpful, avoid eating fresh fruits after dark, as they will be very gas producing then. Avoid drinking coffee or black tea within 30 minutes before or after meals.

Constipation rarely happens to people that move about a lot, even though it can still happen. Increasing movement in our lives on a daily basis may be essential. Especially walking helps by aiding gravity in making food stuffs move down. In case of transit issues, walk for at least 10 minutes after every meal, at an average pace.

However, in the one or two hours after meals one should never bend over. If we need to pick up something from the floor, we bend the knees instead. After food, any pressure on the belly should be maximally avoided, which also means most *Asana* practice is not allowed→7.2.2. Avoid wrong sitting postures that create such pressure - no slouching. Avoid tight fitting clothes or belts in the belly area. Often constipation also creates a cramped bladder, so we should pay special attention to use relaxation and gravity to urinate, rather than pressure.

Never stop the body when it naturally tries to expel gases through burping or passing wind. Better we are impolite to the people around, than to our own body.

Never sleep within 2 to 3 hours after food. Sleeping stops the digestion process, which will create a lot more gases. Stay upright after food, maximally keeping a hollow lower back.

One exception is if low digestive fire is an issue and after food the left, lunar nostril is dominant. Then it is advised to lie down on the left side for no more than 20 minutes after food to open the right, solar nostril→8.5.3, which aids the stomach fire. Usually less than 5 minutes will do the trick.

If for some reason we really need to lie down after food, we never lie on the right side. It will tilt the stomach the wrong way, the entry valve hanging upside down. Preferably we do not lie down for more than 20 minutes, so we do not fall asleep.

A very good yoga posture for digestion to be used after eating is the seated Thunderbolt Pose(VAJRASANA)→P11. Please also read the chapter on proper bowel movements→5.3.2.

4.6. A Few Home Remedies

Like the one on food, this could be quite an endless chapter. The following remedies mostly address common issues that affect our meditation practices quite directly. All of them have been used on myself and the patients in my healing practice, so what follows is based on experience. Many more home remedies are available in Harish Johari's very first book[37].

I have limited myself here to some simple tricks that are relatively mild in nature and thus can be used without much information. When an imbalance is present, if we hit it hard with some remedy, we may easily cause more imbalances. So mild remedies work best, applied over a longer period of time. The use of strong remedies should be monitored by a specialist.

If the underlying emotional issues discussed elsewhere in this book←4.1.6 are not addressed, using the related remedies may actually lead to a more enduring imbalance. They are very helpful in the process of restoring physical balance, nothing more.

4.6.1. DIGESTION ISSUES

Constipation & Gases

Grated raw carrots are a very good remedy. Take two average carrots daily, which can be made into a kind of salad easily by mixing in some yoghurt^(RAITA)^. It can both be combined with fruits to make a sweet dish, or with some other mushy vegetables in a salty dish or side dish.

Prunes and figs are generally a very good remedy. When using a dried form, they should be soaked in water a few hours before consuming them, or made into a stew.

Use the skin that forms on slowly boiling raw milk^(MALAI)^ : take two teaspoons with a dash of freshly ground black pepper each night before retiring.

Use *Sat Isabgol*, an Indian remedy made of flea seed husk, also known as psyllium husk: take one or two teaspoons in water or yoghurt before retiring. Do not overdose.

Some other regulating remedies found in Indian shops are *Chyawanprash and Triphala.* They may create some discomfort in the beginning, as they push out gases. Adapt the dosage if necessary to avoid putting too much stress on the digestive system.

---

[37] 'Dhanwantari' by Harish Johari, Rupa Publications India 2001.

A very useful spice mixture to take on the road in case we have to eat something quite imbalanced is called *Lavanbhaskar Churna*. It can be sprinkled on any dish to assist proper digestion.

In case the constipation problem includes hemorrhoids (piles), it becomes many times more serious. Consult my related page online[38].

Aside of all movement, a fast way to expel some airs is by eating or drinking something spicy. Another consists of lying down on the belly for a while, with a cushion underneath for some gentle extra pressure on the intestines. Keep slowly and gently moving position until some wind can be passed.

Acid reflux

Drinking several glasses of lukewarm water every day is a very good remedy.

Taking about 3 tablespoons daily of purified Aloe Vera juice is an effective natural treatment.

Low Digestive Fire & Chronic Cold

In any case of common cold, rinse the nose regularly with salt water(NETI) →4.8.2.

All following heating remedies can be used to treat chronic cold as well as to stimulate the digestive fire.

Mix 7 freshly grounded black pepper balls with a teaspoon of honey and a few drops of ghee. Eat this not-too-spicy mixture daily before breakfast.

Eat about 2 cups of grated red beets daily, which are very heating to our system. They can be mixed with some yoghurt, prepared as salty or sweet.

Put of few drops of mustard or black sesame oil in the navel before retiring.

Swallow 1 to 3 garlic cloves daily, as if taking a pill with some water. Used in this way, garlic will hardly create a smell on the breath and will very effectively heat the body.

Grate fresh ginger and press it to make ginger juice, using a filter to remove all fibers. Add in some honey to taste. Especially for chronic cold, take up to 3 tablespoons daily for no more than a week.

4.6.2. OTHER ISSUES

Nervousness

Make a 50/50 mixture of *Ashwaganda* root powder and a rather thick honey, producing the consistency of marzipan. If not too liquid, it can be stored without spoiling for about a fortnight. Eat 2 tablespoons daily for about 40 days to restore natural calmness and *ojas*.

38 See leela-yoga.org/healing_hemorrhoids_piles.html.

Keep water during the night in the moonlight and drink it in the morning, for at least 40 days. Moon water will even be more powerful when using a silver cup.

Regularly put almond, sesame or another oil on the entire body.

Wear a pearl necklace.

Joint Pains & Stiffness

Especially for painful knees while sitting in meditation, use the *Ayurvedic* medicine called *Mahayograj Guggul* – it is miraculous.

Regular use of anti-inflammatory spices may also be needed: turmeric, basil, cinnamon, ginger, black pepper, etc. – tip: these are all tasty *chai* spices.

Chronic Tiredness

Mix 7 freshly grounded black pepper balls with a teaspoon of honey and a few drops of ghee. Eat this not-too-spicy mixture daily in the morning, before breakfast.

Make a 50/50 mixture of *Ashwaganda* root powder and a rather thick honey, with the consistency of marzipan. If not too liquid, it can be stored without spoiling for about one week. Eat 2 tablespoons daily for about 40 days to restore natural stamina and *ojas*.

The combination of both these remedies is most effective.

Balancing the Doshas

Whenever some imbalance in the *doshas* manifests as a physical or mental/emotional problem, one can stop it by immediately changing the dominant nostril→8.5.3.

An uncomplicated way to directly change the *doshas* is to use some water and/or fresh ginger[39]. Excess in mucus can be easily reduced with some strong and hot ginger tea or by chewing about 1 cubic centimeter of fresh ginger, rinsed down with just a sip of water. Excess bile can be reduced by drinking some water, best without added ice or the effect might be reversed. Excess gases must be tackled with a subtle combination of heat and moisture. Use a milder, lukewarm ginger tea or by eating some fresh ginger, rinsed down with a full glass of water.

4.6.3. PSYCHOACTIVE SUBSTANCES

People commonly use these 'home remedies' to fix their mood or even stimulate special spiritual experiences. They are part of many cultures and have been quite popular in both ancient and

[39] Compared to other hot spices that might also work, fresh ginger has the particular advantage of not being too much drying, which is especially useful when the gases are imbalanced.

new spiritual circles, from coffee to *Ayahuasca*.

All foods and environmental input, as in colors, sounds, smells etc. have some influence on our psyche, changing our mood, affecting our thoughts. So-called psychoactive substances are simply more powerful in these effects than others, which also means we can more easily come to depend on them. Some may also have adverse health effects. Yet we are still free to use them or not, preferably while taking all consequences into account. Here we will look mostly at the impact on our spiritual practice.

Tea & Coffee

Black and green tea are less strong than coffee, while all increase *rajas*. They may help to some degree in concentration, removing *tamas*, yet when used in excess they destroy the ability to concentrate. They easily produce nervousness and when taken too late in the day, sleeping problems are the result.

Their effects are individual and habit dependent. I personally like one *chai* in the morning before starting to meditate, while two cups of *chai* are clearly not producing better meditation.

The main issue is with people taking too many cups of coffee in a day, which then seem surprised that they can no longer calm down their mind. Many modern energy drinks are even worse, especially when based on Taurine.

Nicotine

Nicotine is commonly used as a calming and concentrating agent, but smoking is obviously very harmful for health. In some people including myself, it creates a strong dependency in the body, while others may use it without getting too much hooked. In case of real addiction, quitting may produce extreme nervousness, so any attempt must be well prepared and supported by lots of relaxation. Something to avoid of course, what more to say?

Alcohol

Alcohol at first stimulates the third *chakra* and gives the Ego a boost, while later on people's energy descends to the first *chakra* level, bringing out their most primitive animal nature. It can be used in moderation and as medicine to treat colds and digestion issues.

However, getting really drunk is having a very powerful negative long-term effect, especially on the subconscious. It binds our energy to the lower *chakras* and whatever more subtle vibrations we have created in ourselves may easily be destroyed by it. It also reduces our natural defenses against negative spiritual influences, as in all cases where our soul loses control over the bodymind.

Getting rid of habitual anger or depression is quite impossible in case of regular abuse of alcohol. A real alcohol addiction is also physically very difficult and literally painful to overcome.

Cannabis

As Cannabis products are very much part of the *sadhu* culture, many people involved with spirituality follow their example. This is quite a complex subject, which I have discussed at length[40].

Basically, Cannabis strongly promotes the lunar energy, which means it will activate the mind and reduce the Ego, making people more creative and mellow. Its common use in the West, combined with all kinds of entertainment, stimulates attachment to second *chakra* pleasures.

To stimulate the heart *chakra* in *Bhakti Yoga* it is traditionally mostly used in foods or drinks, where the effect is milder over a longer period of time and does not carry the health risk included in smoking.

Cannabis cannot be used for real meditation except by advanced practitioners, who already have gained firm control over mind. In others it will make real meditation impossible. As it makes the mind more active, it is used by *sadhus* to exercise mind control, much like they may exercise detachment from sound in a crowded place.

The increased agitation of the mind allows us to more easily separate our awareness from it, the practice of 6th *chakra*. It may thus bring a clearer experience of the Self, which may be useful in contemplation. Yet the fake bliss created by Cannabis through the famous neurotransmitter *Anandamide* is not the bliss(ANANDA) of the Self, so we better figure out what we really want.

Dosage is a major issue and microdosing is advisable most of the time. Using Cannabis is generally not suitable during the day, when we need the solar energy and usually cannot afford to be lunar, undisciplined, incompetent or lazy. Cannabis may certainly amplify those 9 impediments of mind←3.3. The more Cannabis is part of our lives, the more we will need to be otherwise disciplined.

To believe that one should not practice while under the influence of Cannabis or that it will facilitate the practice, are thus both wrong ideas. Watch out for too much fantasizing, as it creates wrong understanding←3.3.7, especially about our own spirituality. On the level of the body, it is fortunately hardly addictive, so to do some fasting is quite easy if the habit becomes excessive.

40 See 'Is there a Spiritual Use of Marijuana ?' on youtube.com/youyoga.

Cannabis should definitely be avoided by people that have excessive anxiety, as it may seriously increase paranoia. Cannabidiol or CBD oil on the contrary may be helpful to relax and without creating any high.

Psychedelics

A variety of psychedelics like LSD, mushrooms or *Ayahuasca* have been widely used to produce special spiritual experiences. They might create a rather *rajasic* state of *Samadhi*→13.2.6, which is not the real *yogic Samadhi*.

As psychedelics bring us more in contact with the subconscious and the spiritual world, something can be learned and maybe some subconscious issue can be resolved. It may profoundly demonstrate the relativity of words and opinions, which may produce a rather naked view of our dear Ego. Yet without proper preparation and support, it can produce serious mental issues.

Traditionally the use of psychedelics for spiritual growth has always been protected by shamans, especially to avoid negative input from the spiritual dimensions. Having treated quite many people after their wrong use of psychedelics, my personal opinion is that without support of a real shaman, of which there are few, it is best avoided. In a more subtle way, it may negatively affect our ability to really meditate for a long period of time.

In youth I experimented quite a lot, yet after my first real *Samadhi* experience ←Story27 I lost all interest in psychedelics. Neither the actual experience of *yogic Samadhi* nor its after-effects on our personality can be compared to the use of psychedelics.

4.7. Fasting

Every second of life gives us the opportunity to fast(VRAT) from something. Meditation means fasting from thought. *Asana* practice in essence means to fast from movement→7.2.2. The main breathing practice is to fast from breath→8.6. So fasting is definitely not limited to food fasting. Some *sadhus* will fast from moving by always staying in the same location and others will fast from attachment to any place, by not sleeping more than one night in the same place.

Fasting from food does not mean that food is bad and neither are we fasting from thought because thinking is bad. Whatever we feel is too much present in our lives, we can fast from it for a while, whether it is chocolate, talk, social media, chairs or *chai*.

First and foremost, we fast because we want to gain more control over our attachments, which will also increase our confidence. Second, this practice will bring us many new insights into ourselves and our attachments. Third, fasting is also a purification, a resetting of our system. The one who adopts regular fasting will never have a boring moment in life, so fasting is also a kind of spiritual entertainment.

It is generally advisable to start with simple, small fasts before doing any serious long-term fasts. We do not want to mess with our self-confidence by being overly confident. Even not eating for only one day might be quite a challenge for some. We will discuss here the 3 most typical *yogic* fasts from food, speech and sleep. These will provide general insights that can be applied to any kind of fasting.

4.7.1. FOOD FASTING

Fasting can be used to lose weight, but only if after the fast new eating and living habits are durably implemented. The first *yogic* reason to fast is to gain control over the desire to eat. The desire for taste is the first aspect to tackle, even if only skipping a meal or ignoring the idea of some snack. The longer we fast, the more we will go against the much more fundamental urge of the body to get some food inside. And since the body's protest will be mostly communicated through the mind, food fasting also teaches us mind control. As identification with the body is the primary attachment of the Ego, the practice of fasting helps us to let go of ourselves. For anyone having problems with enduring pain while sitting in meditation→7.6.5, fasting is a good way to learn how to ignore the body.

Second, food fasting is a means to boost our connection to the cosmic intellect. When after a few days of fasting the mind is no longer so much influenced by the digestion process, it works so much better. We will feel calm and focused, allowing us to reach much deeper in meditation, as well as to really get what the scriptures are saying. Freed of the many 'highs & lows" produced in our mind and mood by a variety of foods, awareness of the Self becomes so much easier.

Third, we can use food fasting to purify the body and reset the bodymind. By eliminating toxins, general health & mental wellbeing will improve. Food fasting can definitely be a great way to get out of some lengthy emotional cramp. The elimination of waste products and toxins will gradually remove *tamas* from our energy field, and with it also sadness, fear and depression may be released. After a few days of not eating, also the *rajas*-based anger will literally run out of fuel.

Food fasts can be used to treat some yet not all more serious physical conditions related to the digestive system.

Purification of the digestive system mainly consists of the elimination of rotting waste products stuck in between the many folds of the intestines. In its effort to find food, the body will clean out every nook and cranny, much like when spring cleaning a house. As food in the intestines gets scarcer, the body will also start using the energy stored in the body, mostly in the form of fats. As fats are often a storehouse of toxins, the body will be forced to truly eliminate them. That process may however temporarily produce unpleasant side effects such as headaches.

Yogis may also fast from food and water, but that is a highly advanced practice, with only some really transcended people being able to stop drinking for more than a few days. It is very unhealthy, only meant for achieving a higher state of consciousness through advanced control over body, mind and Ego. Many other *yogic* practices exist that are unhealthy, such as standing on one leg for a year or something. These people no longer care about damaging their body, having only the spiritual end goal in sight. The risk of the Ego attaching to such hard practices is nevertheless not negligible→7.1.

According to *Ayurveda*, fasting from food and water for more than 4 days is considered to produce irreparable damage and might even be life threatening in some conditions. Some *yogis* are known to endlessly fast from everything, yet these are not normal people. They magically nourish their body with pure *prana*. For other people, it is advisable to consume decent amounts of water while fasting, especially to assure the proper elimination of toxins.

Duration of a Fast

Mucus dominated people will the most slowly move through the purification phases associated with food fasting and can more easily fast for long periods of time. Wind dominated individuals, who usually have not stored much food in their body, will move forward much faster. Bile dominated bodies are somewhere in between. It means that the duration of a food fast must be limited according to the body type. The timing given below uses averages for a full food fast, while we will also look into fasting on a particular food, which works very differently.

Fasting one day every week is a practice that was very much advocated by Harish Johari. It is definitely advisable to start the fasting game here, so that we can gradually learn how to handle fasting and so that our digestive system is already quite clean when starting the longer fasts.

For most elderly people, fasting longer than 24 hours is not a good idea, since their ability to regenerate tissue is much more limited. Beginners may fast from sunrise to sunset, preferably eating something really light in the evening. Best we choose a day in which we are quite free from work and in some spiritual fasts there will be particular days of the week that are the most suitable.

The first two days of a longer fast are actually the most difficult and can be rather unpleasant. The stomach will gradually shrink to a much smaller size, creating cramps in the belly. We may experience all kinds of stress signals from the body, such as shortness of breath, sudden heat rushes, dizziness, heart palpitations and a lot more.

The main challenge will be emotional in nature, with bursts of panic, anger or sadness and depression requiring to be ignored. We may also experience that we cannot stop thinking about food and our fast, which we should. Serious headaches may also develop as toxins are recirculated before being eliminated. This is where we will benefit from doing many one-day fasts in preparation.

During the third and fourth days the body becomes more calm, the feeling of hunger will go and we may experience increasing clarity of mind. To get to the point where our fast becomes a basis for enhanced spiritual understanding, to fast only for 2 days is thus somewhat of a waste. It may not bring us what we want since there may be too much disturbance from the body.

As we move beyond resistance to the fast, we easily become wiser and might even start having visions that profoundly change our perception. It depends on the person, but many may have the experiences often sought in the spiritual use of psychedelics←4.6, yet in a much more refined, calm and useful way.

4 to 7 days of fasting is most advisable for spending a spiritual holiday in retreat→5.6. Most of that time we will truly benefit from the spiritual exercise, before profound weakness becomes more of an issue, depending on body type.

That is definitely the case when a fast is taken to the typical 40 days observed in real serious food fasting. It may decrease will power and overall presence, producing delusions and maybe also severe emotional states. Such advanced practices are for advanced practitioners, who have the control over the bodymind needed to still make it into a positive experience. Fasting longer than 40 days produces an increased risk of irreparable damage, again depending on body type.

Coming Out of a Fast

Whenever planning a food fast, we should consider the time needed to come out of it. After a real food fast, our digestive system will be sensitive like that of a baby. Suddenly starting to eat normally again should be totally avoided, as it may create serious digestive imbalances. We should first restart our system with lesser amounts of easily digestible foods and gradually build up to a more normal diet.

Generally speaking, as much time as we have fasted should be used for coming out of a fast. A seven day fast should be followed by seven days of gradually moving towards our usual diet. The foods to use for coming out are the same ones described below for fasting on food.

Some people will come to resist putting food in their mouth, especially after a really long fast. It means they have too much attached to the light feeling of not digesting anything and dislike the heaviness digestion brings. Still the body needs food, so we then have to force ourselves to start eating normally again. Our taste in food may anyhow have changed quite fundamentally.

Related Activities

While it might not matter for a one-day fast, we definitely need a holiday for longer fasts. Serious physical and mental activities should be avoided, as they need a continued supply of food. If we cannot avoid working altogether, we might be better off fasting on a particular kind of food, see below. For the same reason, a food fast largely includes fasting from sex, which consumes lots of vital energy. And equally because of energy consumption, full food fasts are not advisable when it is cold – spring and summer being most suitable.

Excessive sleep should be avoided and many make this mistake as a way of trying to ignore the hunger. On the contrary, our sleeping schedule should be quite rigid. Use of intoxicants likewise must be strictly avoided, as the effects on a body that is not digesting are quite unpredictable and potentially destabilizing. The way to take our mind of the feeling of hunger is through the uplifting activities that we can engage in.

Definitely, we should not allow ourselves to keep thinking about food while fasting. During our nine-day retreats with Harish Johari, most of us would fast for at least one day. On that day he would ask us to cook our most favorite food for the others. That would teach us not to get involved with the desire to eat.

For the rest we are free to make this more or less into a retreat of a kind, fasting also from the usual social interaction and concentrating more on spiritual activities, including artistic expression, study of scripture, chanting, meditation, etc. *Asana* practice should be reduced to simple effortless stretching during longer fasts.

It is very nice to fast in nature and if we

take enough water, we can stay somewhere in nature for days without needing anything else. Most of my longer food fasts happened in the caves of the Dordogne area in France.

Fasting on Foods

We can fast on particular foods, usually consumed in smaller amounts, if our duties simply do not allow a full fast. Some foods may also produce a specific kind of purification. All traditions have developed many such practices of which the effects are well known.

Many innovative ideas also regularly emerge in spiritual circles, based on some new information on nutritional value, purifying effects or the influence on our neurotransmitters. Many of these often rather commercial hypes disappear as quickly as they appear, as practice may show a different result from theory.

In any case, foods to fast upon should be easily digestible, no French fries. These are also the typical 'meditation foods', used for example during a spiritual retreat.

The first way to ingest a little more energy during fasting is by adding something to the water we drink. In the *vedic* tradition it is very common to fast on slightly honeyed water, maybe with some added lemon juice. A little more nutritious is to mix some yoghurt in the water. Sometimes one adds some cumin, black pepper, *Hing*←4.5.3, black salt(KALANIMAK), fried in a teaspoon of clarified butter(GHEE), to the yoghurt drink, to aid digestion. That is actually also one of the best drinks with which to come out of a full fast.

I know a *sadhu* named Milk Baba, who fasted for 3 decades on milk, fresh from the cow only. I have known another named Indrajit Puri that fasted on potatoes and yet another who only swallowed 7 black pepper balls a day for years. I do not remember his name, but he had lots of energy. More typical is to fast on juicy fruits or on soup made with easily digestible vegetables such as pumpkin, zucchini, carrot or peeled tomato. Small pancakes made of buckwheat flour are also very easy to digest.

Red beets are particularly heating in colder climates, both in soup as grated raw. For many years I did a spring fast on about 2 cups daily of grated red beets, which really gives a lot of energy and is very purifying for the blood. Another fast I often did is on the pepper-honey-ghee mixture described in the home remedies←4.6, taken 3 times daily.

The longer we fast on some food, the more we need to ensure that the nutritional value and the effect on the *doshas* are not too one-sided. A typical fasting food is the famous Indian *Khichari*, a mix of rice and lentils or pulses, maybe with some added easily digestible veggies.

The freshness of these foods is particularly important, so if we want to fast on porridge, the oats should be flaked on a daily basis, instead of having been stored dead for many months. Fasting on one food for a while brings calmness to the digestive system, as it becomes particularly geared in terms of enzymes and flora towards digesting that food. Yet it better be wholesome enough.

4.7.2. SPEECH FASTING

Speech fasting(MAUNA) is quite popular among *sadhus* and during spiritual retreats. It fits very well in the process of going inside and be less involved outside. Speech fasts are great teachers on all levels of spiritual growth.

Householders can also perform speech fasts, but usually their work requires some communication with others, so they will be more limited to the holidays. Generally speaking, there is no limit to the amount of time that we can fast from speech. Some renunciates do this practice for years, which is a rather extreme choice in terms of relationships.

It does not just mean that we stop speaking. It means we stop all communication. Some people that are speech fasting give people slips of paper to read all the time, which is useless. Written messages can be used in longer speech fasts, if anyhow we need to communicate some unavoidable decisions to others, but it should be limited to that purpose. We should obviously not allow ourselves to post messages on social media. Speech fasting means we stop interacting with others, as also a laugh, a shrug, a nod, a hug or even just a look are means of communication. It usually does not fit well within a teaching role, yet some famous teachers are known for teaching their students very well without uttering a single word.

The first thing we learn is the uselessness of all that usual talk. When normally we are involved with others and they are speaking, we are already mentally preparing our own speeches and responses in advance. When speech fasting that is not useful, which means we start listening in a different way. It may teach us to more seriously look at what other people are saying, what really is their point of view and why.

It will mostly demonstrate that a lot of talk is not needed. We will very clearly see how people's Egos tend to continuously air their opinions and experiences, mostly as a way to manage their public image and gain more self-confidence and self-love. When we stop thus engaging, we have to look inside for a positive self-image.

Since our usual speech generates

sounds that most deeply vibrate in our body, speech fasting is also advised in *Kundalini Yoga*, where the silence will purify many *nadis*.

A main result once the speech fast ends is that we speak less and try to be more precise and purposeful in what we say. A lot of speaking is just nervousness trying to find a way out. Since we do not allow ourselves to speak during the fast, we will develop other ways to manage the emotional, subconscious undercurrents that fuel our thoughts and speech.

When speech fasting somewhat longer, we will naturally spend more time in solitude. It is no requirement, as it just naturally happens. What is the use to stay if we are not engaged with others? The group dynamics that may be really entertaining to observe in the beginning, become quite boring to have to listen to. Yet once we then isolate more, we may still be talking to ourselves all the time inside. Speech fasting ultimately means to stop thinking.

One should not retreat from public life too much in the beginning, otherwise it is not very different from just being at home with no-one to talk to. We have to stop thinking about talking to others and that will be learned much faster when we are around other people, at least part of the day. Only when that part of our inner dialogue disappears, we are ready to continue on our own, at least only thinking thoughts to ourselves about ourselves, nothing to prove to anyone else but ourselves. It is a powerful path towards truth.

Speech fasting should never happen from a negative attitude, as a kind of protest. If faced with untruth, we must keep speaking our truth, so it is then not the right time to fast from speech.

Since all this is not so easy and may be perceived as rather boring by the mind, there may be a tendency to sleep more than usual. Just like in food fasting, this should be strictly avoided. If we sleep too much and at the wrong time, then we will mostly be dreaming and continue our talking to others there.

Reading scriptures may be allowed, yet it should be limited to a particular moment of the day, since we want to largely move away from the world of words. Journaling and other writing normally have no part in speech fasting, even though it can be a good combination in my experience. Some schools will allow a short daily talk with the teacher, so that some questions may be answered and the exchange might also motivate us to continue, as doubts naturally develop.

Mantra recitation←4.8.6 is a good aid in passing the time and while it is also a form of inner speech, it is empty of Ego stories. It blocks the thought trains and the soothing sound energies will help to generate pure silence. All more energetic techniques for relaxation and meditation, such as breathwork, may be put to good use.

Our profound insight into the superficial nature of most talk is then also applied inside and we rest more and more in the silence of the Self. It will bring us plenty of experience with the sound of silence, which we will learn to generate at will→11.3.1. We will discuss the technique of stopping the inner dialogue more deeply in the chapter on meditation objects→10.5.2.

As we thus listen to our thoughts without talking to them, we gain great insight into their subconscious origins. Our programming will be revealed as never before, allowing for more conscious deprogramming. The more we advance, the more our thoughts will appear as pure intuition originating with the cosmic intellect. The work of artists and poets may greatly benefit from it.

To come out of a longer speech fast may not be easy. The vocal cords may need some 'lubrication' with *cardamom* for example, but the main issue is that we have trained ourselves so much not to speak that our speech may be a little blocked. When speech fasting, obviously others may try to trick us into talking, see if they can break our practice. Thus we become really good at not responding. It may feel so very peaceful not to have to communicate and we might get too much attached to not needing to explain ourselves. So sometimes when people come out of a long speech fast, they have to be pushed into talking again.

For those still on the path, life has to continue at some point, and so does speech. The path of going inside is only completed in the coming out←3.5. As they are now purified, our words will also make a lot more sense. And our ability to give real silence a place within our daily schedule will be greatly enhanced.

4.7.3. SLEEP FASTING

Sleep fasts are very much part of *yogic* practice, but should be handled carefully. It is not allowed before adulthood and older people may need to be prudent as well.

The official record by Randy Gardner stands since 1964 at 11 days and 25 minutes, yet the Guinness World Record book no longer contains that information. The organization wants to avoid inspiring people to mentally hurt themselves. In many contestants too long sleep fasting brought decades of insomnia and mental imbalances such as psychosis and hallucinations. Some of these people literally have spent the remainder of their lives in a mental hospital. A ground rule is that whenever a strong lasting pain develops, the sleep fast should be broken.

Partying all night and going to sleep

when the sun rises is not considered a sleep fast. One should stay awake until the following evening to get the real benefits. Most practice is limited to that, while more advanced practitioners may fast for 2 nights, thus including 3 days. More than that is not advised.

Coffee, black tea and other stimulants should not be used to artificially prolong our sleep fast, which is one of the main errors made by people trying to set a new record.

Going to sleep is a very strange thing. Every day we are continuously busy with all these things that we think are very important. Still at the end of the day, we say bye-bye to everybody and go to sleep. We completely forget everything that seemed so extremely relevant. Even if we just fell in love with somebody and it is such a massive thing that we cannot stop thinking about it all day, we forget all of it when falling asleep. That person and that love might as well not exist.

Our body needs sleep, but mostly our mind and Ego need it. Without this daily reset we will literally go mad. That fact alone is proof of the huge advantage of people who can also stop thinking without sleeping. While sleeping thus keeps us sane, meditation may expand our sanity to the next level.

As sleepless time goes by, the body will experience more *tamasic* and more *rajasic* episodes. The trick is to rest during the *rajasic* episodes. When the body feels very tired, moving reactivates the *rajasic* energy. Sitting up all night may be physically difficult, so we lie down now and then, but only when the body least demands it.

Mind will become more erratic and often our train of thoughts will derail. However, we will also experience periods of absolute clarity and pure intuition, yet hard to verbalize. Rationality will somewhat disappear, even when handling menial tasks. As a result, the subconscious will be more free to bring out what it wants to bring out.

This is definitely not the time to deal with our problems, except in learning to observe them and let them go. The one who needs to sleep the most is the poor Ego, with all of its stressful subconscious blockages, fears and urges. So if sleep is prevented, we will have to drop the Ego. Instead of spending all night becoming more and more serious, we need to lighten up.

Sleep fasting is most often done in a group for that very reason. We keep each other awake and light, telling jokes and stories, maybe sitting around a fire. Harish Johari was so good at that, I cannot explain. Who could sleep when he was talking and making fun of us? Since he was only sleeping one to two hours on any day, being around him anyhow meant sleeping much less.

Singing is also a fantastic way for passing the time, yet it should not be too monotonous and repetitive, lest we sing ourselves to sleep. Sleep fasting is often included in Hindu festivals such as *Shivratri*, people spending all night in the temple together, singing most of the time.

Sleep fasting is traditionally considered a great cleansing of the brain, which has been confirmed by modern science. As the brain becomes tired it overheats and in order to cool it down, the body will replace part of the cerebrospinal fluid. When we experience a lot of heat in the head during a sleep fast, we should thus be open to relax into the experience of a wonderful cooling effect afterwards. In a similar way, also the nerves and more subtle energy channels are purified.

Sleep fasts very much belong to the practitioners of *Samadhi*, even if we better try to attain *Samadhi* after a good night's sleep. The basic challenge in letting *Samadhi* happen is when the mind becomes so *sattvic* and peaceful that it finally becomes *tamasic* and stops, falls asleep, and we are still awake. Will we also go or will we stay? It takes practice and willpower to stay alert, awake. Especially if we experience falling asleep during meditation, sleep fasting is advised. We need to get that *tamas* under control.

When coming out of a sleep fast, we have to watch our sleep schedule for a while. Regularity may be adversely affected, which must be absolutely avoided. Sleep is a great gift of nature that must be honored. Harish Johari only slept 1 to 2 hours daily, but that is only possible and advisable when there is not so much Ego left, nobody needing a break.

4.8. Activities

For most people, our *karma* and *dharma*, doing our natural jobs, already takes a major part of the day. And we naturally spend some time on the variety of desires originating in all *chakras*←4.4.1. Yet, as that 6th *chakra* desire for spiritual growth increases, there are many supportive activities that we can engage in, besides actual meditation.

All such activities keep us closer to the Self and thus support our meditation, which for most people will be limited to half an hour up to two hours a day→5.1.2. In spending the rest of the time, we can maximally retain Self-awareness while being engaged in our jobs and social interactions, as discussed throughout this book. The subject here is thus more about what to do in our free time, besides meditation.

Uplifting activities must be balanced

with the restraints that we will discuss in the next chapter. Yet too often when we think about improving ourselves, we concentrate on the activities that we feel we should stop. And while that may be well needed, that is not where our overall emphasis should lie.

The activities that tend to bring our energy down in the long run originate in desires to get a quick fix for our unpleasant emotions. If we first focus on producing more positive feelings, it will make us feel better and thus reduce the desire for those less helpful activities. The more we stay in tune with the truth and the feeling of the Self, the more we will be able to let go of those actions that are anyhow less and less fulfilling.

As discussed before, our spiritual evolution can be seen as our *karmic* evolution←3.6.1. As *karma* means action, it ultimately stands for the evolution in what we actually do. Thoughts and feelings centered in love, peace and bliss are obviously part of it, but if these do not lead to loving, peaceful and blissful activities, it all remains rather non-committal. As these uplifting activities will support our meditation, the effects of that meditation will also support our spiritual activities. It is here that we come full-circle and may lead a more and more connected, fulfilling life.

In *Ashtanga Yoga*, five such activities 'to keep alive'(NIYAMAS) are defined, which are also the five first activities discussed in this chapter. Yet *yogic* scriptures also suggest many other auspicious activities, of which I have included a more personal selection.

One often named activity is fasting, which I did not add here as it has its own chapter←4.7. Yoga postures→7, breathing exercises→8 and the purification of the senses→9 are discussed in other chapters as well, even though they also represent beneficial free time activities. However, they are so important that in *Ashtanga Yoga* they are not optional, but separate and to some degree necessary limbs of the meditation process.

4.8.1. CONTENTMENT

I have always thought it a really good joke that contentment(SANTOSHA) is named by Patanjali[41] as one of the main uplifting activities we should spend our free time on. It is somewhat strange to call this an activity, as contentment seems to be more of a feeling. Does not 'to be contented' simply mean 'to be happy'? Yet it is maybe the greatest wisdom that is hidden here. To be happy is an action, an activity. It is something we are totally free to do. And thus it is also the choice for happiness that we have discussed before←4.1.3, made

[41] Yoga Sutras of Patanjali, verse 2.42.

again and again in every second, which makes it into an activity.

Contentment means the continued effortless effort to smile and can be combined with any other activity. It rests upon emotional balance and very much involves the science of the 9 emotional essences, but it is more basic.

Narvada Puri→Story28 taught me that 'Contentment is Self-sufficiency', which has a double meaning. It means that the Self is sufficient for us to generate that smile. And it also signifies how that smile makes us self-sufficient in the sense of not needing anything or anyone else. Like the Buddha, we do not need a reason to smile, while reasons belong to the things that come and go in our lives. That which is always present in our presence not only deserves that smile, it is that smile. We know that we know, so we know how to smile.

It is not so easy sometimes of course. Yet most of the time it should also not be too difficult, meaning it can be 'done', putting in just a little effort.

For people who find it really difficult, the related practice of gratitude can be helpful. When it feels too hard to stay happy, it means that the more unpleasant things in life dominate our perception. Yet we all have so much to be thankful for. Like in the news media, controversial,

Story 28 *I Have a Mantra for You!*

Once upon a time, a few years after Harish Johari left his body, I met Narvada Puri Mataji at the Santoshpuri Ashram near Haridwar. This lady from Germany lived as a sadhu in India for decades[42] and was the first teacher with whom I connected after Dada. She most importantly guided me through a number of solitary retreats with Gayatri. She was a mother to all, Bhakti, Karma, Jnana and Ashtanga Yogi all in one, with a humble sense of humor and tons of dedication. Once at home I dreamed asking her for a mantra, dismissing it as an Ego game upon waking. Few months later, upon arriving at the ashram, the first thing she said was 'Oh hi Peter, I have a mantra for you'. She is my Gayatri Mantra Guru and I can still taste the feeling of singing this beauty for hours together with her, my luggage still just stacked beside me. She is no longer in the body, but her 3 children are now passing on the teachings, as well as those of their father of course, a remarkable Indian sadhu→Story35.

[42] See 'Tears of Bliss, a Guru-Disciple Mystery' by Narvada Puri, Santoshpuri Ashram 2009.

negative stories tend to be more popular in our mind. Thus we make the effort to focus more on the positive, in expressing gratitude.

Even if our life feels more difficult than on average, we are still breathing. Our *prana* means we embody the great gift of life. And as life means growth, we have the eternal gift of growing, our problems merely pointing in the opposite direction. So even for those we can be grateful←3.6.2, as long as we understand that this is again an action. It is a repeated activity of being aware of the miracle of life and feeling that totally deserved gratitude.

As not everyone easily finds the courage to smile, gratitude is traditionally practiced by groups in all kinds of feasts and festivals. We can help each other there, in that practice of smiling for so many good reasons, followed by smiling without reason. Nevertheless, the celebration of the sunrise or a new season also has other functions that relate more to adapting to the natural rhythms discussed further on→5.2.

The practice of contentment is supported by the attitude of equanimity, dropping the game of like and dislike. Contentment means the direct practice of the end objective of yoga, to be happy independent of what happens. And as practice makes perfect, while it may be too hard at first to be contented all the time, slowly it becomes more natural, less forced. Yet it still remains a choice, saying no to unhappiness and smiling our sweetest smile, just because we can. It is clear that this is not about smiling on the outside, while feeling unhappy on the inside.

As discussed before, whatever other action we then undertake from the happy feeling which we created and maintain, will be more successful as well←4.1.3. We definitely have to choose that little smile at the beginning of every meditation session, which is part of the intention phase→6.3.

4.8.2. PURIFICATION

Purification of the bodymind is all over this book, so it is a very broad subject. The purification(SHAUCHA) meant here is mostly of the physical body. The original objective of purifying the body according to Patanjali[43], is to keep the energy clean, so that pure *sattva* stands a chance. Impurities in the physical body send stress signals to the mind that reflect in more unpleasant emotions coming to the *pranic* body, which also activate the desires of the lower *chakras*. That way also our more sensitive issues in the subconscious are easily triggered.

As an environmental engineer, I have studied a lot of research on the effects of

[43] Yoga Sutras of Patanjali, verse 2.41.

pesticides on animals. While most scientific conclusions were based on mortality and physical abnormalities, these reports would very often contain notes on depressive and/or aggressive behavior at the lower dosages. It means many physically toxic chemicals are already emotionally toxic at low concentrations. This just to say that we cannot underestimate the effects of the body on the mind and on what we are trying to achieve on the *yogic* path.

Practicing purity these days thus involves how we keep harmful chemicals out of our system. However, it should also concern the production of harmful chemicals inside the body, especially during digestion. So purity involves the subjects of food←4.5 and food fasting←4.7.1 that we already discussed. It requires regular movement to improve circulation and elimination, including bowel movements. Yet it also starts with basic body hygiene.

An example by excellence is when the teeth are not properly kept clean. Decaying food particles will create a bad taste in the mouth, thus continuously sending distress signals to body and mind. The disturbed sensory input to the tastebuds will trigger electro-biochemical signals that are transferred to the brain and the entire body. This continuous murmur of stress signals will affect our sense of calmness and well-being, reduce our ability to concentrate or relax. Needless to say, healthy teeth are essential for general well-being, as underlying teeth issues may easily undermine our immune system and support inflammations all over the body.

Purity is also required to some degree in our house and meditation environment, for exactly the same reasons. So we keep our body, house and mouth clean and pleasing. And if we want to train ourselves in ignoring bad smells, sights and sounds, we do not need to create those at home, as there are plenty of places in the world to go to for that practice.

Purification may include avoiding dirty words. Every word creates an image in the mind, which in turn will also emotionally affect us. To some degree, saying 'sh*t' creates the smell of it in the mind of whoever hears it. Some people seem unable to stop themselves from using bad language in basically every sentence they speak. Some cultures and subcultures have become so used to it that they no longer seem affected by it, yet they are.

Our Daily Bath

Honestly, many Westerners traveling in Asia are nicknamed 'hippies' by the locals mostly on the basis of their body odor. The habit of showering at least daily is maybe typically Asian and related to hot weather and dust. The truth about the West is that as a supposedly highly civilized culture we have no clear opinion on the subject of bathing. Until the 1800s our culture was actualy quite against it.

Still today many Western aspirant *yogis* do not have the habit of daily bathing and there are some theories about the 'naturalness' of it. Yet when we look around in nature, we see most animals quite excessively cleaning themselves every day, even flies.

We do not only sweat to regulate temperature. Sweating is a way to eliminate toxins from the body and washing these off completes the process. Irregular bathing will mostly cause distress signals through the sense of smell. On a subtle level, maybe all day, bad smells coming off our own skin will affect our mood.

Water is largely sufficient though to clean our body. There is something to say for maintaining a stable microbiological skin environment, moderately acidic, not disturbed by fairly aggressive chemicals like soap. Yet water is needed and it is such a great conductor of energy that it will also very directly remove waste energy. Its profound purifying effects produce like a rebirth every time we shower. From the *yogic* perspective, that energetic purification is the highest benefit of showering.

A shower definitely helps to revitalize and relax. It is an important follow-up of any physical exercise. It does not just wash off sweat, but also eliminates excess energy that we have loosened through our practice, and might still be clinging to the body. A shower helps us to let go of the *tamasic* energy of sleep in the morning. It can definitely help also to release the *rajasic* stress energy accumulated during our workday. One or two short showers a day can be seen as a minimum to keep our body and energy pure, depending on climate and activities.

An important trick for removing an unpleasant feeling, provided it has been around for no more than a few days, can be applied during the daily shower. Just let cold or lukewarm water run evenly all over the head for a few minutes, especially running over the face. Hot water does not have enough *prana* inside to do the job. Meanwhile using some protective *mantra* will also be helpful. From experience I can say that there is at least a 50% chance that this emotion will be changed afterwards. Similarly, fully submerging our body in the bigger waters of lakes and rivers can be very purifying, with some waters like the Ganga River having truly magical cleansing powers.

Oiling the body before or after bathing is very beneficial for the joints and nervous system, while generally producing calmness. Since most oils are cooling, we should make sure not to get cold afterwards. Special oils can also be used to affect the *doshas*[44].

In all traditions purity of body and clothes is required when partaking in any ritual that involves the other dimensions. Bad smells are well known to attract unhealthy energy and repulse the higher energies. For the same reason, we should be relatively clean while meditating and even minor rotting smells should not be allowed to persist in our homes.

Yogic Purification

All cultures have developed a wide variety of more occasional purification activities, such as saunas, special bathing techniques, herbal fasts, etc. They all really have a place, yet are not the subject of this book. For a more health-related purifying detoxification, *Ayurveda* offers the world famous 5 actions^(PANCHA KARMA)^, including medical vomiting and diarrhea, nasal and rectal cleaning as well as blood letting, usually preceded by steaming, oleation and massage.

Experience shows that people's bodies these days are polluted way more than in ancient times. It means that deep purification is best preceded by more moderate purification practices such as fasting or the use of detoxifying herbs. If not, intensive purification practices might be unable to sufficiently eliminate the toxins that are liberated from the places in the body where they have the least impact, such as in fatty tissues. It explains how some people are worse off after a *panchakarma* treatment.

Different *yogic* traditions have also developed a variety of special *yogic* cleansing techniques. In some schools there will be five, in others ten, while in traditional *Hatha Yoga* six particular purifications^(SHATKARMAS)^ are usually put forward. We will discuss their purpose below, so that the reader may feel invited to practice them. Yet I am not giving detailed instructions for most of them, as they are best practiced under close guidance:

- Throat Cleansing^(DHAUTI)^: swallowing a thin and very long muslin cloth and gently drawing it back out - cleans the alimentary tract, solves diseases caused by phlegm and also issues of the skin and spleen.
- Rectal Cleansing^(VASTI)^: drawing water, oil or herbal preparations in through the anus and releasing again – cures chronic diseases related to a disturbed wind *dosha*.
- Nasal Cleansing^(NETI)^: cleaning the nasal tracts and sinuses using salted water and/or a buttered thread – cleans the nasal passage, energizes breathing, stimulates the nervous

[44] See 'Ayurvedic Massage', by Harish Johari, Healing Arts Press 1996.

system and improves vision.

- Eye Cleansing(TRATAK): gazing with fixed eyes on some object without blinking until tearing occurs - cures eye diseases, stimulates the pineal gland and enhances concentration power, which is why I describe it in full detail in the chapter on concentration→11.3.4.
- Abdominal Rotation(NAULI): rotating the abdominal muscles after a full exhale, which takes quite a while to master – restores digestive fire, rejuvenates and balances all *doshas*.
- Skull Shining Breath(KAPALABHATTI): quick exhalation exercise – provides nasal cleaning and makes the brain light up, removing tamas from the head, which is why I describe it in full detail in the chapter on breath→8.7.5.

4.8.3. HARD PRACTICES

The original term means 'to roast' (TAPASYA), indicating a rather straightforward purpose. The objective is to burn away any remaining weaknesses, especially those nine impediments of mind←3.3. The word is sometimes translated as 'penance', yet that is an all too Christian interpretation, based in the guilty feeling of paying for some sin.

So here we roast ourselves on the barbecue, seeking to quite forcefully boost our level of fortitude, tolerance, discipline,

Story 29 — A Little Discomfort

Painting by Pieter Weltevrede →A9

Once upon a time, about 30 years before I met him, Kathia Baba put on his 'Kathia', a wooden belt reinforced with copper. The lock was broken and he did not take it off again until shortly before he left his body. It prevented him from lying down 24 hours a day, thus only allowing him to sit or stand. When asked about its purpose he answered that 'this little discomfort' reminded him always of being on the path. He was really casual about this tradition among a small school of renunciates. He was a truly miraculous person←Story3 and it was always amazing to see what impact he had on people. Many Indian visitors would be overwhelmed by his presence, while most Westerners that I brought to him did not have that much devotional attitude. And yet, even the most disturbed of them, and there were some, became quiet within minutes, without Baba uttering a word.

forbearance and confidence. There is a wide variety of practices in which people overcome some serious discomfort or even pain. Examples are using beds of nails or broken glass, maintaining postures for a very long time, excessive fasting, sitting for hours in the sun surrounded by a ring of fire, meditating on snow, bathing in ice water and a lot more←Story29. It is a very direct practice, seeking to really destroy some attachments to the body→7.1. It may also have great use in helping people to snap out of long-term unhappiness.

I have worked quite a lot with pain myself and as it helps to overcome the pain of long sitting in meditation, I discuss it in the chapter on sitting→7.4. Harish Johari often warned that too much attachment to hard practices constitutes a big Ego trap→7.1, as they require a lot of Ego and produce feelings of wonder and adoration in others.

4.8.4. SELF-STUDY

Self-study(SVADHYAYA) has been discussed already←2.6.2. Remember how repetition is advised here, for example in copying scriptures. It is very much an attitude of observing everything, including the observer. It is the practice of *Jnana Yoga*←2.6.3, the path of knowledge.

4.8.5. SURRENDER

Surrender to our preferred form of the divine(ISHVARA PRANIDHANA) is put forward by Patanjali quite directly in order to prepare us for the state of *Samadhi*. To sink into deep meditation, we need to give up all control, surrender to whatever happens →12.2. We need to trust that the one who will meet us there will take care of us, as we are no longer doing that ourselves. That is really quite a great deal of trust, going against our usual nature as control freaks. Thus it is advisable to exercise surrender to the divine, existing inside as well as outside of us.

As discussed at length before←2.5.3, we are entirely free to choose the form that best symbolizes the formless supreme for us, including some more abstract form of the Self. That form will also be our principal meditation object→10.1.2. It is thus advisable to also spend time with it outside of our meditation practice. That may start with hanging an image of our meditation object in our meditation room. And since the one that needs to give up control very much resides in the subconscious, we may use rituals to repeatedly train our reptile brain to let go←2.7.3.

Here we thus spend time in *Bhakti Yoga*←2.5.4, becoming lovers of the divine. Surrender is also very much an attitude towards our actions and their results, the essence of *Karma Yoga*←2.4.4. And it definitely is essential to *Jnana Yoga*←2.6.3. as well, as we accept the inherent ignorance in our thinking and surrender to the knowing beyond words←3.4.2.

Surrender is the last of the 5 activities prescribed for all *yogis* by Patanjali. Those below are a more optional, personal selection of beneficial activities, especially suited for householder *yogis*.

4.8.6. MANTRA RECITATION

Whether or not we use a *mantra* as our main meditation object→10, we are advised to regularly recite *mantras*(JAPA) in combination with our more worldly activities. Our usual train of thoughts is replaced by the repetition of the mantra, whether recited silently or out loud. That in itself is an exercise of surrender and very helpful to pacify the mind when our thoughts are less constructive.

Regular practice engraves the *mantra* in our mind, where it will start circulating by itself. The moment we stop thinking, we hear the *mantra*. The sound syllables of the *mantra* will very much affect our energy centers as well as the 'rumbling' of the subconscious. It is purifying and calming every level of our being.

One thing to remember is that when in our mind we start a *mantra*, we should always finish it. We do not stop halfway through, as that will have a negative effect on its resonation inside of us. While this practice is destined to become quite relaxed, we will nevertheless need to really concentrate at first, stay glued to that *mantra*.

Inner *mantra* recitation can thus be present whenever we do not need our mind very much for whatever we are doing. It goes along well with household chores, as well as when walking or driving somewhere. Depending on the energetic power of the *mantra*→10.3.2, our energy will also be harmonized by it. The practitioner that might only have half an hour for actual meditation every day, can add to that maybe one or two hours of *mantra* recitation 'on the fly'.

As it will strengthen the neural pattern of the *mantra*, it will make the actual *mantra* meditation a lot easier. It is definitely a main way to always stay somewhat at a distance from whatever is happening. The more advanced practitioner will be able to use the *mantra* when listening to someone, or ultimately even while speaking, a form of mental multitasking→11.2.

Another very useful application is when we feel like lying down for a short break from the business of our life. Instead of then maybe worrying about stuff, we put our mind on a *mantra* and can get a real holiday. Synchronizing the *mantra* with the breath can also be very helpful, lying on our left side→7.3.3, with a long slow inhale and a short fast sigh through the nose on the exhale, which is a soft form of the Shining Skull breathing technique→8.7.5.

I must admit here that the teacher who taught me that breathing technique was actually a dog. Dogs are real experts at napping, using this technique, which is extremely relaxing and somehow allows to stay alert while napping, not really fall asleep. Anyone who lies down with a resting dog and synchronizes breath with that of the dog can experience it.

I very often advise people the practice of *mantra* walking, where we synchronize our steps with the *mantra* recited inside. Walking is anyhow an important physical exercise, especially upon getting older, when we may no longer be so much suited for more challenging physical exercises. Most people will experience that it is easier to concentrate on the *mantra* while walking than when sitting in meditation. That is because the mind can still enjoy the experience of walking and seeing whatever there is to see. Yet instead of commenting on whatever we meet, or being somewhere else in our thoughts, we can do the *mantra* and give ourselves some time off. Silently reciting the *mantra* inside, we let that music bring some swing in our step, nothing too much exciting, supportive nonetheless.

Even though *mantra* recitation 'in life' is also very common among renunciates, it is especially useful for householders as it does not take time off our busy schedules. Another practice, which does take time, is in writing *mantra*, as shown in Image 33. It engages both hemispheres very well and is an excellent practice to improve our concentration abilities.

Image 33 - Written mantra for Hanuman by Harish Johari.

4.8.7. SHARING

Whatever wealth we have, we can share at least some of it with others, in which we but copy the main attitude of our mother nature→10.5.1. The activity of sharing takes many forms and relates to our family and neighborhood. Another typical expression is found in giving a donation to some charity(DAAN) or doing some *Karma Yoga* for some organization that promotes *dharma* or harmony in society. It is a typical practice for householders and teaches selflessness.

Even if often charity is performed from a more egocentric point of view, supporting our public image, still the giving will bring the energy to a higher level. The main power at work is that of the gratitude of others, so we should not only express gratitude to the divine, but to all who support it somehow or other for whatever reason.

Especially whenever we do not feel so much motivated towards actions that support ourselves, we can find satisfaction in helping others. Thus sharing our free time with the divine surely beats wasting time in just hanging around thinking darker thoughts or seeking distraction in empty mental consumption of videos, games, etc. So whenever we do not know what to do for ourselves, we can do something good for others. It will always bring a better feeling, provided it can be done without expectation. It is a way out of enduring sadness and depression.

4.8.8. MASSAGE

As part of his family tree belonged to a tradition of wrestlers, Harish Johari very much promoted *Ayurvedic* massage. In ancient times, *Ayurvedic* therapists would usually not offer massage to patients, as most people were able to get that from their family. Everyone in his family knows how to massage and it is such a simple decision to start some massage, creating a cozy atmosphere. I can very much recommend his book on the subject[45].

Massage promotes circulation, relaxation, elimination and rejuvenation. It will balance all *doshas* and especially helps to reduce issues with the wind *dosha*. It is one of the best ways to treat nerve pains and to remove stress, which is the main reason why it supports meditation practice.

Our feet are the most important part of the body to massage, as they connect us to the earth. Daily foot massage is one of the best remedies against lack of grounding. Many pressure points can be unblocked here, supporting all parts of the body through the lymphatic system. And the good news is that while for massage we usually depend on others, massaging our own feet is very easy. The following rules apply:

[45] 'Ayurvedic Massage', by Harish Johari, Healing Arts Press 1996.

- Without oil, we can press the feet and twist our joints, yet should never rub the skin, as this will aggravate the wind *dosha*.
- Using some vegetable oil, we rub the feet mostly in the direction of the toes.
- Without going into the detail of the pressure points shown in the picture below, we can use our thumbs to press for a few seconds on any harder, painful spot, and then suddenly release that pressure. We can do this a few times until that pressure point becomes soft, including circular motions to promote circulation.

In this process pressure and temperature will liquefy the crystals that occur as blockages in the lymphs. Their sharp edges actually produce the pain we feel when applying pressure. Removing them restores the natural circulation and elimination of waste products. The main pressure points[(MARMAS)] are related to particular organs, see Image 34.

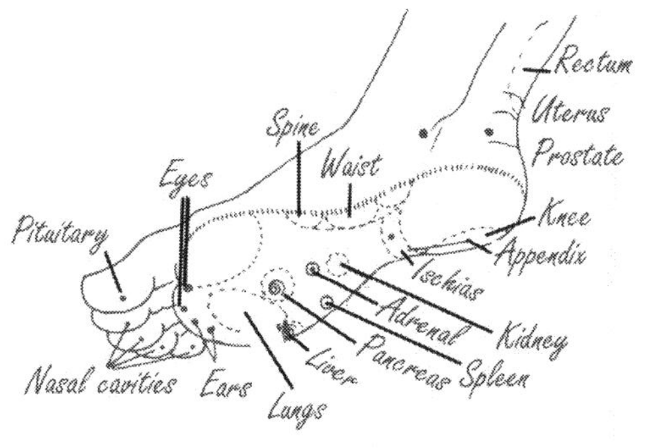

Image 34 - Pressure points in the feet.

4.8.9. ARTS & MUSIC

Visual Arts

Also very much part of the householder practices taught by Harish Johari is the regular involvement with a variety of visual arts. It is very much needed to compensate for the left hemisphere dominance in modern society, which also makes meditation so much more difficult←4.2.4. It enhances emotional balance and counters excessive rationality.

As art is a wordless communication or uses only poetic words, it teaches us to move beyond rational thinking and listen to the divine inspiration inside. That in itself will activate the central, neutral energy channel that we equally need for meditation←4.2.5.

Creating art is an excellent practice in *Bhakti Yoga*, spending long hours in painting the object of our meditation, while reciting the related *mantra* for example. To create impermanent art is the best way not to let the Ego corrupt the practice, like in the tradition of creating images with colored powders[(RANGOLI)], brushed away afterwards, see Image 88.

The old teachings mostly come to us as poetry, stories, paintings and *mantras*. They are all artistic expressions, rather than being dry intellectual, leaving no room for the imagination. While art is nice to decorate our homes with, it can help to express our emotions, especially in difficult times. It is principally a more lunar way to work with our understanding.

As a picture says more than 1000 words, we should include changing our inner pictures in the reprogramming of our understanding. How to understand the *chakras* without a picture? How perfectly is the lightness of spirituality expressed in the image of a dancing Ganesha, that smiling elephant-headed deity with a twinkle in the eyes shown in Image 35? What does it mean for our subconscious mastering of that lightness to have spent many hours painting it?

Image 35 - Ganesha by Pieter Weltevrede→A9

The objective of spiritual art is to inspire ourselves and others to pursue the path. While it can also communicate about the more unpleasant or unjust aspects of life, the end result should always be uplifting, auspicious. Otherwise it is not considered the work of a true artist, someone who is really connected inside, as the seers of old. Truth is never purely negative.

Music

Householder and renunciate *yogis* both have a habit of frequent chanting, whether in group or alone. Group chanting(KIRTAN) of *mantras* and spiritual songs(BHAJANS) is another great way to release and communicate emotions as well as understanding. It allows us to express our love for the divine, as well as the related *rasas* of joy, wonder, courage and ultimately peace. We thus chant to awaken the divine in our heart.

It is a practice of feeling and producing unconditional love, which is a little more difficult in a traditional love song, where the love can always be doubted. Aided by the joy of togetherness and the harmony of voices and maybe also instruments, the awareness comes to a different level. Contrary to meditation, where the mind is an obstacle, here our mind can be an enthused ally and as a result the Ego feels very light afterwards.

I made many 'Singalong' recordings

available online with easy Indian songs, so that people can enjoy some of that even when alone at home, in the car, etc.[46]. Whenever we are not into creating inner silence, some uplifting and calming playlist sounding in the background may certainly help to maintain a nice mood. We will enjoy it all the more when singing along.

4.9. Restraints

When *sadhus* are initiated, traditionally they vow to uphold five restraints(YAMAS) as promises 'to kill' certain activities. These are often mistaken by society as generalized moral rules, yet they are a matter of meditation technology for *yogis*. Without maximally respecting these restraints, the practice of deep meditation will be disturbed for sure. Anyhow, just like with *dharma* in general←2.4.3, how we interpret these restraints is a matter of personal freedom and duty. *Sadhus* nevertheless take that 'killing' quite literally.

4.9.1. NO VIOLENCE

The aspirant *yogi* is required to remain non-violent(AHIMSA) in word, deed and thought. So we do not think bad about anybody, we do not speak hurtful words to anyone, and we also do not hit them. This practice was very well demonstrated by Mahatma Gandhi, who launched the *yogic* idea of non-violent resistance into politics and used it in a very effective way to finally get the British colonizers out of India.

The first reason why it is important not to be in a violent relationship with anybody is to protect the meditator. When we enter *Samadhi*, we become utterly defenseless, even a lot more so than in sleep. The feeling of vulnerability may stop us from entering that state. If we believe to have reason to fear violence, maybe as retaliation for our own violence in word or deed, how to even close our eyes? That was of course even more true for the practitioners of old, often meditating in nature or in some unlocked hut or house.

When sitting down in nature, the practice of non-violence was regarded as the best protection from wild animals. Many examples exist of *yogis* that have developed non-violence to such an extent that also animals can feel it. Thus even wild snakes and tigers become totally

[46] See the 'Singalong' videos on youtube.com/youyoga.

harmless and peaceful when meeting such a person.

Moreover, the feeling of anger, which is the *rasa* that supports most violence, is opposite to the peace and bliss that we want to embrace in our practice. If we carry violence in our heart, it will have to be suppressed when meditating, which ultimately never works. Even if we can push these thoughts away during the concentration phase, they will return whenever we start releasing our Ego and will power in the phase of real meditation→12.1.1. That will effectively block our sliding into any deeper state. How can we reach the Self if we still harbor anger inside?

On a very subtle energetic level also, anger is a destroyer and consumes plenty of *ojas*←4.2.3. Harish Johari used to say that one minute of anger can destroy the subtle results of one year of meditation. We already described how to let go of anger for some time←4.1.8, yet here we are thus invited to let go of any violent resistance altogether. This will gradually become true and as explained, the first requirement is to be fearlessly straightforward in clearly communicating our boundaries to others←4.1.5.

In Buddhism and Jainism, non-violence is a very central practice, often extended to avoiding any kind of hurt to other beings, even accidental. That is a freedom, yet as we cannot even walk, eat or breathe without hurting something, there is no absolute solution that will avoid all suffering, which is natural←3.6.2. When we hurt without selfishness or the intention to hurt, it is a *karma* that produces no bad *karma*.

Only when accompanied by feelings of guilt, accidentally hurting another will require some *karmic* repercussion. The same is true when hurting someone to protect another, like a child, for whom we feel responsible. Sometimes *dharma* itself will require us to fight, while if we can be uninvolved, a mere instrument of the divine, it carries no consequence. This was beautifully explained in the famous discussion between Krishna and Arjuna in the *Bhagavad Gita*.

4.9.2. NO LIES

When *sadhus* are a witness in an Indian court case, their testimony carries high value. There is no reason to speak untruth, as there are no attachments, not even in relationships. To always tell the truth(SATYA) and nothing but the truth is a companion of non-violence. This straightforwardness was also very much used by Mahatma Gandhi in negotiating with the British. He never accepted any compromise, as it would be based in the untruth that the British had some right to rule India.

While I presume the readers to avoid straight-out lying, still we might not always tell the truth. Some little untruths are often permitted in whatever we are thinking, saying or doing. These are our Ego stories and they basically rest upon not fully accepting who we are or what is happening. People thus easily bend the truth a bit, to make ourselves seem better than we are, to make our problems seem more or less important, even to escape responsibility for the results of our actions. Life is a theatre, yet to play our role well, we are advised to stick to the truth as we know it.

The untruths that we have been telling ourselves or others will eat our self-confidence. It will create an expectation in others that is based in untruth and thus will cause us to fear being exposed, which will destroy our self-confidence. Fear about those big or little lies may also disturb our meditation, whenever we come to the point where we can relax our concentration, just like with anger. This is also very related to our marketing as teachers←3.7.8, as our embellishments of the truth of our own achievements will undermine the honesty with which we are committed to our practices. Integrity is a treasure to fiercely protect.

Being true about whom we are, where we stand, is thus essential. We can only be confident about what we are doing when we accept what we are able to do. We also accept what we have as yet been unable to do, even as we accept that we might very well succeed in the future. So we do not entertain any stories about our progress. Only when accepting something as it is, we can work on changing it. Not accepting ourselves as we are will typically lead to inappropriate and ineffective practices.

In meditation, we are trying to find the truth. All that effort serves only that one purpose, as the truth will set us free from unhappiness←4.1.4. We seek a connection to the cosmic intellect←2.6.2 and the Self, which both are alien to untruth. So whatever untruth we keep alive will stop us from reaching our goal.

To think and speak only truth we have to be very watchful of what comes out of our mouth. If we really do not want to state any untruth, then we better remain silent. The Ego itself is a fundamental untruth, an illusionary identity. We can try to be as truthful as possible and communicate at least some uncertainty whenever we recognize it in our understanding. The key lies in acceptance.

Sometimes we may believe to have good reason to lie, to protect something or someone dear to us. Doctors as well as healers know that some patients are not ready for the truth and when forced to recognize it, their self-healing capacity may be very negatively impacted along with their self-confidence. Likewise we may lie to save the hearts of our friends and family, as well as their attachments. It may also not feel it is our place or duty to reveal some truth to them, even if they will usually be best served by it.

It is obviously easier for renunciates than for householders. These are individual choices to make, yet as we evolve towards the truth and learn to think and speak from the cosmic intellect, it will anyhow become very difficult to say anything untrue. So we just need to give truth our best shot and the rest will be resolved by truth itself.

4.9.3. NO STEALING

Non-stealing(ASTEYA) means being truly honest in our exchanges with others. It is not so easy because we are all involved in some kind of business. We naturally prefer to get the most return out of the least effort.

So when we say 'business is business', it can mean that everyone should receive what they are due, even when we are in business with friends or family for example. Some people however believe that 'business is business' means that whatever they can take, they will take it. So that is where the difference between honest and dishonest business lies. How greedy and selfish are we? Only the divine purely gives, yet are we takers, thieves, or are we mature human beings, honestly balancing give and take?

As *yogis* we will not take that which is not ours, because we know that the cost is too high. Whatever stories we might tell to hide our dishonesty, in our heart we will know the truth and the immediate loss will be in our heart connection. Without heart connection, *Samadhi* is impossible, because then we cannot even trust in our own heart. And of course dishonesty creates *karmic* debts and the fear of discovery may disturb our meditation.

The basic understanding is that we get what we deserve, both in the short-term honesty of a deal, as in the long-term *karmic* effects at play. It does not mean we should not help others by pointing out any dishonesty in dealing with us. To be honest means not to try bypassing our own *karma*, which brings deep peace. It is based in the knowledge that the stealing of something is *karmically* impossible and that the price will far exceed the normal rates when honestly obtaining something.

It is said that if we can always be fully honest, we will walk a path of diamonds, meaning we will be taken care of by the universe. And yes, in the long run, that natural abundance is where our honest spiritual evolution *karmically* leads us←3.6.1. Without being honest to others, how can we be honest to ourselves? And without honesty in our walk, which path may lead us to the truth, and to loving ourselves?

4.9.4. NO POSSESSING

The prescribed possessions of a *sadhu* are limited to basic needs, such as a set of clothes, a blanket, a pot, a rosary, etc. Very rare are the renunciates that are called sky-clad(DIGAMBAR), carrying not even clothes nor any other possessions, like most other animals. So 'no possessions'(APARIGRAHA) does not literally need to be equal to not owning anything. It mostly depends on the feeling of possessing.

We cannot regard anything as being ours anyhow. The concept of me and mine is essentially wrong, part of the illusion. What will we take with us when we die? We are merely caretakers of things, users and consumers of stuff, which belongs to nature and everyone. What matters most is how much we identify with them. Is our car a thing that helps us to drive from one place to another or is it part of who we are? We let things be things and not make more out of them, while still taking good care.

All possessions take time and work to be acquired, protected, maintained, upgraded, etc., which is the main reason why *sadhus* avoid them. Not to hoard so much stuff removes a lot of clutter from our mind and a lot of work from our daily schedule. A few years ago, I reduced all my possessions to what could be stacked on a two square meter space. I can live comfortably with what I have left and have hardly missed anything since. And I received a lot of peace in return for my disinvestment.

It is nevertheless possible to see *sadhus* becoming very possessive of whatever they have left, like the mobile phones with which they are often gifted these days. So it is definitely not only about how many things we keep. We can have many things without attaching to them, yet if we are not attached and they are not really needed, why hold on? Once more, it is personal. Even the things that have some emotional memory attached to them, we can let go off, as we let go our past and attach to our present unlimited potential.

Our attachments to things also exist in the subconscious, and even on the level of the body we will attach to our possessions. To lose the connection to the physical body at the onset of deep meditation, it matters. To really go inside and no longer be aware of sitting there, also relates to our attachment to the things that surround us, which we will have to let go.

Letting go of our more superficial attachments also means that our deeper attachments will become clearer. The reasons for which we were born in this life will be more easily revealed, both in life and in deeper meditation. This is the principal reason for this restraint put forward by Patanjali[47]. What will really and durably fulfill us in this life? Our soul's true happiness has little to do with whatever we can find, make, buy or store. Yet each of these things might weigh down on what truly matters.

4.9.5. NO SENSORY ATTACHMENTS

The last but not the least of the *yogic* restraints is very hard to translate without already expressing an opinion. The original meaning(BRAHMACHARI) is to be a master(ACHARYA) of the Self(BRAHMAN). More poetically, it is often translated as 'dancing in the Self', referring to finding our enjoyment in the Self.

For the *sadhu* it represents sensual and sexual abstinence, while sex and other sensory enjoyments are a natural part of the householder life. As explained before←1.7.3, the universe is created for our entertainment, which starts on the sensory level. The senses are just a game of chemicals and energies, yet who will deny value to the beauty of a flower, however fleeting?

The main issue again is in our attachment to that sensory pleasure. Even *sadhus* cannot avoid enjoying the taste of their food, or the touch of the first sunrays warming their skin→Story30. It is personal and since attachment to sensory enjoyment comes so easily, most spiritual teachers point in the opposite direction. Nevertheless, it is the attachment that is the main issue, not the enjoyment.

To some degree, this is yet another matter of meditation technology. Withdrawing inside means letting go of sensory perception→9.4. If our engagement with the senses is moderate, they will more easily shut down when our attention is withdrawn. If the senses are very excited, they will continue to send signals to the brain. If we are 'high' on our sensory input, it will be harder to concentrate. Moderation is logical.

Sensory enjoyment and especially sexual enjoyment consume a lot of energy and *ojas* in particular. When in the practice of deep meditation breath stops, that *ojas* will be needed to stay alive→13.3.1, which is the main reason for sexual abstinence in the *sadhu*. It may definitely also apply when the householder *yogi* goes on a meditation retreat.

Sexual abstinence can be a kind of ritual sacrifice to the divine as well. To offer up our sexual energy is a very potent *tantric* way to get more support from higher beings in the other dimensions. One should be careful however not to overdo it, as the longer we abstain, the more the sexual energy may produce restlessness and even anger. Then there is no point, as that anger will destroy the

[47] Yoga Sutras of Patanjali, verse 2.39.

Story 30 *Agreeing to Disagree*

Once upon a time, I was sitting with Mataji Narvada Puri on the banks of the Ganga river after meditation. We enjoyed a beautiful sunrise, with nature waking up everywhere. When I expressed the happiness that I felt in response to it however, she just waved it aside by hand and said 'pff'. As a real sadhu, she thus indicated that all of it is rather worthless compared to what was joined inside during our practice. I found myself agreeing to disagree, feeling insufficient reason not to be grateful for what nature offered, while keeping the feeling produced in meditation. There is a divine complementarity between the beauty inside and outside. I looked at Mataji and she smiled in return, revealing that we could perfectly disagree on this matter, that choice which we are all free to make. Her own story expressed in 'Tears of Bliss[48] *reflects how after searching to renounce all for about a decade, one might decide to spend another 2 decades building a beautiful family and then move beyond.*

very spiritual connection we seek. Having practiced sexual abstention for quite some periods of time, I can totally advise it, yet there are limits. These are definitely also age dependent, meaning it gets easier. The letting go of sexual energy is nevertheless also a release of emotional energy, which is healthy if not excessive.

It very much goes against our nature to make a morality out of sexual abstinence, treat sex as a sin like in Christianity. Especially as young adults, we are preprogrammed to become quite stressed when the sexual energy cannot be released, as we are forced by nature to seek potential mates.

The sexual energy is essentially part of the reproductive system, which is the most explicit expression of the life force. It is about making love grow, a celebration of life and togetherness. In a world devoid of sex, there are no fruits, flowers, nuts, seeds, rice, wheat or eggs and the birds might be much less brightly colored also. Neither would any renunciates be born.

For sure the ultimate enjoyment is found in the Self, yet that awareness also allows us to enjoy whatever comes our way. We are back to the concept of detached attachment. To most people it is mainly advisable to give spiritual practice a place in life, make life spiritual, not to give up on life. And as we can make

[48] See 'Tears of Bliss, a Guru-Disciple Mystery' by Narvada Puri, Santoshpuri Ashram 2009.

spiritual art out of anything, we can also fine-tune our love making, which relates to the *chakras* that we activate or not[49].

I am certainly enjoying what is there to enjoy. I am not a teacher who is celibate or not allowing himself to taste his *chai*. I will not be caught in the trap in which so many spiritual teachers seem to have fallen, unable to live by the standards that they set for others←3.7.6. I am doing my spiritual work and I am enjoying this divine game of life, seeing no real opposition between them if attachment can be avoided.

Nurturing the Self in that place in our heart means nothing can be forced in getting what we would enjoy to have. This way our enjoyment will not cause any avoidable pain in others or ourselves, as we remain unattached. We remain connected to our spiritual heart, which we cannot if we voluntarily break the heart of another. For sure, sexual desire is very powerful, so this attachment must be well controlled, in *dharmic*, respectful relationships.

4.10. Relationships

This is such a huge subject, which I can only touch upon briefly where it directly affects the meditator. Nevertheless, imbalances in relationships may be the biggest threat to our inner peace and progress in meditation. The people we love the most can also make us the most unhappy.

So the main message is that as we try to balance our emotions, energy, body, food, activities, etc. we better equally make sure to live in relatively balanced relationships. As the truth of the Self is a message of universal love, harmonizing our relationships is definitely a major part of the practice of life. Neglecting our relationships in favor of spiritual practices will easily backfire, while our meditation may also help our relationships evolve.

A main guideline is that *dharma* comes before *sadhana*→Story31, meaning that our duties towards others take precedence over our spiritual practices. It remains a choice of course how we spend our free time and maybe the time spent on some less interesting relationships can be invested in more time for practice.

Yet we should never feel that our social duties stand in the way of our spiritual

[49] See 'Yoga & Bhoga (Enjoyment)' on youtube.com/youyoga.

progress. Duties are generally the natural consequences of our own choices and many of the practices described in this book do not consume time. When there is lack of time, we focus more on matters of attitude, thinking processes and feelings →5.1.1. And we can anyhow defend the need for some time to withdraw inside, which can always be found→5.1.4.

While a few relationships are for life, many are optional, such as in employers, colleagues and friends. If these are particularly toxic to us, we should step out, whatever the consequences. Some people may just be unable to respect our boundaries, which is nothing personal. If some relationships always destroy our emotional balance, we better let go. It is said that our enemies make us grow and this is true, yet some harmony and basic respect, equality, honesty, must be maintained.

As our heart opens more, empathy might become somewhat of a problem in our relationships. We might find ourselves sort-of incapable of saying no to people who are actually leaning on us too much. Their emotional struggles might affect our own emotions more than we know, as we connect to them from the heart. The main rule here is simple: when we feel unhappy ourselves, solving that must be our first priority and responsibility. The Self exists in everyone and so our primary job is to stay connected to it ourselves.

Story 31 *Dharma Before Sadhana*

Once upon a time, while I attended a class at some new location in Brussels, Harish Johari stormed in and went straight for a lady who had been solemnly meditating till then. He loudly asked her if it was true that she had left her husband and kids at home, while following him around Europe for the past 2 months. She said 'Yes, but...' and could say no more, because he immediately forbade her from seeing him for the next two years. He later explained how we can never sacrifice our natural duties to our spiritual pursuits. We held over a dozen nine-day workshops with him in Belgium. He always insisted that people would live there along with their kids. And even though some youngsters were earning a buck to animate the children during classes, the kids were always allowed to disturb the proceedings, which they liked to do. Not in the least as he always play-acted with them, easily bringing out that incredible lightness of spirituality that naturally glows in a child's heart.

I remember being really angry at some trees making lots of sounds above my head, while I was trying to meditate in the forest. None of the people we live with disturb our inner peace but ourselves. Whatever others do, it does not change ultimate reality and our standing divine invitation to connect inside.

4.10.1. SPIRITUAL PRACTICE & KIDS

If we made the choice to have kids somehow, the *dharmic* consequence is to take care of them. As a kid has only two parents, really trying to escape from that duty is impossible without feeling miserable inside. Thus we accept this responsibility as a main spiritual practice for as long as it takes.

Especially in the modern model of nuclear families, often one of the parents can feel nevertheless so overloaded by the needs and desires of their kids that they have no time for themselves. The advice is to anyhow defend the right to a minimal time for relaxation and practice. Kids can learn to respect that, which is especially needed in single-parent families.

I was taking care of my son on my own for a long time. I used to get up very early in the morning, so that I would have time for practice. But if then anyhow he awoke and came down and I was not finished, he knew since the age of 3 what was expected. He would come and lay in my lap and be quite still and enjoying togetherness and maybe some extra nap. Meanwhile I could finish my meditation or at least gently come out of it.

Having kids is one of the best practices for the Ego. Once we have kids, then we are no longer number one. Until we become a mother or a father, then generally speaking most will look upon themselves and their desires as the most important thing. When we have kids that totally changes. First we need to make them happy and only if they are happy, maybe we will get some time on our own, to do what we like to do. Some new parents really need to fight with themselves for a while to keep their own desires in check and not feel like this is so much of a problem.

Anyhow kids grow up and let's say from 10 years old onward, they will start more and more taking care of themselves. 10 to 15 years later, we are happy to see them once in a while. So then we will have time for all that practice and we will benefit from the fruit of ignoring many of our own desires for 10 to 20 years. Most of those dear wishes that felt really important when the kids game started, may now seem quite irrelevant.

To have kids is thus a major spiritual practice. It is a great opener for the heart *chakra*, because we are pushed beyond the basic desires of the first three *chakras*, which are more selfish by nature←3.8.3. The love for our kids is naturally unconditional. Even when angry with them, we still love them. We feel so connected and in that way it is a beautiful thing to experience.

Kids will teach us so much to be here and now. Stepping into our kids' world, we learn to distance ourselves from yesterday and tomorrow, which is basically how kids are. We learn so much about ourselves by seeing them evolve, feel invited to enjoy the many little things. We are still not done with many of the problems that they are facing, while the same basic answers apply. Teaching them, we teach ourselves.

Taking care of our kids means following *dharma*←2.4.3, which in a way is the most principal *Karma Yoga*←2.4.4. It offers plenty of opportunities in the other yogas as well. To think and speak truth, also to our kids, is *Jnana Yoga*←2.6.3. To chant together in *Bhakti Yoga*←2.5.4 is very appreciated, as well as all kinds of pretty rituals→6.4. While they are painting whatever they want, we can paint *yantras*→10.4.5. Keeping inner silence or doing inner *mantra* recitation are other main practices that are perfect to do with kids, as their chitter chatter doesn't matter much. *Asana* practice can very easily be done alongside or together with them. They love getting a massage as babies and love giving massage as youngsters. Nothing stops us from holding our breath, from breathing more slowly or even do some alternate nostril breathing. We can moderately fast from all kinds of things without our kids standing in the way. The more we can generate inner peace while we are with them, the less they will bother us. And as for the actual meditation on our mat, we will find a trick to create at least one hour of extra time in most people's schedules→5.1.

Maybe it is essential that kids learn that loving presence and attention are not the same thing. It is not because we are in the same room with our kid, that we have to be directly involved with what the kid is doing. We are there for them if needed, while doing our own thinking, reading this book why not. When taught early enough, most kids also really appreciate this kind of peaceful, free togetherness.

Maybe one last thing to say is that having kids is quite a lot of work, especially in the first years. If people keep working full time, usually as a couple both, I believe they are making a mistake. Then we may end up with kids that crave attention and start behaving quite badly, really destroy our peace. Western society totally underestimated the impact on children of ending the era of the housewife, even if that end was due. The only correct way to rectify this is if both partners work less than full-time, even if there may be a difference between them.

The more lunar partner will most enjoy the mothering role, whether man or woman.

4.10.2. SPIRITUAL LOVE RELATIONS

Listening to people, kids are often less of a problem than partners. If we are looking for a partner and spirituality is really an important part of our life, then we better look for a partner to whom that is also true. As a general guideline, *sattvic* people should not partner up with *tamasic* people←4.2.1, as in the light fairy falling in love with the dark loser. All other combinations of *tamasic-rajasic* and *rajasic-sattvic* can be seen as quite complementary.

Mutual spiritual interest makes things a lot easier. Whatever we then do in terms of practice, which may take time away from the relationship and our duties, will easily be understood and accepted. As we regard each other as works in spiritual progress, we can act as a mirror of love and also truth. We are in loving support of each other's growth, without expectation. We should always avoid becoming our partner's therapist or spiritual teacher←3.7.8.

Whatever we are doing together as a couple, we will never be the same. Even if both are spiritually inclined, one may have more a liking to Buddha and the other more to Christ. Much more important is if there is an open heart *chakra* on both sides, and the morality related to that. We do not want to have to be very defensive at home.

Anyhow, if one already has a partner that is not spiritually inclined, it can still work. If there is love and no big complaints, then we better hold on. It is quite a rare gift for love between two people to blossom into maturity these days. Everyone has their strangeness let's say, yet if the relationship generally works, then there is no need for the spiritual desires to match. The only requirement is a certain openness, the freedom to pursue what we think is important, without having to defend that choice all the time. And as our practice changes our behavior, some communication about what we are trying to achieve must be possible.

The spiritual issue may be very important to us and also really a good, timely focus. Yet at some time we ourselves might need to refocus on the more material aspects of our life. Thus why should we then look on a more materialistic partner as being an issue?

Some people do not want to look at life's more fundamental problems, while causing lots of these problems. Yet some are the lucky ones, more and more rare in a way, just happy the way they are, without being troublesome to others. They might someday also encounter some bigger issue and then they will start asking some important questions. Yet for now, why not let them be the way they are if that is not causing disharmony? We have to be careful for our spiritual ego not to push us into the role of missionaries, especially at home.

It is natural in a love relationship for partners to have more solar or lunar roles. Solar and lunar←4.2.4 are a main power of attraction. Sometimes men complain about how women are and dream about withdrawing to their man-cave. And women may do the same, except they might prefer their man to stay in that woman-cave as well. We should all realize that we like each other's differences and are supplemented by them. Solar and lunar will also interact verbally, while it should thus not become a quarrel.

More later, as a book on love relationships is anyhow on my to-do list.

4.10.3. THAT WORLD WE LIVE IN

As we open the heart *chakra* more, the pain of others is more acutely experienced ←1.7.1. Looking out into the world, we see so much unnecessary suffering, bickering, dishonesty, depression, ignorance and loneliness. It can feel quite overwhelming, especially when we fail to understand why humanity seems unable to evolve away from entirely illogical selfishness, inequality, environmental destruction, mental imbalance, wars, etc.

Many lose faith in the path or feel that our meditation makes no sense when faced with these problems. Should we not stop everything and deal with the world first? We have to see that it all relates very much to our practice and that we cannot expect humanity to grow up very rapidly, given the rate of population growth over the past centuries.

When I was a kid, there were about 3 billion people living on this planet. Now there are more than 8 billion. The spiritual question is, where did these 5 billion 'extra' souls come from? A few new ones might be aliens or highly evolved beings descending on earth. Yet the obvious answer is that most of these 5 billion new human souls came from the animal kingdom. They were mostly cats and dogs and other animals living close to humans, who upon dying felt attracted to the upgrade of that apparently miraculous human life. About 5 billion unclaimed human fetuses became available over approximately half a century, so easy pick.

Animals have much of the naturalness that we lack, yet they mostly vibrate in the lower *chakras*. There are some great exceptions of course, of animals that show superior wisdom and unconditional love, said to be higher incarnations in animal form. Most animals however just want to survive, to have fun and maybe take pride in some social status, the lower *chakra* desires. They may have a love in the fourth *chakra* for their family or clan, especially among birds and mammals. Yet they usually don't feel much love outside of their peer group. Animals often respond negatively to what is unknown or simply different, may show greed or aggression easily, act very much in terms of 'us' versus 'them', easily identify with some group-Ego, sounds familiar?

One might say that animals also have the big advantage of not overthinking all of that, of acting quite naturally and instinctively, of accepting reality as it is. So then what happens when that new human brain suddenly allows these souls to question everything? What is the result when the desires of these new humans are no longer limited by instinct? What does it mean to be able to truly question ourselves as individuals?

Today we thus have these 5 billion former animal souls in their first human incarnation, having to learn how to live with this complex brain of ours. It is a huge asset and a huge problem both. These souls now have to evolve much more consciously, since that brain gives them real freedom of choice. It simply takes time to open the heart *chakra* more, feel empathy for the suffering of others, be less ego-centered, get some glimpse of the reality beyond.

If I would say that more than half of the people on this planet are actually quite selfish, I do not feel to be exaggerating. They first need multiple experiences of happiness and unhappiness both, to come to the point of asking the really transforming questions. Honestly it will take a while for humanity to change as a whole, which does not stop us from reprogramming ourselves.

Stopping human population growth on this planet will anyhow be needed if humanity wants to survive itself. If we continue to have more and more people, then these 'first incarnation problems' will stay. And the more population growth will meet its natural limits in terms of energy and resources, land, water, air, etc., the more our world will seem on fire.

At some time this unsustainable growth will be stopped, whether willingly or not. On the level of spiritual maturity, it will then still take a generation or two to see some fundamental changes in society. So even if hard to accept, we cannot expect a world of peace and love in our lifetime. The work we do prepares the world for a more distant future, yet we can definitely help ourselves forward right now and enjoy doing so, why the hell not?

The evolution of desire in the *chakras* is a natural process, so our species is predestined to become more wise, considerate and unified. And we can all contribute towards that day through our example and by teaching those that are willing to listen. It is advisable not to waste time and energy trying to force this growth of consciousness upon people that are simply not ready. Timeless patience is the only answer.

It is useless anyhow to become too much impressed by the illusion of suffering←3.6.2. We can do as much *Karma Yoga* as we want, yet should avoid being too much involved with imbalanced people, especially if we feel particularly weakened by it. Neither should we be overly impressed when their antics make headline news. The unhappiness these people create and feel ultimately leads them to the changes we are hoping for.

All the world's problems are only Ego problems of the individuals the world is made off. That same Ego explains why since the dawn of written history, not a single day has been registered when there was no war anywhere in the world. The most essential task in yoga and meditation is to transform the Ego. The state of the world is thus no excuse to question our practice, quite the contrary.

So we keep working on ourselves, which is the first thing to do. Whatever we can do to help and bring change in the world comes second. To be too much focused on what is wrong with the world is not useful to anybody. Instead we should focus on the beautiful truth of the Self, which remains ever available in everyone.

As a youngster I was a punk, totally disappointed with humanity, believing in

Story 32 Do Not Insult My Mother

Once upon a time, Harish Johari gave a class on 'Ego, Mind and Intellect', which I interrupted with the question 'Should we not be more involved with the destruction of Mother Nature, rather than only talking about ourselves?'. I was studying environmental engineering and very frustrated by the lack of attention in society for the pollution of nature. His answer was really challenging: 'How do you dare insult my Mother Nature? Who do you think you are in believing you can destroy her? Even if mankind might kill itself, some bug will always survive. Nature will be back before you know it! This problem is just an Ego game and that is exactly what we are talking about'. I couldn't handle it and ran off in anger. The next day we talked about it in private and that is where he explained to me how a majority of the population is in their first human incarnation, revealing why many do not care for the environment. I deeply understood how all our Egos need time to evolve into connecting to everything and living in harmony. That quarrel truly saved me from becoming a bitter punk.

'no future', getting involved with rather violent resistance against nuclear power and environmental genocide. Fortunately Harish Johari explained the above understanding when I was in my early twenties, after we had the only fight of our relationship←Story32.

Since then, I expect nothing of the world except some natural fluctuations, while nevertheless contributing to spiritual and environmental awareness. I focus on my own practice, as well as on sharing what I have learned with all who are interested.

Unhappiness is the root cause of all misbehavior. The main wisdom is that whatever happens around us, there is absolutely no reason not to smile. Losing that smile is where all problems of the world start.

5

PLANNING OUR PRACTICE

Most people's lives are so busy that if we do not schedule our meditation session, little will get done. Many practices that do not require time are available, and for others some tricks can help us to make the time. Also the cosmic rhythm of the day has a plan for us. We are free to develop a flexible schedule, mainly fix the timing of our basic practice. Whenever on holiday, we might boost our progress during a retreat.

5.1. Making Time

Making time for practice is a matter of choice, yet I will never say it is easy, especially for householders. On the other hand, I believe everyone can find the time needed for practice, especially given some tricks that follow in this chapter.

Of course, when we have many responsibilities, so many jobs seemingly left undone, it might feel like this is impossible. The reality of not having a lot of free time easily partners up with our mind's resistance against practice. Lack of time may rapidly become an excuse for lack of will power, perseverance, motivation, confidence, as discussed.

We should not forget the obvious. All habitual and occasional unhappiness represents an inefficient use of good time, inevitably increasing incompetence←3.3.4. Our practice is a good time investment that will gain us lots of time in the end, making us way more efficient in handling our duties by training to be focused and maintaining emotional stability.

Making time is also about not having too many projects running. If our desires are unlimited like an ocean, always a storm will happen somewhere and there will never be time for peace. Yet if we can limit our projects to the size of a pond, lotus flowers included, most of the time only a calm ripple will disturb the waters and it will be easy to find peace. The more we want to do, the more timelessness will elude us. All the time we will be running out of time.

Life is not very serious←1.7.3, but a little seriousness in giving peace a chance is needed. Then the remainder of the day we can be more joyful, relaxed and efficient. We recognize this as the way in which we can have a lot more fun in our lives. Those with whom we may have to negotiate about our time spent in practice may certainly experience that if we get that time, we are more fun to live with as well.

We anyhow cannot steal time and should not try to force this. It should never fundamentally disturb the relationships that we hold dear, so maybe we go step by step. If we do what we can with what we have, then life will provide the time to do more. Doing the practice that we can do is the most powerful way to make the law of *karma* work for us, as it is the truest expression of our desire to do even more. The universe always listens.

5.1.1. TIMELESS PRACTICES

Whatever limitations we find in creating time for the practice of complete withdrawal inside, we can compensate for them by more practicing in life. Many practices are a matter of attitude, like in focusing on a perfect, unmoving sitting posture→7.4 while watching Bambi with the kids. Or by fasting from sweets for a month, if these became somewhat of an issue. After a while, spiritual practice becomes a 24 hours a day habit. Even just trying to correctly deal with some more difficult people is already a great thing.

Some main examples of practices that do not consume time at all are mindfulness→9.3, self-observation←2.6.2, awareness of awareness←2.6.4, the 5 restraints←4.9, following *dharma*←2.4.3, moderate food←4.7.1 and speech fasting ←4.7.2, as well as the fasting from unhappy *rasas* or on happy *rasas*←4.1.8.

Some practices may consume time, but can also be practiced to some degree without losing a minute of our day. The main examples are in balanced cooking←4.5, *Jnana*←2.6.3 and *Bhakti Yoga* ←2.5.4, chanting and inner *mantra* recitation 'on the fly'←4.8.6, maintaining correct physical posture→7.5, exercising slow and deep breathing→8.4, as well as moderate breath retention→8.6.

Practices that are difficult to do without consuming some time are *Asana*→7.2.1, *Karma Yoga*←2.4.4, *Tantra Yoga*←2.7.1 and sleep fasting←4.7.3. These are all optional to some degree, so if we cannot spare the time, there is no real need for it.

For the one that truly aspires to reach *Samadhi*, some time investment will anyhow be needed for the meditation phases of relaxation, concentration, meditation and deep meditation. Thus if time is really limited, we will only need to make some time for our actual meditation practice, while a lot more spiritual practice can happen without consuming time.

5.1.2. TIME NEEDED FOR MEDITATION

It pays to make our quest for meditation time more concrete. Renunciates have the most free time for practice and yet they will usually not spend all day in practices that require withdrawal from life. There may be periods in which they go in full retreat, while to my experience most of the time the majority of them will spend only two to four hours a day in meditative practices. That duration may be significantly increased during particular periods, probably scheduled by their teacher or through astrology. Only the ones that already can sustain long *Samadhis* may lose all connection to life for weeks, months, years. One has to be ready.

For many householders that are still new on this path, spending half an hour a day on meditation is probably where to start. The main thing is to have some daily practice, even if only 15 minutes a day. At least one may have the experiences needed to become motivated to spend a little more. Yet in most people half an hour can already bring a reasonable relaxation of the bodymind and even include some time where we actually concentrate in meditation.

To my experience, practicing meditation for about one hour a day is a minimum requirement to seriously aim at mastering *Samadhi*. It is the time most people need to relax and concentrate until the focus can be softened into actual meditation.

The real steps into that unseen realm will then probably happen when we occasionally spend maybe two hours, like on a free day. Those more sporadic deeper experiences may then make it easier to reach deeper meditation within our daily one-hour practice. They will make the practice feel less like a mental workout and more like a holiday. For the one who occasionally meditates for two hours or more, the challenge of one hour of daily meditation is easily handled.

If we can maintain that one hour of daily practice, boosted by occasional longer sessions, we can aim at Samadhi, even if more than time is needed in the process→13.2.3. After a period of months or years, *Samadhi* may be expected to occur and then start to deepen. Occasionally, a deeper Samadhi phase may take 3 hours or more. Having then already brought a major change in our personality, we will anyhow need to digest it in life→13.3.3. The need for sleep will become much less, which will ultimately solve the time issue→13.2.3. Increasingly we will also experience 'natural *Samadhi*' within life→13.5, which will not consume time at all.

So the way forward is to start maybe with half an hour and end in one hour or more of daily meditation practice. And on our free days, we spend two or more hours now and then to make some extra progress. And then whatever happens, happens.

The above durations are based on a practitioner with sufficient determination to use the available time well. When we have less time, our will to focus can still make a big difference in terms of result. I learned this the hard way, as one of my teachers once gave me the assignment to restart the rosary→6.2.1 from the very beginning whenever I would detect a thought to have disturbed the *mantra* recitation. It took days to finish that first rosary.

That one hour does not however include *Asana* practices beyond some stretching and proper sitting. Many spiritual people these days are used to spending one to two hours daily in *Asana* practice, while not having a meditation habit. They will experience that if they can spend half of that in more meditative practices, the relaxation attained through a shorter *Asana* practice will be deepened. The tension of the body starts in the mind. As the meditation will be more efficient to maintain mental balance, the stress level of the body will already be lower when starting the *Asana* practice. This understanding has been proven true numerous times in working with students individually. *Asana* mainly releases stress, while meditation better prevents it.

We thus have narrowed down the beginner's question to finding half an hour to one hour in our daily schedule, to spend on more meditative practices. For those already established on that path, a lot more becomes possible. As it will then also be sincerely desired, it will happen. Yet first we may need to use some tricks to create some extra time for one daily hour of going inside.

5.1.3. IMPROVED RELAXATION

Most householders are awake 16 to 18 hours daily, of which on average in Belgium only 8 to 10 hours are needed for the full-time job that brings bread on the table. That leaves 6 to 10 hours that are rather flexible, even if household chores and other responsibilities may not be optional. While some people may work for 12 hours every day, most people will hopefully be quite free in how to spend 2 to 6 hours. They are usually reserved for relaxation, mostly in the evening.

So how much time do we spend on social media, in front of TV, in all kinds of supposedly relaxing distractions? We naturally feel that need to distract ourselves as Egos from the struggles of life, do something without effort or objective←3.3.5, go for some passive entertainment, any story but our own. Yet this kind of relaxation of our Ego is usually not very relaxing for our mind. Especially modern media are so hectic in trying to catch and keep our attention, that they actually stress and exhaust the mind.

Everything may have a proper place and time. Watching a good movie for say two hours may be quite a nice way to relax, yet some people binge-watch on a regular basis for 3 to 4 hours. It is not only a waste of time. It will effectively create so much more stress in the bodymind that we will need more sleep, may sleep less deeply and need more time in the meditation process to relax.

We can thus choose to upgrade some of our relaxation efforts, so that they not only relax the Ego, but also the mind. *Asana* practice can be a workout, but it can also be great fun, effortless wellness. The same can be said for many breathing practices, like heart breathing while lying down→8.1. We can chant *mantras* and spiritual songs←4.8.6, create art←4.8.9, do *mantra* walking←4.8.6, enjoy nature and gardening, spend quality time with our loved ones, etc.

These optional wellness practices are endless and it is for good reason that they represent one of the 8 limbs of *Ashtanga Yoga,* known as the *niyamas*←4.8. Sensory withdrawal(PRATYAHARA) ends in withdrawal from mind and the senses, yet starts by calming them with soothing and nourishing input→9.2. Modern types of jobs are quite mental, so we really need more activities that relax the mind, rather than excite it.

As our aim here is to simultaneously relax the Ego, we just need to keep ourselves from expecting any results. We should not be too serious about our hobbies, as that is not what they are for. This is true even for people who are totally absorbed in art for example, which requires remaining lighthearted.

So we go for a higher quality of

relaxation, which will reduce the need for time to relax the bodymind in meditation and sleep. In my experience, if our mind can be relatively relaxed and balanced in life, the advised time for the relaxation phase on our meditation mat may be reduced to just a few minutes. Then we can already start concentrating on our main inner meditation object→11. Either way, we gain some time for real peace and thus also the craving of the Ego to escape in empty entertainment will be much reduced.

5.1.4. DREAMING LESS

For the busiest people that hardly get time for entertainment and relaxation, there is still a magical formula, aside from weeding out their probably too numerous projects. The solution is quite simply to sleep less, but more deeply.

The understanding of both *vedic* as Western science describes how we sleep in cycles of roughly 90 minutes. In the first sleep cycles we are largely in deep sleep, moving from one cycle to the next through just a few minutes of dreaming. The in-between dream state is detected as the Rapid Eyeball Movement or REM phase. Then the movement of the eyes is visible behind the eyelids, as we watch stuff in our dreams.

The longer we sleep, the longer the dream phases become, and the shorter the actual phases of deep sleep. For most adults, after 4 cycles or about 6 hours, the dream state largely takes over, so from then on we are mostly dreaming.

Dreams are useful and needed in processing some of the experiences activated in the subconscious. This is also shown in people that have a sleeping problem. They experience excessive dreams, from which they also frequently wake up - a problem we will look into later→5.3.12.

Less dreaming is needed in people that are not so restless. Yet if we sleep 2 hours longer than 6 hours on average, 2 hours of dreaming is what we will do. Excessive dreaming is however very tiring for the mind. When the mind needs no more sleep, it becomes bored and starts dreaming quite at random. Before we know it, we are chased by some monster that has no good reason to visit our dreams. Even people that are quite emotionally balanced may experience strong unpleasant emotions when sleeping for too long. It is thus not because we sleep more that we will feel more rested.

We all know this fact from the experiences that we had when sleeping for a very long time, like on a holiday. When sleeping 12 hours in a row, we usually wake up like zombies, tired, groggy, heavy, *tamasic*. This is logical, since for the past 4 to 6 hours we have been 'enjoying' quite useless and possibly disturbing dreams. We may not remember their content, but their feeling may remain or our energy might simply be quite down upon waking. Occasionally a longer nap may be needed, yet if it becomes a habit it will make us more tired.

Now we have come to the conclusion on sleep that will gain us some real time for practice, straight from the teachings of Harish Johari:

Most people will experience having more energy if they sleep one hour less than usual and spend it in more meditative practices.

I have seen this work in countless students. We replace one hour of that more excessive dreaming at the end of sleep by activities that will efficiently help us to relax and rest in a different way. And that one hour of practice will also help us to lose less energy during the day in unpleasant emotions, which are highly energy consuming. Thus we will also need less sleep afterwards and that sleep will itself be deeper and less disturbed. That is the magical formula to find at least one hour of extra time and it will work for most people.

Western society usually points towards a minimum of 8 hours of sleep for adults. It does not however take into account the potential of meditative practices to bring another kind of relaxation. From the *vedic* viewpoint, most adults will need only 6 hours of sleep daily, provided one to two hours of the day are spent in truly relaxing and meditative practices.

These are of course averages, with people that do hard physical work requiring more sleep. When ill, we should sleep as much as we need. Most people will need less sleep when they get older. It is called the owl age, awake when others are asleep←3.8.5.

We are all free to sleep as long as we want. Clearly some people use sleep as an escape from life for the Ego, much in the same way as they use social media. And they are free to do that, but it will not be much of an escape given that excessive dreaming will bring out their unpleasant emotions anyhow.

For those that are used to sleeping more than 6 to 7 hours daily, I suggest reducing that time by one hour and spend it in meditation. It may be difficult for a week or two as our system needs to adapt, yet we should persevere since we are trying to achieve a new balance. We will have to be disciplined about it, because if we feel a little tired during the day and we take a nap, then again the sleeping rhythm will be disturbed and we will not attain that deeper quality of sleep we are aiming at.

There are exceptions, but most people experience that after a while they have much more energy than before. And they can then build on improving their overall performance in that one hour of daily meditation practice.

In conclusion, sleeping less but more deeply, and relaxing more efficiently both Ego and mind, we can easily find one to two hours a day for meditation and related spiritual practices. If we also add the practices that do not consume time, we can transform a life with relatively little exercise into effective progress through practice. As time is thus not the issue, it is our freedom to make that choice. Below we will go through a step-by-step process that will help the reader to make that real in their daily schedule→5.5.

5.2. The Cycle of the Day

When planning our daily practices, we should be aware that the day already has a plan for us. Tuning into the natural cycles of the cosmos may be essential to avoid doing the right thing at the wrong time.

The one who wonders how free we are just needs to try flying. We clearly cannot escape the gravity of the Earth, yet also the other bodies of our solar system impact us beyond our direct experience. While this is actually a highly complex science of astrology, the main effects are created by the sun and the moon. They will largely determine when best to plan our meditation practice and other spiritual activities. It is about going with the flow of what comes naturally, accepting to be part of nature.

5.2.1. THE GUNAS OF THE DAY

The presence of sunlight during the day and its absence at night directly affect the principal *guna*←4.2.1 of the *prana* that we absorb by breathing. During the day the energy is more *rajasic* and at night more *tamasic*. The energy becomes more *sattvic* in between, meaning at sunset and sunrise.

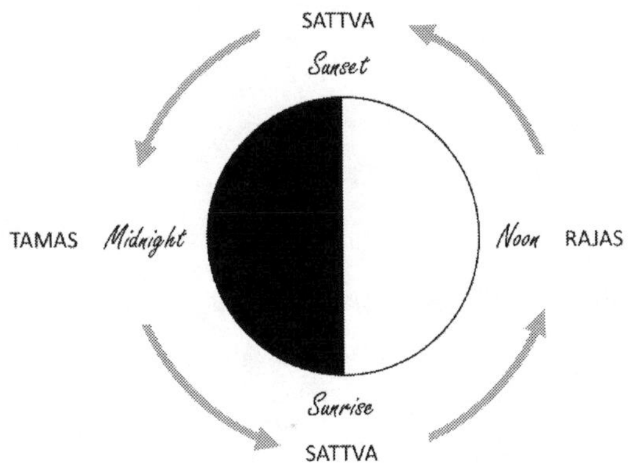

Image 36 - The gunas of the day.

At sunrise this *sattvic* effect lasts quite a few hours, while at sunset it is less pronounced. *Sattva* is more easily established when we are rested rather than tired, easier following a *tamasic* night, rather than after a stressful *rajasic* day.

We are thus basically advised and enabled by nature to focus our *rajasic* activities in the daytime, relax and rest at night and schedule our *sattvic* activities in the early morning. Some animals have found a competitive edge in doing things the other way around, mostly predators and scavengers. Most animals however follow the advice of nature.

5.2.2. THE DOSHAS OF THE DAY

While many lifestyle factors affect the *doshas*←4.3.1, since the night is colder than the day, the *doshas* will also be affected by the time of the day. Bile tends to be more dominant during the warmer day, while mucus and wind are more dominant during the colder night.

They are however also very dependent on the presence of moisture, so during a cold rainy day the mucus *dosha* is quite well supported and the bile *dosha* might still be more triggered by a hot and dry night in the tropics.

The wind *dosha* is somewhat connected to sunrise and sunset in the sense that the purest *prana* will be available then. Yet it is mostly aggravated in cold and dry weather, especially if windy, independent from night and day.

The *doshas* are thus much less directly dependent on the time of day than the *gunas*. It is still their combined effect that will mostly impact our mood, as well as our health. If our body chemistry is too cold, this may well aggravate as the night sets in. If we are overheated, maybe also emotionally, midday is the time to very consciously cool down.

5.2.3. THE RASAS OF THE DAY

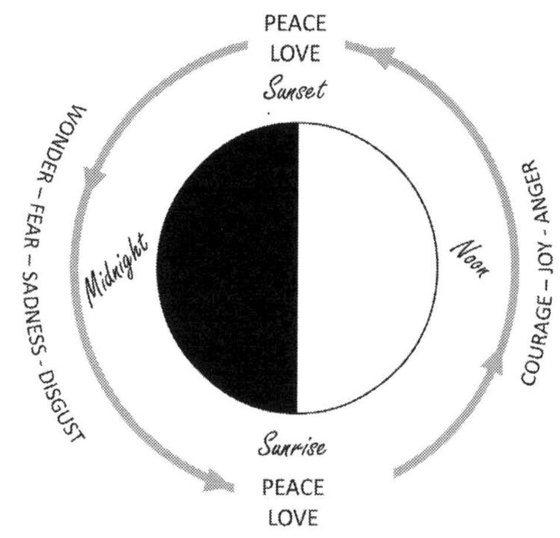

Image 37 - Correlation between the rasas and the time of the day.

Our essential emotions←4.1.5 are affected by so many parameters that do not depend on the time of day. Yet we may experience that some *rasas* are more easily produced at certain times, if we engage in the related activities. This correlation is directly affected by the fluctuations in the *gunas* and the *doshas*.

The only truly *sattvic rasa* is peace, which thus comes most easily and most deeply in the early morning. It is also the best time to produce the more *sattvic* versions of the other agreeable *rasas*. The *rasa* of love and art in particular may benefit from the inspiring presence of subtle *prana* in the wind *dosha* around sunrise.

The agreeable *rasa* that most fits to the *rajasic* daytime is courage, necessary for doing our various jobs. Another that comes easily is the bile dominated *rasa* of joy, allowing us to combine business with pleasure, empowering the life force with the satisfaction of success in our work. As our actions meet obstructions, the fiery anger *rasa* is also easily activated and supported by the *rajasic* energy and bile *dosha*.

As the *rajasic* energy is much reduced after sunset, it creates a *tamasic* feeling of weakness and tiredness. This may trigger the unpleasant *rasas* of sadness, fear and disgust in people that are not so happy. Joy and courage are less easily available. Coming on top of feeling maybe rather stressed from our workday, this effect can be quite strong. Thus we are advised to especially activate the enemy *rasas* of humor, love and art, maybe in some light entertainment. This may be spiced up with the magic of a story, producing the *rasa* of wonder and mystery, which is also related to the twilight of sunset. As the evening moves towards the sleep of the night, these uplifting activities should become more peaceful. Meditative practices can equally lighten our evening mood and especially the more healing practices can be very successful.

5.2.4. THE POWER OF SUNRISE

About 90 minutes before sunrise a first energy wave arrives, which somewhat breaks the darkness of night and wakes up most animals. Birds will start moving and making little sounds.

Between 30 to 10 minutes before sunrise, a second energy wave from the sun reaches us, the light clearly increases and most birds start singing. Equally according to Western science, a strong thinning of the blood then naturally occurs. The blood can thus really penetrate even the hair thin blood vessels and our entire system is invigorated and flushed out. It is called the 'time of the nectar of life'[(AMRIT BELA)].

During sunrise our two nostrils will open evenly for about 10 minutes, which can be easily recognized when we observe them during this time→8.5.1. As a result, even without alternate nostril breathing→8.5.2, the solar and lunar hemisphere of our brain←4.2.4 become naturally balanced for a while, making meditation a lot easier. If our meditation is really peaceful, balanced nostril breathing→8.5.2 will continue automatically throughout our meditation session, the energy flow securely locked within the neutral channel←4.2.5.

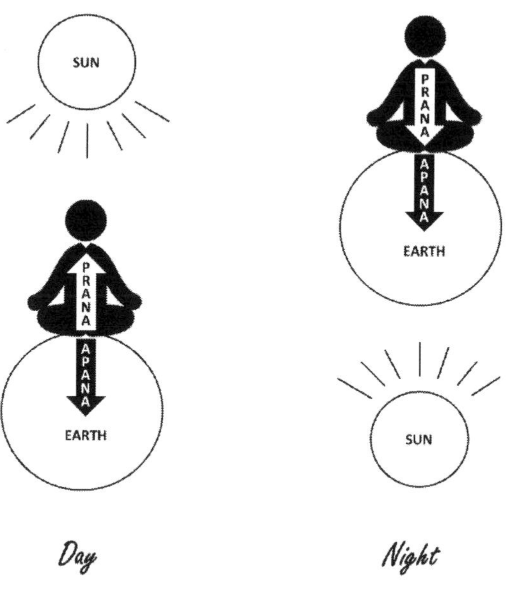

Image 38 - Impact of day & night on prana & apana.

After sunrise, the gravity of the sun will pull the *prana* in our body upward, while the *apana* will continue to be pulled downward by the gravity of the earth. During the night, both the energy of the sun as that of the earth are downward pulling, so *prana* and *apana* are more mixed. This relates to the particular density and ionization of *prana* and *apana*. It means that it is best to sit upright during sunrise→5.3.2.

In India, the morning schedule will be very much centered around sunrise, given its unique power. Even in the north of the country sunrise times do not vary much between summer and winter.

In Belgium where I live, the situation is very different. Sunrise varies from 5:29 am at midsummer to 8:45 am during midwinter. People that live even more close to the poles might not have a sunrise for a few months in winter and the same again during summer. While we can try to make sunrise work for us, it might simply not be possible all year around. So I am not taking it as a basis when describing the typical *yogic* daily rhythm below. It is still absolutely advisable to maximally take sunrise into account, even if only part of the year. Sunrise and sunset both are excellent times for changing anything, so it pays to be aware of their timing.

5.3. Daily Rhythm

We all like to do whatever we want whenever we want. It is what makes a good holiday and so we also like to have this freedom when spending our daily free time. Yet that means we look at the work for our daily bread, butter and stuff as the real work, compensated for by the idleness of our free time. If we are more spiritually ambitious however, we see that material work principally as that which allows the real work to happen. So then our free time is where we put effort into our spiritual progress, which means it cannot be spent too liberally.

We are free to make that choice and nobody needs to make it for us. Anyhow we do not need to schedule all of our free time, so for some of it we do whatever we want, maybe today this, tomorrow something else. We only need to somewhat plan the part where we want to consciously relax the Ego as well as the bodymind. Equally here some flexibility and variation is advisable. The practice of really withdrawing inside through meditation needs to be timed to a more strict degree, especially if the available time is really limited.

After messing around with my daily schedule for over 40 years, the conclusion is quite clear. It may be rather personal, related to my sort-of inborn absent-mindedness, yet here it is: without proper timing it has been nearly impossible to keep some regular practice going, except when having really a lot of free time.

Very much like with children, our activities will benefit from some routine. If every day we meditate around the same time, it will become a good habit, also for the bodymind. If we do not have that regularity, then every day we have to answer the question whether we will meditate or not, how tedious. Giving it a place in our daily habits means that we no longer have to go through this decision-making process, setting doubt aside for a while. And if we have a habit to meditate at a particular time, leaving enough time for our other duties, then everyone in our household will easily accept it, without needing to negotiate and renegotiate.

Another important relationship exists between meals and physical exercise, which should never happen after eating→7.2.2. Most people these days have breakfast, lunch and dinner and I am using this also as a basis for the schedule below.

Yet if we want to have a more *sattvic* lifestyle, we might also switch to 2 meals a day, reducing digestion time. It usually means a brunch in the late morning and having the main meal in the late afternoon. It is more suited for renunciates or when on holiday, since society is quite organized around 3 daily meals.

The most important suggestion given by scripture and from own experience, is to shift part of our relaxation time from the evening to the early morning. It will allow our system to wake up more slowly and the more *sattvic* quality of the energy will be more suited for some more inspired relaxation and meditation as well. That time is thus removed from the evening, where the more *tamasic* energy will render our entertainment more passive and less rewarding.

As they say in India, the beginning of something determines much of what happens afterwards. Many people run off to work within 30 minutes after waking. If we want to have a stressful day, that is how to start. I strongly advise to wake up earlier, so that we have 2 to 3 hours before having to move into the more *rajasic* energy of the day. And since we are going to create at least one hour of extra time for meditation by sleeping less but more deeply←5.1.4, it does not necessarily mean that we need to go to sleep that much earlier, maybe just an hour or so.

So shortly after waking we meditate, yet ideally we should also have some time left for wellness, as in togetherness, arts & music, bathing, massage, reading, enjoying nature, etc. That way, we will also be ready for some inspired, joyful, concentrated *rajasic* action at work, as we already have 'made our day'. The one who tries this will come to treasure it.

I advise reading the following overview without immediately deciding what would fit or not. Later we will go through the decision making in a step-by-step process→5.5. Better first we understand all questions and options.

5.3.1. WAKING UP

When we wake up, we do not want to wake up too hurriedly. As we move towards our meditation practice, we want to get rid of the remaining *tamasic* energy of sleep, without moving into the *rajasic* energy of work. People with more *tamasic* energy upon waking, which usually means sleep has been disturbed or too long, might need a little more action to become alert enough to meditate.

Most people upon waking should avoid whatever triggers the more *rajasic* trains of thought, such as conversation, the news, social media, etc. Many people use these distractions in the early morning to relax the Ego, trying to avoid having to think about their life, yesterday, today or tomorrow. Yet it too much agitates the mind and often the interaction also brings stress to the Ego. Looking at how the world is doing is usually not very uplifting←4.10.3.

As our waking up time defines much of what is possible afterwards, we need to wake up on time. Again, this can be more of a battle for some than for others. When using some alarm, it should mix *rajas* and *sattva* accordingly, like I use a gentle chimes sound, gradually increasing in volume. As I usually get up at the same time, I normally wake up before the alarm goes off.

One of the most important things to do is to immediately sit up upon waking. When we sit up, our energy will also move up. It will be easier to generate a *sattvic* feeling, both focused and peaceful. It is also a great way to prevent us from falling asleep again. If it is rather cold, we can pull up our blankets all around us, making a warm nest in which to wake up.

We try to keep our thoughts calm or even absent and should continue to do so until we start meditating. Some will focus on breath in the heart *chakra*→8.1, some will use some *mantra*, etc. Our main energetic practice←4.1.3 usually comes in handy here.

When then we open our eyes, it is advisable that the first thing we see is something really *sattvic*, such as flowers or maybe some white cloth, our garden, a spiritual painting, whatever gives us a good, calm feeling.

If possible, we wake up between 90 and 45 minutes before sunrise, depending also on how we schedule our meditation practice around it, see below. If impossible, forget about it. If difficult, it is still worth a try.

5.3.2. BOWEL MOVEMENTS

Soon after getting out of bed, we empty bowels and bladder, releasing the *apana* energy←4.2.2. This way a minimal amount of waste products is recirculated in the body. That discipline alone may significantly increase our energy and good feeling during the day. Once the body has this habit, it will happen more and more easily.

If we are not that regular, sitting in Thunderbolt Pose for 2 to 3 minutes with a nice hollow lower back may help→7.5. Walking barefoot in the garden for a few minutes may also do the trick.

Another method I learned to actually make the bowels move when on the toilet is to press index and middle finger downward along each side of the spine, from about 10 centimeters above the tailbone all the way down. Doing this a few times using strong pressure may remove gas blockages from the last part of the intestines. It is no use to try more than a few times.

People for whom bowel movement in the early morning is really difficult should follow the guidelines for removing constipation←4.6. They may also try squatting rather than sitting on a toilet seat. Indian and French style toilets are actually much better for our system. Whatever toilet is used, we should not bend over but keep the lower back hollow. Another beneficial Indian habit is to clean the anus with water rather than toilet paper.

While some pressure can be used during bowel movements, the main task is to relax and let go. Never push too hard, for this is a major cause of piles. If after a few minutes still nothing has happened, better we do not keep trying. Some more movement of the body may be needed first. It is literally counterproductive to become irritated about this objective. Gradually it will become easier.

If possible, we should complete the bowel movements at the latest 30 minutes before sunrise. This way, our body will be clean before the second energy wave of the sun produces that thinning of the blood and the recirculation of energy and waste products←5.2.4. It will very much reduce the absorption of toxins in the intestinal tract and the stress these will cause throughout the system.

By the time we will come out of our meditation, the sun will usually already be well above the horizon. Thus our *prana* and *apana* will be slowly and nicely separated during about one hour←5.2.4. If we are still sleeping and thus lying down long after the sun rises, that separation cannot happen. It will suddenly occur when we sit upright, and thus will not happen very cleanly. Then the dirty *apana* energy will pollute our pure *pranic* energy the remainder of the day.

5.3.3. WAKING SCHEDULE

There are many more options for mild waking activities that Harish Johari describes in his famous teaching 'The Glory of Waking Up'[50], like some strolling in nature or sitting by an open fire. They may all help to become more alert for meditation, without becoming too active.

One might also take a shower, yet that is generally seen as too activating. It might come in handy when we are really quite sleepy, maybe because of getting up earlier than before. The more common minimum cleaning needed comes as the so-called '5 baths'(PANCHA SNANAM), where we clean our hands, feet and face, including eyes, mouth and teeth. Very good is to make some funny faces at ourselves in the mirror, relaxing the facial muscles as well as our dear Ego.

There is also the possible use of coffee and black or green tea←4.6.3, which is personal, yet at least we should try to dose these correctly as not to absorb too much *rajasic* energy that will disturb meditation. Good alternatives are herb tea, lukewarm water or moon water←4.6, adapted to temperature and our balance in the *doshas*.

Again, we are free in all of this. Why not first play a hectic videogame to spice up

[50] 'Dhanwantari' by Harish Johari, Rupa Publications India 2001.

the difficulty of our meditation practice? Or have a nice quarrel with our beloved? We are equally free to choose the easier path towards our meditation.

5.3.4. OUR DAILY MEDITATION

It may be advised to do some simple stretching before meditation→7.6.3 if sitting is an issue. Further on, we will look into more detail on how to develop an optimal series of meditation phases and practices.

If possible, it is ideal if about 10 minutes before sunrise we already enter the concentration phase of our meditation exercise series. Then we will benefit the most from the natural neutrality in nostrils and brain hemispheres, as we move to the soft concentration of real meditation.

5.3.5. STRETCHING & BATHING

After meditation, we enter into a period of free morning time that is more flexible and personal. Some stretching is logical following the long motionless sitting in meditation. Auspicious at this time are a few sun salutations, greeting the day. Relaxing in the corpse pose for at least a few minutes is also advisable→7.3.1.

At this time it is certainly possible to do a more intense *Asana* practice→7.2.2. People who really have a lot of time in the morning might even do that prior to their meditation, yet among householders this is not very common. Other interesting times are available for *Asana* during the remainder of the day anyhow, see below.

Logically following physical exercise, we take the time for our daily bath←4.8.2, maybe after first doing some necessary cleaning of our home. We put on fresh clothes or at least fresh underwear, habits differ. It is all about not carrying around the energy of the previous day.

5.3.6. OPTIONAL MORNING RITUALS

Now that everything and everyone is relaxed and clean, we might think a little on the day to come, maybe decide upon some particular spiritual intention. Those who are into that might also perform their daily rituals, as people usually do in India. It is part of setting an intention for the day and getting some support from the other dimensions. Some lighting of incense or a small ritual might already have happened during the intention phase of our meditation→6.4, but that is different since it only should regard the intention to meditate. At that time, we do not want to focus yet on the day ahead.

5.3.7. BREAKFAST & HOBBIES

Breakfast should be light and easily digestible in view of the *sattvic* activities that might still follow. It depends on how much energy we need until lunch. If anyhow we need quite substantial food, maybe better we eat it after spending the remaining *sattvic* leisure time first, avoiding the *tamasic* effect of digestion.

Some may still have a lot of time left before going off to work, some not. It is about seizing the best time of the day for our most inspiring activities, yet one might not have that freedom.

This was such a memorable experience when living with the family of Harish Johari for the first time. Most of them would get up around 6 am and only go off to work at 10 am. So about 4 hours of free morning time they had and I fondly remember spending it together, practicing music and the arts, sitting on the roof in the morning sun, discussing the teachings, as well as enjoying some really great breakfasts.

Even if we can spend just half an hour on some painting, some music, some philosophy, it will give us a joy and a juice to take along. Heart, mind and senses already satisfied, we are ready to perform our *karma* of the day.

5.3.8. LUNCHTIME

How much time we have at lunch is personal and we may not be the one to decide. If we have little time, best is to eat first so that during the very first phase of digestion we do not immediately have to start working again. Initial digestion draws away a lot of our energy, so we should avoid too much activity if we can. Add semi-liquid foods like some spicy soup←4.5.3 to any cold bread meal.

If we have more time available, ideally we take a one-hour break after lunch for some digestive walk and/or togetherness. Joking and laughing are ideal to stimulate the digestive fire. Working leisurely on some hobbies is also an option. If we want to do some *Asana* practice during lunchtime, it must happen before the meal.

Sleeping during the day and especially after lunch should be avoided. Not to disturb digestion, we should remain in an upright position. If we sleep, digestion will stop and when waking we will have a bad taste in the mouth and our breath will demonstrate the smell of *apana*. Because of the *rajasic* energy of the daytime, present in the common mindfield, we will mostly have lots of dreams anyhow, which will not bring us much rest. Some people 'powernap' for 10 to 20 minutes, yet it is still advisable for most to do so in a more upright position. Meditation is always good, yet during the day we will find it more difficult because of the *rajasic* energy around us.

5.3.9. COMING HOME

When we come home, literally or figuratively for those working from home, we remain aware of this shift. If the situation allows, we should at least spend 15 minutes, if not more, to get out of the work energy and stress.

When we have little time, I suggest using the corpse pose with deep belly breathing→7.3.1, followed by some chanting in an upright position to also affect the mental/emotional level. If we have more time, this is the most ideal moment for a more intense *Asana* practice→7.2.1, fully releasing all stress acquired by the body during the day.

Towards others we should defend that minimal coming home time and if we can have more all the better. Most people will immediately engage with each other when coming home, but then that will happen from the work energy. Better if we each first let that go, as then we can reconnect much more nicely. For a couple that so much missed each other during the day, it might just mean lying beside each other in the garden, silently doing that corpse pose, followed by some singing together. It certainly beats starting to complain about problems at work from the minute we arrive home.

Just like the morning, we should start the evening in the best possible way, whatever works for us, like maybe also a nature walk. Again many people will immediately try to escape into all kinds of passive entertainment, while if they can first just relax a little more consciously, then they will be able to enjoy the evening so much more.

5.3.10. HAVE A NICE EVENING

It is advisable to have supper as early as possible, leaving digestion at least 3 hours between food and sleep.

For the second time of the day now, we usually can enjoy being without too much ambition. If we are a bit tired and maybe also drowsy from the food, a good movie might keep us awake with a great combination of the love, joy and wonder *rasas*, that are the basis of any story of old. We might play some games together, just talk, make a fire, uplifting stuff. Remember that the more *tamasic rasas* easily manifest at this time←5.2.1, so we help each other and ourselves not to get into it. Have some fun, play with the kids, visit some friends, join a party, read a funny story, whatever produces good feeling.

Sunset is not as important as

sunrise←5.2.1. Yet it is still a time when the connection to the spiritual world is a little more active and after sunset some more unhappy energies might affect us. It is advisable to attract the right energies, like by burning some incense or evaporating some essential oil, which offer good protection. Sunset is a great time to spend outside, enjoy bird songs, gently move into the night. It is also an ideal time for most healing rituals.

Some people like to meditate in the evening and it is certainly possible if we still have the energy. As the *tamasic* energy is stronger, we may need to use more *rajasic* practices to reach *sattva*←4.2.1. The use of *mantras* to reduce some negative emotions may be advisable→12.3.2. After most people have gone to sleep, the common mindfield will be less active, making meditation again easier towards midnight. It is preferable not to use the more energizing *mantras*→10.3.3, especially at the end of the practice, as their after-effect might disturb sleep.

5.3.11. PREPARING FOR SLEEP

Especially if it takes a long time before we can fall asleep, we should more consciously prepare ourselves. Avoid excess light in the last hour before sleep, including the lights of screens. Avoid any movies that are particularly violent or frightening, because while we know it is not real, our bodymind may doubt it and will still need to process the images and associated emotions to some degree.

We can spend maybe the last hour on more consciously relaxing activities, for example with some meditative music in the background. Massaging our feet with some oil before going to sleep is very helpful←4.8.8. Sleep inducing as well is a not too hot bath or to comb the hair just before sleeping. I usually fall asleep within minutes, yet some end-of-day habits still help to let go.

5.3.12. SLEEP

A person that lives centered in the 6th *chakra* needs only one to two hours of sleep daily, like Harish Johari. As we evolve spiritually, going through a number of *Samadhi* experiences, our need for sleep will become less. As long as we do not feel tired during the day it is no issue and may allow us to practice even more.

When sleep is chronically disturbed, to most people it is a literal wake-up call. The unrest has increased to the point where normal sleep becomes impossible, which also very much adds to the mental unrest - a vicious circle. We become overly tired and the bodymind tries to overcome it, which again makes it more difficult to sleep. Insomnia produces a negative spiral that stresses the nervous system and may lead to many other disturbances of bodily functions. Moreover, our sleeplessness affects our job, our mood, our relationships and our meditation.

Fortunately, sleep studies also show that people usually sleep more than they think they do. People believing they have not slept all night might still have slept for an hour or two. So there is no need to dramatize, but there is a need to act. It usually does not get better with time, especially as worrying over one's sleeplessness itself tends to become a major cause of not being able to sleep properly.

Sleep means to let go of everything, so whatever comes to our mind, we may need to more consciously let it pass by, without engaging with it. Sleeping problems might also have a more literally spiritual cause, especially when we fall asleep easily, yet often wake up restless in the middle of the night. Some shamanic healing may be required→A3.

Following are some tips & tricks for insomnia based on the understanding of *Tantra*, *Ayurveda* and the ancient Indian science of dwelling and architecture(VASTU):

- Re-installing the sleeping rhythm is a priority. We always go to bed at the same time and get up at the same time, regardless of how we slept. We avoid any in-between naps.
- If our bed is positioned in such a way that our head points to the South, we change the position of the bed or ourselves, so that our head points in any other direction.
- If the bed is very soft, consider getting a harder mattress. On a soft mattress our body may have difficulty to fully relax, as it is always moving, wobbling.
- We make sure our system experiences enough natural light during the day, especially on darker days.
- If our job is not really physical, we make sure to exercise our body daily.
- If we experience a lot of stress in life, we must make relaxation a daily habit and also consider how we can more generally reduce the causes of stress that we experience.
- We avoid caffeine from the afternoon onwards and screens at least from one hour before going to sleep.
- We make sure our sleeping room is as dark as possible, except if fear of the dark is an issue, which can be healed.
- We avoid disturbing sounds during sleep and maybe also turn off the Wi-Fi and mobile signal.
- If we already have some experience with slow breathing exercises or *mantra* meditation, use these in the bed to fall asleep. As long as we are not yet sleeping, at least we are relaxing in a different way, doing something useful.

- Avoid any worrying in bed, especially about our sleeping issue.
- Burning incense or evaporating essential oils in the bedroom is advisable in case of spiritual unrest.

5.4. Sustained Practice

Sustained spiritual practice is called *sadhana* and we can see how important that term is by realizing it is the source of the word *sadhu*. A *sadhu* or *yogic* monk is someone doing *sadhana*, much like being an accountant is based in doing accounting. *Sadhus* are renunciates that largely reduce their lives to doing *sadhana*. A householder *yogi* is free to engage in many activities, yet definitely *sadhana* is part of it.

Sadhana is based in the understanding that practice works by repetition. Performing the same practice repeatedly is needed to learn how to do it, really master it, as well as to overwrite our subconscious programming and thus bring about a durable change in our energy. Most practices thus require to be sustained for some period of time to do their holy work, instead of being the quick fix that people may hope for. *Sadhana* means to do a specific practice, for a certain period of time, having a particular aim.

We have already discussed many potential *sadhanas* that are restrictions, such as in the chapters on fasting←4.7, restraints←4.9 and hard practices←4.8.3. *Sadhana* can however also mean to do some uplifting practice for a period of time, such as a particular *Asana* practice, a breathing exercise or of course that one hour of daily meditation.

To get involved with *sadhana* is the difference between saying no to chocolate today and fasting from chocolate for 40 days. Or between 'I could meditate now' and 'I will meditate one hour a day for 3 months'.

Aside of repetition, *sadhana* offers the great advantage of being able to stop thinking about practice, as it is decided upon, at least for a while. And it also offers the mental rest of not having to see that practice as something which we need to do for the rest of our lives, even if some *sadhanas* may be promised for the entirety of this life. If we always keep some *sadhana* going, big or small, we become that work in progress←3.5.2.

A *sadhana* represents a promise, whether to ourselves, to the divine or to the teacher. And since most students these days are not really ready to accept just any such assignment by their teachers←3.7.4, they will have to first of all make that promise to themselves.

It is an extremely empowering decision to start the game of *sadhana*, taking our spiritual progress in our own hands. The more these *sadhanas* are successfully performed, the more our inner peace and confidence will grow. Without *sadhana*, gaining stability in *Samadhi* becomes very difficult.

Sadhana means that we do not only practice when we feel the need, upon experiencing some stress or unhappiness. Instead of being thus quite stingy and calculated about it, our practice becomes generous. We know that if we can sustain a practice it will make us grow, increase our abilities and insights, prevent issues from becoming problems.

Each *sadhana* is also like an experiment that we conduct upon ourselves, a kind of spiritual entertainment as in 'oh how would I feel if I practice breath retention 20 minutes a day for a week?'. It definitely also is about gaining control over the bodymind and our dear Ego.

Many people may frown upon all this, as in their experience life already provides enough *karmic* challenges. Yet *sadhana* very directly interacts with our *karma*. Instead of life creating challenges for us, with *sadhana* we create challenges for ourselves. Thus we do the work of *karma* by ourselves, with the advantage of being a little more in charge of the process. To some degree, *sadhana* thus has the power to soften our *karma*←3.6.3. The changes that *karma* is meant to produce in us are already produced through the *sadhana*.

Definitely growth in our meditation practice requires steady action, as in daily meditation. Just like when a toddler learns to walk, perfecting that 'walk towards the Self' requires perseverance and getting back up whenever we fall. *Sadhana* is what it truly means to move to the 3rd step towards enlightenment←3.8.4, bringing the theory into sustained practice.

An important rule in *sadhana* is to talk about it as little as possible. Maybe some people in our household need to know for practical reasons and the teacher may also be involved. Yet aside of that, the fewer know, the better. Again this is a matter of protecting our confidence and not letting the *sadhana* be corrupted by the Ego←2.8.3.

In *sadhana* the Ego challenges itself. Once the promise is made, the Ego wants to stick to it. It knows it will hate itself for not keeping it up without good reason. *Sadhana* is usually not result-oriented, as it only defines a certain effort. Some exceptions are there in *tantric sadhana*, see below.

5.4.1. DEFINING A SADHANA

When deciding upon our *sadhana* we have to be careful. We cannot mess around with our self-confidence. A *sadhana* that fails may damage our self-esteem quite seriously. We will need to define exactly what we are going to do and for how long. We want to give ourselves a real challenge, yet we should not overreach. We also remember that *dharma* comes before *sadhana*←4.10.

A smoker who decides to quit on an impulse may succeed, but the chance is rather slim. Better to be absolutely sure about why to stop, why now, how to deal with the side effects, how to keep performing in life as required, how to stay motivated. The same way, we better think our *sadhana* through.

So we decide upon the practice and its duration, both in the time spend on each session and in the number of days we will have these sessions. While we want to be rather ambitious, better we make a promise for something a little below an optimal performance. Like if we feel that 1 hour of meditation a day seems possible, it may be wise to make our promise only for 40 minutes. What we have decided upon is the minimum that we will do every day, which does not prevent us from doing more on days when we have extra time and motivation.

5.4.2. DURATION OF SADHANA

40 days is the usual minimum duration of a *sadhana*, yet beginners may certainly experiment with shorter *sadhanas*. 40 days however is said to give the full potential result of a practice, which is related to the moon cycle, see below→5.4.4. When we want to bring about an even more durable transformation, we go for 3 months, 6 months, one year, many years or life.

The more precisely our *sadhana* practice is defined, the shorter the duration should become. Like, we can decide to meditate for at least one hour daily during the coming year, while we also define a specific one-hour series of meditation practices for the first 40 days of that year. This way, the particular practice may evolve upon evaluation, while the overall minimal effort is maintained. We will discuss later how to evaluate and adapt our meditation series→6.2.3.

5.4.3. A WAY OUT OF SADHANA

In any case, we always need to define a way out for any kind of daily practice. We might get ill, be prevented by family or work or sometimes just not feel up to it.

In my case with *mantra* meditation for example, if I decide to do 5 rosary rounds of a *mantra* every day, I also decide upon a way out, just in case. If for whatever reason I skip a day, the next day I will do 2 times 5 rounds to compensate for it, plus the 5 rounds for that day. Since that is 3 times the usual number of rounds, I will not lightly decide to skip a session, yet I do have a way out.

If needed, we can thus accept 'not today' without feeling particularly guilty about it, without losing self-confidence. Thus also the *sadhana* itself will be much more easily maintained, since many people may stop their *sadhana* altogether after just missing it for one day. Their dissatisfaction with themselves then so much degrades their self-image that they lose the confidence to continue. We are human, so we need a way out and will thus also more easily decide on a more challenging *sadhana*.

5.4.4. THE MOON CYCLE

Full and new moon have been added to my agenda for decades. It is one of the main factors determining when I will do what and especially when to take an important decision, like starting a new *sadhana*.

On new moon, the gravity of sun and moon pull in the same direction, which brings the solar and lunar energy more in balance←4.2.4. Thus on new moon our emotions are more calmed by our rationality, which also means we are more *sattvic* and less passionately *rajasic*. If our general energy anyhow is rather *tamasic*, it will be the most down around new moon, which may aggravate the *rasas* of sadness, depression and worrying. If we are quite happy around new moon, then we can enjoy the more calm and subtle flavors of all pleasant *rasas*. Since our energy is less agitated, it is also easier to meditate, provided we can gather the willpower to give it a go.

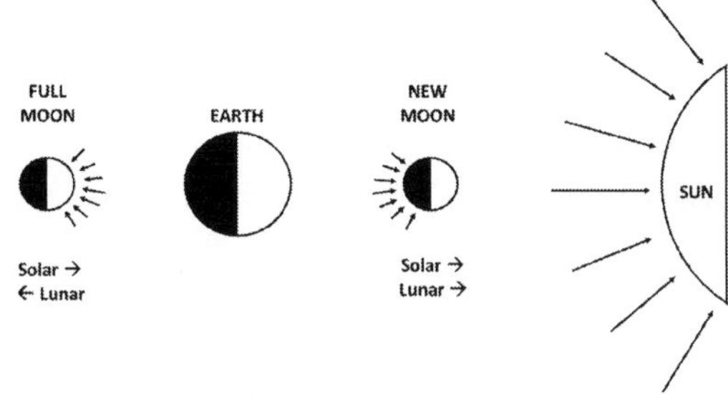

Image 39 - Impact of the moon cycle on solar & lunar energy.

On full moon the gravity of sun and moon pull in opposite directions. This brings more imbalances between the solar and lunar polarities and increases the *rajasic* energy. We will be more passionately emotional, while calmness will be more difficult. If our energy is anyhow rather excited, it will be the most active around full moon, which may aggravate anger and panicking as well. If we are quite happy, full moon is a great time to party on the *rasas* of love, joy, wonder and courage. Since our energy is more agitated, meditation is more difficult, but we will have more will power to do it.

On full moon our energy is thus more *rajasic*, while new moon offers opportunities for *tamas* and *sattva* both. Both new and full moon produce a stronger connection to the spiritual dimensions, which may disturb our sleep.

Decisions about *sadhana* are best made between moving from new moon to full moon. We will then have enough willpower to take a good decision, and that power will still increase until full moon, giving our *sadhana* a good start.

A *sadhana* decided upon new moon is said to be doomed to fail, while new moon is a good time to contemplate on our *sadhana* without taking any decision.

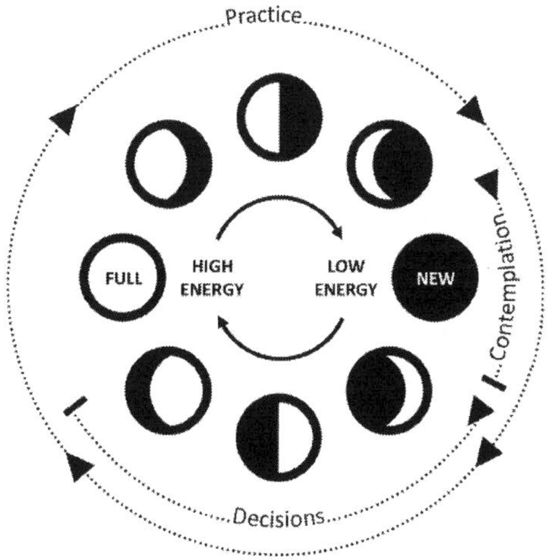

Image 40 - Synchronizing sadhana decisions with the moon cycle.

A *sadhana* is sometimes started officially on full moon, yet that relates more to the *tantric* approach of getting spiritual support, see below→6.4.1. In other cases it is not so advisable, since we might be overly ambitious about it, while our energy will go down for the first 14 days of the practice, which will thus become exceedingly difficult. Usually, if we can maintain the *sadhana* for the first third of its duration, we will also be able to finish it.

The typical 40 days duration of a *sadhana* represents one and a half moon cycle. When we start in the middle between new moon and full moon, we will end in the middle between full moon and new moon. Then we have a break for 2 weeks, giving us time to contemplate on our next move after new moon again.

Having such a break between *sadhanas* is considered auspicious in my householder tradition, while other traditions may have other opinions. We can then still practice, but there is no promise, no obligation and we can experiment with new practices that we might include in our next *sadhana*.

As the practice is thus also maintained during all solar and lunar fluctuations of at least one moon cycle, it will be most durable in its effect. 40 days is also the typical time taken in *Ayurveda* for the duration of a particular medical treatment that seeks a long-term durable effect.

5.4.5. SADHANA RITUALS

The more challenging the *sadhana*, the more important it is to make a formal decision. We might hang something on the wall to remind us, tie a knot in our hanky so to speak. We might count down the days by moving beads from one pot to another. Whenever deciding upon a particular series of practices, we best write it down, including timing.

Since the subconscious will produce the main resistance to our *sadhana*, working with rituals can be very helpful for our perseverance←3.2.6. Since *sadhana* rituals represent a promise made on the level of our soul, it may also bring support from the other dimensions.

The typical ritual for starting and ending a *sadhana* is very similar to the optional ritual for starting our meditation→6.4. There is just the added message about a *sadhana* starting or ending, including a request for support. Of course, when working within a particular tradition, we should follow the more detailed habits when announcing a *sadhana* in ritual.

In more *tantric* practices, *sadhanas* become a very specific deal with some spiritual energy. In return for the practice offered, that energy will explicitly support our spiritual pursuits, healing power, the removal of blockages, improving health or even more worldly projects. The start and end rituals then seal that deal.

These *tantric* rituals are usually very particular to the tradition they belong to, so they cannot be taught in a book. Moreover, one cannot just propose any such deal, as a spiritual connection must already be established for it to work. If the aspirant does not yet have such a connection, the teacher might have. There must also be sufficient insight into the level of *sadhana* that should be performed in return for a specific result, which is like a "pricing' system existing within the tradition, also beyond the physical dimension. It is here that we find for example traditions of doing 24,000, 108,000 or more repetitions of a particular *mantra*.

Some *sadhanas* are maintained until the expected result manifests, which is like an open-ended deal. This form is particularly used in support of the highest spiritual pursuits, which are basically priceless.

5.4.6. FIRE RITUALS

Fire rituals(HAVANA, HOMA, YAGYA, AGNIHOTRI) are very common at the start and end of *sadhana*. They are described in the earliest *vedic* scriptures and are present in most ancient cultures. While there are many aspects, the main practice is the offering of *mantra* to the fire, along with oblations of clarified butter(GHEE), rice, nicely smelling herbs and woods(SAMAGRI), black sesame and the more optional fruits, grains, pulses and seeds.

Especially in *tantric mantra sadhana*, up to 10 % of the total number of rounds done in meditation is usually offered to the fire at the end of the *sadhana*. For example, a *sadhana* of 108 days including 10 rounds of a *mantra* daily, totaling 1,080 rounds, will be finalized by offering up to 108 rounds to the fire, which may take several days. I have personally experienced many times how this will incredibly amplify the result of the *sadhana*.

Fire rituals create a powerful portal to the spiritual dimensions←2.7.2, which must be protected from negative energies. While these rituals are very popular on spiritual festivals these days, without adequate protection it can be really damaging. One just cannot ask anybody out there for help, as it allows interference with our lives and potential misuse by lower energies that have their own agenda.

In the *vedic* way this protection takes lengthy preparation rituals, usually performed by a priest(PANDIT). For the *tantric* it is more simple to start a fire ritual, as the personal connection to some higher spiritual energies will ensure the protection needed. Outside of these two options, I absolutely advise against just doing this by oneself. If one does not believe in these things, then why do it at all? And if one does believe in the other dimensions, then why ignore this warning, which is repeated in all traditions?

5.5. Planning the Day

So now we have all information needed to actually start planning a new kind of day, fitting within a certain *sadhana*. Our daily schedule will usually contain a variety of sustained practices, both on the mat and in life. Like with a *sadhana*, such daily schedule is then best defined for a certain period of time, while details can change along the way.

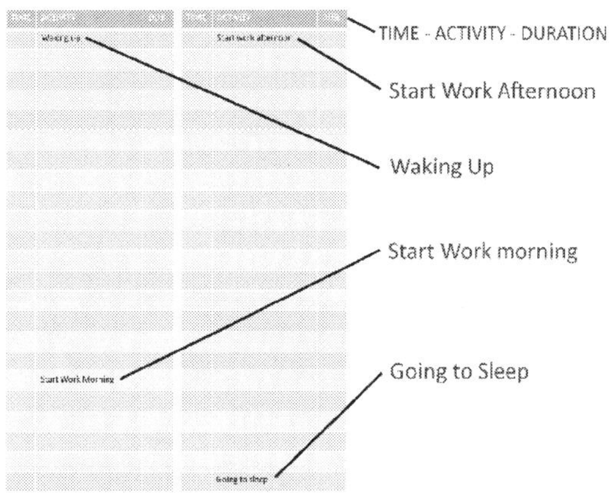

Image 41 - Example format for deciding upon a new daily schedule.

It is advisable to see this first as a theoretical exercise, before actually making any long-term decisions about it. It may take some time to feel confident about our plan, discuss it also with those affected by it, try out things.

For this exercise, I base the daily schedule on 3 meals a day. We can use a starting format similar to the one in Image 41. One may rapidly recreate it from this picture or download it as a PDF→A11. The following 12 steps will thus lead us to a better insight into how our new daily rhythm could look like:

1. Enter the times when you start and end working in the morning, as well as in the afternoon. There should be a lunch break in between and also add any time needed for commuting.
2. Add any other duties with a fixed timing that you cannot escape from, such as bringing kids to school while driving to work or feeding the family animals.
3. Enter the time for waking up at least two and a half hours in advance of the moment that you have to start some lengthy work or duty in the morning, including commuting. It can also be more, but for the sake of this exercise not less.
4. Enter the time when you should go to sleep in order to wake up at the time for waking you entered. Subtract 1 hour from your usual sleeping time, unless that is already less than 6 hours or unless you already have a daily meditation habit of minimum 30 minutes in the morning.
5. Below the waking time, write the activities required prior to your meditation practice: bowel movements, mild refreshing, drinking some water or a cup of tea and optionally a short walk outside, some very basic stretching, *sattvic* activities. Now also add timing to the totality of these activities, which may be called the 'Waking Schedule'. Do not add time for reading a newspaper, consuming social media or unnecessary contact with others.
6. Underneath the waking schedule, enter the time to start meditating. Decide how long you will meditate, between 30 minutes and 1 hour. In case you want to meditate longer, you will probably have to get up more early accordingly – so then you adapt the waking up time, as well as the time to go to sleep.
7. Now enter your 3 meals in the schedule without adding a start time but while indicating the duration for eating and maybe also cooking. Enter breakfast in the middle between your morning meditation and the start of your work. Enter lunch in the middle of the noon break. Enter supper in the middle between the

end of the afternoon work and the start of sleep.

8. Since *Asana* and other physical practices should not be done within 2 to 3 hours after food, it usually comes just before eating. You might thus do *Asana* practice before breakfast, lunch and/or supper. Decide for 1 or more sessions of a certain duration and enter them in the middle between meditation & breakfast, the end of the morning work and lunch and/or the end of the afternoon work and before supper, adding the duration for each session, maybe ending with breathwork.
9. It is logical to take a shower after exercise and before food and it is really advisable to take at least one shower, preferably in the morning. So add one or more showers of a certain duration to the schedule accordingly, after exercise, before food.
10. For the morning time till work starts, now enter the starting times for all activities you have added, depending on their duration. Hopefully it works out and you even have half an hour extra for 'relaxation & hobbies' before or after breakfast (togetherness, art, reading, music, daily ritual, etc.). If you do not have enough time between waking up and going to work for the activities you planned, adapt them or the waking up time, plus sleeping time, accordingly. Now do the same exercise for the lunch break.
11. Think about what other hobbies and things you need to reserve some evening time for. Add them with their duration before or after supper as fits, making sure that there are at least 3 hours between the end of supper and the start of sleep. Remember to leave at least 15 minutes for relaxation directly after work.
12. Check what time remains in the evening to spend whichever way & think about what that means for the duration of activities that are maybe more stressful than relaxing, more passive and not so inspiring. Adapt everything accordingly. For those that have trouble falling asleep, avoid screens 1 hour before retiring and focus on activities that aid in the relaxation of body & mind.

One may obviously add more or less details than in the following example, also in the meditation or *Asana* series. One might make a different schedule for working days and free days. Divorced parents might for example have a different schedule for the week that they are with the kids, and for the week without kids.

Thus everyone can figure this out, making sure that our spiritual and other objectives get a place. We cannot force this too much, should let it grow. The main step forward is to make a start, begin a *sadhana* of this kind. And for people with an anarchistic streak like me, we can be a little more flexible in living such a schedule sure, yet keep it alive nonetheless. Things will anyhow happen beyond our control, so we always have to be ready to adapt.

EXAMPLE OF A DAILY SCHEDULE

START	ACTIVITY	DUR.
6:00	Waking Up Schedule	30'
6:30	Meditation	60'
7:30	Feed the Cats	5'
7:35	Take Ashwaganda Honey	5'
7:40	Short Stretching	10'
7:50	Shower	10'
8:00	Householding	10'
8:10	Breakfast	20'
8:30	Commuting	30'
9:00	Work Morning	240'
13:00	Lunch	30'
13:30	Work Afternoon	240'
17:30	Commuting	30'
18:00	Householding	30'
18:30	Asana & Breathwork	30'
19:00	Shower	5'
19:05	Feed the Cats	5'
19:10	Supper including Cooking	60'
20:10	Free Time Family & Cats	140'
22:30	Evening Ritual & Chanting	20'
22:50	Foot Massage	10'
23:00	Sleep	420'

5.6. Retreats

Whether we have a free day or a few weeks or even months of holiday, we can turn it into a spiritual retreat to boost our progress. The combination of being able to practice that much more, as well as avoiding the usual work-related stress, may certainly do that. Whether we retreat at home or in nature, in an *ashram* or a cave, the first main objective must be to withdraw from life as much as possible, which will make it so much easier to withdraw inside.

Maybe we stay 24 hours a day in a darkened room, with an adjacent small bathroom so we never have to go out, food being regularly and silently delivered. This service we find in many monasteries or *ashrams*. There is neither internet nor light, usually mostly sounds of nature around, no communication allowed or requested, nothing to do but be with the Self. Or maybe we prefer to retreat a little less.

One can really do a fruitful retreat even at home, preferably located in somewhat of a quiet area and with minimum interactions with others, even if living in the same house. Just cut off that Wi-Fi, shut down the phone and go in total lockdown, ignoring everything but ourselves. A home retreat is free and does not need to be booked in advance. One can also more easily slide out of a home retreat back into normal life, yet with some fundamental new habits and practices developed during the retreat.

On the other hand, some really peaceful other location, where we are totally cut off from our usual life, has plenty to offer as well. Some places have particularly high value, whether because of their spiritual history←Story27 or because of the energetic field produced by a highly evolved teacher living nearby←3.7.3. It may be motivating to know that there are others all around doing a similar retreat, like in many *ashrams*.

Beginners may certainly benefit from following the particular daily schedule and the prescribed practices of some *ashram* for a while. Yet I do advise to choose a place where at least the meditation techniques used are free and personal, as one set of techniques cannot cover all people's needs←2. It is less of an issue if the remainder of our schedule is more practically aligned with *ashram* life. People that are more new to all this, may anyhow be better off following some *ashram* schedule within a group. Even if that is not a real retreat, communication allowed, it may be great fun while ensuring plenty of practice and learning.

Many of the practices and disciplines that may be hard to even consider during a normal workday, come into play during our retreat. Non-vegetarians might stop having animal food products for a while. We best exclude alcohol and other intoxicants, avoid foods that are particularly wind producing←4.5.3, as well as *rajasic* treats like sugar or black tea. We might also use some home remedies and wellness therapies on a continuous basis. Fasting from or on food is common←4.7.1, as is speech fasting←4.7.2. All main restraints proposed in classical yoga←4.9 can rather easily be maintained, as they are mostly difficult in our relationships.

As for our meditation practice, we should at least double or triple the usual effort made. If one is used to meditating one hour daily, it may anyhow be too much of a jump to start meditating all day. That also leaves room for many other activities that will support our relaxation and withdrawal in meditation. Overall, we challenge ourselves of course, but also take time off from the challenge of life, in part take a real holiday, within the restraints of a retreat.

Rasa Sadhana definitely has a great place here and why not give it a shot to postpone all unhappiness until after the retreat←4.1.3? Just the decision for example to really try not to get irritated or angry by people and things might create quite a different kind of holiday.

If some inner shadow work is actually due, it should receive some time within our daily schedule, yet it should never dominate our retreat. We focus on generating as much light as possible, and then temporarily let it shine within the dark←4.1.9. This is a matter of energy, not about the stories we tell ourselves, even though they are part of it. Seen in the light of *sattva*, the darkness of *tamas* has no power.

The practice shows that anything is possible and that in no way someone else can tell us how to do our retreat, provided we have some idea ourselves. As inspiration, here are some examples of retreat schedules that I have used.

I followed the first retreat schedule below for 40 days, on my own at a cabin in the forests of the French Dordogne area. It happened during the last lockdown of the Covid pandemic, so I saw more deer than people.

There were many restraints in place, including intoxicants, social media and sex. I was eating quite a lot, which was needed because at the time my body was weak, needing exercise and nutrition. That equally explains the *Asana* & breathwork, hiking over endless hills and swimming in a great nearby freshwater lake.

The morning meditation was silent *mantra* meditation on a particular *mantra*. The fire rituals were part of a more *tantric sadhana* related to the healing energies and largely consisted of offerings to the fire using that same *mantra* silently←5.4.6. Some of those rituals were done under an outdoor roof of my cabin, some in one of the many nearby caves. It often froze at night, another reason to get enough to eat.

RETREAT SCHEDULE 1

START	ACTIVITY	DUR.
5:30	Waking Up Schedule	30'
6:00	Meditation	150'
8:30	Shower, Breakfast	30'
9:00	Householding	15'
9:15	Optional Choice of Chanting, Guitar playing, Self-Massage, Swimming & other Wellness	105'
11:00	Asana	60'
12:00	Breathwork	30'
12:30	Lunch	60'
13:30	Hiking in Nature	180'
16:30	Gathering Firewood	30'
17:00	Preparing Fire Rituals	30'
17:30	Shavasana & Shower	30'
18:00	Fire Rituals	150'
20:30	Small Supper	30'
21:00	Free Time around the Fire	120'
23:00	Sleep	390'

Besides getting totally into that *mantra* energy, staying happy was another major promise made for that duration. So I definitely took a retreat also from my Ego's problems, which changed when I finally decided to stay at that cabin one month longer, yet with some changes to the schedule.

During this second period in France, the time for wellness in the morning was shortened, making room for some 'shadow work'. I would prefer to call it 'light work', but I guess that would be too confusing. Anyhow yes, while I had totally ignored my own inner struggles during the previous 40 days, now for one month, one hour a day, I had some cleaning up to do. It involved some writing also, some truth speaking, some crying and forgiving, some massaging of old wounds.

RETREAT SCHEDULE 2

START	ACTIVITY	DUR.
5:30	Waking Up Schedule	30'
6:00	Meditation	150'
8:30	Shower, Breakfast	30'
9:00	Householding	15'
9:15	Optional Choice of Chanting, Guitar playing, Massage, Swimming & other Wellness	45'
10:00	Shadow Work	60'
11:00	Asana	60'
12:00	Breathwork	30'
12:30	Lunch	60'
13:30	Hiking in Nature and/or Coaching Videocalls	150'
16:00	Gathering Firewood	30'
16:30	Preparing Fire Rituals & Healings	60'
17:30	Shavasana & Shower	30'
18:00	Fire Rituals & Healings	150'
20:30	Small Supper	30'
21:00	Free Time around the Fire	120'
23:00	Sleep	390'

I mostly remember that the shadow playing was surprisingly easier than I had expected. It essentially means to focus quite concretely on our pain, reliving it, yet keeping peace and love in our heart←4.1.9. The principal discipline of looking those problems straight in the eye for an hour and then to stop thinking about them until the next session, is really powerful. Not all pain went, while I felt more human and fresh afterwards. A lot of old stuff was left behind, making room for the future.

Another major change was that I started long-distance coaching and healing again, needing some income. That largely replaced the daily hikes with video calls and the healings partially took over the fire rituals. Energy-wise that changed a lot, but I had a great time and largely used this schedule as the blueprint for the one that I maintained when back in Belgium afterwards.

RETREAT SCHEDULE 3

START	ACTIVITY	DUR.
5:00	Waking Up Schedule	60'
6:00	Gayatri Mantra Meditation	450'
13:30	Silent Lunch with Mataji	30'
14:00	Gayatri Mantra Meditation	360'
20:00	Free Contemplation	180'
23:00	Sleep	360'

The first two schedules above are actually still quite nice and easy, yet there have also been others that were more strict, like the retreat I did a few times for a few weeks at the great Santoshpuri Ashram in Hardwar-India. Later on, I basically used the same schedule nr. 3 for most Sundays during roughly 2 years.

My meditation practice was at the time fully centered around the Gayatri *mantra*→10.3.3 and involved silent meditation alternated with chanting. Basically, we meditate silently and when we become too tired of the effort, we remove the *tamasic* energy with *rajasic* chanting of the same *mantra*, including energizing breathwork→8.3.1. The chanting then leads to a new trance state that produces a more *sattvic* silent meditation on the *mantra*. Part of the time one moves beyond doing in *Samadhi*, otherwise it is honestly really tough to keep up that kind of effort all day.

There was only one light meal a day and this silent lunch with Narvada Puri←Story28 was very supportive. It was allowed to ask any practice related questions at the end of it, and sometimes that was very welcome.

The contemplation in the evening before going to sleep had no particular subject except the Self, as Gayatri energy very much enhances Self-awareness. The *mantra* anyhow had a tendency to keep playing in the back of my head. Use of social media etc. was not allowed. At the end of that contemplation, I allowed myself to write down one sentence daily.

Definitely all of these retreats have helped to propel me inward and I pray that each reader finds some time for some of this, which is a grace.

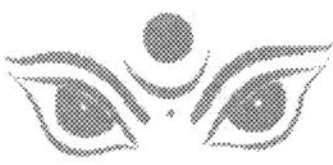

please continue to

SAMADHI

THE DEEP MEDITATION HANDBOOK

Volume 2 – SAMADHI PRACTICE